The Williamson Reports of 1921 and 1923

including
Training for Library Work (*1921*)
and
Training for Library Service (*1923*)

The Scarecrow Press, Inc.
Metuchen, N.J.   1971

ISBN 0-8108-0417-4

PREFACE

This volume includes two reports on library education prepared by Dr. Charles C. Williamson. The first, Training for Library Work (1921), is reproduced from a typewritten copy shared with Miss Sarah K. Vann by Dr. Williamson. This report, which has never before been published, was prepared for the Carnegie Corporation of New York, and is here reproduced with the consent of the Carnegie Corporation of New York.

Part II of this volume consists of a reprint of the 1923 Williamson Report, Training for Library Service, originally published by D. P. Updike at the Merrymount Press, Boston, and long out of print. The 1923 report is a revised and edited version of the earlier unpublished report of 1921.

The two are published together here for comparative purposes and have been produced in this facsimile form to facilitate easy reference to specific pages or passages from Sarah K. Vann's comparative study, The Williamson Reports, which is being published concurrently by the Scarecrow Press.

TRAINING FOR LIBRARY WORK

A REPORT PREPARED FOR
THE CARNEGIE CORPORATION OF NEW YORK

by

CHARLES C. WILLIAMSON, PH. D.

Advisory Committee

Herbert Putnam
J. H. Kirkland
Wilson Farrand

NEW YORK
1921

TABLE OF CONTENTS

Chapter		Page
	Table of contents	2
	List of statistical tables	4
1	Introduction	5
2	Types of library work and training	9
3	The library school curriculum	21
4	Entrance requirements	42
5	The teaching staff	53
6	Methods of instruction	60
7	Text-books	70
8	Field work	76
9	Joint courses, academic credit, degrees and academic status	96
10	Financial and statistical studies	100
11	Relation of library salaries to improvement of library schools	117
12	The professional library school and the university	121
13	Advanced or specialized study	127
14	Placement of library school graduates	143
15	Recruiting for the library profession	149
16	Training in service	154
17	Correspondence instruction	159
18	Standardization and certification	168
19	The problem of trained service for the small library	181
20	The library school situation in New York City	187
21	The proposed library school in the Portland (Oregon) Public Library	196

TABLE OF CONTENTS

Chapter		Page
22	Library service for small towns and rural districts	202
23	The Riverside Library Service School	207
24	The Library School of the Carnegie Library of Atlanta	215
25	Other Library Schools	223

APPENDIXES

I	General information in regard to the fifteen library schools studied in this report	232
II	Map showing location of library schools	238
III	A. Specimen entrance examination questions, Library School of the New York Public Library; B. Typical entrance examination questions, various schools	239
IV	Paper entitled "Some Present-Day Aspects of Library Training," containing original proposal for national certification board	247
V	Report of the special A.L.A. Committee on Certification, Standardization, and Library Training, 1920	249
VI	Report of A.L.A. Committee on National Certification, 1921	255

LIST OF TABLES

	Page
Number of hours of classroom instruction given by eleven library schools in the major and more important minor subjects in the curriculum	30
General education, technical training, and library experience of library school instructors, including only those giving courses of at least ten classroom hours, in 1920-1921	54
Library school budgets, showing total for all purposes and amount of salaries	100
Salaries of the directors, principals, and leading instructors of library schools, in 1921	102
Tuition and other fees	103
Statistics of library school students, showing initial salaries of graduates	104
General statistics of graduates of library schools	106
Salaries of graduates of five representative library schools . .	115

CHAPTER 1

INTRODUCTION

The study on which the following report is based was undertaken in accordance with a resolution of the Board of Trustees of the Carnegie Corporation of New York, April, 1919, authorizing such an inquiry and inviting the writer to undertake it, in cooperation with an advisory committee consisting of Dr. Herbert Putnam, Librarian of Congress, Dr. James H. Kirkland, Chancellor of Vanderbilt University, and Mr. Wilson Farrand, Principal, Newark Academy. It was understood that active work on the inquiry could not begin until the writer had finished his service as statistician for the Study of Methods of Americanization. Not until April 28, 1920, it was possible to call the members of the Advisory Committee together. An outline of the scope and method of the study laid before the Committee and discussed at that time has been followed in the main. It was found to be necessary, however, to limit the scope of the original plan by confining attention largely to the so-called professional library schools - fifteen in number - and dealing only incidentally with training classes, summer schools, and other types of training agencies.

During the summer of 1920 certain preliminary studies were made and a complete outline prepared of the topics on which it was desired to obtain data and opinions from library school officials and teachers. During December, 1920, and January, 1921, all of the library schools except two were personally inspected and conferences held with the principals and directors. In April and May the remaining schools - the Carnegie Library School at Atlanta and the Syracuse University Library School - were visited. Unexpected delay in the final preparation of the report has been due to a number of causes but principally to the necessity which the writer has been under of devoting the major portion of his time to other duties which could not well be put aside for an extended period.

This tentative report is being submitted to the Advisory Committee for its criticism and suggestion in advance of presenting it to the Carnegie Corporation. The author has keenly regretted that the circumstances under which the work has been done has made it impracticable to consult with the Committee more frequently. He is conscious that the report as it stands is susceptible of improvement at many points and that differences of opinion will necessarily arise in regard to many of the subjects discussed. He has endeavored to uncover and present the facts necessary to form opinions in regard to the general problems of professional library training. At the same time he has attempted to interpret these facts in their relation to what he conceives to be a sound program for the improvement of library service. Little time has been given to tracing the history of individual schools and none at all to the details of library school administration.

The primary purpose in the author's mind has been to present the library situation in this country with reference to the training problem so that the educator and the layman interested in educational problems may be able to form a correct judgment as to what the present situation demands. The possibility has also been kept in mind that if the report in some form should come to the attention of library school authorities, they may find in it some suggestion or constructive criticism that will bear fruit. As it stands, the report contains much matter of a confidential character designed solely for the information of the Carnegie Corporation. With this confidential matter eliminated, there would seem to be no reason why the rest of it should not be published or put into the hands of library school faculties, which have generally expressed a strong desire to examine it. Before that is done, however, the author would wish to have it submitted to a few of the outstanding leaders among library school officers and teachers for their comment and advice.

No extended description or criticism of individual schools or school projects has been undertaken except in the case of those supported in some form by Carnegie funds or seeking such support. In some of the statistical tables, as well as in the text, the names of the schools are omitted. This was necessitated by the fact that certain of the schools prefer not to make public all of the information asked for. It is believed that in their present form most of the tables could be published without violating any confidences.

The following fifteen library schools were visited, including all that claim to give at least one academic year of instruction.

New York State Library School, Albany, N. Y.

Pratt Institute School of Library Science, Brooklyn, N. Y.

University of Illinois Library School, Urbana, Ill.

Carnegie Library School, Pittsburgh, Pa.

Simmons College School of Library Science, Boston, Mass.

Library School of Western Reserve University, Cleveland, Ohio.

Library School, Carnegie Library of Atlanta, Atlanta, Ga.

Library School of the University of Wisconsin, Madison, Wis.

Syracuse University Library School, Syracuse, N. Y.

Library School of the New York Public Library, New York City.

Library School, University of Washington, Seattle, Wash.

Riverside Library Service School, Riverside, Cal.

The Library School of the Los Angeles Public Library, Los Angeles, Cal.

The St. Louis Library School, St. Louis, Mo.

University of California, Courses in Library Science, Berkeley, Cal.

A very brief historical sketch of each of these schools will be found in Appendix I. All but two of these - the Riverside Library Service School and the University of California library courses - are considered approved or accredited schools; that is, they have been admitted to membership in the Association of American Library Schools, an organization described in some detail in the chapter on standardization. Other schools are in the process of development. In the University of Texas and the University of Buffalo instruction has been organized which looks forward to recognition as a library school. Portland (Oregon) and certain other cities are considering plans for the organization of schools.

All except three or four of the fifteen schools covered in this report began as training classes for some particular library. In order to admit students from other libraries they were transformed into library schools. The transformation, however, has not in every case been fully accomplished. Many of the schools, as is pointed out at various points in later chapters, still exhibit some of the characteristics of training schools, much as a college may which has developed from a secondary school by changing its name, adding a new instructor or so, and lengthening the course, without making substantial change of personnel or equipment.

CHAPTER 2

TYPES OF LIBRARY WORK AND TRAINING

This chapter enters into a general discussion of the appropriate education, general and vocational, for different types of library work. Much use is made throughout the following chapters of the words "professional" and "clerical". Before entering upon any systematic description or critical discussion of vocational training for library work, it is desirable to make as clear as possible the meaning which will henceforth be attached to these terms. As the word "professional" is used in these pages, it is not synonomous with vocational, though that has been customary in library literature. Nor is the word "clerical" as used here confined to that part of the work in a library which is essentially the same as the so-called clerical labor carried on in business and other organizations. Much of the necessary work in a library is peculiar to libraries, yet it is distinctly of clerical grade. Those who do this work, however, have not been called clerks, but have been lumped with all other library workers in one vocational group of "librarians."

For clear thinking on the subject of training for library service it is necessary to understand the different kinds of work which must go on in a library. In this report we recognize two distinct types which, for want of better terms, we call "professional" and "clerical". Each of these types or phases of library work demands general and vocational education of a particular character. The distinction between the two is only vaguely understood and seldom applied in library organization and practice. It therefore seems desirable to dwell upon it at some length before proceeding to an examination of the library schools and other training agencies. While in one sense this is an introductory or preliminary chapter, it will be apparent that it is also a summary of some of the most important conclusions of the whole study.

In library work of nearly every kind efficiency requires careful attention to a large amount of detail. The supreme importance of attention to detail in records and the necessity for skill and accuracy in routine operations have apparently been allowed to obscure somewhat the real nature of professional library work and the kind of training required to fit for the highest type of success. Library schools originated at a time when methods of handling the detailed record work of libraries were being worked out with scientific care and precision. The difficulty of supplying libraries with assistants who were skilled in handling such detail and possessed of enough general understanding of the significance and importance of care and accuracy seems to have led the first schools to shape their curricula to meet the needs of the time, which was natural and desirable. The unfortunate result is that an attempt has been made ever since, more or less unconsciously, to give to manual labor of a purely clerical and routine nature the dignity and importance of professional work. This has made and continues to make library work unattractive and distasteful to men and women with the proper educational and general equipment for successful service in types of work which are of real professional character.

A shortage of persons trained for library work has been felt for some time and will no doubt continue to be felt until some differentiation is recognized by library administrators in the organization of library staffs between duties of clerical and routine character and those requiring professional outlook and attainments. A "trained" worker in a library may be of either one or the other type, but at present it is commonly assumed that all "trained" workers are of the same general grade. There are many kinds of work in any library which can be performed just as well (perhaps better) by young women with a high school education and a little appropriate instruction and experience as by a college graduate with the best library school training that can be devised.

Two main types of training for library work are required. The first is the broad general education represented at its minimum by a full college course which has included certain important subjects, plus at least one year's graduate study in a library school properly organized to give a thorough preparation for the kind of service we describe as "professional." The second type calls for a general education represented approximately by a high school course followed by a course of instruction designed to give a good understanding of the mechanics and routine operations of the library, together with sufficient instruction and practice to insure proficiency and skill in one or more kinds of the clerical and routine work which we may call "sub-professional" or "clerical."

Library administrators appear to be making little or no effort to keep these two types of work distinct; or, if they do recognize such grades of work, they assume that the clerical worker will in the course of time and solely by continued experience in clerical work, develop capacity for the higher or professional grades. Occasionally this has occurred in the case of exceptional individuals, but the assumption that the difference between the clerical and professional worker is length of experience only is vicious and has much to do with the low state of library service and the absurdly low salaries offered for even important positions of professional character.

Since the library administrator does not organize the staff in such a way as to make clear the qualifications needed for different types of work, the library schools have not been under the necessity of making the distinction and many of them have not done so. They have admitted to the same classes students who by no possible chance could give acceptable service of any except to a clerical type along with those well qualified to enter the highest grade of professional work. Exactly the same instruction has been given to both groups. In other words, they have been trying and are still trying to train clerical workers and professional workers in the same classes and in the same way. The results could not possibly be satisfactory and they have not been. The time has now come to apply the remedy for this fundamental defect. The situation calls for a proper organization of library service and the provision of separate facilities for training both classes of workers.

Graduation from an accredited college after four years of study leading to the bachelor's degree should now be recognized as the minimum of general education needed for successful professional library work of any kind. Much of the record keeping and routine in libraries of all kinds can be carried on very well by persons who have less than this amount of general education and even by those who have had only a high school course. For the sake of the library profession and to elevate the standards of library service, some distinction between professional and sub-professional or clerical grades of library workers is essential.

College education is now required of the high school teacher in practically every part of the country. How can the library even in the smallest town be expected to serve intelligently the needs of all classes unless the librarian is at least as well equipped as the high school teacher? The librarian, indeed, should be equal in his educational and general equipment to the high school principal, the superintendent of schools, the minister, the editor, and all other educated persons upon whom the community depends for leadership. The librarian must be the intellectual equal of the best educated classes in the community if he is to live up to his opportunities.

The need of training for librarianship, even for the smallest libraries, is almost universally recognized but the mistake is often made of assuming that the training needed is confined to matters of library technique and clerical routine. It is true that to be successful a librarian must understand library methods, but no amount of training in library technique can make a successful librarian out of a person who lacks a good general education. The most essential part of training for librarianship is that general education which is ordinarily secured nowadays through a college course. Some knowledge of foreign languages and literature, history, sociology, economics, government, psychology, the sciences, every librarian worthy of the name must have. Moreover, he must know more than the average college graduate about the literature and sources of information in all the principal fields of interest and have at his command the bibliographical tools and devices for unlocking the printed sources of information on any subject. It goes without saying that the high school student cannot do this. If he could, a college education would cease to be important as a background and preparation for any profession. The time required for the specific training for librarianship is comparatively short - usually but one year - because the most important part of the equipment is general education and a knowledge of men and books which can be acquired in a variety of ways but which is most likely to be found in those who have completed a college course.

A person with the general intellectual and personal equipment for librarianship can ordinarily get in one year from a properly organized library school the specific training needed to take up any type of professional library work. In order to do the highest grade of work, however, and make rapid progress in any specialized line, the student should have a second year of special study, not following the year of general technical study immediately but after at least one year of professional library work.

No amount of study in a library school can fit for successful library service the individual who lacks the fundamental educational equipment. On the other hand, many persons having the necessary education and native fitness and capacity have taken it up with complete success in spite of a lack of technical training. It is far easier for an intelligent, educated person interested in books and people to make a success of library work than it is for one having all the technique the library school can give him but lacking in general intellectual and cultural background.

Some discussion has been occasioned in library circles by the fact that many of the most successful librarians are without library school training. The question has been raised as to whether a library school course is helpful, whether indeed it may not be an actual hindrance to the highest success in types of librarianship requiring initiative, originality, resourcefulness and large administrative capacity. Two possible conclusions are indicated. In the first place, it should be perceived more clearly that the least important part of the librarian's equipment is that which the library school gives him and that therefore a high standard of general education should be required for admission to the professional school. Secondly, it is probable that the schools should so adjust their methods of teaching and the content of their curricula that students with adequate education and capacity will not find that in the process of acquiring a knowledge of library technique they are in danger of missing the broad professional outlook, and suffering a certain deadening of initiative and imagination which is likely to result from an excessive attention to minute detail.

Library technique should be presented to men and women, properly educated for professional library work, from the point of view of principles and policies. Too often even in the best of schools such subjects as cataloguing and classification have been taught as if the student had no mind. "Do it this way and don't ask why", has frequently been the instructor's attitude. Granting that such a method may legitimately be used in dealing with a class of apprentices, it is ridiculous when applied to college graduates who suppose they are being educated for a profession and in a professional spirit.

To the library school of a graduate and truly professional character we should look for workers to fill all positions requiring extensive and accurate book knowledge, advice and direction in the use of books, skill in organization and administration, and expert technical knowledge in many special lines. Being professional schools, these institutions will in no case aim to train specifically for any one library staff.

To another type of library school, commonly called a training class as conducted by the larger libraries, we must look for trained clerical workers. The subjects covered by the two kinds of training agencies will be to a certain extent the same. Clerical or sub-professional workers will need instruction in cataloguing, classification, and in all kinds of record-keeping topics, including filing, indexing, alphabeting, typewriting. They can be taught such things as the nature and uses of subject headings, not with the idea that they will be responsible for the subject heading work in any important library, but that they may be more intelligent and efficient with their own range of duties. For this type of training a large amount of drill and practical work will necessarily accompany the class room instruction. An intelligent person with a high school education should on the completion of such a course be able to give efficient and satisfactory service, especially in the library in which and for which she has been especially trained. It should not be possible to say of her, as library administrators now often say of library school graduates, that they have been taught a great many things and have hazy ideas about library work in general but cannot do any kind of work acceptably well.

The professional library school is the type of training agency which, in the writer's judgment, should receive consideration from the Carnegie Corporation. The benefits of aid given to the better type of professional schools are not confined to the immediate community in which the school is located. Municipal libraries should not be expected to devote their resources to training professional librarians. That is in reality a state function, to be supported by the state along with other kinds of professional education. Many important states, however, do not have a public system of higher and professional education. Where this is the situation, as in New York, Massachusetts, Connecticut, etc., progress and efficiency in library service seem to demand private support for professional library schools. Under the leadership of those who come forth from such schools, the purely local problem of recruiting and training clerical workers will be comparatively easy of solution.

Some of the so-called library schools at the present time are not equipped to do more than give a good thorough training for clerical workers. Under certain conditions that is the most important thing that can be done and the school which neglects to do it well in an attempt to achieve the impossible and give a professional training with inadequate resources and ill-prepared students is doing the cause of library service more harm than good.

In the last analysis every library will have to make its own decision as to what positions on its staff require professional training. The number and proportion of such positions will be determined by the size and character of the library, as well as by the money available for the payment of salaries. A reference library will require a larger proportion of professional librarians than a circulating library of the traditional type. The large library system will require a smaller proportion, though perhaps a higher grade, of professionally trained librarians than the small library, for the reason that the greater specialization made possible in the large organization permits the professional worker to supplement and supervise the work of a larger number of workers of clerical grade.

The mere recognition of this principle will do much to solve the training problem. In the first place, it will considerably reduce the number of people which the professional library schools will be called upon to turn out. Assuming, as has apparently been done by many library executives, that practically the entire body of library workers, even down to pages, should have a full library school training, the impossible task would fall upon the library schools of training all library workers by means of one general type of curriculum. At the present moment the demand for trained workers, which is alleged to be far in excess of the supply, is in reality not solely a demand for fully equipped and professionally trained workers, but for both types. When this fact is recognized, professional library work will make a far stronger appeal to college men and women as a career, not only because the professional type of work will be more attractive in itself but also because it will make possible more adequate salaries. The confusion of clerical and professional work tends inevitably to keep salaries down to the clerical grade. No matter what the financial resources of an institution, it is not justified in paying clerical workers much, if any, more than those of equal education and experience receive in commercial and competing fields of work. In many cases the law of supply and demand will make it possible to maintain efficient clerical staffs at salaries even lower than those offered by commercial and private employers.

Until the distinction between clerical and professional workers is sharply made and adhered to, the demand for adequate salaries for the professional group will prove ineffective because unnecessary and economically impossible. A careful inspection of the duties actually performed by many workers for whom professional salaries are demanded will show that they are often in large part clerical and not entitled to higher remuneration. Until such time as library work is organized so that professional workers devote all their time and energy to professional tasks - tasks which workers with less adequate general and technical equipment cannot perform without permanent damage to library service - it is not worth while to expect librarians to be paid on a professional basis. When library work is so organized, and for this and other reasons is adequately remunerated, library schools able to offer professional training of high character will not need to worry about the difficulty of securing enough students to fill their classes, nor will librarians have cause to bemoan the dearth of trained assistants for professional work.

The inherent attractions of professional library work will never fail to produce the necessary supply of workers when working conditions and salaries are properly adjusted. Neither will the call for trained clerical workers go unanswered when the type of worker and the type of training required are clearly defined. At no time during the last three years would the library schools have had any great difficulty in filling their classes with a good grade of high school graduates, who with proper training would have made excellent clerical workers. Some of the library schools conducted by public libraries, should confine themselves to this task and let their libraries look to the professional schools for the other type of trained workers.

Some of the stronger library schools may find it possible and desirable to offer both types of training, in separate classes of course, and perhaps to some extent by a separate corps of instructors. In general, however, workers of the clerical grade can and will be trained for the larger libraries by their own training classes. Any library finding it necessary to add to its clerical staff as many as ten new members a year is likely to find it wise to maintain a training class. With one competent person in charge of the class and doing most of the teaching, aided as required by other professionally trained members of the staff, a library can provide its own clerical workers more economically and quite as efficiently as if it should attempt to conduct a library school.

To such a program some library executives will make the objection that they wish their entire staff to have full professional training. This is at best a counsel of perfection, though in reality it probably reveals a lack of understanding of the principles of economical and efficient administration. If it is true that the high school graduate is not fitted for the professional work, it is also true that the college graduate will not give the best service in strictly clerical positions. If a person with college education is satisfied to spend his time or any considerable part of it on tasks the high school graduate can do equally well, he will probably give no better service than the latter, and will actually be inferior and likely to be dissatisfied with his position and remuneration.

Small libraries find it somewhat more difficult than large ones to provide a properly trained personnel. For professional workers they will of course look to the library schools, but a supply of trained workers of the clerical grade will not be so readily secured. Requiring too few persons of this grade to warrant the expense of conducting a training class, they will have to resort to some other agency for competent clerical assistants. The easiest but least desirable source will be apprenticeship. Young women residing in the community will be taken on the staff and expected gradually to learn the work by doing it under direction. In some cases this may prove fairly satisfactory. The amount of instruction that can be injected into such apprenticeship will necessarily depend on the size of the professional staff and the time and teaching ability available for the task.

In many cases it should be possible for smaller libraries to make arrangement with larger ones within easy reach to train their clerical assistants. There would seem to be no good reason why the training class of a large library should not accept students from libraries in smaller adjacent towns and cities, charging a proper fee, to be paid, not by the student perhaps, but by the library benefited. In other situations a group of smaller libraries in the same neighborhood may conduct a training class cooperatively. Still other small libraries may find a solution of the problem by sending their assistants to attend short courses and summer schools conducted for that purpose by state assistants may also be offered through properly conducted correspondence courses.

Whatever the method employed for recruiting clerical workers, it is of the greatest importance not to overlook the fact that training is necessary for the best results. Without the trained clerical assistant the professional worker will be overburdened with responsibilities for detail from which he should be free in any properly organized library. A certification system should recognize the grade of clerical assistant and admit to that grade those whose general education and library training meet the standards provided. Under a certification system which makes the essential distinction between professional and clerical grades, there will be little or no danger than individuals qualified for clerical work will be able to pass themselves off for the higher grade. There will be no reason, therefore, why accredited and standard training classes cannot, if they choose, accept for training students not under appointment or pledged to accept appointment on the library's own staff at the end of the period of training. In such a case it would be proper, of course, to charge a reasonable fee for the course.

CHAPTER 3

THE LIBRARY SCHOOL CURRICULUM

In order to make as clear as possible to the general reader the scope and content of library school curricula, the following brief descriptions of courses have been compiled from the current issues of the announcements or catalogues of the leading schools. These statements are not designed to be a complete outline of the courses given in any one school; they constitute rather a composite summary of the descriptive statements which seem best adapted to convey a fair idea of the subjects on which it is deemed necessary for the professionally trained librarian to receive instruction in the schools.

It may at first strike the reader that we are introducing here a mass of detailed information which should have been relegated to an appendix. This matter is deliberately brought in at this point, however, in order to give at the outset a good idea of the scope and content of the library school curriculum. It serves also, it is believed, to give point to the contention made throughout this report that professional library training should be based on a broad, general education. The different courses are arranged in the order of the average amount of time given to them in the classroom schedules of the eleven schools which reported on this point. Each paragraph under a subject is taken from the statement of a different school.

Cataloguing

"The course includes lectures, recitations, and practice work in dictionary cataloguing and alphabeting. Each lesson is followed by an exercise in actual cataloguing, the books used being selected to furnish illustrative examples of the rules given in class. The exercises are revised from sample cards and corrections discussed in class. The corrected cards are converted into sample dictionary catalogues, which are indexed to bring out examples of rules.

The A. L. A. rules mimeographed on cards for convenience in study and reference are followed with minor modifications."

"A study of mechanical devices and supplies used in cataloguing; methods of duplicating cards; problems in ordering cataloguing supplies."

"Practice is given in alphabeting and in the ordering, handling, and use of Library of Congress printed cards.***Each student keeps the revised cards for about 200 books, correctly arranged and furnished with guides, as a sample catalogue for future help. Additional lectures are given on cataloguing of children's books, cataloguer's reference books, supplies, cataloguing of foreign books, music scores, and maps. Lectures and practice in the use of fuller collation and imprint are given***."

Book Selection

"Designed to familiarize, so far as possible, with books and writers, their scope, qualities and respective values in certain leading classes of literature, and with sources and aids in book selection in these classes; to define and analyze the principles underlying discriminating selection of books for library use; and to cultivate the power of judging books according to their value and suitability for different types of readers and libraries."

"(a) Principles of book selection in Biography, History, Travel, Sociology, Nature and Popular Science, and Religion; study of standard and current aids and book reviewing publications; study and practice in annotation and evaluation; exercises in compilation of special lists; study of editions and series desirable for library use. (b) Survey and analysis of modern fiction (in English), covering principles of critical judgment, aids and guides, and study and practice in annotation, for modern fiction, historical fiction, foreign fiction in English translation, 'borderland' fiction, short stories, fiction of the current year."

"Translation of the works of the leading French novelists are read and reported upon, followed by a survey of representative novelists of Spain, Italy, Germany, Scandinavia, and Russia. Recent poetry, the short-story, and modern drama are studied.*** The class examines about forty new books each month, and attention is given to current publications by reading and checking the issues of the Publishers' Weekly. The large amount of reading required in this course may be expected to encroach upon the time which a student usually gives to general reading."

"Aims to cultivate further the power of judging books as to their value and adaptability to various types of libraries and people. Practical problems in the selection of translations of the classics and foreign fiction, series, editions, quick selection of new books, etc. Reading of selected modern novelists, dramatists and poets is required and problems of selection in these fields discussed. Facility in estimating books is developed further through the writing of booknotes and reviews. The economical spending of book funds is taught through the checking of second-hand, remainder and other bargain catalogues of American and English dealers."

"After considering the qualities of a good edition, the various editions of the standard authors are studied and those best suited to library use are recommended."

"The evaluation and selection of periodicals for library use are considered briefly."

Reference Work

"A study of the standard works of reference, general and special encyclopedias, dictionaries, annuals, indexes to periodicals, ready reference manuals of every kind, special bibliographies, and the more important newspapers and periodicals. Works of similar scope are compared, and the limitations of each pointed out. Lists of questions made up from practical experience are given, and the method of finding the answers discussed in the class. Problems in selection of reference books, especially for the small library, are assigned and talked over. The aim of this course is not only to promote familiarity with a considerable number of well-known reference works, but also to give the student some idea of the method in the handling of books, to familiarize him with the use of indexes, tables of contents, and varying forms of arrangement, and, finally, to suggest some method of comparison and evaluation."

"Lectures and problems from the standpoint of college and university libraries, large reference libraries or departments. Principal topics: interlibrary coordination and cooperation in reference work; organization of reference material; law libraries and law books; care and use of manuscripts; medical libraries; patents publications; legislative reference; local history and genealogy; publications of learned societies; dissertations; indexes to foreign periodicals; trade and professional journals."

Classification

"The Dewey Decimal classification is used as the basis for a thorough consideration of the subject matter of books, with a view to their arrangement on the shelves, both of the large and small library. Lectures are given also on the Cutter Expansive and the Library of Congress classifications."

"***Practical work in classifying selected lists of books, considering the various requirements of large, small and special libraries; brief history of classification; comparison of the principal systems; use of the Cutter-Sanborn tables for assigning book numbers."

"The importance of adapting classification to the need of special localities and types of libraries is emphasized through the discussion of specific books. Methods of simplification, especially in biography and literature, are taught. The study of book numbers is included in this course."

Administration

"This course includes the administration of large libraries, the administration of small libraries, and a short course in business methods.*** In the consideration of the administration of small libraries, practical details of management and the adaptation of methods to the needs of a small library are emphasized. The principal topics are: library finance; statistics and reports; relation of librarian to trustees; the staff and the reading public; the place of the library in the community; cooperation, publicity, and extension of the use of the library."

"Library legislation."

"Work of a library organizer; office systems; accounts and bookkeeping; business correspondence."

"Forms and supplies."

"An analytical study of reports and statistics in their vital relation to the practical work of the library, including the graphic presentation of these."

"Methods of bringing public and library together. Outside publicity, including reaching the business men, newspaper publicity, miscellaneous printed matter and its distribution, placards, car cards, movie slides, outside bulletin boards, window displays and exhibits; and inside publicity, including lectures, exhibits, book displays, and bulletins."

"Methods and problems of city extension by means of branch libraries, deposit stations and smaller agencies; rural extension, including county and township systems and the book automobile; state traveling libraries and other work of library commissions."

Library Work with Children

"This course aims to give the principles of library work with children, and comprises a series of lectures on management and training of children; equipment of a children's room; books for little children; books for younger children; how to judge fiction for boys and girls; historical stories; boys' reading; girls' reading; program of a children's department."

"Book selection for children; administration and equipment of children's rooms; library work with schools and playgrounds; cooperation with other educational and social agencies."

"Principles underlying the art of story-telling, applied to the selection, adaptation and oral presentation of stories. Students electing this course will tell stories in the playground and other branches of the library."

"History of children's literature. The purpose of the course is to trace the development of children's literature in England and America and to study the forces which affected it and determined its characteristics at different periods. Beginning with the time of Aldhelm and Bede, typical books of each period are discussed, the chap-books, old-fashioned books for children, and facsimile reprints in the Library School collection being used for study and comparative purposes."

Current Events

"As an aid to the student in following the affairs of the day, attention is given to the events chronicled from time to time in the daily newspapers and in the weekly and monthly periodicals."

"Round table devoted to the review of important current activities and events, designed to give practice in the use of periodicals and to develop judgment of the value of the material presented."

"Survey of the history of general American periodicals, also the best in special subjects, as Science, Fine Arts, and Education; English and widely-known continental magazines."

Public Documents

"A study of the publications of the United States Government, with a consideration of state and municipal documents, as illustrated by the publications of the state of ---***. The Executive Departments, Congress, and other government offices are considered as sources of information for libraries. The printing and distribution of documents, their indexes, and their use in reference work are taken up. Emphasis is laid upon the documents of most value to the small library."

Subject Headings

"Principles of subject indexing as applied to the dictionary catalogue are discussed and the relation and correlation of subjects are studied both in relation to the entry of books in the catalogue and to the arrangement of books on the shelves."

"Assigning subject headings on the basis of the A. L. A. List of Subject Headings and the Library of Congress lists."

"In studying subject headings, analytics, cross references, and the headings assigned specific books by the students are discussed. The A. L. A. subject headings is checked by each student."

Subject Bibliography

"The best and most available bibliographies and selected lists in various departments are considered as to their authority, date, content, arrangement, merits, defects, and adaptation to different uses. Special topics, such as the scope, utility and limitations of bibliography are also treated. For graduation each student submits a selected and annotated bibliography that tests the ability to collect, arrange, and definitely to evaluate the literature of the subject chosen. Methods of work, authorities used, and results obtained are examined and criticised. A study is made of the organization and work of those societies and institutions of America and Europe which are interested in the stimulation of bibliographical movements, in the perfecting and unifying of bibliographical methods, and the production of bibliographical material. Special attention is given to cooperative undertakings and international bibliography."

History of Libraries

"History of European libraries, early and present, American library movement; library associations and library periodicals; great American libraries and their specialties; American library biography".

"Development, characteristics and tendencies of the American library movement, different types of libraries; library associations, national and state; library commissions and their work; library training."

"*** Origin, materials and development of writing; origin and spread of printing; methods of book illustration; history of bookbinding."

"Book illustration, title-pages, printers' marks, and famous printers and presses."

Fiction

See Book Selection

Lending Systems

"Discussion of the principles underlying the relations of the library to the public brought about by the loan of books, and the character of the service to be rendered; a study of the various necessary and desirable records connected with this work, representative loan systems suitable for various types of libraries, and rules, regulations, and practices incidental to the service."

"History and principles of charging systems, with detailed study of Browne, Newark and Columbia University charging systems. Circulation of periodicals, music, pictures and books for foreigners. Besides loan work routine the following topics are discussed; access to shelves, rent collections, book disinfection; distribution through branches, stations, schools and home libraries, interlibrary loans."

"Registration, infectious diseases vs. library books, fines, reserves, renewals, rules for lending, pay collections, training of staff, and apprentice classes."

"Consideration of the business principles which should underlie routine and of the social principles which should govern relations with borrowers forms the basis of the course."

Trade Bibliography

"Historical development, national book-trade bibliographies of Europe; English and American book-trade bibliography, general, national, and special; related bibliographical aids, important catalogues, and special bibliographies."

"Aims to give *** a working knowledge of about thirty-five American, English, and foreign trade publications which are of constant use to libraries in their dealings with book-sellers and publishers and in the acquisition of books in general."

Binding and Repair

"Lectures treat of materials, processes, and methods of binding; practice is given in judging materials and workmanship as to strength, durability, appearance, and cost. Students become familiar with all processes by inspecting books in various stages of binding, and by visiting binderies. The necessary technical routine and the preparation of serials, pamphlets, and books for binding and re-binding are also considered. Mending is taught by practical work and demonstration."

"Publishers', and re-inforced bindings, and history of the art of bookbinding (with slides)."

"Practice in mending; in preparing books and periodicals; in giving specifications for binding of a varied assortment of books; in estimating wearing qualities of different editions."

"Mechanical processes necessary in preparing books for circulation, mounting pictures and clippings, binding pamphlets, magazine covers, etc."

Order Work

"The subjects included in this course are book-buying, discounts, ordering books, checking and entering bills, the accession book and its substitutes, the shelf list, serials and continuations, exchanges, gifts, duplicates, pamphlets, clippings, the history of copyright and the copyright law."

"Importations; second-hand auction purchases."

Printing and Publishing

"Lectures discussing the features of a printed book, such as the parts of a book, type pages, illustrations and color printing, the printing of books from plates, etc., are given to cultivate an appreciation for well made books. Further, the characteristics of the best known American publishers and their works are discussed to familiarize the students with the standards of publishing and the value of imprint."

"Lectures and practice aim to give the student the information most needed in preparing the simplest library publications. Includes the preparation of copy, mechanical editing, routine and processes of printing, correction of proof, library stationery and blanks and forms, and examination of library reports and bulletins as to waste and economy, types, indentions, etc."

School Libraries

"The value and place of the high school library; types; relations to the public library; selection of books and periodicals; modifications in classifications, cataloguing and other records; charging systems; aids in reference work; the administration and use of the school library; special problems of the school librarian; making and use of a clipping and picture collection; the vertical file; lessons on the use of books; vocational guidance; special features such as lantern slides, stereographs and music records."

"Previous pedagogic training or teaching experience are desirable for this course."

"The work of the school and teachers' department, deposit stations in the schools, educational theories and books are discussed in order to give an intelligent understanding of the possibilities of cooperation with teachers."

Library Buildings

"Methods of planning and equipping library buildings, with discussion of the form and arrangement of rooms for various library departments and calculation of book capacity."

"Shelving, lighting, furniture and fittings, decorations, equipment for social service purposes."

"Principles are illustrated by lantern slides and photographs showing plans of library buildings."

Community Relations

"Study of library work and possibilities of a definite city or other community. The topography, population, political, financial, industrial and other social conditions will be considered in their relation to actual and potential library work in the community."

"Designed to give the student a knowledge of the library's relation to the community as a whole and of the various agencies for industrial, social and civic betterment with which it may cooperate."

"Municipal and government activities and problems, methods of working with local organizations, neighborhood survey, etc."

Shelf Work

"This course includes practice in assigning book numbers by the Cutter-Sanborn author tables; lectures on the shelf-list, showing its value for inventory and statistical purposes; methods for checking continuations and government documents, and caring for pamphlets, pictures, slides, etc."

"Book supports, shelf labels and other appliances; preservation and arrangement of pamphlets; inventory; shelf-listing. Model shelf-lists are made both on cards and on sheets."

Languages

"Technical French and German. A study of an extensive list of

German and French book titles, customary abbreviations, etc."

Accessioning

"The condensed and loose-leaf accession books are used, and other systems of keeping accession records and of withdrawing books from the library are taught. The mechanical preparation of books for the shelves is included."

Indexing

"Marking matter for indexing; choice of headings; form of citation; verification; filing; full and brief indexing; periodical indexes; indexing documents; correlation of entries; cross references; editing for print; form of printing; labor-saving methods and devices."

Notes and Samples

"Each student is required to submit for inspection a collection of material on the various phases of library work. This collection includes books and pamphlets on library economy, bibliographies and reading lists, library periodicals, publications of individual libraries, blanks and forms used in library administration and the problems, notes and other required work of the regular courses. No certificates or diplomas are awarded to students who do not present well-selected and well-arranged collections of reasonable size."

Special Libraries

"Information regarding the important and rapidly growing work of industrial, commercial, financial, and other special libraries, by visiting librarians, and experience in such libraries."

Books for the Blind

"Lectures are given on library work for the blind, the history of types for the blind, books, magazines, games, writing appliances and music, and other subjects of interest to the blind."

Although no less than twenty-five distinct courses are recognized in the curricula of the library schools, about half of the student's time is devoted to four subjects - cataloguing, book selection, reference work, and classification. These four subjects may well be called the heart of the curriculum, for although the actual time devoted to any one of them varies greatly from school to school, these are the subjects on which all the schools lay primary emphasis.

The following table shows the actual number of classroom hours de-

Number of Hours of Classroom Instruction Given by Eleven Library Schools in the Major and More Important Minor Subjects in the Curriculum

Subjects	School											Average for 11 schools reporting
	1	2	3	4	5	6	7	8	9	10	11	
Cataloguing	44	57	105	90	57	45	35	66a	43	61	61	60
Book Selection	57	60	27	60	36	52	50	60	76	45	32	50
Reference Work	53	47	44	60	30	50	30	44	36	69	60	48
Classification	42	47	44	25	35	30	20	33b	28	32	33	34
Administration	76	25	20	18	36	37	20	40	27	17	34	32
Children's Work	15	6	18	30	9	18	35	12	c	27	24	18
Current Events	15	c	35	c	18	c	15	c	30	24	32	15
Public Documents	13	12	10	25	10	15	10	16	12	11	20	14
Subject Headings	30	17	15	20	10d	e	10	e	e	19	30	14
Subject Bibliography	f	30	6	g	13	10	12	10	26	32	f	13
History of Libraries	3	30	14	32	10	2	10	5	10	8	8	12
Fiction	6	gh	25	5	gh	10h	10h	24	gh	16	32	12
Lending Systems	6	10	5	7	6	19	10	8	13	16	18	11
Trade Bibliography	10	17	4	30	7	10	8	gi	6i	16	f	10
Binding and Repair	7	12	7	9	10	10	23	5	4	6	12	10
Printing & Publishing	13	10	8	9	2	5	18	c	5	9	6	8
Order Work	4	9	6	6	5	5	5	16	12	8	3	7
School Libraries	2	26	1	g	6	1	20	gj	c	j	2	5
Library Buildings	4	9	4	6	k	6	3	3	8	5	6	5
Filing	2	L	8	6	4	1	10	g	10	2	4	4
Community Relations	g	g	3	g	g	9	15	g	10	8	g	4
Shelf Work	2	7	9	3c	2	2	3i	d	8	2	2	4
Language	m	m	23	m	m	m	m	m	m	m	20	4
Accessioning	3	2	3	g	4	8	2	i	i	2	2	3
Indexing	3	9	5	g	3	1	g	g	n	c	3	2
Inventory	1	o	o	o	p	1	1o	g	o	2	1	1

a - includes shelf listing
b - includes subject headings
c - not given
d - included in cataloguing
e - included in classification
f - included in reference work
g - not segregated
h - included in book section
i - included in order work
j - included in children's work
k - included in library administration
L - included in indexing or cataloguing
m - required for entrance
n - included in filing
o - included in shelf work
p - included in accessioning

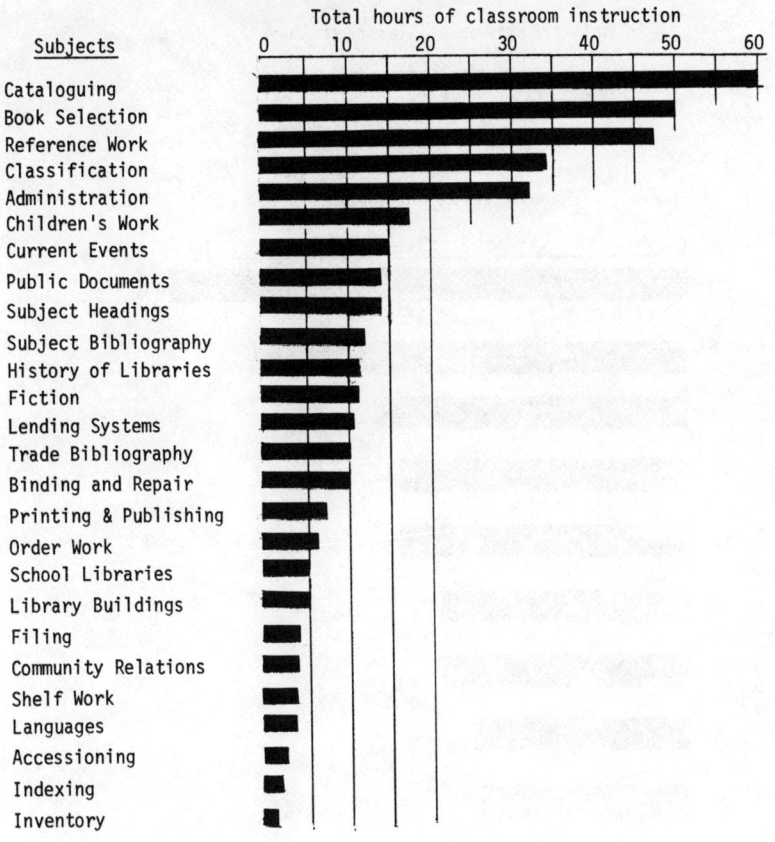

Amount of Time Devoted to Instruction in the Various Subjects in the Library School Curricula. Based on Statistics from Eleven Schools.

Relative Number of Classroom Hours
Devoted to Instruction

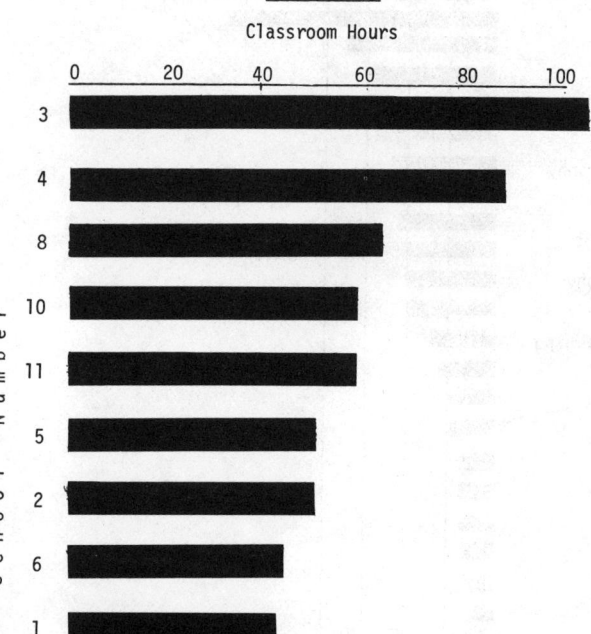

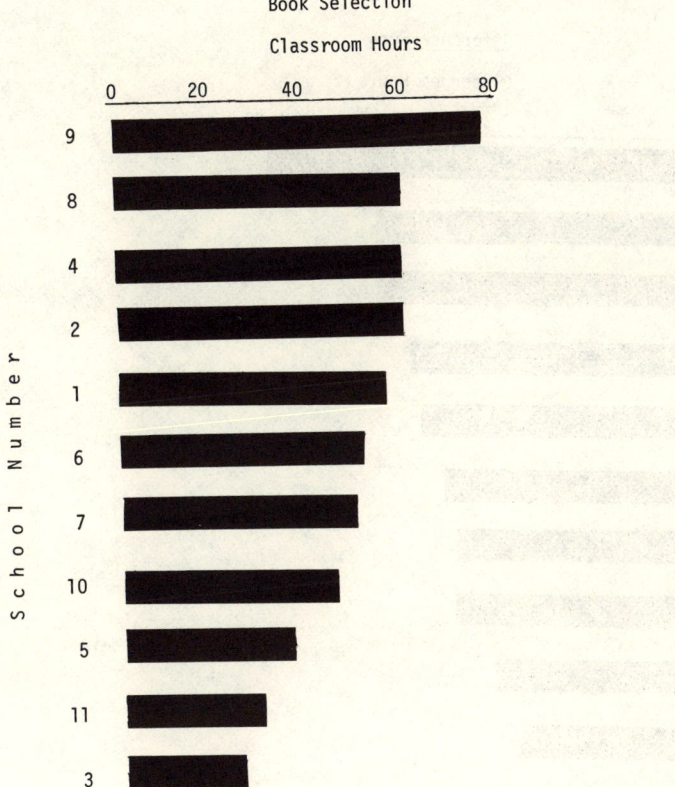

Relative Number of Classroom Hours
Devoted to Instruction

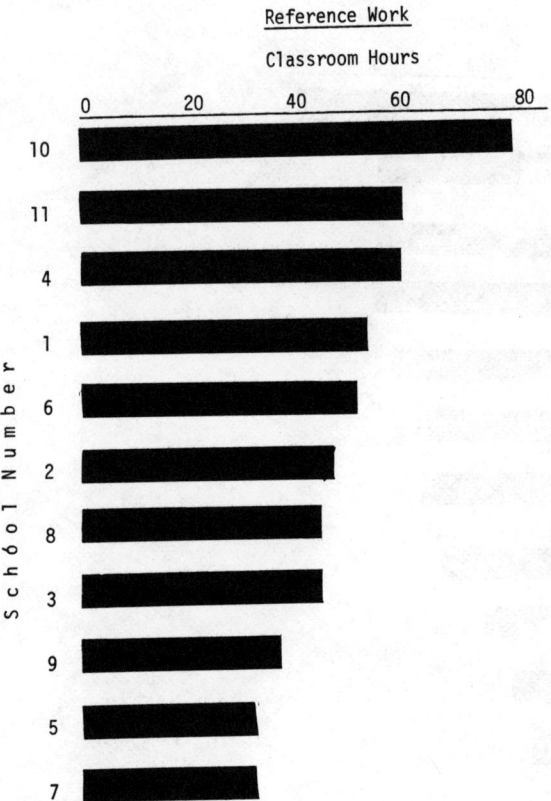

Relative Number of Classroom Hours
Devoted to Instruction

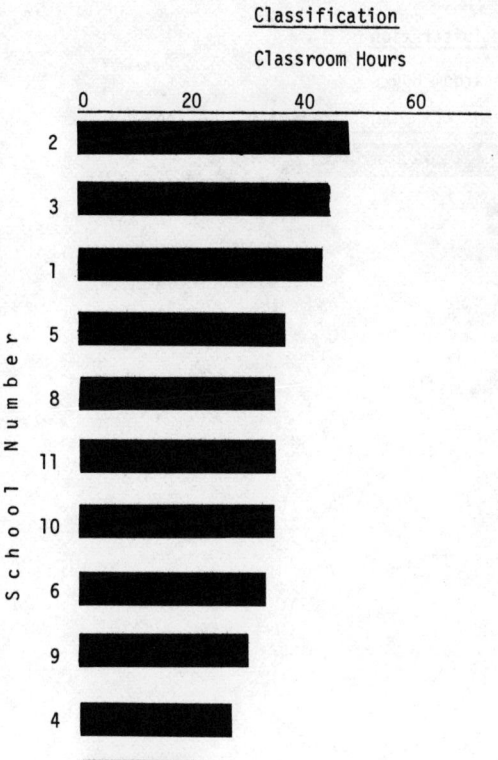

Relative Number of Classroom Hours
Devoted to Instruction

Administration

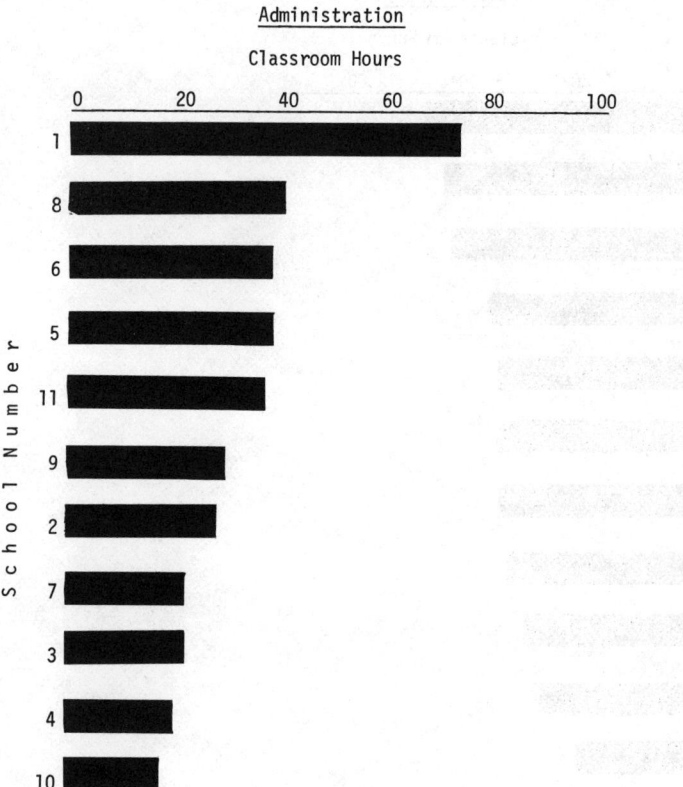

voted to the major and most of the minor subjects in the curriculum of the eleven schools from which reports were received. Differences of terminology and the variety of groupings and combinations of subjects encountered make it impossible to arrive at strictly accurate averages or to compare one school with another at every point. The table, together with the series of charts, does serve, however, to indicate the remarkable variations in the time given by different schools even to the major subjects. Cataloguing, for example, gets 105 classroom hours in one school and only thirty-five in another, the average for the eleven schools being sixty. One school devotes seventy-six hours to book selection and another only twenty-seven. Time allotted to reference work varies from thirty to sixty-nine hours. Classification claims forty-three hours in one school and only twenty in another. In the minor subjects variations are naturally still more pronounced.

Several conclusions of possible significance may be drawn from these facts. Obviously there is no agreement among the schools as to the relative importance of the different subjects in the curriculum. The time given to a subject seems to depend on the personal opinion or desires of the instructor or the principal. While considerable interest has been manifested in discussions as to what should constitute the minimum essential instruction in cataloguing, apparently no effort has been made by the Association of American Library Schools to arrive at minimum standards for the course in cataloguing. Complaint is common that the curriculum is overcrowded while important new subjects are clamoring for admission. The school that succeeds in giving its students the essentials of cataloguing in thirty-five hours, while others require two or three times that amount, can take up other subjects that may be more important for the general professional course. Teaching skill, as well as equipment and methods, is an important factor in determining the amount of time to be given to a subject.

While it would manifestly not be desirable to bring about strict uniformity in the content of the various courses in the curriculum, there does seem to be need for a certain degree of standardization of both the major and minor courses given in the first year of professional library school study. Nomenclature should be standardized and standard courses worked out and officially adopted by the proper professional body. The term "book selection" means far different things in different schools and terms used in presenting the subject do not have at all the same meaning everywhere. The situation is similar in other parts of the curriculum. It is impossible to tell what instruction a student has had in book selection from the mere fact that he had a course in that subject in an accredited library school. The fundamental courses in library schools, as in schools of law and engineering, should all have the same scope. To bring this about should be one of the important duties of the certification board recommended elsewhere in this report. Before such a board can accredit a library school for the certification of its graduates, it must satisfy itself that standard courses are given. Development of training in service for library workers through other training agencies than library schools will require the formulation of minimum standards as to scope and content of courses which are to be accepted for certification purposes.

   The library school curriculum has passed through something of an evolution and is quite likely to see even greater changes in the future. The schools at first confined their attention largely to technical library subjects, such as cataloguing and classification. Later cultural and other studies were introduced to make good deficiencies in the student's general education. The present tendency is to eliminate the general cultural and informational courses from the library school curriculum, requiring for admission everything of that nature considered essential for successful library work. Courses in literature are still given in some schools, but usually in a limited way as a part of the subject of book selection. A "fiction seminar", or special course in the study of fiction, is still given in about half of the schools. Where this is considered important, it is not looked upon as a cultural subject, but rather as a part of the technical equipment of the library worker, needed equally by those who have and those who have not had adequate college courses in literature. There is no doubt that such a course is valuable for the librarian who is called upon to select and purchase fiction for his library and to guide the reading of its patrons. The point that seems to be overlooked, however, is that for similar reasons the library school student needs instruction in the literature of scientific, technical, business, social, economic, and political subjects. Instruction in such subjects is even more important than in pure literature, since the standard library reference books and current guides for book selection in fiction and pure literature are more numerous and of higher quality than in scientific and practical subjects in general. Neglect of these large, new fields of interest on the part of the reading public may be due in part to the one-sided character of the library school curriculum. Too much attention is still paid by the library schools to pure literature, both in their entrance requirements and in their curricula. The traditional view of the library as the workshop and playground of the literary and leisure classes persists, though social and economic subjects are now competing for first place in the interests of book selection experts.

It is impossible, within the library school curriculum, to give instruction in the wide range of subjects which must claim the attention of the professional librarian. To be equipped for his work he must enter upon this professional training with nothing less than a good all-round college education. Many library schools still consider it desirable to give a course in current events in order to create an intelligent interest in the more important subjects that engage the attention of the reading public. For the most part, however, these are the schools which require only a high school education for admission. Schools with higher standards of education look upon the teaching of current events as they would upon a course in elementary economics or general history - necessary, of course, for the skilled librarian but a prerequisite to, and not a part of, library school training.

The library school curriculum as it stands represents in the main the current demands of the librarians who employ the graduates and the experience of the graduates themselves. Most library school teachers and principals are keenly alert to discover any new topic of interest to librarians or any new development in the library world, in order to bring them into the curriculum. One school has an active advisory committee of three graduates to which the question of changes that may be desirable in the curriculum is regularly put. Another school circularizes its graduates periodically to get suggestions for new courses or new topics to be introduced. Everywhere library school officials have an ear to the ground for any sound of dissatisfaction with what the schools are teaching. This attitude, however, does not make for radical changes in the curriculum. Rather, it results in excessive conservatism and conformity to custom and tradition. The suggestions which come back to the schools are only echoes of what they have been doing.

No school has ever attempted or is now prepared to disregard what has been done in the past and make a thorough, scientific analysis of what training for professional library work should be and build its curriculum upon its findings, instead of following tradition and imitating others. A more aggressive leadership is needed. If the Carnegie Corporation is to take an interest in promoting training for library work, it should see to it that men and women of energy and initiative are brought into the schools. Some of the pioneers in the library school movement were of this type and they left their mark.

It would be ungracious to criticize the schools for not doing more to put library service on a higher plane. Within the limits of their pitifully small resources they have probably done all that can fairly be asked of them. Not, therefore, as a criticism, but as encouragement to push on to better things I would point out to the library schools an opportunity which is theirs to wield a potent influence in bringing about a new library movement. Some of the epoch-making advances just ahead in the library world are discussed elsewhere in this report. Standards of service are to be worked out; a certification system inaugurated; methods of training in service for library workers devised, including an effective system of correspondence instruction; and county libraries and library extension promoted to the point where "books for everybody" will be a reality. In university, research, and other types of libraries equally rich opportunities await the advent of leaders with vision and enthusiasm to set new standards of service. It is to the library schools that we should be able to turn for inspiration and guidance, but it must be confessed that trained leadership of the quality now demanded is not likely to be produced by the present curriculum and personnel of the professional schools.

CHAPTER 4

ENTRANCE REQUIREMENTS

Within certain limits it is probably true, as Mr. A. E. Bostwick, librarian of the St. Louis Public Library, says, that the greatest service of the library schools is in selecting people fitted for library work.[1] Certainly schools can not turn out a satisfactory product with only one year of instruction unless the students selected have the necessary education and special aptitude for library work. To the selection of their students all the schools pay special attention, though the methods employed seem to warrant careful scrutiny and possibly considerable revision. Little or no attempt seems to have been made to utilize modern vocational and psychological tests. Except as to age of applicants admitted (and minimum educational requirements) there is little agreement as to what entrance requirements should be.

As a rule, applicants must be at least twenty-one years of age and not over thirty-five. Two or three schools put the lower limit at twenty years, while one specifies thirty and another forty years as the age beyond which a person should not attempt to enter library work through the schools. Though persons above thirty-five are seldom rigidly excluded, they are strongly advised against taking the course unless they have been continuously engaged in similar intellectual pursuits. Persons over thirty-five are said to find the work difficult and to be at a decided disadvantage in finding positions.
.....

[1] Proceedings of the American Library Association, 1912, p. 155

A four years' college course is required for admission to only two schools, the New York State Library School and the University of Illinois Library School. The Los Angeles and the Carnegie Library Schools require a college degree only for the special course in high school library work. Even the college course is not considered sufficient by the better schools unless it has included two foreign languages. "A knowledge of foreign languages is always necessary," says the New York State Library School, "and each additional language with which the student is acquainted is a direct professional asset." The "best preparation for general library work is a college course which includes a rather wide range of subjects." Most of the schools recognize the value of a college education, but do not find it practicable to require it for admission. In the Los Angeles school "two years of college will ordinarily be required. Four years of college is strongly advised and is essential for school library work." The Wisconsin catalogue states that "the importance of a four years' college course as an educational equipment for library work can not be too strongly emphasized."

Admission to all the schools, except New York State and the University of Illinois, is by examination, although applicants having a degree from an approved college are accepted without examination in practically all others, with the reservation by some that the college course must have included a broad training and modern languages. In all cases applicants for examination are required to have had four years of high school, or its equivalent. The examinations of all the schools cover about the same range of subjects - history, literature, general information and current events, and one or more modern languages. The purpose and scope of these examinations are well expressed in the following statement from the circular of the New York Public Library School:

> The entrance examination is designed to rest the candidate's qualifications for professional library training, and particularly to determine whether he possesses the habits of mind and the funda-

mental knowledge essential to the proper performance of his duties as a librarian. It involves answering questions on history, current events, general information, and literature, together with translation of French and of one other modern foreign language, preferably German, the choice of which is subject to approval by the Faculty. The questions, while allowing fair range of choice, assume reasonable familiarity with the main facts and names of literary and general history; and as regards the present, an intelligent interest in local, national, and international affairs."

Typical lists of examination questions are given in an appendix to this report. To the ordinary, educated person, and even the experienced library worker who has been out of school or college for a few years, the questions asked in many entrance examinations may seem too difficult and varied, expecially in history and literature. But the examinations follow practically the same lines each year, so that a candidate in possession of a series of questions from the different schools can form a pretty close estimate of what he must do to pass. It does not appear to be the practice of the schools to mark the papers closely or to hold to any definite passing mark, the theory being that the examiners can learn what they need to know about the candidate whether he answers the questions correctly or not.

Two possible criticisms may be made of these examinations. If the questions are used primarily as mental or psychological tests, they are very crude and unscientific. Far better tests could be devised for selecting persons with the requisite general information and personal qualities to fit them for library work; and tests, too, which would not appear so formidable that many excellent persons are deterred by the fear of failure and disgrace from attempting to enter a library school. On the other hand, the kind of examinations commonly used can not be considered as an adequate means of testing the candidate's general education and information. They cover too narrow a range of subjects and in too superficial a way.

Languages and general information are of fundamental importance for all professional library work. Special knowledge of literature and history, on the other hand, are not more important for many kinds of library service than social and applied sciences. As an educational preparation for library work nothing has been discovered which can take the place of a thorough college course of varied content. The University of Illinois and certain other schools suggest in some detail a program of college studies which should be followed in preparation for library work. A high school graduate may often pass the type of entrance examination given by the library schools as readily as the college graduate. Nevertheless, the college graduate of equal native ability has a breadth of view and an ability to attack new problems and master them which is very important for the professional library worker, but which is seldom found in one whose education has not been continued beyond the high school.

We do not mean to imply that every college graduate is fitted for library work. It may well be that even when the college degree is required some properly constructed selective test should also be applied. The point that should not be lost sight of is that a high school education does not fit anyone for professional library service, and that no entrance examinations can be devised which will serve as a substitute for four years of college education.

Entrance examinations are usually held in June, though several of the library schools which admit by examination also hold another in the fall. By the cooperation of local libraries candidates who live too far from the school may take the tests in or near their own home town. Since the examinations of all the schools using that method cover approximately the same range of subjects and hold to about the same minimum standards of education, the desirability of uniform examinations or a single examination for all the schools suggests itself. Some of the schools have felt the need for such a system. It is increasingly difficult to prepare examinations without repeating questions previously asked by some school. A uniform system would put all candidates on the same basis and make it unnecessary for a student to take the examination of two schools or more so that if he fails to pass for one he may still enter another. Some school authorities believe a higher grade of student would be secured by uniform tests. If scientific and approved tests are to be employed, it is particularly desirable to have them worked out cooperatively. The uniform college entrance examinations need only be cited to show the advantage and possibilities of such a system. A student who passes the general examination could select the school he prefers to attend, while the school itself would be free to accept or not accept those who pass the general examination.

As matters stand at present, however, there is little likelihood that separate examinations by the schools will be abandoned. Some of the schools take a seemingly unwarranted pride in their own particular questions; others find it advantageous to use flexible standards in rating the papers of applicants. The heads of some schools state that they seek a particular type of student and for that reason could not dispense with their own examinations. The latter objection would be more convincing if some clear description of the special type of student sought were given. Should the national certification board, recommended elsewhere in this report, become a reality it may be possible to work out uniform admission tests that will satisfy all parties. For the time being, local conditions, jealousies and rivalries stand squarely in the way of this as of many other desirable improvements.

Perhaps the most mooted feature of the entrance requirements of library schools is actual experience in library work. The views of those who insist on the desirability of such previous experience are well expressed in this statement which appears in the catalogue of the Library

School of the University of Wisconsin: "It is desired that as many as possible shall come to the school with library experience. Practical work in a good library for a year or more, in addition to the educational and literary attainments, is the best preparation for the year's work in the school. It tests the candidate's aptitude for library work, gives a knowledge of library terms, and familiarity with library processes, and makes a student more eager for, and appreciative of, what the library school has to offer. ... While it has not seemed wise as yet to establish an absolutely rigid requirement of library work extending over a definite period, still this preliminary library experience is considered so important that applicants without it are strongly advised to spend much more than the required several months in apprentice work before entering the school." The New York State Library School also considers previous experience so desirable that "all admitted students without such experience are strongly urged to spend as much time as practicable in voluntary or other staff service in their local libraries or elsewhere before entering school." "Some library experience," it is further stated in the latest catalogue, "will in all probability be an entrance requirement in the near future."

On the other hand, one of the most important library schools does not require previous experience and the head of that school, a person whose judgment is to be trusted, does not even recommend it. The head of another school of high standing states that he "prefers to get students before they are spoiled." The same view is taken by still another leading school principal. Many could agree with Miss Alice Kroeger, formerly principal of the Drexel Institute Library School, that "students with experience often do no better work than those without and they often have much to unlearn."

It is obvious that the disadvantages of previous experience which these three or four leading school authorities have in mind relate to actual employment in libraries of inferior standards, unsupervised, and unrelated to the student's actual need of preparation for school work. Unless the school can plan such practical work and actually supervise it (and this is, of course, seldom practicable), previous experience is very likely to prove a positive handicap.

There is no doubt, however, that the wholly inexperienced student does need an orientation in the library business before being plunged into the maze of technicalities of the professional library course. He needs to become familiar with the ordinary library tools and terminology, and to get some insight into the aims and methods of library service. This orientation is accomplished by several schools through a preliminary period of practice work for inexperienced students just before the opening of the regular school year, usually in the library with which the school is connected. This preliminary practice ordinarily covers two weeks.

It is not clear that this short practice period is always so organized and supervised as to accomplish efficiently the desirable or necessary orientation. It would seem that if this is as important as many authorities believe it to be, special pains should be taken to give the student in this preliminary course as good an introduction as possible through lectures, readings, inspections, and individual conferences. It is to be feared that at present too much is left to chance in this preliminary period. Unless full advantage is taken of the opportunity offered through the preliminary course, it is of doubtful value.

Many of the schools have much to say about the "personality" qualification for admission. Several of the circulars announce that in considering applications for admission personal qualifications and natural aptitudes for library work are taken into consideration. The usual method of applying this personality test is an interview with the head of the school. The following quotation from the circular of one of the schools illustrates the stress laid upon "personality" and the "interview."

> "Personal qualities and a more or less discriminating sense of literary values are, however, essential considerations.

> It follows, therefore, that an interview ... is an important entrance requirement. Despite the expenditure of time and money involved by such an interview, it is insisted upon, except under unusual conditions."

Undoubtedly it is very important to give much weight to personal qualifications and natural aptitudes. It is impossible, however, to put much confidence in the personality tests as now applied. In the first place, no attempt has been made to determine scientifically what personal qualities are essential. It seems to be assumed that library work is of a homogeneous character and that consequently the same personality tests can be applied to all who desire to enter library service. It may be questioned whether there is any such thing as "library work" in general. There are many kinds of library work, and if there are any special capacities and aptitudes which make for success, they must be considered in relation to each distinct type of work. It will probably be found that any qualities which are necessary for library work in general are just those qualities required for success in most other occupations.

The first thing for the library schools to do is to tell us what qualities they look for in candidates. The next thing is to give some assurance that they are able through a brief personal interview by one person to detect the presence or absence of those qualities with sufficient exactness to justify giving weight to the result. The impressionistic method of the interview seems likely to reflect the personality of the interviewer as much as that of the interviewed. If it were possible to arrange independent interviews by several competent persons, the result could be accepted with much greater confidence. Whatever the method of selecting applicants, misfits in library work will occasionally occur. It is not apparent that the personal interview does anything more than eliminate those who are physically unfitted for any kind of library service.

As conducted at present the personality test may actually be responsible in part for the acute shortage of competent library workers. Those who are applying the "personality" test have their own background of experience and acquaintance with types of libraries and library work. Their undefined ideal personality seems likely to embody the qualities they would seek for the kinds of library work they know best. By eliminating all others in the selection process, school officials may unconsciously and unintentionally deprive libraries of those who would make excellent workers in special positions. The impressionistic, or interview, method cannot disclose temperamental defects. These come to light later and every school has among its graduates persons who constitute perpetual "problems" for school principals who assume, as most of them do, a large measure of responsibility for keeping every graduate in employment and contented.

Much can be said in favor of simplifying entrance requirements by specifying a full college course for all students in professional library schools and at least a high school course for admission to training classes. If desired, the school can call for the applicant's college record and accept only those whose work is of high grade. If classes must be further limited other tests can be applied to applicants, but any effort to base selection on personal qualities and aptitudes for library work should be discouraged until such qualities are carefully and clearly defined and more accurate methods of detecting the possession of such qualities are worked out by vocational psychologists. It does not appear that up to this time any of the library school authorities have approached their problem in the scientific spirit or made any use of scientific methods.

Before leaving the general topic of admission requirements, some reference may be made to certain minor features. The earlier schools concerned themselves largely with training in technique, and even the mechanics, of library work. With the lapse of time a differentiation, not clearly recognized, however, has taken place between the broader or professional type of training and the training necessary for those who are to do the actual clerical work of record keeping, etc. The development of library work as a profession has been hampered by the tendency on the part of the public to look upon it as wholly clerical in nature. The library schools and the actual organization of libraries have not only done little to remove this handicap, but have even done much unconsciously to perpetuate it. Some of the library schools still require students to acquire the vertical or library handwriting, while nearly all of them lay great stress on skillful use of the typewriter. Several schools require the ability to operate a typewriter with fair accuracy and speed before admission; others permit students to make good the deficiency during the year's course, often providing machines for practice.

There is much to be said, of course, in favor of ability to operate a typewriter as a part of the general equipment of any educated person. Any intellectual worker is likely to derive considerable advantage from the ability to make skillful use of the typewriter, but it is not clear that such skill should be required as a part of the professional librarian's equipment any more than that of the teacher, the engineer, or the business man. The typewriter is far more indispensable in every business office than it is in the average library, yet the professional schools of business do not make typewriting an essential part of their course. That is left to the schools for training the clerical staffs required in every business office. The same general relations should obtain between the library training class and the professional library school. It would not be surprising to find that able and ambitious college men and women hesitate to look to library work as a professional career when assured by the catalogues of the so-called professional training schools that "a ready ability to use the typewriter is an important part of a modern librarian's equipment" and is "necessary in almost any library position."

CHAPTER 5

THE TEACHING STAFF

A detailed analysis of the training and experience of members of the teaching staffs of twelve of the library schools seems to indicate a quite definite lack of fitness of a large proportion for giving instruction of high professional character to students with college or university education. The table on the following page tells the whole story. About half (48 per cent) of the instructors giving ten lectures or more during the year 1921 were not college graduates. Many, it is true, had a partial college course, while others had carried their studies somewhat beyond the high school in educational institutions of some kind.

It should not be inferred that a college degree is considered an absolutely indispensable part of the equipment of the library school instructor. Certainly some of the most successful teachers now on the staffs of the library schools are without the college degree. The bachelor's degree is, in general, however, a fair measure of an individual's intellectual equipment and has come to be regarded as the minimum essential for all kinds of teaching above the elementary school. In no part of this country would instruction in a well-organized high school be considered acceptable if half of the teachers were not college graduates.

Library school instruction, moreover, should rank not with the high school but with the college. In respect to college faculties the best opinion is even more insistent on full college education and in the better institutions an advanced degree is usually a _sine_ _qua_ _non_ for instructors. It does not seem probable that a few small library schools will get better

General Education, Technical Training, and Library Experience of Library School Instructors, Including Only Those Giving Courses of At Least Ten Classroom Hours, in 1920-1921

School number	No. of instructors	No. of college graduates	Graduates of a library school	No. teaching in same library school from which graduated	No. having previous teaching experience	No. having any teacher training	Experience in library work of value in teaching	
							Good	Apparently inadequate
1	6	2	6	1	2	1	5	1
2	17	11	16	13	0	0	10	7
3	5	1	5	4	0	0	4	1
4	5	3	4	1	2	0	4	1
5	9	5	5	2	2	0	7	2
6	8	5	6	3	3	1	5	3
7	9	6	8	6	3	2	7	2
8	11	5	7	2	1	1	9	2
9	5	4	3	0	3	2	4	1
10	9	4	8	4	1	0	7	2
11	8	4	5	0	3	0	3	5
12	8	2	8	6	0	0	3	5
Total	100	52	81	42	20	7	68	32

results from a teaching staff of which 50% are without the bachelor's degree than would a college. No self-respecting college would attempt it. Some of the protagonists of things as they are attempt to justify the existing condition by belittling the value of a college education and arguing that some instructors are better without it than others would be with it.

As a matter of fact, the present situation is due almost entirely to economic necessities and inadequate standards. College graduates of fair ability are not attracted by the kind of salaries paid by the library schools. Consequently library schools have to recruit their staffs from a group which is not eligible for attractive positions in other fields. If proper salaries were paid in all library schools and the best instructors possible were secured, it would not be long before at least 90 per cent would have the college training.

Most library schools also still retain something of the flavor of apprenticeship training in which beginners are put into the hands of those who have not yet risen to the higher ranks, but who have become proficient in some part of their craft. If the library schools hope to take rank with other professional schools of the higher grade, they must accept the existing academic standards for all teaching above the elementary schools. Throughout this report is has been pointed out that professional library work requires a college education. College graduates going into library service should not be asked to take their professional training under a group of instructors one-half of whom are without the college viewpoint.

The library schools have been more careful, in recruiting their staffs, to get technical training than general education. While only 52 per cent of the instructors are college graduates, 80 per cent have completed some kind of a course in a library school. It is significant also that 42 per cent are teaching in the same school in which they took their own library training. Certain schools, by choice or necessity, choose nearly all their instructors from their own graduates. The obvious disadvantages of this practice are an inevitable inbreeding and a certain imperviousness to new ideas or methods.

It is not at all surprising that among library school instructors special skill in teaching is not conspicuous. Only 7 per cent of the instructors have had any kind of training in the science or art of teaching. It seems safe to assume that none at all have had the slightest instruction in the methodology of the teaching of library subjects. In recent years the growth of vocational education has drawn attention to the need of special teacher training for each of the many subjects to be taught. The need of preparation for teachers of agriculture, for example, seems to be well recognized. A recent report of the United States Bureau of Education does not regard the work of a state agricultural college as *bona fide* "unless the curriculum includes at least a two-hour course in special methods of teaching agriculture and at least one three-hour course in either psychology or education." Is that an unreasonable standard? Is special preparation for his work any more important for the teacher of agriculture than for the teacher of library theory and practice?

Only 20 per cent of library school teachers bring to the library school any experience in teaching. The outstanding successes on the faculties are found almost entirely within this 20 per cent who had behind them good teaching experience in school or college before taking up library school instruction.

Opinions may differ as to the desirability of requiring actual experience in library work as a qualification for teaching the various subjects in the curriculum of the library school. Some teachers lacking extensive experience in any kind of professional library work may prove more satisfactory than others whose experience has been excellent but who lack teaching ability. Granted a scholarly attitude of mind, a thorough knowledge of the subject matter, an interesting personality and ability to teach, an instructor's work must benefit very greatly from a considerable period of somewhat varied experience in library work. Long experience alone, however, is no evidence of qualification for library school teaching.

An examination of available information as to the practical library experience of these one hundred instructors indicates that a little over two-thirds (68) have held library positions of such a character for such a period and with sufficient bearing on subjects taught as to make it possible to describe their experience as "good." The experience of thirty-two of the instructors, on the other hand, must be characterized as "apparently inadequate." This is not surprising, however, in view of the very low salaries paid. A man or woman with fair qualifications for teaching and good experience can ordinarily command a much larger salary in practical work.

Almost without exception the library school principals complain of extreme difficulty they experience in securing new teachers. Low salaries are probably at the root of the problem. On the surface, however, it does not seem to be primarily a question of salaries. A strong disinclination toward teaching pervades the library profession, largely as the result, perhaps, of the fact that so many librarians were formerly teachers who have found library work more congenial, if not more remunerative. A further difficulty in finding persons to fill the comparatively few positions on library school faculties is, that of those who are not disinclined to teach not many are qualified. Few of those who have the necessary professional knowledge and experience have either the essential personal qualifications or the training or experience required for successful teaching. As shown in the preceding table, very few members of library school faculties have been teachers, and yet this is most important.

Concerted effort should be directed toward raising the quality of instruction in the library schools. Though an increase in salaries will not of itself bring relief, other measures are likely to be of no avail so long as salaries remain at anything like the present level. A teaching position on a library school faculty must in some way be made to carry at least as much professional prestige as the higher administrative positions in public libraries. It must be made possible for men and women of the highest quality, who can also teach, to find a permanently satisfactory career in library school instruction. The schools themselves must be put on a higher professional basis and an opportunity offered to instructors, through longer vacations, freedom from excessive drudgery and overloaded schedules, to make contributions to the scholarly or practical sides of some branch of library work.

Library school teaching may be less attractive than college teaching because of the comparative lack of freedom as to the content both of the curriculum as a whole and of the individual courses. The tendency has existed from the beginning for library schools to be more or less dominated by a single personality. The ideas and ideals of that personality, consciously or unconsciously, mold the content of the courses and even determine the methods of instruction. Most school principals are conscious of exercising control only to the extent required to prevent over-lapping of courses and direct conflict as to rules and practices taught in the schools. As a matter of fact, actual control probably goes much farther - so far, indeed, that little scope is left for originality and the enthusiasms of the gifted teacher.

In a one-year course this is almost inevitable. The time is so short for covering the wide range of topics with which an acquaintance is considered essential, that the curriculum must be very closely planned and organized. In the curriculum of any professional school, the necessity for covering a specified range of subjects is likely to seem more compelling than in a college of liberal arts. In library schools particular effort seems to be made to give the student a speaking acquaintance with every kind of library work and every problem he is likely to meet. This tends to reduce the teaching to routine and to make the work unattractive to the genuine teacher to whom it seems more important to give the student a professional attitude toward his work, to awaken his enthusiasm, and to develop his power of attacking problems, than to race superficially through a prescribed list of topics.

For apprenticeship and training classes a minute control of the content of the course and the rules taught may be quite proper. For the professional library school it is at least an open question as to whether better results would not follow from a greater use of the project method, with less lecturing and a much less strict adherence to syllabi, which years of use have made well nigh exhaustive on every subject.

We should probably cease to expect the library schools to send out graduates crammed with information about every conceivable subject, from incunabula to color-band filing and demand, rather, men and women of liberal education, well grounded in the fundamentals of library practice and ideals, familiar with the librarian's tools and resourceful in attacking and solving problems as they arise. Instead of suppressing differences in the views of library school instructors, it might be well to encourage them to emphasize their own opinions and points of view. Otherwise students, having little incentive to think through the problems and form their own opinions, take them ready made from the instructor who teaches what the principal has decided to be the official policy of the school.

CHAPTER 6

METHODS OF INSTRUCTION

The lecture method predominates in all library school instruction, although the better the school the fewer the lectures and the larger the use of other methods. In catalogue descriptions of courses, lectures are usually said to be supplemented by readings, problems, recitations, seminars, class discussion, class practice, quizzes, or individual conferences with students. While the proportion of lectures and other forms of instruction necessarily varies somewhat, depending on the nature of the subject, the size of the class, etc., nevertheless, most of the library schools apparently place an excessive dependence on the lecture. This is frankly admitted by most of the library school authorities, who are quite ready to agree that in general the best schools and the best teachers to the least lecturing.

Although it is freely conceded that the lecture method is overworked, it is claimed that the worst abuses have now disappeared and that under existing conditions further improvement is scarcely possible. This problem is not peculiar to library schools. In all higher and professional instruction the lecture has proved to be the line of least resistance for the poorly prepared, overworked and unskilled teacher. Yet even the skilled teacher in the library school finds a measure of justification for much lecturing. Inadequate preparation of a part of the students in a class seems to put a natural limit on the effectiveness of other methods. Library school classes in which college graduates with excellent library experience are mixed up with students having only a high school education and no acquaintance with libraries drive even the best teachers to an excessive use of the "pouring in" method. None of the schools are large enough to permit of a classification or grading of students on the basis of education and experience.

As the curriculum has developed it contains subjects of somewhat minor importance to which only a few hours of instruction can be given. The necessary orientation, for which the lecture is probably the best method, requires so much of the time allotted for the subject that in order to cover the ground in the little time that is left, the instructor persuades himself that he must lecture continuously. While a conscious effort on the part of the administrative and teaching staff to economize the students' time is entirely praiseworthy, it is doubtful whether the desired result can best be reached by emphasizing the lecture method. The general use of mimeographed syllabi represents a vast improvement over the old lecture system. Yet one still finds occasionally that library school students are required to write into their notes verbatim the language of the instructor. The need of better text-books and manuals to save the students' and teachers' time and improve the efficiency of library school teaching is so acute that it will be discussed in more detail in another chapter.

It must also be made clear, in fairness to the library schools, that methods of instruction of which more use might advantageously be made, are out of the question because of the heavy demand they would make on the instructor's time in the holding of individual conferences and the reading and revision of written work. It is particularly important, not only in teaching all of the so-called "record work", but also in such courses as book selection and reference to require the student to express himself in writing. In the professional school this should not be allowed to degenerate into a mere drill in routine processes for the sake of acquiring skill and speed, but should be used judiciously to insure rapid and firm grasp of principles involved. One of the results of the common failure to distinguish between professional library training and the training for routine and clerical work is that library schools which should be conducted on the professional plane do not stop at giving their students a grasp on principles and methods, but are deadening their initiative and enthusiasm by drilling them in the routine processes of hand work and the memorizing of rules and classes. The professional library schools have need to be on their guard against over-emphasizing skill in clerical technique. There is danger that by forcing upon their students a perfection in detail, they will stifle the indispensable qualities of enthusiasm, imagination, and initiative.

The wholly legitimate and desirable use of written work is limited in the library schools today by lack of proper assistance for the instructors. Each school has one or two "revisers" who assist the instructors in reading and correcting written work. Not much improvement can be made in library school instruction until money is available to employ a sufficient number of competent revisers to free the instructor from the detailed work which now takes time that should be devoted to study and research and contacts with practical library work and his colleagues in the profession. The reviser is the laboratory assistant which in important scientific schools may outnumber the teaching staff itself, but which poverty has all but denied to the library schools.

We cannot refrain at this point from noting that what has just been said about the nature of instruction in library subjects shows that it is peculiarly adapted to the correspondence method. Even in the residence schools where student and teacher can meet and talk, the best instruction in many courses is carried on by means of written communication between them. Correspondence instruction as a method of "training in service" is fully discussed in a later chapter.

One of the curious results of low standards for both instructors and students and a lack of contact of many schools with institutions of learning is the incongruous adaptation of the methods and terminology of the university. One who, being accustomed to think of the seminar as a group of students engaged in original research under the guidance of a scholar and investigator, comes upon the "seminar" of high school students engaged in acquiring a modicum of elementary information on book selection or some other subject in the curriculum under a teacher without college training or experience in research can understand a certain reluctance on the part of university faculties to accord the library schools the recognition which their field of work and general relations to intellectual pursuits abundantly entitle them. It is fortunate, however, that the schools do take themselves with the utmost seriousness and by dint of patient and devoted, if not brilliant, effort do achieve results which are surprisingly large when measured by their resources in personnel and equipment. Better teaching equipment, higher standards of education and experience on the part of the teaching staff, and more attention to methods of instruction, are obvious needs of all the library schools, though, of course, in varying degrees.

On no question in the administration of the library schools is there a wider diversity of opinion than on the use of part-time as against full-time instructors. As library schools have virtually all developed in close connection with some public or university library, their direction and most of the teaching have been in the hands of the members of the library staff. Certain of the schools have separated the school staff from the library staff and are convinced that no other plan is practicable. Other schools, on the contrary, have no full-time instructors at all and seem equally confident in the superiority of that method. Most of the schools have one or more persons giving full time to instruction, a larger or smaller share of the teaching being done, as a rule, by members of some library staff in the vicinity. The unanimity with which each school principal defends its own practice suggests that library schools have acquired the convenient habit of making a virtue of necessity.

There can be no doubt that the part-time and full-time systems, each have their peculiar advantages, as well as disadvantages; that under one set of conditions the balance may be in favor of part-time instruction, while under other conditions full-time service may give the best results. For the most part, the actual practice of the schools is not determined by theory but by finances. Schools in a financial position to employ a corps of full-time instructors usually do so.

The great advantage claimed for part-time instruction, and usually the only advantage mentioned by its advocates, is the opportunity through constant contact with actual library work to keep abreast of library progress. It is alleged that the full-time instructor is in danger of becoming an impractical theorist and even a formalist or reactionist. The claim is made in some schools that under the part-time system a better type of person is secured for both sides of the work than either school or library alone could hope to secure. Unfortunately, the results of actual experience under the two systems are far more conclusive. The two schools which give a two-year course and require a college degree for admission pursue diametrically opposite policies. The University of Illinois school has a separate faculty, believing that the greater part of any professional course should be in the hands of instructors giving full time to the work and that it is difficult to secure persons who can give first-class service on both the library staff and the school staff. The New York State Library School, on the other hand, depends for its instruction almost entirely on the staff of the state library and holds that any other method would be far less satisfactory.

Serious disadvantages inhere in the part-time method. The instructor gets no continuing contact with the student and is not available so freely for consultation and informal discussion. Part-time instructors are not likely to view their teaching in a broadly professional spirit or to take a deep interest in educational problems. In any such division of work, one part or the other, or both, are almost certain to suffer.

Not many of those whose opinions have been sought fail to recognize the need of one or two full-time instructors, at least, to look after details of organization and administration and to give the technical and major courses - cataloguing, classification and perhaps book selection. The part-time instructor in such subjects as cataloguing and classification is in too great danger of teaching the methods he uses in his own library. For training schools that is perhaps acceptable, but for strictly professional instruction a broadly comparative and detached point of view is essential. Many of the minor subjects in the curriculum can well be taught by librarians fresh from their professional duties.

Perhaps it would not be altogether fair, under present conditions, to use as a basis for ranking the schools the proportion of the teaching staff giving full time to the school. That, however, is coming to be a practical method of appraising other kinds of professional schools and must sooner or later be applied also to the library schools. This is, in a sense, inevitable because the part-time instructor is usually a result of an attempt to conduct a school with insufficient funds. The school with an adequate income, other conditions being the same, will be the best, for it will employ the best instructors, who will give all their time to their school work.

It appears from all the available evidence that a library school of high professional rank should be large enough and provided with sufficient funds to require the full-time services of at least four instructors to give the major courses, particularly the so-called technical courses. Being conscious of the dangers pointed out as inherent in full-time service, the school should shape its policy and the individual instructor should make definite plans to get the necessary contact with actual library work and problems by vacation service on library staffs, in making library surveys, by sabbatical years, etc.

The special or visiting lecturer, even more than the part-time instructor, is an outstanding characteristic of nearly all library schools, though in some cases the difference between special lecturer and part-time instructor is not very clear. Ordinarily the special lecturer gives only one or two lectures. He may be either a resident or non-resident specialist who is brought in from year to year to supplement the regular instruction in some definite way. The special lecture of the right type is considered quite essential in the conduct of many of the minor courses, but satisfactory lecturers are difficult to secure.

Sometimes a course, such as library administration, is made to consist largely of these special lectures, the instructor's part being to correlate and supplement them as best he can. In theory the special lecturer, like the part-time instructor, is supposed to bring to the classroom the practical point of view and to help in making a vital contact between theoretical instruction and actual library work.

Certain special lectures, usually classified as inspirational, may have little or no direct relation to the work of instruction, while still others are conceded to be neither instructional nor inspirational, but are considered to have value in introducing the students to the leading personalities in the library profession. In the latter group are found library administrators who are invited to talk to the students solely for placement purposes. Impressed by the merits of the school which urges him to become a special lecturer, the prospective employer is likely to seek no further for candidates for positions on his own staff.

The best authorities frankly confess that the special lecture feature of library school instruction has been overworked. The better schools have consequently in recent years virtually abandoned or greatly limited the number of such lectures. When put to the test, they have been found to have very little either of informational or inspirational value. This is particularly true of the single lecture. The value of special lectures is said to increase with the number given by one individual on the same general topic. It has been found difficult to correlate single lectures, even when they are excellent in themselves; but too often they have been entirely disappointing. Speakers classed as specialists frequently fail to develop their subject as desired. One library school principal, admitting the futility of special lectures, holds that they do nevertheless have a good effect by giving the students more respect for and confidence in their regular instructors.

For some schools the expense involved constitutes the principal objection to the special lectures. Casual lecturers, usually librarians of professional standing who happen to be at the school or in the vicinity and are asked to talk to a class, are ordinarily not paid, but as a rule the special and visiting lecturers receive an honorarium of $5 up to $25, traveling expenses also being paid, at least for the single lecture.

To reduce the item of traveling expense and yet secure desirable lecturers from a considerable distance, the library schools in the eastern states have cooperated informally in arranging lecture circuits. The principal of one of the schools is designated each year to arrange a schedule for one or more lecturers, usually of the inspirational type. Traveling expenses which would make one lecture or two prohibitive for a single school bear less heavily when shared by three or four schools. The difficulties of finding lecturers acceptable to several schools and of arranging satisfactory schedules tend to confine the lecture circuit system, even in the east, to rather narrow limits.

In the central and far west, distances are so great that it is seldom feasible for as many as two schools to cooperate even on a single lecture.

A more ambitious plan of cooperation among library schools proposed from time to time combines to some extent the system of part-time instructor and visiting lecturer. It seems desirable that many of the minor subjects in the library school curriculum should be taught by specialists. Local specialists not being available and the work covering only a few weeks each year so that a full-time member of the faculty is out of the question, it naturally occurs to anyone to suggest that a person who combines the required special knowledge or experience and teaching ability should be engaged to go from school to school repeating a short intensive course. In theory it would be possible in this way for each school to enjoy the best instruction. Too often the minor subjects have to be presented by some local librarian not especially qualified or by some regular member of the school staff who is not a specialist in the subject and is already over-burdened with the range of subjects he is expected to teach.

In a very limited way cooperative effort of this kind has been employed. The Los Angeles School and the Riverside School, for example, both employ Mr. W. Elmo Reavis, of Los Angeles, to teach bookbinding. Perhaps the two other schools on the Pacific Coast would benefit by engaging the same excellent teacher. Serious difficulties, however, at once arise. Mr. Reavis might find that his business would not permit a month's absence in Berkeley and another in Seattle. It might not be practicable to give up his business and spend his entire time going from school to school. To most persons such an occupation would be distasteful and there is some question as to whether the quality of a teacher's work would be maintained through even a short period of such teaching. Again, there is the difficulty, at times insuperable, of the inflexible schedules of individual schools. On account of the time lost between courses and extra traveling and living expenses, the cost to each school of securing such specialists might prove prohibitive with their present budgets. Similar difficulties also stand in the way of exchange of instructors, even for short intensive courses, though undoubtedly much benefit would result from such exchanges if they could be arranged.

Such considerations may perhaps render any extensive scheme of cooperative instruction impracticable at the present time. But as the schools raise their standards and undertake more specialization they will probably be forced to seek for opportunities to cooperate in this way. With fewer and larger schools and more adequate budgets, it may also become possible to do many things, which, under present conditions, seem impossible, however desirable in theory.

CHAPTER 7

TEXT-BOOKS

The efficiency of library schools and other training agencies would be greatly increased by satisfactory teaching aids, particularly text-books. For the most part, the volumes which students are required to buy, such as the American Library Association Cataloguing Rules, the Decimal Classification, American Library Association List of Subject Headings, and Kroeger's Guide to Reference Books are not text-books at all, but manuals of practice and reference books for the practicing librarian. The student must, of course, learn to use these tools of the trade, just as the engineering student must learn to use engineering handbooks, books of formulae, the slide rule, tables of logarithms, and other aids to computation. But, while familiarity with such tools, an understanding of their purpose, and some skill in their use is indispensable, an engineering school could hardly use them as text-books in courses devoted to mastering the principles of any branch of engineering.

The emphasis given here to the lack of text-books should not be construed as a recommendation that library school instruction be conducted by the text-book methods, the teacher assigning "lessons" and hearing recitations. Perhaps that obsolete method, however, has as much to commend it as the extreme form of the lecture system under which the instructor attempts by the classroom lecture to give the student all the information he is supposed to need. Most of the subjects taught in the library school involve the presentation of much detailed information.

In bibliographical and technical subjects, such as cataloguing and other record work, much importance attaches to the precise form in which the facts are written or printed. In many of the fundamental subjects, also, free use should be made of illustration in the way of reproduction of forms and records, photographs, plans, etc. Much of the content of the curriculum needs, like the subject of architecture, to be presented to the eye, so that ordinary lectures are a peculiarly inappropriate method. The student needs to have placed before him an unusually large amount of printed matter, much of it especially prepared for instructional purposes.

Two types of printed matter are needed, the text-book and the treatise, the first designed particularly for the student in training and the latter more of the nature of an encyclopedic compilation of practice and procedure, methods and policies adapted to the needs of both the beginner and the experienced library worker. From the pedagogical standpoint virtually no text-books are available for the library schools and other training agencies. The efficiency of all types of library training agencies would be incalculably increased by well written manuals presenting a reasonably complete exposition of the theory and practice of the various subjects, with enough concrete description and illustration to fix the principles and the main facts in the student's mind, the whole presented in such form and arrangement as to lead the student into the subject by the easiest path and onward through its more difficult phases in the shortest time with the least effort on his part.

Every library school instructor has now to utilize some unsatisfactory substitute for the kind of teaching tools that should be available. In the hands of a skillful teacher the A. L. A. cataloguing rules or the Decimal Classification are better than no text-books at all, but without a teacher few students, however serious and capable, could make much progress with them. One of the chief difficulties that must be met and overcome in establishing the system of correspondence instruction recommended in this study is the lack of proper text-books. When such volumes do become available, they will mean much to the untrained, isolated worker everywhere.

Some teachers attempt to make up for the lack of text-books by preparing reading lists of the best available material on the topic, in the form of periodical articles, reports, papers, etc. On many important subjects, however, useful literature is not only inadequate, but scattered and inaccessible. The attempt to use it results in such waste of the student's time that some schools have abandoned required readings altogether.

The lack of text-books has resulted in a very extensive use of syllabi in mimeographed form prepared by each instructor for his own courses and revised from time to time. These syllabi, containing outlines of lectures, bibliographical matter, definitions, etc., are indeed a great step forward from the time when everything the student got was given to him in the form of lectures. Important points, definitions, and much detail regarded as important were dictated to the class slowly enough to enable the student to write it out precisely in longhand. Notebooks slowly and laboriously compiled in this way the student was taught to regard as indispensable, not only for the purpose of his school work, but also for guidance in dealing with problems to be met later in his active library work[1] - a kind of <u>vade mecum</u> or cyclopedia of library practice.

Adequate handbooks and treatises covering many phases of library administration and practice would relieve the schools of the necessity that seems now to confront them of presenting to their students largely through lectures a systematic and comparative description of library practice and procedure. The lack of a suitable professional literature of a cyclopedic nature seems to have a tendency to force the library schools to develop

-----
(1) One library school states in its catalogue that "the lecture notes of the students are examined from time to time, as to their form, content, orderly preservation, and <u>availability for future use.</u>"

their lecture courses in that direction. The effort to cover the subject comprehensively and completely to the last degree tends to obscure principles and policies by the very mass of detail, and to substitute the acquisition of facts for an understanding of their significance. If accessible and authoritative treatises were available, it would be easier to put professional instruction on a higher plane; the instructor would be relieved of the feeling of responsibility for systematically presenting every detail of the subject. This would also relieve the curriculum from extreme pressure and make it possible to devote more time to accumulating information on subjects which cannot easily be worked up from printed sources whenever the need arises.

It was apparently the need for something of this kind that prompted the publication of the A.L.A. Manual of Library Economy. This "manual" consists of some thirty-two chapters by different authors, all but three of which have appeared as preprints, these three being still in course of preparation. Eight of these chapters deal with types of libraries, eighteen with problems of organization and administration, and six with special forms of library work. Some of these preprints are used for instructional purposes in the schools, but none of them are adequate either as text-books or as manuals of practice. They are too brief and sketchy. On each important subject treated a volume instead of a pamphlet should be prepared.

If text-books and systematic treatises are so much needed, why are they not forthcoming? One reason is, perhaps, the comparatively small demand. The financial return does not promise to be sufficient to stimulate either their preparation or publication. The experience of the A. L. A. Publishing Board indicates, however, that such publications can be made to yield a small profit, though of course not enough to compensate the author for his work. The preparation of such works should not have to wait upon

a financial stimulus. Professional interest and service should be sufficient
and doubtless would be, save for the fact that comparatively few librarians
have either the capacity or the time for authorship. In education, engineering, medicine, law, accounting, and many other professions, technical
treatises and text-books multiply, regardless of slender financial returns
to the authors.

We must look to the leading experts in the library profession and,
above all, to the instructors in the library schools to produce an adequate
and worthy professional literature. Library schools must be able to pay
salaries that will secure for their instructional staffs the leaders in the
profession, who not only can teach but can contribute to library progress by producing useful and much needed publications. This will help to
give the library schools the prestige in university faculties which they now
lack and will aid in drawing a better class of students to the schools.

In my judgment a very important contribution could be made at
this time to the improvement of instruction in library schools by a comparatively small amount of money used to stimulate the preparation of textbooks and manuals adapted for instructional purposes. On the faculties of
the library schools are a few men and women who have been hoping for years
to have an opportunity to put into shape for publication the results of their
study and experience in a special field. Teaching schedules are heavy, however, and not many library schools can afford to give their instructors
sabbatical years. I would therefore recommend that the Carnegie Corporation
appropriate for a period of years a sum of money large enough to pay the
salary, and perhaps an allowance for traveling expenses, of one library
school instructor on leave of absence each year for the specific purpose
of enabling him to complete for publication a work which when published
will be useful to the schools and to the library profession generally.

Such a prize or fellowship should be made competitive and awarded by a properly constituted committee instructed to select the person who has in hand the piece of work most needed by the schools and so near completion that it can be finished within the year. The A. L. A. Publishing Board (endowed by Mr. Carnegie) would doubtless find it profitable to publish any book written under these conditions. The stimulating effect of this would not be confined to the prize winner of the year, but would extend to all who might hope by hard work to win it in some future year and would therefore begin at once to lay their plans to capture it later. I believe the entire effect on the teaching in the library schools would be good. Such a "fellowship" might be offered for a period of five years in the beginning. Toward the end of that period it would be easy to determine whether it should be continued or modified or abandoned. If the certification board recommended in this report should be organized, that would be an ideal body to entrust with the responsibility for awarding the fellowship.

CHAPTER 8

FIELD WORK

All library schools supplement their classroom instruction given in the form of lectures, readings, discussions, problems, seminars, etc., by bringing students into contact in one way or another with some phase of actual library work. The methods of accomplishing this differ very considerably, but the methods are no more divergent than the terminology used. The following terms, since they are met frequently and are used with different meanings, need to be defined: "Practice work," "practical work," "field work," "laboratory work." The Association of American Library Schools has made some effort to standardize the terminology, with the result that "practical work," as distinguished from "practice work," is now the accepted term for describing the activities supposed to be carried on by the student under actual library conditions. In some cases this is done under the supervision of representatives of the school, while in others practical work means actual library work done altogether outside of the supervision of the school. "Practice work" thus comes to mean class practice, or the work done by the student either in preparation for or following and definitely related to the classroom exercises. In cataloguing, classification, book selection, and other courses there is ample opportunity for class practice, that is, for work not done under actual conditions, but in accordance with assignments made by the instructor and later corrected or revised. "Field work" in some schools has exactly the same meaning as "practical work." Simmons College, for example, does not use the term "practical work" at all, but calls all work in outside libraries "field work." In general, however, the term tends to be used to describe that part of the practical work which is done in a library other than that with which the school is connected and frequently seems to be restricted to work in libraries at some distance from the school. But the terminology is not settled, some schools, Wisconsin for instance, using the terms practice, field practice, and practical work, interchangeably. Certain schools use the term "laboratory work," with the idea, apparently, that such a simile tends to put their field work on a more scientific basis or on a little higher plane. As a matter of fact, the class practice, such as can well be carried on apart from any actual operating library, bears to library instruction the same relation that laboratory work does to instruction in the natural sciences. Class practice is therefore as appropriately labeled laboratory work as is the field work.

"Practical work" is not a satisfactory term. Practical this part of the training is, as compared with the theoretical or abstract instruction of the classroom, but it need not be actual library work carried on under normal conditions, as the term implies. "Field work" is a much better term, since it carries no implication as to the student's relation to the library in which he makes his observations, nor does it imply that the student when he has finished his course is fully equipped for actual work without further experience.

In the course of his instruction the student should come into close contact with actual library work of many kinds. In doing this through his field work he may actually serve as a member of a library staff or he may be present merely as an observer, working out problems assigned by his instructor. If in the instructor's opinion he can carry on his observations better, can get a better insight into the problem assigned and do it in a shorter time by working as a member of a library staff, there can be no objection to that plan. But there must be many points in a professional library course at which the student can gain far more through a very short period of purposive observation than through a long period of actual service on a library staff. This point will be elaborated a little later.

Every library school recognizes to some extent the desirability of supplementing its theoretical instruction by contact with or active participation in some kind of actual library work. It does not appear, however, in the published or oral statements made on behalf of the schools that there is anywhere a very clear understanding of the underlying pedagogical principles involved. Certain schools seem to proceed upon the assumption that the classroom instruction itself may be expected to make of some of the students, at least, skilled librarians, and that the practical work is designed merely to demonstrate their skill or reveal the lack of it. "It is necessary and important," says the catalogue statement of one school, "that students be brought into contact with actual library conditions and their ability tested." Another aims by its practical work to give the students a "chance to measure themselves under actual conditions and coordinate what they have learned."

Other schools proceed on the theory that the practical work is merely a means of clinching the classroom instruction by giving a better understanding of theory and principles and a firmer grasp on the essential facts. This view is expressed by the statement of one school that its practical work is designed "to assist the students in understanding the subjects studied in instructional courses," while another leading school explains that its practice work or "laboratory work," gives "an opportunity for the demonstration of the principles presented through class instruction." Still another school bases the need of practical work on both the test-of-ability and the aid-to-instruction theories. Its brief period of supervised practice "serves not only to test the ability of students when confronted with actual conditions, but also makes clear much of the class work."

Most of the schools give no explanation at all of their reason for devoting from an eighth to a quarter of the year's work to practice; perhaps there is no reason why they should. But several of the best schools do attempt to explain the basis for their practical work, and these explanations seem to show clearly that so far as the program of the library schools is based on any conscious philosophy it relies almost entirely on formal instruction. In theory the practice work is merely an adjunct to, or one phase of, formal instruction.

In one or two cases, however, the casual use of the word "experience" in reference to practice work suggests the possibility that some of those in charge of schools may be thinking of the field work as a means of acquiring skill of some kind. One school, while clinging to the idea that the practice work "enables the student to test the theories discussed in the classroom," actually goes on to make a fair statement of the way in which at least the beginnings of skill in library work may be acquired by supervised practice. Explaining the purpose of its practical work, the Library School of the University of Wisconsin says that by means of it students "acquire poise and confidence in meeting and serving the public, and ascertain for themselves how library work reaches out to all interests in a community, and becomes a vital element in its life." This is the nearest approach that has been found in any of the printed matter issued by the library schools to a recognition of the fact that skill in the performance of any kind of library work must be wrought out by actually doing the work.

The amount of practical work included in the one year library school course appears to have no scientifically determined basis. It actually varies in the different schools from a total of four weeks in one school to approximately twelve weeks in another, counting a week as forty hours. No better illustration can be found of the complete lack of carefully determined standards for the library school course. Some schools find that the best results can be secured by four weeks of practical work, while others find it desirable to extend the period to twelve weeks and correspondingly reduce the amount of class instruction. It does not seem possible that both methods can be equally sound, yet it would doubtless be difficult by comparing the work of students trained under the two methods to say which is more effective. The reason for the difficulty is that so many other factors are present in the final result. Not only are the ability and previous experience of the student to be considered, but the amount and character of classroom instruction and, in the matter of practical work itself, the efficiency with which it is adapted to the needs of the particular student and the amount and character of the supervision which he gets.

The amount of practical work varies greatly; but the point in the course at which it is introduced is subject to even greater variation. The two main types are:(1) the "blocked," or full-time practice, usually in the months of February or March, or both; and, (2) an equal or larger amount scattered irregularly throughout the year or with a given number of hours per week. The first is illustrated by the library schools of the New York Public Library and of the University of Wisconsin, and the second by the University of Washington. Various combinations of these two methods, along with still other devices, are found, as the following tabular statement shows:

Summary Statement of Amount of Practical or Field Work
and Position in Year's Course

New York Public Library	: Four weeks' "blocked" practice, in February, usually in two assignments.
New York State Library	: Fifty hours during year in State Library and local libraries; "blocked" practice during March, outside of Albany.
Pratt Institute	: Throughout year; outside field work during spring vacation.
Simmons College	: Two weeks in March; two weeks in summer vacation between junior and senior years.
Western Reserve University	: One hundred hours, distributed throughout

		the year; eighty-one hours of "blocked" field work latter part of second semester.
University of Wisconsin	:	Eight weeks of field work, February and March.
University of Illinois	:	One month of field work.
Los Angeles Public Library	:	One week in the months of November, February, and March; and the month of June.
University of Washington	:	Six hours a week for five quarters for undergraduates; twelve hours a week for thirty weeks for graduate students.
St. Louis Library School	:	Three hours a week throughout the year; four weeks in February.
Carnegie Library, Atlanta	:	Three hundred sixty-six hours distributed throughout the year.
Carnegie Library School, Pittsburgh	:	Three hundred forty-eight hours scattered throughout year, with two weeks "blocked" practice in February.

The wide variation in methods followed grows partly out of theoretical and partly out of practical considerations. Those in charge of some schools believe that the results for the student are better if he is allowed to concentrate on his classroom work for the first semester, and then for a month or two give all his time to practical work, coming back to the classroom again for the most of the year, except for occasional observational assignments. Others proceed to scatter the practical work throughout the year on the theory that the assignments can be so correlated with class instruction that students will benefit by having their theoretical and practical work on each subject at about the same time. No effort seems to have been made to weigh the merits of these two diametrically opposed methods by careful experimentation or scientific procedure. It seems very doubtful whether it is ever possible for any school to arrange schedules of instruction and practical work so that students will actually have their practical and theoretical work on every subject at the same time. Most schools would certainly find it quite impossible. It may also be somewhat easier in a small library to give a large amount of practical work to many students if their assignments are scattered throughout the year. Where practice students are not relied upon to supplement the regular staff, and especially in the larger libraries, "blocked" practice is doubtless more convenient. It would seem that, on the whole, the time at which the practice work is given has been determined with reference to the convenience of the practice library or of the school rather than from any consideration of educational theory.

Particular inquiry was directed to the methods of making assignments for practical work. The results, as on other points, are disappointing. No clear-cut and well-defined objective was discovered. Among the points considered was the method of determining to what type of library and to what particular library a given student should be sent for his outside practical work, or "field work." Shall the student be placed in the kind of work in which he is already interested, which may be taken to mean his probable future work, and perhaps the kind of work in which he already has some degree of skill? On this point two diametrically opposed theories emerge. Certain schools assert that assignments are based on the needs of the student, which would necessitate placing him in a type of work in which he is not especially interested but in which his class work shows he needs to strengthen his equipment in order to go out with a well-rounded training and general acquaintance with professional library work. Another group of schools pursues the opposite policy and places the student for practical work in that particular type of library in which he is most interested and to which he looks forward for permanent service. The latter usually leave the choice of a library for practical work to the student's own initiative; unless his choice is obviously unwise, it is approved. In a few cases an effort is made to divide the practice period and follow both methods. The earlier part of the practice work would thus be devoted to strengthening some weak point, and the later to some line of work in which the student is strong and already well-equipped.

Schools which provide a large amount of practical work in one library - usually the one with which they are connected - and a relatively short period of "field work" in outside libraries make more or less effort to distribute the former work among all the principal types of service. Thus the Pratt Institute School of Library Science devotes to practical work in the cataloguing, circulating and reference departments about one hundred hours each, sixty-six hours in the children's department, and twenty-one hours in the reading room. The outside work or field work can then be chosen with reference to the student's future work, if that is known; and if not, with reference to his interests and preferences.

Still another basis of selecting a place for practical work disregards both the student's needs and preferences and strives to place him under the supervision of particular persons. This may be sound philosophy and a safe policy to follow if superior individuals can be found who have the time to devote to practice students. Unless the standards for this personal basis of choice are very clearly defined and strictly adhered to, there is grave danger that it will do harm. It would be easy, for instance, for a school to assume that any field work must be good for its students if done under its own graduates, no matter what the type of library.

The fundamental purpose of the practical work should determine the method of making assignments. If the purpose is to acquire skill, then future work and present interests should be the determining factor. If grasp of principles and better understanding of subjects taught is the purpose, then the practical work, if it cannot cover all subjects, should be selected to represent the branches in which the student has not shown proficiency. For example, if his class work in cataloguing has been weak and uncertain he should be put into cataloguing for the practical work. If the aim is to try him out, to see whether his success in actual work is what could be anticipated from classroom work, then the type of practical work does not greatly matter, and nearly everything depends on the skill of the supervisor and the kind of reports made to the school officials.

Practical work in a one-year professional course as a means of acquiring skill should be left out of consideration. Grasp of principle and a clear understanding of subjects taught are the objects of classroom instruction. If only students of first-class ability and maturity are admitted to the schools and then if the instruction is of high quality, the student should be able by the aid of systematic and detailed observation in contact with actual library work, under the instructor's supervision, to get sufficient grasp of the principles of every phase of professional work. A prolonged period of practical work should not be necessary as a test of the student's general capacity. The faculty should be able by means of classroom exercises and the so-called class practice to gain adequate insight into the student's ability. If it cannot be gotten in this way, certainly the chances are small that it will be gotten at all, if reliance has to be placed on the so-called practical work.

If a long period of practical work under actual library conditions is not necessary or desirable as a part of the first year's professional instruction, neither should much time be given to it as a means of helping the student to find the type of work he desires to take up. In the first place it may be that his mind is already quite made up on that point, but even if it is not, he is very likely to find the first openings in other and quite different fields. As the practical or field work is usually managed, the student would not have sufficient opportunity to make an adequate experiment in all the different possible lines. Furthermore, as to the student's actual choice, the testimony of school principals seems to show that this does not after all result from the practical work but rather from his general range of interests and tastes, aided most of all by the impressions gained from the observation made on expeditions.

From the report forms furnished by the schools for the use of librarians who supervise practice work it may be inferred that one important object of the practical work is to secure information about the student which will be useful in placement. This purpose is nowhere avowed in print and is suggested only by inference in oral statements and in the report blanks alluded to. It may be an open question whether the school is justified in taking very much of the student's time to discover, if possible, some of his personal qualities which may have a part, even though a very important part, in determining his professional success. Even if it does nothing else, the year's study must lay broad and deep the foundations of knowledge, insure grasp of principles, impart an appreciation of the ideals of library service, and develop a professional attitude toward the work. It seems impossible to escape the conclusion that the school cannot be expected in one year to do all this and find time for the prolonged practice necessary to produce a skilled professional librarian.

Is the school justified either in taking much of the student's time to gain information to be used principally for placement purposes? So long as the schools feel called upon to give so much attention to this phase of their work, undoubtedly all the information they can get about the student from the reports of supervisors of practice is valuable. But there are at least two large questions involved here: the first is whether the schools are not assuming too much responsibility for the placing of the student, especially in view of the fact that they cannot pretend to turn out skilled workers. The other point of doubt relates to the fullness and reliability of their information about the student's capacity and fitness for any kind of library work which the school actually gets at present from reports on practical work.

Does the use of the practical work for placement purposes justify the time devoted to it? Much depends on: (1) the skill used in putting the student into an environment which will elicit the desired information about him; and (2) the skill of the supervisor in taking the student through those experiences which will furnish an adequate and reliable test of his capacities and in reporting on them. The latter requires on the part of the supervisor a full and sympathetic understanding of the aims and methods of the school, a fairly intimate acquaintance with the student's previous training and experience, and, above all, plenty of time to devote to the student under his supervision. As these conditions are seldom or never fulfilled, it becomes necessary to question the value of practical work as a means of gaining information needed for placement purposes. Still other considerations point in the same direction. Not only do the reports of supervisors fall short in quality, but they are inadequate also in point of quantity. Reports are based on brief contact with a student who is not and cannot be given an opportunity to take responsibility, who, feeling himself on trial, does not do himself justice.

It may well be urged that the task of the school is simply and solely to give the student instruction, inspiration, and stimulus, and not to assume responsibility for any other element of his success. As it is, the schools seem to feel responsibility for (1) selecting only students who are certain to succeed; (2) giving instruction; (3) analyzing character, ability and special aptitudes of students in order to place them successfully at the end of the year's study or remedy mistakes as soon thereafter as possible; and (4) for developing a degree of skill in several lines of library work, so that the student can enter upon the practical duties of almost any type of position offered at the close of the course. In the discussion of entrance requirements we have already expressed doubt as to the success of the selective process as now carried on. The primary and fundamental responsibility which the school cannot escape and by which it must be judged is its work of instruction. It probably should assume less responsibility for placement and disclaim any pretense of being able in the one-year general course to add to instruction the experience necessary to turn out skilled library workers. The best thing the school can do for the student and for the library profession is to devote itself to instruction and to drop students who do not show the mental capacity to maintain a high standard. The professional library school should not permit itself to be turned aside from its main purpose to experiment with the student and plan for launching him on his professional career. It will do well to confine itself to selecting students of the highest ability and broad education, and free from obvious defects of character or physique and then give them the best possible instruction, making the work of so high a grade that differences in capacity appear in the records of scholarship. Then let the student's school record and the judgment of instructors, added to the student's own preferences and desires, be the basis for recommendations to employers.

Many schools take particular pains to emphasize the fact that students are sent into libraries to work as a member of the staff under <u>actual</u> library conditions. Practice work should not be <u>actual</u> library work under normal conditions. Actual library work is not carried on for the benefit of the staff or to give instruction to students. Incidentally an intelligent member of the staff gradually acquires information and skill in some kind of work, but that is purely incidental to a vast amount of routine work, and some very intelligent people work all their lives in a good library without getting a professional outlook. The thing to be avoided ordinarily is putting the student to work under <u>actual</u> conditions. He should not even be treated as a new member of the staff. His work must be planned and supervised, not with reference to his present or future usefulness to that organization, but solely with a view to giving him an opportunity to observe and learn at first hand and as rapidly as possible everything he needs in order to acquire a broad grasp of a wide range of library problems. If his work is so organized as not to waste his time, it is not done under actual conditions; it then closely resembles class practice in purpose and method. To treat the library school student as a member of the active staff is to exploit him or, at best, to waste his time.

Field work carried on by the student as a member of a library staff is in most cases wasteful of his time and unsatisfactory because it does not give an opportunity to observe minutely, and critically, and comparatively all phases of the work of a completely organized library unit. It is assumed that, no matter what he is doing, he is getting experience to help him when he takes a position, whereas his future work may be very different; and even if it is not, it may be so unlike in detail that what he has acquired by practice may be an actual hindrance or no help at all.

Student practice is in general poorly supervised and inadequately analyzed and reported to the schools. To give the best and largest results, field work needs as competent guidance as class work. Comparatively few head librarians or heads of divisions and departments have the time, the desire, the knowledge or skill to supervise student's field work. The ideal supervisor must be a real teacher, a skilled library worker, fully informed as to the other work of the school and well acquainted with the student's attainments and needs. Such supervisors are so rare that it would seem as if the schools must needs keep the supervision of the field work pretty much in their own hands. This is quite practicable where the instructors are members of the practice library staff and can also supervise the field work. This dual function puts more responsibility on the instructor and requires more of him in the way of allround practical ability.

If, however, field work must be supervised by some one not a member of the school staff, the school must see to it that the supervising librarian is qualified for the task, has the time to give to it, and is possessed of the essential facts about the student. Some schools pay considerable attention to this; others very little. The librarian selected to supervise a student's field work should be given a full account of his previous education and experience, his work and record in the school, his strong and weak points, etc.

Certain schools do this with some degree of care. The instructor talks with the students either as a class or individual, about their field work and then writes to the outside supervisor more or less fully. This is all helpful and good so far as it goes. Supervisors usually report either by means of a blank form or by letter. The chief use made of these reports, as pointed out above, seems to be to gain information for placement purposes. They add comparatively little to what the instructors already know as to the student's ability and habits of work.

There is no doubt that the long period of field work during which classes are entirely suspended gives some relief to overworked instructional staffs. The poverty of the schools, however, should not be translated into poverty of professional equipment on the part of the student. The year's study is none too long to lay well the foundations for professional work. The curriculum is crowded and other important subjects are pressing for recognition. It is exceedingly important therefore that the student should not put more time than necessary into his field work, that it be so organized and supervised that he will gain from it the maximum concrete information and breadth of view and resourcefulness. If more instructors are necessary, they should be forthcoming. If a more competent director of field work is needed, school authorities should press for the necessary funds. If satisfactory supervisors of field work not connected with the school can be found, they should be paid for their services. It is not reasonable to expect librarians to devote themselves to students without compensation. The service that can be rendered by even the best student in the course of his field work in a properly conducted library is not adequate compensation for the attention that should be given to him. To try to balance the account in this way is certain to result in improper exploitation of the student. Only one school, so far as inquiry has shown, pays the outside supervisors anything for guiding students' field work and even in this one case the pay allowed is wholly inadequate.

One of the weakest points in the practical or field work is the common failure to require adequate reporting from students. Even in some of the best schools students doing field work make no reports at all or no regular reports. In some cases the instructor later discusses the work with the student, but this is evidently not a satisfactory substitute for frequent, regular and careful written and oral reports by the student. It would seem to be self-evident that nothing should be left undone to induce the student in the field to think about what he is doing and to relate it to what he has learned in the lecture and classroom. The mere spending of a certain number of hours a day in a library for a certain period carries no assurance that the student is conscious of his surroundings. He should not be sent to any post except for a definite purpose. He should be told what he is expected to get and should make as definite a report as on any assignment in his course.

This would require a different system and higher standards for supervision of practice work. As a matter of fact, the field work should probably be planned by the various instructors, each one laying out a program as definitely related to the instruction given in his own courses as the so-called class practice. This is necessary if the field work is to be regarded as a supplement or aid to instruction. Too much is now left to chance in definitely relating field work to instruction. If observation is to clinch class instruction the two must be very closely correlated.

The time which can be devoted to supervised practical work in the course of one year's study is entirely too short to produce skilled library workers. The most important thing - the really essential thing - is to give the student during the one year as thorough a grounding as possible in the principles underlying library practice and methods. There is not enough time to give him the background of facts and principles which are essential for the highest skill and also to make it possible for him actually to acquire some degree of skill in the only way it can be acquired, namely, by doing actual library work, preferably, at least in the beginning, under the supervision of a skilled worker. The schools should be quite frank to admit that they cannot turn out skilled workers, and merely attempt to give instruction which can be relied upon to make the acquisition of skill speedy and certain. With this clear understanding, the schools may properly continue to include in their one-year, general course a small amount of so-called practical work, solely as a means of increasing the efficiency of classroom instruction, and not at all with an idea of producing skilled library workers. In the best sense, the average graduate of a one-year course in a library school is not a trained librarian; he should have had the best of instruction, but he should not be expected to have acquired special skill.

A large amount of practical work in a general professional course of one year is open to serious question on several counts. The primary purpose of the school is to lay a broad basis for skill in some type of professional work, not to develop that skill and certainly not to impart skill in the routine processes which belong to the clerical grades of library service. The latter is a very important consideration. It is the function of the training class to give the student skill in the performance of the duties of some particular position in a particular library. The relatively small amount of instruction which accompanies the practice is not calculated to give any professional equipment, but to make the acquisition of skill in routine clerical work easier and more certain. One instructor with the aid of members of a library staff can give all the instruction required by a training class. Professional library work should be organized on a very different basis. The large part which the practical work has hitherto played in the professional course is additional evidence that no clear distinction has yet been made between professional training and clerical training.

The place for the practical work as a means of imparting skill in professional grades of library work is not in the one-year general course, but in a second year devoted to advanced study in some special field. This is the real counterpart of the extensive practice which necessarily forms a large part of the training class work. The years immediately following the general professional course, together with the second year of specialized study, correspond to the medical student's internship. The medical four-year course is not interrupted by short internships or periods of practical work. Throughout the period of instruction, and particularly toward its close, the student is brought close to practical work by laboratory and clinic and given full opportunity for observation under the guidance of the instructor, but there is no thought of turning him loose to "practice" under the actual conditions which will confront him after he has his degree and is licensed to practice.

It will be said, of course, that a student who has not done much practice work will be a mere theorist, without practical knowledge and unable to do anything well. It is a _little_ theory that is the dangerous thing. The present system of practical work does not sufficiently clinch and check up theories learned from lectures and reading but it does seriously interfere with thorough instruction. Thorough comparative study carried on under the supervision of competent instructors and held up to a high standard will be the best safeguard the school can have against turning out half-baked theorists. The present system of practical work in the one-year course certainly gives no such assurance.

The proposal to do away to a large extent with the so-called practical work as a part of the first year's study does not mean that a successful library school can be conducted apart from good library facilities. On the contrary, it assumes the widest possible range of libraries and library service of high standards for observation purposes. Training class work can be conducted in a single library, and even in a very small library, but professional training requires a wide acquaintance with library methods and organization, to be acquired only by systematic observation and reporting under the guidance of a skilled instructor. In passing, it ought to be said that a supervisor of field work should be the most experienced and practical library worker on the staff of the school, and at the same time a trained teacher. The failure to recognize the fundamental difference between professional training and the sub-professional type of training is nowhere more apparent than in the assumption that adequate professional education can be given in a small isolated library, however excellent that library may be of its kind. No worthy professional school can be conducted out of easy reach of many libraries of different types and sizes, maintaining high standards of organization and service.

An important feature of the program of several of the older and best known library schools is the annual library "visit", or tour of observation and inspection made by the entire class and lasting a week or more. The classes of the New York State Library School, accompanied by some member of the faculty, spend about ten days visiting, in one year the leading libraries of Washington, Philadelphia and New York and vicinity, and in the alternate year the libraries of Boston, Springfield, Worcester, and Providence. Pratt Institute, the New York Public Library, the Carnegie Library School of Pittsburgh, and the University of Illinois Library School make similar class trips each spring. Other schools, not able for one reason or another to provide for such expensive trips, seek to accomplish the same result by means of one-day visits to nearby cities, while still others are able to extend their observations no further than to libraries in their immediate locality.

There is no question that these extended trips are of very great value, if not absolutely essential, for professional training. The school authorities in every case report that students return from such trips enthusiastic about what they have seen and enter into the class work with keener interest and greater appreciation. They give students an opportunity to become acquainted with different types of libraries, to appreciate the need which gives rise to them, and to observe their methods of operation. Many students have a very limited acquaintance with large library systems and the more important kinds of special libraries. On the basis of the observations they make on the trips, they are sometimes able to decide definitely what line of library work they wish to enter. Another very practical end not lost sight of by the school authorities is the introduction of students to leading workers in the profession and even to prospective employers. Various other advantages accrue from these trips, in the nature of by-products, perhaps. Thus one school finds the annual trips help to keep the school instruction abreast of library progress, while another finds that the instructor in charge of the excursion is able to get an intimate acquaintance with the students such as could be gotten in no other way.

These trips are not designed to be mere pleasure junkets. The students are held responsible in one way or another for showing definite additions to their professional knowledge and outlook. In some cases topics are assigned in advance for each student to report on. Other schools organize the class into various committees, each being responsible for reports on special topics; and after their return the presentation of reports may be followed by discussion and quizzes. On the whole, the aim is very much the same as that of the so-called practical work - to reinforce and illustrate class instruction, to fix important facts and ideas in the student's mind, and to instil in him the habit of taking a comparative view of methods and procedure.

With some schools trips of inspection and observation are not differentiated from practical work or field work. In the University of Wisconsin there are no library visits apart from the practical work, but the libraries studied are reported on in great detail, following a standardized, elaborate outline.

Schools which because of their location or other unfavorable conditions cannot make the class trips for observation are still able to realize a large part of their advantages by means of planned visits by individual students to libraries within easy reach. While something of the enthusiasm and inspiration which comes from the extended class trip is likely to be lost, the student stands to gain on the other hand by the more leisurely inspection and more detailed reports made possible.

If our conclusion as to the real object of the practical work is valid, it is not practice in actual library work so much as directed and supervised observation that is to be sought. This is also the purpose of all kinds of library "visits" and inspection trips. Any course designed to provide a thorough professional training should include both the extensive observation afforded by the brief trips to other cities and the intensive observation which must be secured in local libraries. Whether the extensive or intensive observation should come first is largely a pedagogical question. Tentatively, it may be assumed that the local and intensive observation, related somewhat closely to the class instruction, should precede. With this as a background the student will go on the extended trips with seeing eyes. The outline of points to be covered in the more rapid surveys will have been fixed in his mind by his detailed comparative studies in local libraries.

CHAPTER 9

JOINT COURSES, ACADEMIC CREDIT, DEGREES AND ACADEMIC STATUS

A considerable proportion of the 50 per cent of library school graduates who have the college degree did not take a four years' college course and then the library school course, but took both in four years, receiving college credit for the library courses. About two-thirds of the graduates of the Simmons College School of Library Science have taken the library training as a part of the general college course. In the University of Washington and the University of California the library school admits students who have completed the junior year in the undergraduate college. After spending his senior year in the library school the student gets his bachelor's degree. In the University of Wisconsin and Western Reserve University the library schools receive a few students from the arts colleges under a joint course arrangement which enables the student to receive both degrees in four years. In some instances colleges in the same locality with the library school, though not parts of the same institution, have arranged similar joint courses. Thus Occidental College in Los Angeles gives the A. B. degree for three years of work in the college and one in the Los Angeles Public Library School. A similar arrangement has recently been made by Carnegie Library School and the University of Pittsburgh.

Graduates of any accredited library school may in individual cases be permitted to offer certain library courses for the bachelor's degree, but college faculties are not always willing to give full academic credit, particularly for technical courses. In the University of Illinois, for example, college credit is given for the courses in the history of libraries, reference work, and sometimes, though not always, in book selection. A representative of the faculty of one college which has refused to consider a joint course with the library school explained that his college had certain standards of scholarship for its own faculty which the library school did not maintain and that since it did not attempt itself to instruct seniors and freshmen in the same classes, it did not care to credit seniors for library school work taken with a class a majority of whose members had had no college study at all. While this position may seem ultra conservative, it is undoubtedly reasonable and exposes a real danger that the joint courses may seriously dilute the college course.

The fundamental viewpoint of this report is that professional library work requires a college education or its full equivalent. Three years of college study are better than two and two are better than none, but not so good as four. So far as the joint courses have served to raise the average education of library school students, they can be approved. Certain library schools have frankly sought to effect joint course arrangements with neighboring colleges with the hope of getting more students and raising the general level of their preparation. Even the joint course, however, should be considered a temporary expedient. Every professional library school should make definite plans to pass on to a strictly graduate basis.

The joint course plan as described above, in which three years of college work are followed by one year devoted exclusively to library school study, seems to me to be preferred to the Simmons College plan in which the library courses are spread throughout the four years. While comparatively little of the vocational work in Simmons is given before the junior year, in my judgment it would be much better to postpone all vocational courses until the senior year and better still until after receiving the bachelor's degree.

Only seven, or less than half, of the library schools recognized in this study, have the power to confer degrees or are connected with degree-conferring institutions. Students in the schools which cannot confer degrees usually receive a certificate on satisfactorily completing the one-year course and a diploma at the end of the two-year course. The degrees conferred for work in library schools are B. L. S. (Bachelor of Library Science), B. S. (Bachelor of Science), A. B. (Bachelor of Arts), B. L. E. (Bachelor of Library Economy), and M. L. S. (Master of Library Science).

A committee of the Association of American Library Schools has recently considered the subject of professional degrees for library courses. In its report it is recommended the B. L. S. degree be recognized as the professional and technical study, admission to which requires a four-year college course. This has been the practice in the past. The New York State Library School and the University of Illinois are the only schools which have given the B. L. S. degree (with the exception of two by Syracuse University). The B. L. E. degree formerly conferred by the University of Washington and Syracuse University as a professional first degree on the completion of one or two years of study has been dropped as recommended by the committee. It was also recommended (by the committee) that the degree of M. L. S. be conferred whenever the character of work done in library schools which are on a graduate basis meets the requirements usually set for graduate work leading to a master's degree. Seven M. L. S. degrees have been conferred by the New York State Library School and one by Simmons College.

Approval of the Association is given to the general practice of conferring the degree of A. B., or B. S., either with or without the addition of "in Library Science", on the completion of one year of professional and technical study, when that year forms a part of a four-year college course, or one year of such study in addition to four years of undergraduate college work. The B. S. degree has been conferred in this way by Western Reserve University and Simmons College, and the A. B. by the University of Illinois, the University of Washington and the University of Wisconsin.

In library schools affiliated with a municipal or state library and not organized as a part of a university, all members of the teaching staff have the rank of instructor, regardless of salary, length of service, or experience. This fact may perhaps have had some influence in keeping all salaries low. If different grades of teaching service were recognized, it is possible that the higher grades would command larger salaries. In schools organized as an integral part of a university, members of the faculty in most cases have the same grades and salaries as in other departments or schools. The head of the university library school usually has the rank of professor. In certain cases the rank of assistant professor is found, but with few exceptions every one on the staff, except the director, ranks as an instructor and has only the salary of an instructor.

Every existing university library school is a negligible part of the institution, unnoticed or looked down upon by the other faculties and especially by departments in which research is emphasized. The causes for this lack of prestige seem to be the smallness of the library school, the brevity of the course, the predominance of women in both faculty and student body, the preponderance of teachers having only the rank of instructor and the total lack of anything recognized as productive scholarship. All of these conditions are remediable and will tend to disappear as the standards of the library profession are gradually raised, increasing the size and importance of the professional schools.

CHAPTER 10

FINANCIAL AND STATISTICAL STUDIES

Only ten of the library schools were in a position to give any information in response to a request for the total amount of their budget for 1920-1921. And of the ten schools included in the following table only two, apparently, pretend that the figures give anything more than a rough approximation of the total cost of operation. Only two or three schools have independent budgets, the others being operated as an integral part of a library or an educational institution. Probably in no case do the figures include any charge for heat, light, janitor service, etc.

LIBRARY SCHOOL BUDGETS, SHOWING TOTAL FOR ALL PURPOSES AND AMOUNT OF SALARIES

School Number	1910-11 Total	Salaries	1915-16 Total	Salaries	1920-21 Total	Salaries
1	$15,133a	$9,322a	$16,604	$11,878	$21,500	$14,885
2	7,000b	4,828b	7,500b	4,936b	19,048	15,120
3	12,602c	7,830	11,506c	7,525	15,309c	11,930
4			11,181	10,066	11,540	10,590
5	8,050	4,950	8,970	5,520	9,360	6,260
6					7,190c	4,290
7	4,764	3,976d	5,145	4,300	6,650	5,850
8				2,390	5,553e	5,895
9	4,500	2,939	4,500	2,950	4,500	3,455
10			2,050	1,410f	3,350	2,730f

(a) For the year 1911-1912
(b) Represent part of budget only; balance not segregated from library budget
(c) Approximate only - based on estimates.
(d) For 1911-12.
(e) For year 1919-1920.
(f) Not including service of library staff.

The extreme poverty of most of the library schools is clearly revealed by this table. The sum total of the budgets of the fifteen schools probably does not exceed $150,000, or only about 50 per cent more than the income which such a library school as ought to be established in New York City would require annually in a short time.

The budgets of 1920-1921 compared with those of ten years and five years earlier reveal a comparatively static condition. The schools are evidently not keeping pace with the growing needs of the libraries of the country. The total of the budgets of all the library schools, omitting three or four, does not exceed the salary of the head librarian of the public library in one of the larger cities or the salary of the superintendent of schools in many cities of less than 100,000 population. It is small wonder, in light of the figures as to salaries of principals and leading instructors shown in the following table, that service on library school faculties does not make a strong appeal to successful and ambitious librarians and educators.

The Western Reserve University School is the only one which has its own endowment. The Library School of the New York Public Library and the Library School of the Carnegie Library of Atlanta receive annual grants from the Carnegie Corporation. The schools in Pratt Institute, Simmons College, and Syracuse University are supported in the same way as other departments of those institutions. In the state universities of Illinois, Washington, and California, the library school is carried in the budget of the university library. Similarly, the New York State Library School has no financial status apart from the State Library. In Wisconsin the library school is carried in the budget of the Free Library Commission. In Riverside, Los Angeles, and St. Louis, public library appropriations are used to supplement the income from tuition fees.

Tuition fees in all the schools are very moderate, in keeping with library salaries in general. The Simmons College fee of $200 a year is the

Salaries of the Directors, Principals, and Leading
Instructors of Library Schools, in 1921.

	Director	Principal or Vice-Director	Best Paid Instructor
New York State	$5,500a	$3,200	$2,000
Pratt Institute	b	2,500	2,000
Un. of Illinois	4,500c	2,700	2,400
Carnegie Library, Pittsburgh	8,000d	3,000	2,180
Simmons College	4,000	e	2,530
Western Reserve University	3,000	e	1,920
Carnegie Library Atlanta	2,550	e	2,100
Un. of Wisconsin	b	2,500	2,100
New York P. L.	e	3,300	2,200
Un. of Washington	4,400	e	3,500f
Los Angeles P. L.	e	1,920	1,800
St. Louis Library	9,000g	2,280	1,500
Un. of California	b	e	1,800

a - Total salary as director of State Library and director of the Library School.
b - Information not available.
c - Total salary as librarian of the University and director of the Library School; one-fourth time to Library School.
d - $6,000 from the city as librarian of the Carnegie Library of Pittsburgh, and $2,000 from the Library School budget.
e - No position by this title.
f - Total salary as reference librarian of the University and instructor in the Library School.
g - Salary as librarian of the St. Louis Public Library.

highest in any school, while the lowest is found in the Atlanta school with no tuition fee at all. Tuition and other fees of twelve of the schools are shown in the following statement:

Tuition and Other Fees

New York State	: $100 for two years; $150 for non-residents.
New York Public Library	: $45 for first year for residents of New York City or those living within commuting distance; $75 for others in first year; $25 for second year.
Pratt Institute	: $100 a year (one-year course). $5 registration.
University of Illinois	: No tuition fee. $50 a year incidental fee (two-year course). $10 matriculation fee; $10 diploma fee.
Simmons College	: $200 a year (four-year course and one-year course).
Western Reserve University	: $100 a year (one-year course). $5 registration.
Carnegie Library, Atlanta	: No tuition fee. $5 registration.
University of Wisconsin	: $50 a year (one-year course) for residents of Wisconsin; $100 for non-residents. $5 registration.
Carnegie Library School, Pittsburgh	: $100 a year (one-year course). $5 matriculation.
Los Angeles Public Library	: $50 a year (one-year course) for residents of Los Angeles County; $75 for others. $5 matriculation.
St. Louis Library School	: No tuition fee for residents of St. Louis; $45 a year (one-year course) for residents of Missouri outside of St. Louis; $75 for residents of other states.
Syracuse University	: $120 a year (two-year course). $5 matriculation: $6 university infirmary; $8 athletic fee.

Light is thrown upon the question of a need for more library schools by the fact that the fifteen schools examined are being utilized to only about 60 per cent of their total capacity. These fifteen schools reported a total maximum capacity of 612 students enrolled at one time. This includes three schools in which some students take a second year's work, so that if all the schools were filled to their capacity, the number finishing the course each year would be somewhat less than 600. The total number of students enrolled

Statistics of Library School Students, Showing
Initial Salaries of Graduates.

Name of School	No. of students school could accommodate	Students enrolled in 1920-1921	No. completing course in 1921	Average initial salary of graduates		
				1914	1921	Percent of increase
New York State	75	35	26	$ 922a	$1728	87.4
Pratt Institute	30	26	24	764	1413	84.9
Un. of Illinois	42	34	25f	1200	1585	32.1
Simmons College	60	30	18	683	1233	80.3
Un. of Wisconsin	40	26	25	780	1394	78.7
Carnegie Library School, Pitts.	50	27	21	720	1320	83.3
Western Reserve University	30	22	28	1260	1580	25.4
New York P.L.	60	36	26	776	1412	82.0
Library School, Atlanta	25	8	8	600	1200	100.0
Los Angeles P.L.	30	27	25	720	1190	65.3
Un. of Washington	20	12	12	780	1200	53.8
St. Louis Library School	40	17	16	b	943	
Un. of California	30	30	21	b	1250	
Riverside	30	15	15cd	900	1200	33.3
Syracuse (d)	50	26	14de	e	e	
Total	612	371	304			

a - For 1915.
b - School not yet established.
c - Does not include "short course" students.
d - Approximate.
e - No report received.
f - Only seven of these completing the two-year course.

in these schools in 1920-1921 was approximately 370, or 60 per cent of their combined maximum capacity. The estimate of maximum capacity for each school is based on the physical equipment, size of rooms, desks available, etc. In a few instances the present staff of instructors would not be adequate to care for all the students the plant would accommodate. Additional instructors or assistants to instructors, usually known as revisers, would have to be added to the staff of certain schools if they were to receive as many students as their rooms and equipment make possible.

Assuming that the existing schools are properly distributed geographically, there seems to be no room for doubting that the most efficient and economical way to increase the number of persons in training for professional librarianship is to fill the schools already in operation to something like their full capacity, rather than to establish new schools with meager financial support and small enrolment.

No attempt has been made to estimate the number of new library workers with professional training which are required by libraries of all kinds each year. When it is considered that a certain proportion of the graduates of these fifteen schools enter and remain in clerical positions, for which the appropriate training is that afforded by the training class rather than by the library school, it seems altogether probable that if most of the schools were to put their work on a strictly professional basis and fill up their classes, they would be able to turn out now, and for some time to come, all the librarians needed.

In most communities the need is not for a professional library school, but for a training class designed to take graduates of the local high school who possess the requisite personal qualifications and fit them in a comparatively short time for the various grades of clerical work which plays so large a part in the operation of most libraries. No institution for professional training is likely to maintain adequate standards if it is mainly

General Statistics of Graduates of Library Schools

Name of School	Year established	Total no. of graduates including class of 1921	Average no. graduates per year	Men graduated No.	Men graduated P.C. of Total	Graduates still in library work - Men No.	Men P.C.	Women No.	Women P.C.	Women graduates who married No.	P.C.	Graduates having a college degree No.	P.C.	College graduates in class of 1921 No.	P.C.
New York State	1887	902(a)	27	176(a)	19.5	122	69.3	387	53.3	140	19.2	692	76.7	26	100.0
Pratt Institute	1890	677	22	24	3.5	16	66.6	437	66.9	145	22.2	83	12.2	8	33.3
Un. of Illinois	1893	671(b)	24	40	5.9	21	52.5	330	52.3	168	26.6	480(c)	71.5	5	100.0
Carnegie, Pitts.	1901	397	20	0	0.0	0	0.0	234	58.9	109	27.5	119	29.9	9	42.8
Simmons College	1902	429	27	0	0.0	0	0.0	263	61.3	125	29.1	429	100.0	19	100.0
Western Reserve University	1904	339	19	5	1.4	4	80.0	217	64.9	64	19.1	88	25.9	5	17.8
Carnegie Library, Atlanta	1905	150	9	0	0.0	0	0.0	89	59.3	38	25.3	6	4.0	1	12.5
Un. of Wisconsin	1906	424	28	6	1.4	2	33.3	275	65.7	78	18.6	155(d)	36.5	6	24.0
New York P.L.	1911	333	33	22	6.6	15	68.1	244	78.4	48	15.4	109	32.7	14	53.8
Un. of Washington	1912	113	12	1	.8	1	100.0	83	74.1	27	24.1	113	100.0	12	100.0
Los Angeles P.L.	1914	130	18	2	1.5	2	100.0	76	59.3	13	10.1	41	31.5	13	52.0
St. Louis Library School	1917	59	15	0	0.0	0	0.0	42	75.9	8	13.5	7	11.8	3	18.7
Un. of California	1919	40	20	0	0.0	0	0.0	37	92.5	1	2.5	40	100.0	21	100.0
Riverside (Public) Library	1913	(e)	(e)												
Syracuse Un.	1908	(f)													
Total		4664		276	5.9	183	86.3	2714	61.8	964	21.9	2362	50.6	141	46.3

(a) Matriculants; number of students receiving first-year certificate, 493; B.L.S. degree, 262; M.L.S. degree, 7; Diploma (those completing course before college degree was required), 52.

(b) Students registered; 299 completed two-year course.

(c) Estimated

(d) Fifty-four of the 155 took the joint course in the University and the Library School.

(e) Data furnished not comparable

(f) No report received

engaged in fitting residents of the same community to meet a local need.

Approximately 304 students completed in 1921 a course of one or two years in our fifteen library schools, which is about the average number of graduates of the same schools in the last few years. Reports of enrolment for the year 1921-1922 indicate a considerable increase over 1920-1921.

The total number of graduates of all the schools from their beginning, not including summer school and short-course students, is approximately 5,000. Of this number only 276, or between 5 and 6 per cent, were men. Nearly half the schools have never had any men students at all. Over 60 per cent of all the men trained for library work by the library schools studied at the New York State Library School; while of the 183 men still engaged in library work 122, or 67 per cent, are graduates of that school. This is a very significant fact in view of the need for attracting more men into library work. If we are to judge by the statistics, college men prefer a school of the highest standards which comes most nearly to meeting the requirements of a professional school organized on a graduate basis.

The statistics of graduates still engaged in library work have no special significance. One would expect to find that for the older schools a pretty large proportion of all the graduates have died or taken up other work. The figures show that 62 per cent of the graduates of all schools are still actively engaged in some kind of library work. Of all the schools established ten years or more ago, the New York Public Library School makes the best showing, with nearly 78 per cent of all its graduates still in the ranks. The women make a better showing in this respect than the men, not only in the New York Public Library School, but also in the two other schools which have had an appreciable number of men graduates.

The rather high proportion of women graduates who marry and leave the profession seems to be matched by the greater tendency of men to take up other work, due perhaps to the larger opportunities opened to men in administrative and other intellectual pursuits at larger salaries than have been customary in library work. Taking all the schools together, and including the most recent classes, about 22 per cent of all women graduates have married, very few of them continuing in library work after marriage. The percentage differs materially among the different schools, being the lowest for the Los Angeles School and the highest for Simmons College.

Unfavorable comment has been made at times on the seemingly large proportion of women graduates of library schools who marry. The question has been raised as to whether vocational training not utilized is a good investment either for the individual or society. A fair interpretation of the statistics presented here seems to leave little ground for criticism of library school graduates on this score. In the first place, as the figures show, men graduates drop out of the profession in about the same proportion as women. If statistics were available, it would probably be found that women trained for teaching and other professions marry in even larger proportion than those trained for librarianship. It is also claimed, and with some plausibility, that library school training is excellent preparation for the duties of homemaking and the social responsibilities of married women. Certainly it would be a mistake to assume that a woman librarian who marries is lost to the cause of library progress. Not only has she in most cases given a longer or shorter period of service in return for her training, but as a responsible citizen, perhaps as a member of the board of trustees of her local library, the ex-librarian may be able to do more to improve library service than she could as an active member of a library staff.

While we may therefore conclude that library schools cannot justly be criticized on the ground that too many of their women graduates marry and are lost to the service, it may still be in order in comparing the standing of the different schools to assume that those whose graduates remain in the profession in the largest proportion have succeeded best either in the selection of students with the special qualifications needed or in imparting to them the kind of training and inspiration which hold them in the ranks of the profession against all other attractions.

Throughout this report stress has been laid on the view that for professional library work, as distinguished from the more mechanical, routine or clerical aspects of the operation of libraries, a college education should be a prerequisite. Two of the best schools do require a college degree for admission, while two or three others give both the bachelor's degree and the library school degree for a course of four years' study which combines three years of college and one year of library instruction. In several of the schools which admit high school graduates on examination, the classes have a fair proportion of college graduates. Over 50 per cent of the 1921 class in the New York Public Library and the Los Angeles Public Library schools entered with a college degree. The proportion of students who enter the schools with a college education is steadily increasing. It should not be difficult within a reasonable length of time to make the bachelor's degree an entrance condition for all professional library schools. Schools which are called upon to train for sub-professional grades of service will naturally continue to accept high school students.

Constant reference has been to the low salaries paid to library workers. Accurate statistics of the salaries of graduates of all the library schools are not available. For five representative schools, however, complete and fairly comparable data have been secured and are shown here in graphic form. The following summary table shows that over 40 per cent of all the graduates of the five schools, now engaged in library work, earn less than $1500 a year. Only 15 per cent receive as much as $2,000, while only 3.6 per cent are holding positions which command as much as $2,500 a year. These figures are all based on recent reports and include the general increases

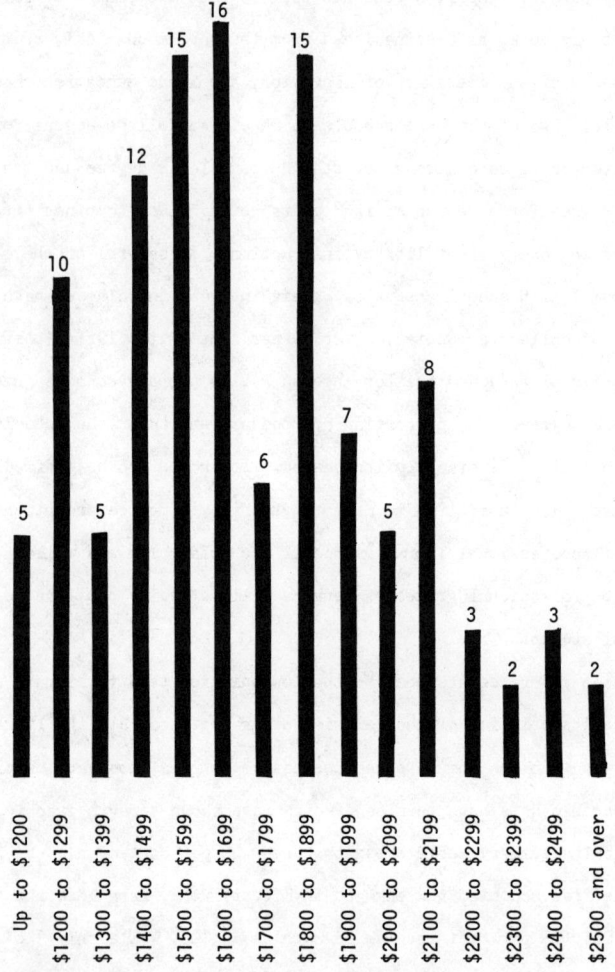

Chart Showing Distribution of Salaries of Graduates of a Western Library School. Fifteen Classes Have Been Graduated. Twenty-eight Percent Receive Less Than $1500.

Bars indicate number of persons in each salary group.

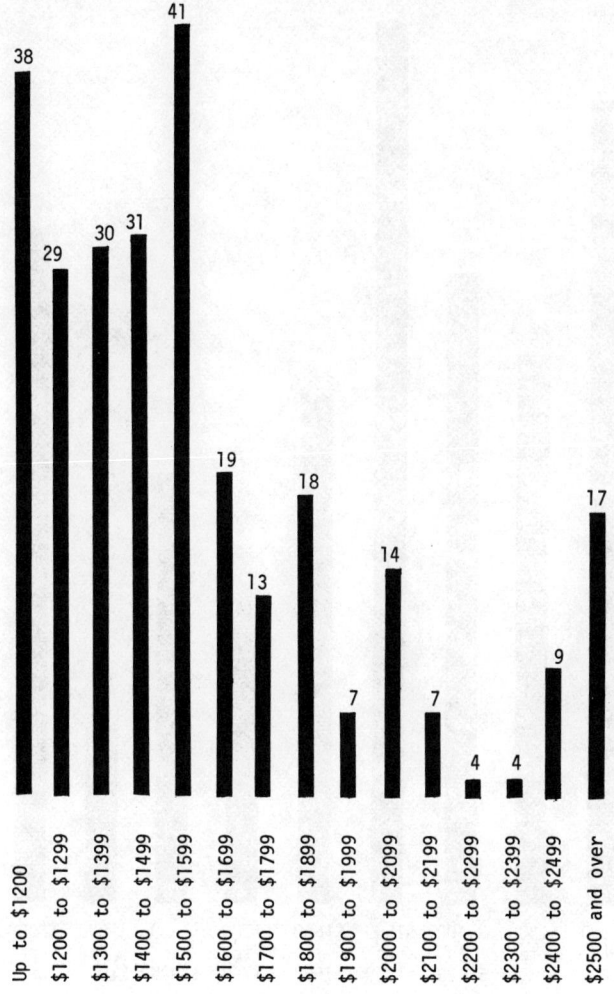

Chart Showing Distribution of Salaries of Graduates of one of the oldest Library Schools. Forty-six percent receive less than $1500 a year.

Bars indicate number of persons in each salary group.

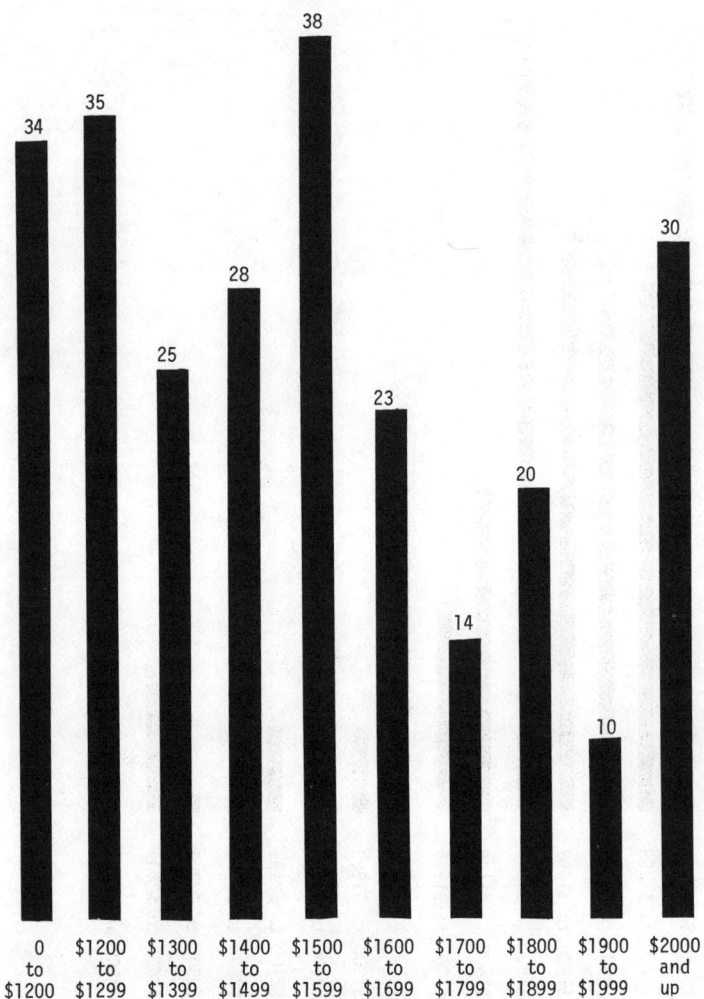

Chart Showing Distribution of Salaries of the Graduates of One Library School, Showing a Fairly Typical Distribution. Sixteen Classes Have Been Graduated. Nearly Half of the Graduates Are Receiving Less Than $1500 a Year.

Bars indicate number of persons in each salary group.

Chart Showing Distribution of Salaries of Graduates of One of the Smaller Library Schools. Seventeen Classes Have Been Graduated. Fifty-Two Per Cent Receive Salaries Not Exceeding $1500.

[Chart Missing]

Chart Showing Distribution of Salaries of Graduates of One Library School. Ten Classes Have Been Graduated Thirty-four Percent Receive Less Than $1500.

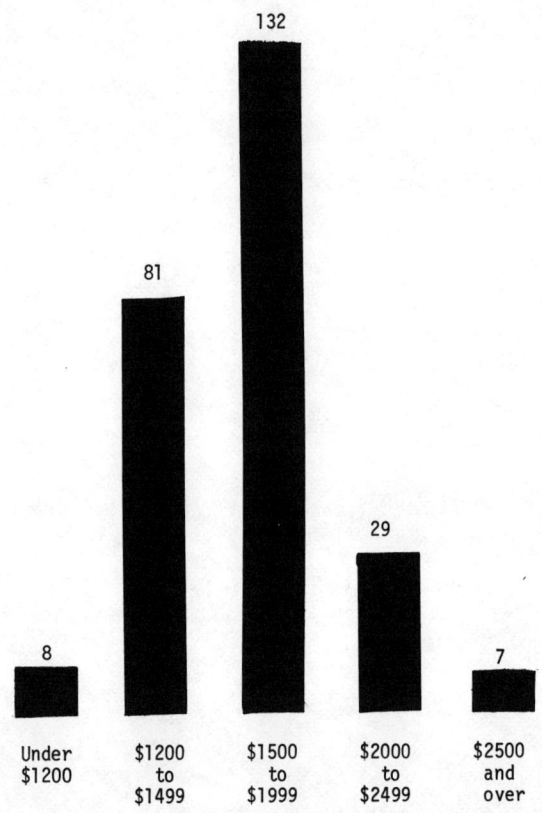

Bars indicate number of persons in each salary group.

occasioned by war conditions. One of the five schools is among the oldest and largest, while none of them has sent out less than ten graduating classes. Salaries of past graduates, however, have not increased since 1914 as rapidly as the average initial salary reported by the schools. On account of the careful attention given by the schools to the placement of their graduates, the initial salaries shown in a proceeding table may be accepted as accurate.

SALARIES OF GRADUATES OF FIVE REPRESENTATIVE LIBRARY SCHOOLS

School Number	No. of graduates reported on	Receiving Salaries					
		Below $1500		$2,000 or more		$2,500 or more	
		No.	P.C.	No.	P.C.	No.	P.C.
1	73	38	52.1	3	4.1	0	0.0
2	257	89	34.6	36	14.0	7	2.7
3	114	32	28.1	23	20.2	2	1.8
4	280	128	45.7	55	19.6	17	6.1
5	257	122	47.5	30	11.7	9	3.5
Total	981	409	41.7	147	15.0	35	3.6

In 1914 the unweighted average of the initial salary of graduates of the twelve schools reporting on this point was $842, or about $70 a month. In 1921, with fourteen schools reporting, it had risen to $1332, an increase of 58 per cent. This increase reflects the shortage of library workers during and immediately following the war period. No similar increase has taken place in library salaries generally. The figures merely show that new and inexperienced workers have been taken into library staffs at a beginning salary approaching, if not exceeding, salaries paid to experienced workers already employed, who are not in a position to demand the compensation the newcomer can command.

The actual salaries paid to some 5,000 library school graduates, who may be called the élite of the library workers, numbering in all probably 15,000, suggest that perhaps library work is not a profession but rather a minor intellectual and clerical occupation. Doubt is cast by these figures on the insistent assertion that there is an acute shortage of librarians. The average increase of initial salaries from 1914 to 1921 of 58 per cent does indeed indicate a relative shortage during that period, but present salaries do not seem to show a condition which calls for many new library schools or as great an increase in the number of trained workers as some library administrators seem to think.

Improvement in library service is more likely to result from a limitation of the product of professional library schools, accompanied by a higher standard of general and professional education, until such time as salaries paid make it economically possible for library work to compete with other professions in attracting men and women of first class ability and qualities of intellectual and community leadership. In other words, not more library schools or larger classes, but a better grade of student and higher standards of instruction are the fundamental needs in professional training for librarianship at the present time.

CHAPTER 11

THE RELATION OF SALARIES TO IMPROVEMENT OF LIBRARY SCHOOLS

A fundamental cause of any shortage of trained and competent library workers is the fact that salaries paid in nearly every grade and type of library service are lower than in other lines of work requiring equal ability and education. Until recently graduates of library schools took their first positions at an average salary of $70 a month. Changes brought about by war conditions have caused some improvement. At present graduates are being placed in their first positions at an average salary of about $1332 a year, but this is considerably less than a college graduate with one year of post-graduate study is offered in high school teaching.

The low initial salary, however, is not so great a deterrent to the capable and ambitious man or woman who finds the work otherwise attractive as the slowness of promotion, the small and uncertain salary increases and the very meagre income which he can expect to receive even after a long period of service. The lawyer and the physician may earn less in the first year or two after leaving the professional school than the librarian; but in the older professions a person of ability, industry, and good training is almost certain of a good income in a few years; and for those whose professional success is marked, an income many times that of the successful librarian is assured.

It is quite possible that library personnel would be improved if initial salaries were lower and ultimate salaries higher. At present persons of mediocre ability, or less, are induced to take up the work by the fair initial salary and then never leave but remain in the ranks to be promoted slowly to the higher positions as the abler workers leave for more lucrative and attractive occupations. In this respect library work is not unlike teaching. "The beginning salary for the teacher", says one educational authority,[1] "is sufficient to hold, sometimes permanently, the teacher who is really a failure, and the upper salary is not sufficient to hold in the profession those teachers who show the greater worth. It thus happens that the professions of law and medicine usually cast off their failures while the teaching profession often casts off its successes."

Comparatively few library positions pay over $5000 and until recently the list of those paying as much as $4000 would not have been a very long one; and this, too, for those who have spent a lifetime in the service. Such salaries as these, moreover, are paid only in administrative positions. It is not surprising, therefore, that those seeking a career have come to look upon library work with disfavor, as a field which, whatever other attractions it may offer, does not promise more than a bare subsistence.

So long as library work as a profession suffers this handicap, library schools will be obliged to give relatively short courses, admit all applicants except the obviously unfit and be content to remain small. A university devoting its resources to vocational or professional training may well hesitate to provide training facilities for a very small group whose services are not likely to be valued as highly, on an average, as many kinds of unskilled manual labor. It is really surprising that more educational institutions have not abolished their library schools, either on account of the small demand for graduates or the low salaries paid.

The Drexel Institute in 1914 did discontinue its library school, largely on the ground that the demand for its graduates was too slight and salaries too small to justify any further expenditure on it. On account of
. . . . .
(1) J. L. Creech, "Why Do Men Turn from Teaching?" Educational Administration and Supervision, October, 1920, v. 6, p. 391.

the small enrolment the per capita cost of the library school students was discovered to be the highest in any department of the Institute. From the time of its organization in 1892 to its discontinuance in 1914, 317 students were graduated (only two of them men), or an average of less than fifteen per year. Nor was there any prospect of being able to increase the enrolment materially, especially since the Institute was designed to be primarily a school for Philadelphia. For some years before 1914 the number of students had been limited to twenty, but the average number from Philadelphia was less than four per annum.

A study of the salary and employment situation in Philadelphia also suggested the discontinuance of the school. On this point Dr. Hollis Godfrey, the President of the Institute, reported as follows:

> "We found in comparing the number of positions and salaries in a selected group of Philadelphia libraries, that there are one hundred and twenty holding positions in selected libraries, drawing from $216 to $600 per annum; thirty-one drawing from $600 to $720 per annum; twenty-seven drawing $900 per annum; and twelve drawing over $900. In five years all the general libraries in Philadelphia took direct from the Library School seven graduates. Total notices on file of vacancies in libraries of the United States for the past five years at salaries of $600 and over, were one hundred and sixty-six. It should be remembered, of course, that this employment field is for young women graduates, but it must be equally remembered that this is the record for five years. On the basis of the facts shown above, the board decided that the Library School should be given up."

The considerations which led to giving up the Drexel Institute Library School might almost equally well be used to urge the discontinuance of all library schools. Enrolment everywhere is small, per capita cost of training high, and salaries paid to graduates uniformly lower than in any other field of work. No one, however, who has the slightest appreciation of the importance of a trained library service would suggest giving up all the library schools. On the contrary, the situation points to the opposite conclusion. The schools should be strengthened in every way, enrolment multiplied, standards of fitness for library work raised, and salaries increased to a point that will lead college men and women to look upon library work as offering a desirable career.

Elevation of professional standards and improvement of salaries will have to go hand in hand. Neither is likely to come about until the teaching staffs of the library schools can command the best talent in the profession. They will then take a somewhat broader view of their function and be able to make their work appeal to the best type of college man and woman. Both the salary and training situations can best be attacked through some system of certification for librarians and an efficient method of accrediting training agencies. The system which seems to the writer most likely to accomplish the best results is outlined in a chapter on standardization and certification.

CHAPTER 12

THE PROFESSIONAL LIBRARY SCHOOL AND THE UNIVERSITY

A library school conducted by a public library, primarily to supply the need for trained workers on its own staff, must necessarily labor under many serious disadvantages in endeavoring to offer a thorough professional education. In the first place, every library important enough to have its own professional school will need also to conduct a training class. The attempt which is often made to combine the two is fatal to both. But the objections to the public library professional school go much deeper. No library is organized for the purpose of providing general professional education. Its object is to furnish library service. If it can be shown, however, that the best way to secure professionally trained librarians is through the service institution, of course any more or less theoretical objection could be waived, but such does not appear to be the case.

There is a fundamental contradiction in the very idea of _professional_ training to fit for service on the staff of any one institution. If the general training is actually professional in character, it cannot be molded in any degree to meet the peculiar requirements of a particular library staff; the only legitimate way that a library supporting a professional school can derive a special benefit from the supply of trained workers created is by paying them as much or more than is offered by other employers. If it is prepared to do this, it can get trained workers at any time without going to the trouble and expense of conducting its own school. The trustees of at least one library which conducts a library school are said to be disappointed that so many of the graduates go to other libraries. The head of any truly professional school will endeavor to place its graduates as widely as possible and at as high salaries as possible. A fundamental conflict arises, therefore, in the conduct of a library school by a public library unless the library authorities, understanding the situation thoroughly, declare their intention to use the public money appropriated for providing a local library service to conduct a library school of professional grade for the sake of libraries and library service generally, without expecting more than incidental and intangible benefit to their own service. They should be prepared to see every graduate of the school find employment elsewhere if service in other libraries should prove for any reason to be more attractive.

As a matter of fact, it is not probable that any library board would make the undertaking, if professional library schools were held up to adequate standards. The expense would be so great that they would at once see the impropriety, not only from an educational view point, but also from the standpoint of their own trusteeship and responsibility to local taxpayers. A training class for clerical workers is amply justified, even in comparatively small libraries, for under existing standards of library schools, the difference in expense of conducting a training class and a library school is so slight that any library board can readily justify the additional cost because of the added prestige that the training class gets if it is known as a library school. When proper standards for professional schools are insisted upon, the financial burden put upon public libraries which have schools will lead either to their abandonment or to seeking outside support, or the schools will be turned over to some educational institution organized and supported for the purpose of providing professional education of whatever kinds the public welfare demands. The training of professional librarians should cease to be the self-imposed task of municipal library boards and be turned over to the universities. There should be no more reason for expecting or permitting the public library of one city to train librarians for a whole state or for the whole country than for allowing the public schools of that city to use municipal revenues to train teachers for the whole state. The state would not permit the latter as a matter of educational policy, and any taxpayer would seem, on the face of it, to have a clear case against a municipal library board which uses money appropriated for public library service to support a professional library school of the type which should prevail.

Let us assume, however, that the public library is able to conduct its school by means of funds which can be legitimately used for the purpose. The question then becomes one of general educational policy and the answer is perhaps not quite so clear. If the public library can adequately support a professional library school, we need only inquire as to whether it can for the money put into it secure as good a result as if the school were conducted under other auspices.

The question of general educational policy involves a consideration of the adequacy of the teaching staff and general facilities, the relative ease of attracting well educated men and women as students and the actual results attained in the long run under different types of schools. Looking at the matter in the light of broad, educational policy, it would seem to require a very exceptional situation in library work to justify a plan which has not proved satisfactory in the case of any other profession. Medical schools conducted as an adjunct to a medical practice or a hospital service have proved to be inferior and have been supplanted almost completely by schools organized as a part of universities. The situation is similar in regard to all other professions. In no other case does the need of an institution for professional services on a large scale justify it in attempting to assume the entire responsibility for offering professional training in that field. The school system of a large city may train its own elementary teachers, but no city attempts to train teachers specifically for its high schools or for the administrative educational services. Universities, state and endowed, can and do maintain colleges of education of the highest professional grade. The principles and general methods of organizing professional education are fundamentally the same for all the professions built on a basis of higher education. University boards and university officials are better fitted to supervise professional education for library work than are public library boards. University authorities are dealing all the time with educational problems - with problems of professional education. Their experience and breadth of view ought to give them a decided advantage over library boards whose main business is of a very different character and to whom a small library school as their sole responsibility in the field of professional education must either be treated as of no importance at all or unduly burdensome.

As to the maintenance of proper standards in the teaching staff, the advantage would seem to lie again with the university school. It should be stated at once that existing library schools not connected with universities have some instructors who would take high standing on any university faculty. Final judgment, however, cannot rest on individual cases. We are approaching a time when the professional library school must be a graduate school. The regular instructors must themselves have college training as well as special training and experience in their own field at least equal to that required in the teaching staff of the best professional schools. Can this be realized in the public library type of school? Granted more adequate financial support, perhaps it can, but it does not seem probable. University authorities are more likely to insist on the graduate school standard than are public library authorities. Putting the instructional staff on a graduate basis does not mean making all of them full-time "academic theorists"; it does mean that in addition to the necessary first-hand knowledge of library technique and methods they shall be possessed of the general education and personality to fit them to instruct college men and women.

College men and women of the type needed in library work will not tolerate the standards of instruction found too often in existing library schools. The instructor who is wholly competent to train clerical workers may fail completely to attain the standards of professional training. The school that does not satisfy the needs of college men and women should not be allowed to take the rank of a professional school, for students in such schools must be recruited from the colleges. This is an additional and very important reason for believing that the university type of school is to be preferred. In the colleges and universities are found the men and women of the future. Many of them are looking forward to a permanently satisfactory career, the gateway to which they will naturally seek in the professional schools maintained by their own or other universities. Able college men and women are more likely to enter the library schools in universities than those in public libraries. The university school seems to offer entrance to the whole field of library work; the public library school to the public library field alone. Though this is not necessarily the case, it must seem so to the student looking at it from the outside.

In respect to the variety of types of library work and highly developed library systems, adequate support and excellence of administration, the advantages are decidedly in favor of the public library. Merely as a laboratory, the public library is usually superior to the university library. It should be assumed, however, that any library school of professional grade will make the fullest possible use of the best laboratory facilities available. A university medical school utilizes the best hospital facilities within reach through some form of cooperation or affiliation. Naturally a university library school would do the same. A good university library school in close proximity to excellent libraries of all the principal types would offer an ideal opportunity for the best professional training.

It is true that the library school will be one of the smallest departments of a university and thus suffer some disadvantage, but it should not be much smaller, even under present conditions, than certain other and well recognized departments. The normal distribution of students in a university with a total enrolment of 10,000 students has been estimated* as follows: Arts and science, 2,500; graduate school, 500; medicine, 200; law, 200; dentistry, 200; pharmacy, 200; various lines of engineering, 1,800; agriculture, 1,500; veterinary medicine, 150; commerce and business, 1,200; education, 1,000; journalism, 200; library science, 50; landscape architecture, 50; architecture and design, 150; music, 100.

---

*President R. H. Hughes, of Miami University, Oxford, Ohio, in Proceedings of North Central Association of Colleges and Secondary Schools, 1920, p. 78-89.

CHAPTER 13

ADVANCED OR SPECIALIZED STUDY

To bring about a reasonable degree of efficiency in library service, adequate provision must be made for specialized training. A glance at the personnel specifications for any of the larger libraries is sufficient to show how diversified and specialized library work has now become. While library service has been growing more and more highly specialized and will doubtless continue to do so, the training afforded by the library schools has for the most part remained general. It is approximately accurate to say that the aim of the library schools at present is to fit every student to take up any branch of library work which may offer an opening when he has finished his one-year course.

In most of the leading professions specialization in practice is promptly followed by a corresponding specialization in professional education. In engineering, for example, specialization in industry long ago forced engineering schools to provide specialized courses. Speaking of this feature of engineering education, Dr. Charles R. Mann says: "Formerly the choice lay among civil, mechanical, and mining engineering; now the selection must be made from aeronautical, agricultural, architectural, automobile, bridge, cement, ceramic, chemical, civil, construction, electrical, heating, highway, hydraulic, industrial, lighting, marine, mechanical, metallurgical, mill, mining, railway, sanitary, steam, textile, telephone, topographical engineering, and engineering administration (1)."

.....
(1) A Study of Engineering Education, by Charles Riborg Mann. 1918. 139 p. Bulletin Number Eleven, the Carnegie Foundation for the Advancement of Teaching.

Library work, to be sure, has not become so highly specialized as engineering, owing in part to the fact that modern library service is a comparatively recent development and in part, also, perhaps to the fact that the library being, as a rule, a branch of the public service, has not benefited by the stimulus toward increased efficiency through specialization which comes from commercial competition.

The schools explain their failure to provide specialized training partly on the ground that there is insufficient demand for it, while librarians reply that there is a potential demand which would become actual if the schools were equipped to turn out well trained specialists. The truth seems to lie somewhere between the two positions. Libraries have too often expected the schools to turn out in one year assistants who can readily fill any position in any kind of a library. Largely for financial reasons the schools have been unable to expand their work beyond the general one-year course; but even had they been able to do so, the low salaries paid even to skilled specialists in library work, together with the lack of recognized standards of fitness for special work, would have kept the numbers seeking the special training so small that the schools would scarcely have been justified in offering specialized curricula.

A point has now been reached, however, where there is apparently sufficient demand to make it feasible to provide specialized professional training. The rapid expansion of public and private libraries, the development of many types of special libraries, and a keen interest at the present time in higher standards of service, put a responsibility on the professional training schools of which they are becoming aware, but for which as yet they have taken no adequate steps to meet. Only two specialized curricula have been offered so far by any accredited library school - one in children's library work by the Carnegie Library School of Pittsburgh, and Western Reserve University, and another in legislative reference work by the University of Wisconsin Library School.

It might be said that a certain kind of specialization has been attained by the two-year schools - New York State and the University of Illinois. Since these two schools admit only college graduates and give a two-year course, it is possible for them to cover more thoroughly all the subjects in the curriculum. As a consequence graduates of these two schools have become especially prominent in the administrative and scholarly aspects of library work. In point of fact, however, these two-year schools do not offer specialized study. Aside from a very few elective courses in the second year, they cover in two years essentially the same range of subjects taken up by the one-year schools. The work is naturally somewhat more thorough, certain second-year courses being properly described as "advanced", but it is nevertheless essentially accurate to say that they attempt, like the one-year schools, to prepare students equally well for all kinds of library work.

Recently the growing demand for workers with specialized training has led some of the schools to deviate slightly from their general program in the direction of specialization. Special and visiting lecturers have briefly described their specialized work; the students have inspected some of the more notable examples of special libraries and have even been permitted to do their field work in very specialized lines. It would be a misfortune, however, if either students or school authorities were to be misled into believing that this slight look into specialties constitutes specialized professional training. These lectures on special libraries and a certain amount of field work in libraries of this type are not only legitimate but quite essential features of a general professional course. Specialized training is a very different thing and is not to be secured by listening to a few lectures followed by a brief tour of inspection.

The specialist is not a beginner but an expert, a master of the history, theory, technique, and practical problems of his special field.

Library school authorities very generally take the ground that no specialization is possible within the one-year course and undoubtedly this is sound policy. Nothing less than one year's instruction is sufficient to provide a broad foundation for professional work of any kind. The primary function of every library school must be to provide this general all-round training and it does not appear that this can be done in less than one full academic year. Two or three schools, indeed, offer a second year's work of general character, while other schools have looked forward to adding a second year of the same kind, but it has always been difficult and seems now to be increasingly difficult to hold students for this second year of general instruction. Apparently, fewer students still would remain for the senior year if two years' work were not required for the desired degree. Many students, moreover, would apparently be willing to forego the degree if the work of the junior year represented in itself a well-rounded introduction to library work.

The opinion of experienced library workers is very decidedly against the two-year general course. It is believed that it would be much better for the two-year schools to crowd into one year all the essentials of a general professional course and then offer a second year of specialized, advanced work. There has been a feeling that it is unnecessary and even a waste of time to spend two years getting the fundamental training. Students who have taken two years for the general course show no marked superiority over those who take both years in one or those who have had their training in the better one-year schools; it is probable that any difference which may be pointed out may be due to the higher educational standard for admission to the two-year schools. Statistics compiled by the University of Illinois show that 152 women students who took the second year's work are earning $89 a year more on the average than 110 women who stopped at the end of the junior year. Nine men who took the two year's work are earning $619 more on the average than eight who took only one year. These figures do not prove, however, that the second year's study was worth while, even from the standpoint of earning power. The best students were doubtless encouraged to return for the second year and get the degree. The poorer students were allowed or persuaded to drop out at the end of one year. The surprising thing is that the difference between the earnings of the two groups is not greater than it is.

Few well informed librarians have any doubt that a second year of training is needed for those who look forward to responsible positions in professional library work. The opinion is very widely held, however, that while the first year of study should be general and basic, the second should be definitely and even minutely specialized in the field in which the student is to take up his work. The actual demand for a year of specialized training has now become strong enough to make it imperative for the schools to give some heed to it.

Probably the most important special group for which specialized training should be provided at once are the school librarians, particularly the high school librarians. In states having the best educational standards the high school librarian must have the qualifications of a high school teacher, which means a college degree with special training in education and some graduate study in the subjects to be taught, plus professional library training. A college education and one year's study in a library school do not give adequate preparation for high school librarianship. A second year of special preparation is coming to be essential, the course to consist of three elements: (1) special study of high school library problems, supplementing and adapting the general course; (2) special study and training in educational subjects, history of education, educational psychology, and the high school curriculum; (3) while the third part of the year's work would consist of a large amount of field work, including extended periods of actual service in well organized high school libraries under the close supervision and direction of able and experienced high school librarians. At the end of this second year's work the student would be much better equipped to organize and administer a high school library than she can be at the end of the second year's work in one of the two-year schools at the present time. A graduate of the full course in either the New York State or University of Illinois School has spent more time than is necessary on various subjects which are highly important for other kinds of library work but of little or no value in a high school library. She will probably have taken only a brief elective course of rather general character on school libraries and a limited amount of "practice" in high school libraries. No opportunity will have been offered for the training in education which is indispensable for acceptable and efficient service as a high school librarian.

For other types of library service requiring special preparation, the present library school facilities are even farther from being adequate than they are for the high school library. Leading librarians in the college and university group have for several years been outspoken in their criticism of the failure of the library schools to provide adequate or appropriate training for the special reference and research work of a scholarly character. A prominent university librarian writes:

> "The best reference people I have met in my own experience are not library school graduates but university-trained people who have somehow gone into library work. I recognize, however, the extraordinary value of the addition to their other equipment of the training afforded by library schools, and I am always seeking persons who have had that training for our staff. In looking for people to take charge of our graduate reading

rooms, however, I have given other considerations foremost place and have made a known scholarly attainment the basis of selection. I would rather have such people with an imperfect knowledge of library technique, than the best trained technician who lacks university training and some graduate study."

"It seems to me that the requisite thing is some such sort of scholastic library work as was given for so many years at Gottingen by Dziatzko. Such work could be done at Harvard, Yale, Princeton, Michigan, Chicago, perhaps at Minnesota and Cornell; but I am absolutely certain that no one of the librarians or chief assistants at those institutions can find the time, under the pressure of their work as now arranged, to give such instruction."

While the demand for this type of training has not been as clearly defined as for high school work and other special fields, it would seem to call for a second year of study carefully planned with reference to the special needs of college and university libraries referred to in the statement just quoted.

The need for specialized training for library work with children has long been recognized and fairly well provided for in the Carnegie Library School and more recently in Western Reserve University. Under the plan of organization proposed in this report, the specialized training for professional children's work would be given as a second year of library school study, consisting of some technical library courses, with much attention to literature for children, thorough courses in education, child psychology and the relations of the library to the public school, accompanied by much field work and practice under expert supervision.

Another important branch of library service which calls for at least one full year of specialized study and training is cataloguing and classification, combined with several closely related divisions of library organization and service. Advanced courses in technical cataloguing and the principles of classification, with a large amount of field work, giving opportunity for comparative study and responsible service under skilled supervision would afford thorough preparation for positions as chief cataloguers and senior assistants in the cataloguing and classification divisions.

Special preparation for order work could be combined with the cataloguing and classification or with advanced training for reference work. The actual grouping of subjects for the year of specialized work in book selection, order work, cataloguing, classification and reference, will require careful consideration. Our purpose here is merely to suggest in broad outline some of the types of specialized curricula which should be among the first to be organized.

Courses in library administration should be provided among the first. Objection is often made to training for administrative positions on the ground that administrators are born, not made. The same can probably be said with almost equal truth of cataloguers, reference librarians, children's librarians, etc. Even the person endowed with a gift for administrative work needs a broad basis of technical knowledge and special familiarity with the problems with which he is concerned. In the general one-year course there is no opportunity to take up many subjects as personnel management, the general principles of organization and management, applied psychology, government and finance should be introduced in this course. Graduate schools of business administration and experiments in training for various types of executive positions show conclusively that training for executive work is practicable.

There is abundant material for a year's work in preparation for executive positions, not only as heads of library systems large and small, but as branch librarians, chiefs of divisions, assistant librarians, college and university librarians, etc. It is not proposed to make executives but to take those who have already shown some capacity for administrative functions and give them instruction and training that will help them to develop their capacity. The futility of trying to teach administration in the general course might be admitted without weakening the case for advanced training for those who have already shown some ability in that direction. And, after all, probably more people possess the combination of common sense and an understanding of human nature, which form the basis of administrative skill, than is ordinarily supposed.

County and rural library work, which might include secretaries of library commissions, state organizers, etc., promise in the near future to call for a large number of workers with special training. The development of county library systems is already being seriously retarded by the lack of properly qualified leaders and organizers.

Some library school favorably located should develop a special course for the training of persons who are to teach library subjects, not only in library schools, but in training classes, summer schools, normal schools, colleges, etc. The inadequate equipment of library school instructors has been referred to in a preceding chapter. At the present time those who find themselves called upon to teach library subjects have nowhere to look for help but must struggle along by means of their own unguided experience. Even a short course in the pedagogy of library school teaching would greatly improve the situation. Unfortunately, the salaries paid to instructors in library schools and training schools are so low that they can scarcely be expected to spend much time or money on special training. Experience with a so-called "normal course" offered by Pratt Institute School of Library Science a decade ago is sometimes cited as evidence that there is no demand for such a course. Better salaries, however, and higher standards of qualification for teaching positions should make it possible for some school in a strategic position to develop a course of such practical value that it could be given in alternate years, if not every year.

A very large field for specialized training is afforded by the business library. While the opinion is still held in some quarters that the worker with a thorough general training can make the necessary adaptations for the business library field, it is clear from the extent to which business library subjects are being introduced in the one-year courses that considerable demand has arisen for special training. It is equally clear that it is impossible to furnish the indispensable general professional training and also any adequate special training for business library work in a one-year course. A second year of specialized work appears to offer the only satisfactory solution. Such a course should be organized as soon as possible in at least one school and in a school, it need not be said, which is so located as to offer excellent opportunity for field work and to command the services of competent instructors of wide practical experience.

A year of specialized training supplementing the general course will eventually be called for in various other special fields. Courses in public documents with statistics and sociology, in chemistry, fine arts, technology, law, medicine, and agriculture are among the possibilities for the immediate future. The two-year schools cannot make this radical change in the character of their second year's work a moment too soon. For the one-year schools the necessary adjustment is simpler. Those which are able to secure sufficient financial support and are so located that they can command adequate opportunities for field work, and secure the services of experienced and practical instructors, can offer specialized courses whenever there is a demand for them.

To provide the kind of specialized training proposed here, it will also be necessary in most cases for the library school to be located in the vicinity of other educational institutions whose cooperation will be indispensable. Thus for the specialized course for high school librarians, the instruction in education and pedagogy must be sought in a teachers' college or department of education of a university. Though not quite so necessary, it would be highly advantageous to have the cooperation of a school of education in the training of children's librarians. For business library training, college courses or, better still, courses in a school of business administration, should be combined with the special instruction in library technique and the field work. A special course in library administration would require the cooperation of college or university faculties. In fact, the lines of specialized work which any library school can offer will depend very largely on the facilities in the same locality for giving instruction in subjects required in the specialized course, but which cannot be given properly by the library school itself without unreasonable expense. No advanced work should be undertaken where excellent facilities for supervised field work do not exist or where it is difficult to secure the part-time services of superior instructors.

Advanced special work of the character here proposed should not as a rule follow immediately the first year of general study. Exception might be made in the case of mature students who have had very exceptional experience before entering the school. Exception might possibly be made also for students who have specialized to an unusual degree in the subject matter of the proposed library specialization. Every one agrees that the second year's work will be taken with far greater profit after the student has spent at least one year in library work. This preliminary experience gives what there is no time for in the first year of school work, a period of actual service long enough for the student to acquire some degree of skill and long enough to enable him to decide in what branch of service he wishes to specialize. Moreover, this period of practical work between the general and special courses should serve to eliminate the less competent, for no one should be accepted for the year of specialized study who has not made a very good record in actual service.

One very important result of this actual experience will be that the student will run no great risk of fitting himself for a special line of work in which later he finds no satisfactory opening for employment. One of the strongest reasons advanced by school officials for not attempting to give specialized courses at present is that very few students know what special kinds of work will be available when they have finished their course. A student who has been in actual work for at least one year would not ordinarily return for a second year without having some very definite assurance of a position awaiting him. Often he will be able to secure leave of absence from some post to which he expects to return, better equipped for efficient service and promotion as a result of the year of study. Library administrators will gradually come to require such advanced training for all of the most important positions in the professional service. Special training should also receive recognition in certification schemes.

It seems altogether probable that advanced study of the kind and quality here proposed would attract enough students to make the plan practicable at once. Less than half of the students in the junior classes of the two-year schools return for the senior year. Fewer still would return if the junior year's work constituted in itself a complete and well-rounded course. To get a good general course many students now feel compelled to take the senior year, though students who leave at the end of the junior year find good positions waiting them and usually "make good." Officials of the two-year schools fear that no students would come back for a second year's work if all were forced to spend at least one year in practical work. And this would probably be so in the case of the existing second year of a general nature. A second year of advanced study of very practical and specialized character, however, once its value is demonstrated, should draw a reasonable number of students, not only from the first year classes of the same institution, but from the graduates of other schools as well.

Under present conditions the senior classes of the two-year schools are recruited almost entirely from the junior classes in the same schools. Very few graduates of the one-year schools take the senior year either at New York State or the University of Illinois. This may be due to some extent to an opinion on the part of certain of the schools that in their one-year course they cover the general essentials of library training as well as the two-year schools do, and that their graduates would therefore find the second year's work largely repetition and not worth the time and expense. No effort has been made to arrange the curricula of the two-year schools so that the second year would make a special appeal to graduates of the one-year schools. Moreover, the two-year schools require college graduation for admission and this in itself necessarily excludes most of the graduates of the other schools.

When all professional schools are put on a graduate basis and the work of the junior year organized as a thoroughly well-rounded and complete general course, graduates from all the schools should look naturally to taking a second year of special training wherever an accredited course is offered in the special field they desire to take up. Graduates from all the schools might go to Western Reserve for children's work, to the New York Public Library School for a special business library course, to Wisconsin for legislative reference, to the University of California for a county library course, and so on. Several schools should offer the year of special training for high school libraries.

Courses in all of the principal special fields of library work should be offered by at least one school and that the one best equipped to give it, by reason of strong teaching staff, presence of cooperating faculties, and exceptional opportunities for field work. Probably no one school should be expected to develop courses in all the specialties, but all should be offered somewhere. In developing its proper specialties each school will naturally be guided largely by its own local demand. The pressure of this local demand, on the other hand, should not be permitted to force specialization too far into the year of general professional instruction.

Such courses need not be given every year, if the number seeking them does not warrant it. They might well be offered only every third year. If definitely announced and made known to all potential applicants, those who desire a special course could make their plans one, two, or even three years ahead and arrange for leave of absence from their posts. It might be found practicable and desirable to plan all second-year courses so that they can be taken one-half at a time, making it unnecessary to devote an entire year to it all at once.

The number of students enrolling for this type of specialized training would not usually be large enough to require formal lecture courses by the library school faculty. The instruction in library subjects would therefore be given largely by readings, problems, discussions, and individual conferences with the instructors in charge. Instruction in related subjects would ordinarily be given through the regular courses in cooperating institutions. Field work should occupy a large part of the student's time and be very carefully planned and supervised by practical experts in the special field. As in the general course, the field work should include a large amount of planned observation and reporting, but unlike the method recommended for the general course, it should also include much actual work carried on under the direction and criticism of a competent expert. In a course of this kind, the acquisition of skill is a definite objective. While skill in any kind of library work is not to be expected or sought as a primary result of the first year's study, a high degree of skill in the chosen work must be the main objective of the year of specialized training.

If organized on some such plan as here suggested, the cost of specialized training for library service, while greater perhaps than for the general work, should not be excessive. The task of organizing and directing the work would rest on the principal or some competent member of the school staff, but would not require the full time of one person until the number of courses offered and the enrolment reach considerable proportions. The specialists who give the instruction in library subjects and direct the field work should be properly compensated for their service; otherwise it will as a rule not be efficient. Instruction given by cooperating institutions would not entail large expense for the library school. The ordinary fees for such courses would have to be added to the library school fee, or the regular library school fees shared with the cooperating institution.

On any other plan of operation the expense of a second year of first-class specialized training is prohibitive at the present time and will be for a long time to come. Elaborate plans have been proposed for a postgraduate library school with a full corps of well paid instructors and expensive equipment. Eventually it may be desirable to develop a school of this character. It is clear, however, that the practicable next step must be worked out at a minimum expense by utilizing fully the resources of the stronger professional schools in cooperation with other educational institutions in the same vicinity, using the services of competent specialists on the part-time plan and effecting a more thorough utilization of opportunities for field work.

It is possible that some specialized training of the character described above could be given *in absentia* by an institution properly equipped for it. Such study might not be acceptable for a degree but might, if properly safeguarded, receive some recognition in a certification system. The subject of training in service by correspondence methods is discussed in a later chapter.

CHAPTER 14

PLACEMENT OF LIBRARY SCHOOL GRADUATES

Library schools undertake not only to select and train those who are to become our professional librarians; they also serve their students and graduates, as well as library boards and administrators, in the capacity of employment agencies. Almost every library school regards this phase of its work as of great importance - so important that, as a rule, the active head of the institution gives it his personal attention and in not a few cases appears to give it a considerable part of his time, particularly at certain seasons of the year. While in their published statements the schools usually disclaim responsibility for placing their graduates, they do nevertheless feel that responsibility keenly. The head of at least one school is said not to feel at liberty to leave his post for the summer vacation until every member of the graduating class is placed.

It is commonly estimated that 90 to 95 per cent of the graduates are placed initially by the officers of the school. In the last three or four years, however, there has been no difficulty in finding places either for members of the graduating class or for the older graduates who are out of a place or desire to make a change. Much effort, on the other hand, has been expended by the schools in trying to find among their graduates persons able to fill the positions open and bidding for candidates.

Most of the schools keep in very close touch with their graduates and former students. Through correspondence, regular reports and various other means the principal usually knows pretty nearly what salary each one is receiving and whether he is contented or desirous of making a change. All this involves considerable correspondence and, especially in the case of the older schools, a large amount of such record work as any efficient employment agency necessarily requires.

Several factors have apparently contributed toward making the placement function so prominent in the conduct of all library schools, particularly of the older ones. In the first place, there has been no other agency to which employers could look for library workers. Commercial agencies have not developed as they have for teachers. Little use has been made of advertising in professional journals and in any case that method has very decided limitations. An unwritten but rather widely observed code of professional ethics forbids one library from "stealing" employees from another. That is to say, subordinate members of a library staff often have only such opportunities to move to another library as the head librarian approves. To a certain extent the library schools bow to this code, yet in the interest of their graduates who are in danger of getting "pocketed", they do not hesitate to open the doors of opportunity for promotion to better positions. Library administrators generally turn to the schools when seeking assistants. Practically speaking, they are the only source of information about professionally trained workers. Even those librarians who have been most skeptical of the value of library school training turn regularly to the schools for aid in recruiting their staffs.

The very success of the schools as general employment agencies and counsellors for their graduates has resulted in a certain prejudice on the part of not a few library administrators against employing the library school product. No sooner has the school trained assistant learned his duties, they say, and become fairly efficient, than his school finds another position for him at an increased salary. To employ library school graduates, therefore, is to have a constant succession of learners. For this reason they prefer to train their own assistants and enjoy some assurance of being able to retain them after they have become proficient.

The proper answer of the library school to this indictment is evident, of course. Any library can retain a competent assistant by paying him what he is worth. Certainly library salaries do not indicate that there has been any objectionable "profiteering." School officials, however, are conscious of the criticism they incur in paving the way to promotion for their graduates and try to keep in mind the interests of employers as well as of their students. It is quite common for school principals to discourage their graduates from changing positions oftener than every two years.

The library schools have also been in a position to give good service as employment agencies because of the intimate knowledge they possess of their graduates. Useful information has been assembled in the first instance in the process of selecting candidates for admission. Classes in all the schools are so small that the principal and members of the faculty come to know each student somewhat intimately and are able to follow his professional career. They are therefore in a position to add to what the school records show, a personal knowledge of the special capacities and defects of each graduate and can make recommendations with a high degree of intelligence and discrimination.

The lack of any generally recognized standards and tests of professional fitness tends to put the employment of library assistants on the sole basis of personal choice and thus the recommendation of the library school principal is naturally sought. The placement function of the library schools would be much less conspicuous if public library staffs were more generally recruited by civil service methods in which examinations, records of experience, and various practical tests formed the gateway to competitive appointment. As library employees, however, are generally the personal choice of the librarian or library boards, great dependence - perhaps undue dependence - comes to be placed on the recommendation of the library school. The library school, indeed, is sometimes looked upon as a substitute for the state and municipal civil service machinery through which other positions in the public service are usually filled. We cannot discuss here the interesting question as to whether the principle is sound of combining in one agency the functions of training for a technical branch of the public service and the testing and approving of that training as a basis for appointment to office.

It is perhaps a cause for regret that conditions in the library field have made the library schools the sole form of employment agency. The primary function of a library school is not, of course, to find or fill positions, but to fit its students for a high type of professional service. Not a few librarians, however, who lack library school training and fail to appreciate its value are tempted to look upon the school as an expensive kind of an employment agency. Recently a group of non-school librarians has organized a Library Workers' Association with the avowed and primary purpose of providing for its members an employment service, which is designed to open up to them avenues of professional advancement now enjoyed only by the proteges of the library school. Unfortunately many of these non-school library workers seem to believe that their chief handicap is not a lack of professional training, but the lack of an <u>alma mater</u> ever watchful for opportunities to promote the personal and professional interests of her sons and daughters.

It would be unfair to give the impression that library schools are unique in the attention they give to the placement of their graduates. Certain teacher training institutions have acquired a wide reputation for success in putting their graduates into important administrative positions in the public schools. It may, perhaps, not be out of place to suggest that the library schools need to be on their guard against an excess of zeal in this entirely legitimate activity. A safe policy to follow is that set forth in the following statement from the head of one of the best of the schools:

> "We do not initiate the correspondence in respect to a vacancy. Our regular practice is to answer those letters that come to us asking for candidates, by recommending one or two or three of our students who appear to us to be qualified to fill the position, and in most instances our correspondence ends with that letter, un-

less the librarian, or library board member, or student, writes for further information. To probably 15 or 20 per cent of the requests during the past year we have replied that we had no one to recommend, though most of the time one or two of our former students were on our lists as needing places. We try not to recommend people unless they fit into the particular place for which we are asked to suggest candidates. Two or three times during the past year I have recommended librarians who never had any connection with this school because I thought they were better prepared for the job than any of our own students who were available."

The latter part of this statement refers to a criticism frequently directed at the library schools for an alleged tendency to recommend one of their own graduates and vigorously push his candidacy even though he is not especially qualified for the post, which might be better filled by some one whose school has not heard of the vacancy or is less aggressive in its placement policy. It would doubtless be easy to exaggerate the extent of undesirable practices of this sort. Library boards and library administrators, too, must share some of the blame because they open the way for such abuses by their uncritical and undiscriminating use of recommendations.

It has long been hoped that the American Library Association might develop an employment service that will serve both employers and employees, trained and untrained alike, and relieve the library schools to a large extent of this somewhat burdensome function. The prospect is not bright, however, for an efficient central agency. The A. L. A. is without funds to organize it properly, even assuming that it might later become self-supporting. It is questionable also whether the country is not too large to be served by a single centralized employment office.

The projected national certification system with its regional agencies, discussed fully in a later chapter and in a section of the appendix, would seem to go far toward solving the problem of securing full and dependable information about all professional librarians. Even if it should not be practicable for the certification board itself to provide an employment service, its cooperation might insure the success of a service conducted in the office of the secretary of the American Library Association.

The acute need of some kind of a clearing house of information in regard to persons engaged in professional library work has led to the suggestion of a librarian's "Who's Who". If any practicable basis were available for determining what a professional librarian is and who should be included in such a volume, it might do much to aid in solving the placement problem by putting at the service of library administrators and library boards information which they find it difficult to now get in regard to the educational qualifications and professional experience of library workers. The problem of selecting those whose names are to appear in such a guide, however, brings us back once more upon the necessity for some certification system for formulating and applying standards for professional library work.

CHAPTER 15

RECRUITING FOR THE LIBRARY PROFESSION

It is a matter of no little urgency that professional library work be disentangled forthwith from the skillful use of hands in the mechanical operations which play so large a rôle in every active and useful library. Until this is done, library work will not make a strong appeal to the better type of college men and women. The almost complete absence of men in library school classes is not to be explained solely by the fact that salaries are low in the assumption that college men are all looking for opportunities to make money. Largely because it is generally looked upon as clerical, library work has come to be known as "women's work." Men generally, and women to a large extent, do not think of it as offering a desirable professional career. The so-called "recruiting problem", brought about by the acute shortage of competent library workers, will not be solved until library service does offer to well educated men and women as desirable a career as other learned professions.

The library schools have heretofore assumed too large a share of the responsibility for recruiting library workers. Part of this error has doubtless been due to their deep professional interest, but in part also no doubt to the necessity for keeping their classes filled, since an important share of the income of every school is derived from student fees. The willingness of the schools to serve as the chief recruiting agents should not be allowed to obscure the fact that the responsibility for keeping up the supply of competent workers rests upon the profession at large. Not only is it somewhat undignified for the schools to be pressing upon college men and women the desirability of taking up library work, but they are not in a position to do it effectively. They are, in the first place, open to the suspicion of "drumming up trade." Moreover, library school instructors are seldom forceful and convincing speakers. Most of them are women, which tends to confirm the impression that library work is a feminine vocation. Many of them are not college trained and for that reason cannot meet the college student on his own level. While, most important of all, the picture of library work given by library school instructors tends to be theoretical; they do not always speak as active participants in the many interesting and worthwhile types of library service. College and university officials have referred to the harm done to the recruiting cause by the type of representative sometimes sent out by the library schools.

Young people in choosing their occupation are probably influenced more by what they see than by what they are told about any vocation. What they ordinarily see in the life of any library worker does not tend to magnify the importance of the work in their minds. This is particularly true of the staff of the college library, which is likely to be the only library the college student knows anything at all about. In too many cases the college librarian is an overworked, underpaid individual, ranking socially and academically below the teaching staff and in no sense a subject for emulation by the ambitious student. Even where the head librarian's position is not inferior to the teacher, the rank and file of the library staff do not occupy an enviable status. Even at its best the college library represents a special type of library work of limited appeal. From it the student would get little idea of the human interest and opportunities for public service inherent in public library and other kinds of library work. Unfortunately the usual vocational advisors of college students are not in a position to overcome this natural handicap suffered by library work. Deans and professors themselves are often ignorant of the rich opportunity for service in the library field; they are much better equipped to discuss with students the opportunities in law, medicine, engineering and other professions, and even in business.

Having in mind this problem of bringing into the schools a larger number and a somewhat higher grade of students, the library school principals were asked what their observation shows to be the chief factor in bringing students to the school. Almost without exception the answer was, "Our own graduates." Sometimes mere proximity, the reputation of the library system used for practice work, the friends of the teachers, etc., determine which school is selected.

In the writer's judgment, the organization and curriculum of the library schools should be modified to any extent that may be necessary to make them the gateways to professional library work for college men and women. The circularizing of college students and the sending of speakers to talk to students will effect little. In the qualifications of the teaching staff, the content of the curriculum, and the methods of teaching, the schools must be brought to the level of a graduate school. More and more, too, it will probably be found that library schools run by public libraries will not attract the best college students. As pointed out elsewhere, the place for the professional library school is in the university which is so located as to command adequate opportunities for field work. Large public libraries will continue to maintain training classes to train local recruits for the sub-professional grades of the service. When professional education of librarians has gone where all other professional education is going - to the university - a long step will have been taken toward a solution of the recruiting problem.

Library schools lack altogether the aid which may be derived from scholarships and fellowships in stimulating the interest of desirable candidates for admission. In some schools tuition is free or the fee merely nominal. In the best schools, however, the tuition fee is a substantial amount. If these schools were provided with the funds for a few scholarships to be awarded on the basis of merit in such a way as to help in bringing into the classes promising men and women who would not otherwise train for library work, the result might be very beneficial.

In addition to scholarships to cover tuition fees it is the general opinion of the library school officials that great benefits would be derived from a few scholarships or fellowships which would cover not only tuition fees but most of the other necessary expenses of a year's resident study in a professional library school. Library schools connected with the universities especially feel the need of scholarships and fellowships to enable them to compete with graduate schools which draw some of the best students into teaching and other lines of work by offering inducements of this kind.

Most of the older schools have small loan funds provided by the alumni for the use of needy students. These funds seem to be wisely administered and very useful. They are comparatively small, however, and the loans that can be made seldom cover more than tuition fees. As the money borrowed is always paid back such funds increase slowly.

In most schools there is little or no opportunity for needy students to meet a part of their expenses by paid labor of any kind. School work is definitely planned to occupy all their time and they are discouraged from making an effort to earn anything during the school year. Two or three schools, however, do permit students to take half-time work, or less, thus completing a year's study in two years or more while serving on some library staff, usually the library with which the school is connected. In general this practice is looked upon with disfavor though it is difficult to see why there should be any objection to it, if it enables capable workers to secure professional training who would otherwise have to forego it.

A very good way to aid in bringing the best college men and women into the library schools might be through fellowships and scholarships in selected professional library schools. They should be awarded, of course, on a competitive basis and used to the fullest extent to stimulate the recruiting of library school classes from the most promising college graduates. I would recommend that the Corporation consider the establishing of a few fellowships in one or more of the best library schools. It would seem to me possible to do a great deal for the development of library service in certain southern and western states by offering fellowships in approved library schools to college graduates from those states who would agree after the completion of their course to return and render their best service to the library cause for a stated minimum period.

CHAPTER 16

TRAINING IN SERVICE

Too little attention has been paid among librarians to the possibilities of professional improvement of workers while in service. In this respect perhaps less has been done in the larger than in the smaller public libraries. The assumption has become firmly fixed that there are only two ways for an individual to reach the upper ranks of the profession - through the traditional type of library school and through the tedious process of learning by experience. Even for the graduate of the library school there is a noticeable lack both of incentive and opportunity for continued intellectual and professional growth and improvement. To some extent this could be corrected by the development of specialized, advanced work in library schools. Little can be expected, however, from merely offering the opportunity unless at the same time sufficient incentive is created.

The main reason for lack of incentive is the failure on the part of libraries to adopt a properly graded scheme of service with definite standards of educational and professional attainments for each grade. It has not been made sufficiently clear that mere length of service does not fit one for the higher and more responsible positions. Very few libraries have any kind of a system of efficiency ratings and it is safe to say that not one has developed rating systems comparable to those commonly used for grading teachers. Of course, also, the narrow salary limits and very small increments place too slight a premium on superior ability and success. Whether the worker enters the service without preliminary training or through the library school, after he is once in the system conditions are not such as to make him feel that his advancement requires continued systematic study and growing efficiency. To some extent the lack of standards of personal qualifications on the part of library workers rests back upon the lack of standards for the service which a community should expect of the library as a whole. Only a few progressive libraries have made a beginning in the work of standardization and classification of personnel. The system of certification advocated in this report should be a very great aid in supplying the stimulus to improvement in service which is now generally wanting.

One of the main objects of the state library commissions has been to provide a little much needed training for untrained and too often uneducated persons actually in charge of small public libraries. In fulfilling this function use has been made of traveling representatives often called organizers; library institutes, modeled to some extent on teachers institutes; and summer schools. In regard to the work of organizers as a means of giving training in service, little needs to be said. While under any properly organized state system of libraries inspectors are needed to visit the libraries frequently and make suggestions and criticisms, it would be financially impossible at present to assign organizers to all libraries having an untrained librarian for a long enough period to make the instruction effective. If the untrained librarian had the proper education and cultural background, an adequate staff of organizers might do effective work. Or if advantage could be taken of a well organized system of correspondence instruction, the visits of the state organizer might become more fruitful.

The organizer working singlehanded with the individual librarian can do so little that a system of local institutes and round tables has developed in some states. The general method and purpose of the institute and round table are well stated by Miss Plummer, who says:[1] "The institute was tried first
---
(1) Training for Librarianship, by Marry W. Plummer, revised by Frank K. Walter, Chicago, A. L. A. Publishing Board, 1920.

and consisted of two or three meetings at some town or village containing a library. One of the meetings was usually open to the public and intended to arouse public interest in the welfare and development of the local library. Librarians from neighboring towns and villages were invited, papers were read, discussions encouraged, and a question box was a usual feature. Usually an official of the library commission, of the state library, or of the state association had charge; the local librarian was chairman of a committee on local arrangements, and a number of trained or experienced librarians assisted with the program. The chief value of the institute was a method of propaganda rather than of instruction, since the best effect was usually through the public session and the making of professional acquaintances outside the meetings. The librarians most in need of help often felt timid and constrained in the meetings and got most of their practical assistance from the individual conversations between sessions. These facts pointed the way to the round table. This is a gathering of librarians living in towns and villages not far apart to whom is sent at their request someone capable of giving help in their daily problems and difficulties. At least two sessions are held at one of the libraries concerned, and attention is concentrated on the immediate expressed needs of these libraries. It is much easier to secure such expression under these circumstances than in the institute meetings. The older type of institute has largely given way to the round table, under whatever name it may be conducted. In New York state a definite state program for the institutes is planned and the state divided into definite districts where the general program is given. At the same time a large force of volunteer conductors insures so much latitude in the form of the meeting and the treatment of the subject as to make each meeting practically local in its application. In states with library commissions the regular conduct of round tables is a common, recognized duty of the state organizer."

The need of the institute and round table to remove some of the handicaps from the trained librarian will pass with the coming of county libraries and a trained service to be brought about by certification and higher standards. Professional conferences - local, state, and national - will necessarily continue to have a very large usefulness for the interchange of ideas and information and the fostering of professional interests and ideals. Untrained library workers as a rule do not attend professional meetings. With the elimination of the untrained worker and the consequent improvement in service and salaries, professional organizations will increase in strength and power for service. These organizations can do and have done much good, but their activities have been narrowly limited by the lack of financial resources. All such organizations depend almost entirely on the dues of individual members which must be kept very low to correspond with library salaries. Libraries, being supported almost entirely by public or institutional funds, cannot well contribute financially to the support of the activities of professional library organizations, however important the work they might be able to do. The most that public libraries can do is to grant their employees, without loss of pay, the time required to visit other libraries, attend professional conferences and do a reasonable amount of professional committee work. An organization of low salaried public servants, designed to promote the public service might ask for public support, but, of course, such a proposal would not be practicable. The possible activities of professional library organizations, whether local, state, or national, offer a fruitful opportunity for private philanthropy. A comparatively small amount of money supplementary to contributions which library workers generally make from their own meagre salaries would accomplish large results in strengthening and supplementing the labors of love which librarians are everywhere giving to their organized efforts.

Training in service in most of its phases is of the nature of a makeshift, a substitute for something better which, for the time being, is impossible or impracticable. The agencies and methods employed necessarily change as conditions which give rise to them change. This is true not only of the types of training just referred to but also of the best known and most commonly used agencies, the summer school, the training class, and apprentice instruction. One method of training in service, of which virtually no use has yet been made, is sufficiently promising for the future that it will be discussed fully in a separate chapter - correspondence instruction.

CHAPTER 17

CORRESPONDENCE INSTRUCTION

Nothing better illustrates the general backwardness in the development of library service and technical training for it than the almost complete failure to make use of the correspondence method of instruction. Commercial correspondence schools long since proved the feasibility of such instruction. It was then adopted and improved by great endowed and state supported institutions and has not developed to an extent unrealized by those who have not had occasion to follow educational developments rather closely.

The United States Bureau of Education reports correspondence work conducted by seventy-three non-commercial institutions in thirty-nine states and the District of Columbia, sixty-one of these being state supported and twelve privately endowed. Both the commercial and non-commercial schools offer instruction in a great variety of vocational subjects, though with one minor exception nothing has appeared for library work. In view of the great dearth of trained workers this is all the more surprising and calls for some explanation.

Apparently the principal reasons for this condition are general unprogressiveness, which may be regarded either a cause or a result of low salaries, an attitude of prejudice or suspicion in regard to correspondence study, and a lack of standards in library service and incentives to increased efficiency. The difference between what a library assistant can earn with and without the kind of instruction and training that would be possible by correspondence has been too slight to bring the commercial school into the field. The endowed institution also has not taken it up because of the comparatively small demand. The lack of demand in turn can be traced in part to the general absence of graded systems of service in which promotion is based on competitive tests of skill and efficiency; and in part, perhaps, to an attitude of prejudice toward correspondence study on the part of librarians. Librarians are essentially conservative. Long overworked and underpaid, submerged in routine duties and free from a strong public demand for efficiency, librarians as a whole have not themselves been innovators nor are they in general inclined to experiment with new ideas. Whatever the reason may be, the fact remains that up to the present practically no use has been made of correspondence instruction in training for library work.

It is not necessary here to describe the methods or set forth the possibilities and advantages of correspondence study. This has already been so well done that we need only cite the conclusions of competent investigators to prove the desirability of making some attempt to apply correspondence instruction to the library field. In the conclusion of his report on "Correspondence Study in Universities and Colleges", Dr. Arthur K. Klein says:

> "Inexpensive methods of quickly reproducing written material in considerable quantity have, in combination with cheap and rapid mail service, enabled correspondence teaching to be carried on extensively and effectively. But more important than these external devices are the pioneer study and practice of the method by the proprietary correspondence school and the universities and colleges supported by public funds. Their work has developed the technique of the method and shown the extent and effectiveness of the service that can be rendered. The experimental state in the development of the general method has now been passed and the results obtained are now available to serve as a basis for the application of the method upon a more extensive and serviceable scale."

As to the general method of correspondence study, Dr. Klein says:

> "The essential characteristic of correspondence study is not the fact that it is instruction by mail; that is in many cases merely incidental. The correspondence method has been tried in resident instruction with results which indicate that the ordinary methods of class instruction may in some degree be displaced profitably by further application of the correspondence method. Indeed, the correspondence method has always been used in resident instruction in certain subjects and in many cases no other method is possible. English com-

position, for instance, cannot be taught in any other way than by correspondence-study methods."

"It is not, then the intervention of the postal system which gives to correspondence study its virtue. The method of instruction is the essential thing. It may or may not be applied through the mails. The chief characteristics of the method are constant efforts by the student and correction by the teacher. As ordinarily applied in correspondence study, the method consists of the assignment by the instructor of definitely planned work, the writing out by the student of the results of his work, the correction and criticism by the instructor of the written lessons, and the suggestion and assistance upon points where the student needs such special help. The student is tested on the whole of every lesson. He not only recites the entire lesson, but reduces it to writing, so that any error may be detected and corrected. The criticism by the instructor is also clearly and definitely written. No slipshod or evasive work, no bluffing is possible for student or for instructor. The hard grind which such methods require from students is such an ever-present fact, so much a part of correspondence study and so seldom found in class work, that this method of working is more truly than postal transmission the essential feature of correspondence study."

In view of the extensive use now being made of correspondence instruction in vocational subjects, the heads of library schools and many librarians were asked to state what subjects taught in library schools could not also be taught by correspondence, what difficulties would be encountered, and whether they would be in favor of having such instruction tried out under proper conditions. No one was found willing to assert that there is any subject in the curriculum which cannot be taught by correspondence, provided the student has access to books. Organized collections of books are indeed the indispensable laboratory for much of the instruction in library methods and problems. Some study of value could doubtless be carried on with the aid of comparatively few books and provision might even be made by the teaching institutions for lending these. In few, if any, of the library school courses is class discussion an indispensable element. Though of unquestioned value, the advantages of class room work are likely to be largely or wholly offset by specific advantages of the correspondence method.

Some of the difficulties assumed by librarians to be inherent in correspondence instruction merely reflect a lack of familiarity with what has already been accomplished in perfecting the methods used. Other difficulties are real and would have to be faced and solved. The very serious need for good text books and teaching material in the library schools has been pointed out in another chapter. Successful correspondence instruction would necessitate some attention to the pedagogy of the subjects taught and would require the preparation of text-books and other teaching material. This difficulty, however, instead of being an argument against correspondence instruction is really an argument in its favor. Instruction in library schools and training classes would be greatly benefited by the improved methods and tools which would have to be produced for correspondence study.

The difficulty of providing satisfactory opportunity for field work for correspondence students is referred to, but this criticism seems to arise in part from a failure to appreciate the conditions under which correspondence study would ordinarily be undertaken. Applicants would usually be actually engaged in library work; if found desirable, enrolment could be limited to those so engaged. This would give a skillful instructor ample opportunity to see that the student relates his study to his work. In certain courses opportunities for field work and observation might be limited for the person employed in a small, isolated library. But so are they limited, and very narrowly limited, for students in several of the existing library schools. If there were any courses from which a student could derive no profit from the kind of field work available to him, he could be refused enrolment. For the student who is aiming to cover the whole ground of a full professional training, such courses could be reserved for the brief period of residence study which it would probably be desirable to require for any professional certificate or academic credit.

In libraries everywhere, large and small, workers are to be found who lack technical training and are unable for financial, or other reasons to leave their work and attend a library school. Training classes and summer schools will not meet their need, even assuming that those are within their reach. With the proper encouragement from library boards and administrators, workers of this kind might enroll for correspondence study in large numbers and derive great benefit from it. For some the benefit would take the form of a broadening of their view so as to include other phases of the work than those in which they are actually engaged.

For others the benefit would lie in a study of the principles and technique of their own part of the service. For those with inadequate general preparation, such study might do something to increase efficiency. For workers of ability and broad education, correspondence study might very well be made an acceptable substitute for library school training for many purposes.

It is indeed the possibility of substituting correspondence study for a library school course that constitutes the objection which some school authorities make to it. They fear that standards of training and service will be lowered. Experience in other fields does not seem to lend support to this fear. The popular prejudice against correspondence study would likely be sufficient to prevent the person with that training from displacine one with better, or even inferior, training acquired in a library school. In other words, a person who has gotten his training through a correspondence school would necessarily have to possess a better equipment than a library school graduate to get the same recognition. It is to be expected also that the best of those who attempt to get some instruction by correspondence will sooner or later find a way to take some residence study.

A well managed correspondence course is likely to pick out and bring into the schools persons well adapted for library work who might otherwise not get to the library school at all. In so far as correspondence study aids those already in service to be more efficient, it would also tend to raise rather than lower standards.

The institution conducting correspondence instruction could exercise any desired amount of control by requiring high standards of preliminary education and fitness, particularly from those who wish their study to count toward a professional certificate or school certificate or diploma. It is not apparent that instruction of a high grade given by correspondence is in any greater danger of lowering standards than are summer schools, short courses, institutes, etc. This also disposes of another difficulty foreseen by some in an assumed inability to choose students with sufficient care. It is believed that the correspondence institution could select its students as carefully and efficiently as any other. However, unless very serious dangers actually appear, it would seem wise to put the instruction in many courses at the disposal of all applicants who show that they can do the work successfully. The proposed system of national certification would prevent the wholly unfit from masquerading under false pretenses.

The principals of library schools without exception have expressed a desire to see correspondence instruction in library subjects tried, if it can be done under proper conditions. None of the schools are in a position at present to furnish these proper conditions. In the first place, none of them has the financial resources to undertake new activities. Correspondence instruction, if attempted, should employ the best obtainable teachers, those who are specially qualified for the task and who would enter upon it with enthusiasm. They should also be well paid for their work. Such instruction could not succeed if expected to be self-supporting. No worthy professional education of any kind can be wholly supported from students' fees. Library schools are all endowed or subsidized or supported by public appropriations. Correspondence students should be required to pay substantial fees, but a large part of the cost of instruction should be met from some other source. To insure the highest degree of economy and efficiency, correspondence instruction should be offered, for the present at all events, by only one institution and that one selected or created with a view to furnishing the most favorable conditions possible.

Actual experience in teaching library subjects by correspondence is too limited to be of real significance, yet the little experience that can be cited does on the whole confirm the conclusion reached on other grounds that this method has large possibilities and should be given a fair trial. The University of Chicago has for many years offered through its correspondence study department a course of twenty-four lessons on "Technical Methods of Library Science", designed to furnish an elementary training in practical library work for those who are unable to attend a library school. While the announcements state that students should have as preparation for the course at least two years of college education or its equivalent, students are accepted who have only a high school course. The tuition and matriculation fees amount to $24, or $1 a lesson. The books required cost $10 or $12 more. At present the average enrolment is about fifteen active students. Most of these are engaged in some kind of library work, some of them being teachers who have to care for school libraries. The instructor in charge of the course states that many of the students get a great deal out of it, short as it is, and confined almost exclusively to the mere routine or mechanical phases of library work. It seems quite clear that if this course were considerably expanded and enriched, it would have a wide appeal. So long as the student has to pay the full cost of the instructors' time and the overhead charges, it will not be possible to do thorough work and assist the student to apply his instruction in such a way as to give him the equivalent of practice or field work. Better text-books, better teaching methods and many specialized courses are needed. Instruction of this sort requires endowment or subsidy quite as much as does resident study.

The California State Library is giving correspondence instruction in cataloguing, the number of students reported in January, 1921, being twenty-six. It was estimated that about half of these were doing good work and deriving substantial benefit from the course. The instructor in charge feels keenly the need of proper text-books and teaching material. To meet the requirement of a Wisconsin law every high school in that state must have a teacher-librarian who has had a minimum of library training in addition to the qualifications of a teacher. The supply of teachers with the required amount of library training was found to be so small that the Extension Division of the State University was called upon to provide the necessary instruction by correspondence. Between 250 and 300 students were enrolled in 1920. Those who had previously had a little library experience or knew something about books and libraries are reported to have done well in the course, while those to whom the whole subject was new got very little out of it. It is also reported that a course on reference books and their use is offered through the correspondence study department of the University Extension Division of the University of Missouri.

One of the most interesting possibilities in the use of correspondence study is its application to graduate, specialized study of the character recommended in an earlier chapter. Dr. Klein predicts that "the practice of permitting graduate students to secure credit by correspondence will undergo a great development during the next few years." Several western universities permit candidates for the master's degree to take a part of their work by correspondence, while the University of Chicago permits candidates for the doctor's degree to "substitute correspondence study for residence work upon approval in advance of the head of the department in which the work lies."

This chapter has been confined to a general discussion of the possibility of using correspondence instruction to supplement and extend the work of the library schools. A specific recommendation looking toward the organization of such instruction is made elsewhere in connection with a study of the library school problem in New York City.

CHAPTER 18

STANDARDIZATION AND CERTIFICATION

At every point in our survey of library schools and other training agencies, the need for higher standards, for standards of any kind, indeed, has been the outstanding conclusion. Practicable methods of formulating standards and putting them into practice must therefore be sought.

So far as the library schools are concerned, it would seem that the need might be met by the Association of American Library Schools which was organized in 1913 with a constitution under which the ten charter members agreed to maintain the following standards: (1) a four-year high school course, or its equivalent, for admission; (2) a course of at least thirty-four weeks of technical instruction in preparation for general professional library work; and (3) not less than two full-time instructors with at least two instructors who are graduates of a library school having such standards. In 1918 an outline of the information to be submitted by schools applying for admission was drawn up, but no change has been made in the formal standards. A two-thirds vote of all members of the Association is required for the admission of new schools. The Los Angeles school was admitted in 1918, the University of Washington in 1920, and the St. Louis school in 1921. Of the fifteen schools reported upon in this study only two - the Riverside school and the University of California - are not members of the Association at present.

It is provided in the constitution that any school failing to maintain the Association's standards may be dropped from membership by a two-thirds vote, subject to reinstatement at any time on proof that requirements are being complied with. So far no machinery has been set up for a periodical examination of the schools and no question has been raised as to whether any school has failed to conform to the requirements. It scarcely seems possible that any institution willing to call itself a professional library school could fail to meet the extremely simple standards fixed by the Association, yet it has been suspected that compliance on the part of certain schools has been no more than nominal, at least.

Having once organized without applying proper standards to its charter members, the Association is now helpless, either to enforce the existing inadequate requirements or to make necessary advances. Motives of self-interest and personal relationships effectively block any attempt to enforce its standards, except perhaps in their application to new schools, and unpleasant feelings are easily aroused by demanding of applicants for admission standards not being maintained by charter members.

If there is to be any effective supervision over the standards of library schools, it must come from outside the Association. This is the opinion of the best library school authorities familiar with the situation and anxious to see standards raised. The library schools seem to be repeating on a small scale the history of American medical schools, which were powerless themselves to raise standards however obvious the need. The Council on Medical Education, on the other hand, a small, outside, sympathetically interested body, controlled not by the medical schools but by the medical profession, has brought about a very remarkable improvement in the standards of medical education in a few years. It seems clear that improvement of library school standards must be sought by some body analogous to the Council of Medical Education.

If the Association of American Library Schools is not the proper agency for formulating and applying standards for library schools, what kind of a body should take its place? No satisfactory answer can be given to this question if considered solely from the side of the professional schools. Their standards are low partly because standards of library service are low. It would be futile to expect any great and sudden improvement in professional training without at the same time doing something to create a demand for improved training. True, the converse could be alleged, namely, that it is not worth while to demand higher standards of service because workers with the capacity and training are not to be had. Standards of service and standards of training are indeed inseparable. In this chapter, therefore, an effort is made to discover where we should begin and what steps should be taken to put professional library training and service on a more efficient basis.

The amazingly low standards of professional fitness of library workers have been pointed out from time to time. Librarians have much to say about themselves as educators and intellectual leaders in their communities - an enviable position which they might occupy if they were alive to their opportunity. Intellectual leadership requires broad knowledge and training. Are library workers qualified for leadership? A committee of the Minnesota Library Association recently reported that outside of the Twin Cities and Duluth only nine librarians of public libraries in the state have a college education, though there are 104 public libraries and 237 high schools. The situation in most other states is not much, if any, better. What can be expected in the way of intellectual leadership from librarians who have less education than high school teachers? Discouragement over the situation is in no way relieved by the fact that many of these uneducated workers are known as "trained" librarians. Through library schools, short courses and summer schools they have acquired some smattering of library methods and technique. In many cases they are doubtless able to manage their libraries with efficiency in matters of routine. The clerical work, in other words, may be well done, but that alone does not give a public library a large place as an educational force in the community.

It is unnecessary to enter at length at this point into a discussion of the effect which low standards of professional fitness have on a library's standing and influence in a community. The facts are becoming clear to the leaders in library work. The remedy proposed by the Minnesota Library Association is two-fold: (1) improved opportunities for training; and (2) certification of librarians. And these are the measures to which the forward-looking library forces are rapidly turning for help. In some ten other states certification proposals have recently been under discussion and some slight experiments are being made. The interest of library workers is keen, though it must be admitted that the public is as yet indifferent. Librarians are ready and waiting expectantly for the creation of an effective system of certification.

It must come as something of a shock to the intelligent layman to discover that for professional library work there are no recognized standards of fitness, by which is meant not only that there are no standards required by law for library workers who serve the public at public expense, but even that the organized library profession has formulated no minimum standards of training and equipment for library workers of any class or grade. Here and there a single library has developed a "scheme of service" with some definite standards of education, training and experience for each grade and position. Such standards are both voluntary and local, however and can therefore be ignored or abandoned at any time.

The formulation and wide acceptance of standards of fitness is clearly the next step in improving library service. Complaint is ever heard of low salaries and inadequate appropriations. Without question salaries of library workers are unusually low and libraries inadequately supported, but also there can be no question that this condition will continue as long as library work stands alone among the professions without recognized standards of personal qualifications for efficient service.

Some system of certification is everywhere in force for public school teachers. The reasons for certification of teachers need not be reviewed here. Many, if not all, of them apply with equal force to library workers. Wherever the incompetent are allowed to compete with the competent, the former will win when competition is waged on a salary basis, as it is so conspicuously in public library service. Men and women of education and ability have no desire to train for a pseudo-profession without standards or for work in which a newcomer without education, training or experience is often accorded the same standing and recognition as the person with the best training obtainable and a long period of successful experience.

It may be argued that library workers are not called upon to concern themselves about standards of library service; that it is the public which is affected by poor and inadequate service and that it is to the public, therefore, that we should look for the initiative. This attitude, though not uncommon, shows a complete lack of acquaintance with the way wholesome standards have been established for other professions. As a rule, the need of a minimum standard of qualification for the practice of any profession has been recognized clearly by its leading members long before the general public reaches the point of demanding it. It is to be expected that the capable and conscientious workers themselves will see the result of incompetency and inadequate equipment before it becomes evident to the layman.

In medicine, law, teaching, accounting, engineering, dentistry, pharmacy, and so on, the initiative in fixing and advancing standards has been taken by farseeing and public spirited practitioners.

Standards may be secured and maintained by law in some professions almost from the beginning, while in others it will be necessary for a long period to rely on the voluntary action of the professional group. In medicine, law, dentistry, nursing, and in general in those professions in which the danger to the public of inadequately trained and incompetent practitioners is easily demonstrated, certain minimum standards are usually embodied in state law without difficulty. On the other hand, professions in which the danger to life, health, or property resulting from incompetency, either relative or absolute, does not make a strong, popular appeal, proper standards may have to be secured and maintained for an extended period by the voluntary action of professional organizations. A good illustration of this is found in the case of architecture. Voluntary action has long been the sole reliance for fixing proper standards. A few states are now passing architects' licensing laws, but for a long time to come the only standards in many states will be those maintained by the profession itself.

It is not uncommon or undesirable to have minimum standards of fitness embodied both in law and in the rules of voluntary professional bodies. This method is well illustrated by accountancy. While every state has its accountancy board or corresponding authority for passing on the qualifications of public accountants, membership in the American Institute of Accountants is open only to those who meet certain professional qualifications prescribed by the Association itself. Neither the American Library Association nor any of the other organizations of library workers, unless an exception be made of the Library Institute, are, strictly speaking, professional bodies, nor could they well be such so long as there are no recognized standards of qualifications for a professional librarian. The American Library Association admits to full membership every person, whether engaged in library work or not, who shows enough interest in it to pay the small annual dues. The same is true of the state library associations. Under these conditions it is obvious that library service as a would-be profession is not only without standards but lacks even the machinery for creating standards.

Starting with conditions as they are, various methods of procedure are possible. The American Library Association might (1) create within its own membership a selected group or class who meet prescribed qualifications (to be determined by examination or otherwise) or (2) it might create or foster some agency for formulating and applying standards in a voluntary way to all library workers whether members of the Association or not. The latter seems to be for many reasons the more desirable course.

A third method by which librarians themselves might elect to begin the work of building up professional standards is through legislation. An examination of the experience of other professions and some understanding of the present situation in the library field, make it quite clear that this is not the line of effort that is likely to produce the best results in the long run or any result at all in the near future. In the first place, library work certainly belongs in that group, along with architecture and engineering, in which it is most difficult to bring home to the general public the necessity for making high standards of personal fitness compulsory by law. That may come in time, but in the meantime and while the public is being educated to appreciate that the librarian, no less than the teacher or the doctor, must be competent, standards will need to be formulated and applied voluntarily. No other method of educating the public to demand a high standard of personal service will be so effective as the simple expedient of creating such standards by the voluntary action of the profession itself.

The idea of certification for library workers is necessarily not new. Teacher certification and the licensing of practitioners of many other professions have inevitably suggested it many times. As a practical matter, however, certification of librarians has but very recently been given serious consideration. For several years the American Library Association has had a committee on standardization and certification, its duties being undefined and its activities limited to brief reports on the general feasibility and desirability of certification of librarians and the formulation of minimum standards of library service.

Under the influence of teacher certification, it was but natural that compulsory standards should be widely adopted first for high school librarians. To California, often regarded as the most progressive of all the states in library as in educational matters in general, apparently belongs the honor of taking the first step in compulsory certification. In enacting the county free library law of 1909, the paramount importance of securing a high degree of fitness in the heads of county library systems led to the creation of a board of library examiners "to pass upon the qualifications of all persons desiring to become county librarians." This certification provision for county librarians was followed by a law requiring all high school librarians to have a special certificate similar to that of a high school teacher. A recent Wisconsin law required every high school in the state to employ a teacher-librarian, which means a person who has the general qualifications of a high school teacher, plus library training equivalent to a four-credit college course.

Aside from a few relatively unimportant beginnings, nothing at all has been done in the way of voluntary or compulsory certification. In a loose sense, library school diplomas and certificates have stood for a kind of elementary certificate of fitness, but many of the best known librarians and a large proportion of most library staffs have not had library school credentials. The schools, too, have differed widely in regard to their standards of admission and training. However, the certificate of a library school can bear no evidence as to success after leaving the school. Library school credentials, therefore, cannot take the place of a general system of certification.

Library workers throughout the country are taking a deep interest in certification as a means of improving library service by raising the standards of qualifications and improving the status and salaries of library workers. This interest has been stimulated to an appreciable extent by a plan for national certification first presented to the American Library Association by the writer in June, 1919. This proposal grew out of the initial consideration given to the present study of training for library work. From his general knowledge of the situation and his preliminary investigations, the writer became convinced that the primary need in any plan for improving library service and training facilities is some adequate and appropriate agency for formulating and applying minimum standards, not only for the library schools but for other training agencies and for all persons engaged in library work. To test the attitude of the library profession toward such a suggestion a paper entitled "Some Present Day Aspects of Library Training" was prepared and presented to the American Library Association at its annual conference in June, 1919. The essential features of this proposal are contained in the underscored paragraphs of the paper attached to this report as an appendix.

This proposal was received with unusual interest and manifest approval and was referred to the Executive Board for early consideration.

Along with all other proposals for enlarging the scope of the Association's activities, the project of a national certification board was presently placed in the hands of the Committee on Enlarged Program and after examination and discussion was adopted and given a prominent place in the so-called Enlarged Program. Because of the wide-spread interest in the plan and an evident desire to have it worked out in more detail and better understood by the Association, the Executive Board appointed a committee "to consider the subject of certification, standardization, and training, and report to the annual conference of 1920." The report of this committee is attached to this report as an appendix. The significant feature of this document is the recommendation for the establishment of a National Board of Certification for Librarians, a specific plan for the composition of a board representing all the library interests of the country and a suggestion for its incorporation under state or federal charter. It is further recommended "That this Board shall investigate all existing agencies for teaching library subjects and methods, shall evaluate their work for purposes of certification, shall seek to correlate these agencies into an organized system and to that end shall recommend such new agencies as seem to it desirable and shall establish grades of library service with appropriate certificates. ..."

"That the creation of such a board shall have for one of its purposes the stimulation, through state and local library commissions or associations, of the improvement of library service and the professional status of library workers. ..."

Pending the necessary constitutional provision, a special committee, constituted substantially as outlined for the proposed board, was recommended and later appointed. This committee has confined its activities to a closer study of the composition of the national certification board and a general survey of its duties and functions. Until funds are in hand to carry on its work, it is useless to create the board. No detailed plan for its work can be adopted in advance of its organization and independent study of the problem.

To summarize the present status of the movement for certification of librarians and standardization of library schools, it may be said that while a few sporadic efforts are being made to secure certification laws, voluntary action seems most likely to be widely effective under present conditions. A plan for voluntary national certification has, therefore, been worked out in the last two years and accepted in principle by the American Library Association. To put the plan into operation funds will be needed. After the preliminary work is completed and the system well established, it may become at least partially self-supporting by a system of fees for examinations and certificates. In the meantime, a few progressive states are going ahead with plans for compulsory certification for the heads of public libraries. Between these local efforts, even where they are successful, and the plans for national certification, there is no conflict. As was pointed out in the original proposal, very little effective legislation can be expected for a long time and to guide such legislation as can be secured, it is most desirable that the library profession should formulate minimum standards of service. The few legislative proposals now under consideration present a bewildering variety of requirements and methods, which is to be expected in the absence of any semblance of recognized professional standards. Once such standards are set up it is reasonable to anticipate that state schemes will conform to them so far as practicable.

In one respect the library profession at this moment is in a peculiarly fortunate situation. In many other professions, such as teaching and medicine, state or local legislation developed in a haphazard fashion and it has proved to be exceedingly difficult to bring about a reasonable degree of uniformity. By the creation of a national board of standards at the very beginning of the movement for state certification legislation, the library systems of the various states can be relieved of the annoying and troublesome variations and complexities.

In earlier paragraphs of this chapter some general reasons were advanced for voluntary action by professional organizations. At this point it may be well to advert to some of the more specific reasons for believing that the situation in the library profession demands that emphasis be laid at this time on voluntary, rather than compulsory methods. The voluntary system proposed can be applied at once to the entire staff and not merely the head librarian, as contemplated in all pending legislation. It can also be adopted by individual libraries in states which will as a whole long be backward in library development. Communities too small to work out systems of service for themselves will find it easy to adopt the national standards. In some cases state-wide legislation, applicable to all cities, is impossible because of an extreme form of home rule charters.

Perhaps the principal advantage of the national voluntary system lies in its second feature, the coordination and accrediting of training agencies. Following the modern system of certification for teachers, it may be assumed that it will be found desirable to certify without examination the graduates of approved training schools. In teacher training the state is traditionally a self-sufficient unit and can properly be so because of the large number of teachers required. The number of professional library workers, on the other hand, is so much smaller that few states can expect to rely mainly on their own library schools. They will necessarily recruit workers, particularly for specialized types of service, from schools located in other states. But how futile it would be for each of the forty-eight states to make its own independent examination and accredited list of the twelve or fifteen or more library schools in all parts of the country and how confusing for the schools to be subject to the separate and often inexpert scrutiny of forty-eight states, to find themselves accredited perhaps by some states and not by others. Evidently the only sensible thing is to provide one central accrediting agency.

A more detailed statement in regard to the functions and duties of the National Certification Board, including tentative suggestions for a system of certificates that such a board might adopt, together with some explanation of the way the system would be inaugurated and applied, is to be found in the 1921 report of the temporary A. L. A. certification committee, appended to this report. As an addition to its primary function, or rather as an important phase of that function, the certification board would exercise a degree of supervision over the library schools and other training agencies. To a greater or less extent it would take the place of the Association of Library Schools, which, as has been pointed out, cannot be relied upon to become an effective instrument for enforcing minimum standards on the part of library schools. The power of the Board to withhold the national professional certificate from the graduates of an unaccredited school would make its rulings and decisions effective. The board should not stop, however, with merely formulating standards and inspecting and accrediting training agencies, and then certifying the output of accredited institutions or admitting to certificate by examination. It should also become a central agency for promoting professional training in the many ways that would be open to it. It should very soon occupy a place analogous to that of the Council on Medical Education of the American Medical Association.

CHAPTER 19

THE PROBLEM OF TRAINED SERVICE FOR THE SMALL LIBRARY

The problem of creating a trained service for the small library cannot be separated from the improvement of library service in general. Free access to books for everybody requires a pooling of book resources and personal service in a way which has not yet been attained. The small library can no more be self-sufficient in personal service than in book resources. Even under the present system much can be done to help the service in small libraries by raising of standards generally. But the only permanent and effective method of attacking the problem of service in the small library is by creating a workable library system and this requires the cooperation of all agencies interested in improving the service in all types of libraries.

No sound policy of aiding the small library should be based on the assumption that of two communities the less populous has less right to expect free and complete access to books than the more populous, if that is practically possible. That to a large degree it is possible for ordinary purposes is substantially true. The high degree of transportability of printed matter and the constant improvement of transportation facilities mean that for practical purposes all that stands in the way of equal access to books is the lack of intelligence, education, training, and capacity for usefulness on the part of the librarian. It should not be assumed that those who live in the small community or in the open country are entitled only to a book service which consists of a purely mechanical exchange of books into whose selection and purchase little or no intelligence, understanding, and appreciation have entered. With the perfecting of library systems and a general improvement of standards of service, every man should be able to command the services of a skilled librarian.

Though the problem of an adequately and properly trained service is far from being satisfactorily solved even in the large library, it is in small public libraries that the situation is on the whole most difficult. Yet the need for an intelligent and active library service is no less acute in small towns and rural districts than in the larger cities. Indeed in many respects the small isolated community has the greater need and presents the richer opportunity. Quantitively speaking, there is less need, of course, though it is probable that in the average small town the proportion of the population able and willing to take advantage of a good library service is just as high as in the cities. And in the small community substitutes for what an active library can offer are less common than in the city. Book stores and newstands do not exist, school libraries are undeveloped, lectures and the ordinary means of popular education are not so abundantly supplied.

In the relatively isolated condition of small towns and rural communities the library has its richest opportunity to cooperate with the schools, to provide for all ages the only adequate means of popular education, and to bring to bear on the economic and social problems of rural life the information and stimulus available now in abundance through a variety of printed matter. The poverty of the schools and the inadequacy of the teaching, instead of proving that books are not needed, only point to the very great need for the educated, professional librarian. The schools at best can only teach the individual to read; the library is the one public agency able to create the desire for reading throughout life and to give wise direction as to what to read. It is not sufficient to provide "something to read." The lower the average of education and natural impulse to find in books healthful recreation, mental growth and the broadening effect of stories of travel, biography, science, etc., the greater the opportunity, the greater the need for the skilled and educated librarian.

A community of well educated people may get on very well with an uneducated librarian, provided she possesses enough technique to purchase books selected by someone else and manage the necessary records and routine clerical work. In the ordinary small town and rural community the uneducated librarian, who does not have a wide knowledge of books and human nature, who does not understand the manifold applications of science to our common life, who is not well informed and deeply interested in social and economic problems, who does not have a real understanding of the problems of community life and organization, who, in other words, has not the education or capacity for community leadership or the special training necessary to make leadership felt through a library service, can be of very little value to the community. In any community in which the average person has enough education to get at the thought and information in the printed page, the librarian has an opportunity for service quite the equal of that possessed by the minister, the doctor, the teacher, or the editor.

It must not be assumed that the small town and rural library have less opportunity to be helpful to citizens in their vocational and business interests than the city library. Governments are spending millions of dollars in this country in scientific study of every phase of agriculture and rural economics. The results are published in both popular and scientific form, but fail to reach effectively the very persons for whom they are designed because an efficient distributing agency is lacking. A well educated librarian, with professional training, can aid in the effective use of the wealth of agricultural literature. The clerical type of librarian can do nothing at all.

What can be done for communities too small or too poor to avail themselves of the services of a professionally trained librarian? There is but one satisfactory answer: make the library unit large enough, and efficient service is possible. This may be done through the county system. The same principle is involved in the consolidation of rural schools; districts too small to maintain a good school are combined. In no other way does it seem possible in this country to give to every citizen the fullest access to books, with intelligent and efficient direction in their use.

But progress towards the county system is slow. What can be done awaiting its development to make the service of existing small libraries more efficient without the danger of putting still farther off the time when "books for everybody" will be a reality?

Three distinct situations have to be dealt with: (1) The community that has a library and is large enough and wealthy enough to employ a professional librarian but does not do so, either because it does not know what an efficient library service and what its value is, or because it thinks it has the best that is to be had; (2) the community which appreciates the value of a library but is evidently too small to have an efficient, independent service; and (3) towns and rural districts without books or library service of any kind and without any conscious need for them.

Until county systems develop, each of these problems require special treatment. The first calls for education and above all standardization and certification. The expected aid from certification in this situation is discussed elsewhere. Improvement can only be made gradually. Certification may eliminate poor librarians but it will not immediately produce good ones. Adequate salaries and better training facilities will in due time produce the type of librarian demanded. Such librarians will not stand in the way of county systems but will be a very strong factor in their development.

Certification will not set aside economic law. Where adequate salaries cannot be paid, certification and a supply of professionally trained librarians will avail little. This is the condition which state library commissions have been hopefully attacking. Little libraries in the hands of uneducated and untrained, often unpaid, librarians offer as hopeless a situation as can be found in the whole range of social and educational problems. By such means as state supervision, state organizers, summer schools, and short courses for untrained librarians, the commissions have thought to improve conditions. Even though the state commissions had adequate funds for their task - which none of them have - they would only be pouring water into a sieve. Fifth years of such effort would not suffice to effect appreciable improvement, except so far as it leads to a change of system or the employment of educated librarians, where the latter is possible.

Indeed it is a serious question whether the superficial acquaintance with those parts of library technique which can be given to persons of limited education through summer schools and other means used by the commissions may not often prove to be a very real hindrance to the development of library service. In spite of the best intentions and ample warning, such a librarian is likely to think of herself as fully equipped for her task, not knowing or being capable of knowing what her real opportunity is. The community so served is in still greater danger of mistaking what is at best an efficient routine library service for the service which could be given by an educated and professionally trained librarian. It is rare nowadays that any community thinks of the librarian as a person of education and a knowledge of practical affairs which, combined with a knowledge of books and good judgment, make of him much more than an efficient book clerk.

Shall we then conclude that it were better to make no effort in behalf of the untrained and often uneducated librarian who, along with her community, is the victim of an inherently inefficient system? Let the answer be "no". While we are putting all our efforts into securing a better system, we can safely, if we understand what we are doing, employ all available means for getting the best results from the system under which we are working. So long as we must have uneducated and inadequately trained librarians and library assistants in small libraries, let us supplement their education and give them such technical instruction as they can be brought to seek through summer schools and every other agency. Only the best of the class will seek such help and the danger of giving a false impression of what is being done and thus helping to intrench a system that must disappear, can be largely, if not wholly, avoided by the system of certification.

The program to be recommended, therefore, while we await the development of the county library system, is this: Secure librarians with college education and professional training wherever that is economically possible; in the smaller places be satisfied for the time being with the best that can be had. Where it is possible to secure as librarian a person with high school education, give her the technical training necessary and a certificate of the clerical, sub-professional class. No library, and no community, will then be in danger of imagining that it has a professional service. No community, it is to be hoped, will look upon such a situation as more than temporary. The mere knowledge that its library service is sub-standard will prove a mighty stimulus to improvement. Other communities, for the most part of smaller size, will find themselves unable to reach even the sub-professional standard of service, but if they are doing the best they can do under the system, that is all that can be expected and every means should be used to help them reach at least the lowest standard recognized in the certification system.

CHAPTER 20

THE LIBRARY SCHOOL SITUATION IN NEW YORK CITY

It is taken for granted that the Corporation will desire something in the way of a special report on the Library School of the New York Public Library, with recommendations in regard to its future support. On May 12, 1911, Mr. Carnegie offered to contribute $15,000 a year for five years to enable the New York Public Library to conduct a library school. The first class was graduated in June, 1912. Since the expiration of the five-year pledge, the Carnegie Corporation has continued the donation from year to year, increasing it to $20,000 for the school year 1921-1922.

The purpose of the school, as stated in the first announcement, was two-fold: "to secure and train the best possible material in the way of assistants for the New York Public Library, and to prepare students as librarians and assistants for other libraries." From the beginning, high school education and passing of an entrance examination have been required for admission. The examination has been waived, however, in the case of graduates of approved colleges. The course of study has consisted of either one or two years. The general one-year course devoted to instruction and a brief period of practice has led to the certificate of the school. The second year, open to certificate holders, and consisting largely of paid practice in the New York Public Library, has led to a diploma.

During the ten years the school has been in operation certificates have been granted to 297 students and diplomas to 160. Of the 160 diploma holders 124 had received the certificate for the first year's work in the school, while thirty-six took the second year course on credentials from other schools. Eliminating all duplication, 333 students have received either the certificate or the diploma or both during the first ten years. Of these, twenty-two, or less than 7 per cent, were men. Fifteen of the twenty-two men, or 68 per cent, are now in library work. Of the 311 women graduated, 244, or 78.4 per cent, are still in library work. Of the 333 graduates, 123, or about 37 per cent, have a college degree. The fields of service into which the graduates have gone are numerous; though public library service has claimed most of them, 51 per cent of those now engaged in library work holding positions in public libraries. College and university libraries come next, with 15 per cent; business libraries with 11 per cent; while high school libraries claim 7 per cent.

In every respect this school has made a creditable record as measured by the work of the best of the other library schools. It has been economically and efficiently administered, relatively high standards of instruction have been maintained, and the graduates have done well in comparison with those of other schools. At the same time, conditions have not been entirely favorable. The school is inadequately housed in the central building of the New York Public Library. The rooms used by the school are on the basement floor. The main classroom and student work room, though large and well equipped, depends almost entirely on artificial light, while the main lecture room and the principal's office have no natural light at all. No rooms are available as offices or studies for members of the faculty. In respect to its quarters, this school ranks below most of the library schools in the country. The other outstanding need which this school has, in common with others, is funds for the payment of more adequate salaries.

There seems to be no reason to doubt that the school has accomplished everything that could rightfully have been expected under all conditions and is entirely worthy of continued and enlarged support. The question should be raised, however, as to whether the time has not come to effect a reorganization which will enable it to take full advantage of the unique opportunity presented to a professional library school in New York City.

Unquestionably the place for a school of the highest grade for training professional library workers is in a large city; and New York City offers unique advantages. A library school needs for its laboratory as great a variety of well organized libraries as possible. This is quite as essential as are adequate hospital facilities for a first class medical school. No city in the world has so much to offer a library school in the way of highly developed and well administered libraries of many types as New York City and its immediate vicinity. For this reason alone the leading library school of the country should be located in New York City. Not only are superior laboratory facilities available in New York, but here also are to be found the competent specialists to give instruction in the library school, supplementing the work of the regular full-time instructors. It must also be considered that New York is in some sense the intellectual and cultural capital of the country. Throughout the United States it has become quite a matter of course to look upon a residence of a year or two in the metropolis as a liberalizing education in itself. Even a short residence in New York has peculiar value for the library worker from every section of the country. The contacts which can be made and points of view gained by even a brief residence in New York have peculiar advantages for the librarian from other states and cities.

It does not seem possible for the Library School of the New York Public Library, under present conditions, to rise to the opportunity presented in New York City. One of the unfavorable conditions is the lack of connection with an educational institution - an institution, that is, organized for general or professional instruction. As has already been pointed out, the general tendency is at present, and should increasingly be, to transfer professional schools conducted by service institutions to the university, whose sole business is general or professional training. The Library School of the New York Public Library presents no peculiar conditions which should make it an exception to the application of this principle which has been discussed at length in the general report. If library schools are to reach proper standards of instruction; if they are to attract the best college men and women; if library work is to take its place with other professions and not fall to the level of clerical labor, the technical and professional training must be co-ordinated with other professional training in the university.

It is not a new suggestion that the Library School of the New York Public Library should be affiliated with Columbia University. For several years the University has been offering instruction in library work through summer schools and extension division. There is reason to believe that it would welcome an opportunity to offer to the library profession the kind of training which Teachers' College has long been giving for the development of educational experts of many kinds. The University two or three years ago gave serious consideration to a proposal for the establishment of a graduate school of library administration. Had the funds been forthcoming at that time the project would apparently have been carried out.

It is the opinion of the writer that the plan referred to, while possessing much merit, had several serious defects. In the first place, in ignoring the existing Library School of the New York Public Library, it would have caused much undesirable duplication of effort. Secondly, the scheme proposed was planned on too elaborate and costly a scale. While there is no doubt that the income of the existing Library School is totally inadequate, it would not seem wise to attempt to expand at one jump to a program calling for an annual income of $108,000 and requiring a building to cost $500,000. The proposed program, though requiring over one hundred thousand dollars a year was not as broad in its scope as a library school established in Columbia University should be. It did not, for example, contemplate extension instruction through correspondence or other methods. The plan referred to must also be criticized for proposing a course of study devoting two years largely to a general training, with comparatively little opportunity to specialize even in the second year. It is believed that the plan proposed in this report will better serve present needs, will attract a larger body of students and cost far less to put into operation.

A library school affiliated with Columbia University would not only have the general advantages of the university relation pointed out elsewhere in this report but would also have special advantages in New York City over a school conducted as a part of the New York Public Library. Greater New York is served by three library systems, the New York, Brooklyn, and Queensborough Public Libraries. A school at the University could cooperate with and serve the three systems in a way that a school conducted by any one of the three cannot. The specialized work of the proposed school would be greatly facilitated by the cooperation of a variety of other schools and departments of the University. The schools of Business, Law, Engineering, Medicine, and many others, would offer the library school student an opportunity to pursue studies which are indispensable to the highest success in many special fields of library service. As has already been said, New York is especially rich in what are known as "special libraries." Experts in charge of these libraries would probably be more willing to become identified with a university school as instructor or supervisor of practice than with the existing school in the Public Library.

If the Carnegie Corporation is prepared to assist in any way in promoting training for library work, it is the writer's opinion that it would be better to develop one strong school than to continue indefinitely to grant small subsidies to many. Besides the schools already subsidized or supported by the Corporation, there are several others whose work would be materially improved by a comparatively small amount of financial assistance, but it is believed that library training and the development of library service in general would benefit more from the existence of one school located in New York City with sufficient resources to set standards which other schools would have to approximate or disappear.

The present Library School of the New York Public Library, either as a separate school affiliated with Columbia University in some such way as Teachers' College, or organized within the University as the schools of Business and Journalism, and adequately endowed, should have the effect of stimulating the development of a few other library schools on a proper professional basis, of inducing others to drop back to their proper status as training classes, and of discouraging an unfortunate tendency to start library schools in public and university libraries without either sufficient demand for professional training or the financial and personnel resources to develop the work properly.

In addition to these general benefits of a strong professional library school in New York City, such a school would be the best, if not the only, available agency for inaugurating important changes in library training. In the first place, this new school should develop experimentally the type of specialized training advocated in this report. More lines of specialization can be developed in New York than in any other city because of the unequalled laboratory facilities. This school should also be expected to develop courses of training for the teaching of library subjects, not only in library schools but in training classes and wherever such courses are offered. Whether such teacher training courses should be developed as one of the specialized types of second year work or as summer school work, or in some other form, remains to be determined. The proposed school should develop short intensive courses for summer school students of such a character that credit can be given for them toward the professional degree. Possibly similar courses should also be given in the winter.

Perhaps more important than the development of specialized work, or training to teach library subjects, or the short courses, is the need of such a school to develop correspondence study. The possibilities and advantages of correspondence instruction were fully discussed in an earlier chapter. No existing school is equipped to inaugurate a correspondence department; it should be attempted by only one school and under conditions which will insure a fair test of what can be done. It is of the utmost importance that correspondence instruction for library work should not be expected to become self-supporting. The proposed school in New York City should be expected to develop this work on a large scale, to put into it the best available organizing and teaching ability. Special attention should be given to the necessary publicity for securing a large enrolment from the start. Cooperation with library authorities, state and municipal, should call forth a large unsuspected desire for training. Nothing else is so likely to create a demand for training as the national certification plan proposed; and the type of library school recommended for Columbia University should shape its regular residence instruction, and particularly its short intensive courses and its correspondence courses, with a view to preparing library workers by training in service to qualify for the national certificates.

In making this recommendation I have not lost sight of the fact that the Corporation may be especially interested in promoting training for the personnel of small public libraries which do not pay salaries large enough to command a well educated and professionally trained librarian. As we have already pointed out, this is a problem which can be successfully met only by the county library system or some other type of organization which will supplant the small isolated library without the funds necessary to provide a skilled library service. Some palliative of existing conditions may be supplied by summer schools and correspondence instruction; and to the latter type of instruction the proposed school should give its best attention. It is believed that more will be accomplished in the end toward improving the service of the smaller public libraries by raising the general standards of professional qualifications and training through certification and a higher type of library school than through a multiplication of summer schools and library schools of the usual type. Professional training that will attract the abler college men and women and develop a progressive leadership will do more for the small library than any other kind of effort that can be put forth. Such is the assumption underlying the recommendation for establishing one professional library school of high grade - an assumption which we believe to be fully warranted by experience in other fields of professional and educational service.

The type of library school proposed for New York City should not confine itself merely to acquainting students with existing knowledge and practice. As a part of its advanced or specialized work leading to the master's degree, it should be constantly conducting surveys and original investigations. Subjects suitable for investigation by advanced students in library administration and similar courses might come to hand through a library information service conducted under the auspices of the school. Such a department under the management of skilled and experienced library workers on the staff of the school could do very much to advance library progress and at the same time provide excellent teaching material. The members of the staff of the school should be recognized authorities in their respective departments so that the school would be called upon from all parts of the country to give advice and to conduct surveys and reorganizations. Some practical contact with the larger problems of library management would be especially desirable for those who attempt to give advanced courses in library administration.

The school (perhaps through its information service) should organize and keep uptodate a permanent exhibit of library equipment and methods, to be used primarily for teaching purposes but freely available also to any one interested. Model book collections for different purposes might be included in the permanent exhibit. Traveling exhibits of various kinds might be prepared for sending out to other library schools, training classes, etc. There is acute need for a well equipped information bureau covering the whole range of library work. A few state library commissions are doing something for the smaller libraries in their own states and the American Library Association is doing a useful work, though greatly hampered by lack of funds. In my judgment it would be advisable to develop an adequate information service in connection with the proposed library school in New York City.

CHAPTER 21

THE PROPOSED LIBRARY SCHOOL IN THE PORTLAND (OREGON) PUBLIC LIBRARY

When this study was first proposed, my attention was called to the fact that the Portland (Oregon) Public Library, officially known as the Library Association of Portland, had for some time been hoping to start a library school. Many leading librarians were inclined to the opinion that there should be a library school in Portland. Miss Frances Isom, the efficient and highly esteemed librarian, since deceased, was untiring in her efforts to interest the Carnegie Corporation in her project. In this desire she had the strong support of her board of trustees. Before going to Oregon I had discussed the subject with Miss Isom and later with a member of the board of trustees who came to New York. Consequently, when I visited Portland in January, 1921, I was not altogether unfamiliar with the main factors in the situation.

It was my conclusion, after the personal investigation and conferences with various persons in position to give helpful advice, that it would be unwise for the Corporation to finance or endow a library school in Portland at the present time.

This conclusion was reached in face of certain conditions wholly favorable for the establishment of a school. In the first place, the central building of the Portland public library is a beautiful and commodious structure with ample and satisfactory quarters for a library school of the better type now in operation. In course of time, doubtless, the library itself will require the space which it is now desired to devote to school purposes, but other provision can then be made for the school. Portland also offers the important advantages of a well organized and efficient library system, covering not only the municipality but extending by contract to the whole of Multnomah County; a state-wide system of county libraries; a well-developed interest in library service and a large demand for trained workers - a demand larger, it was claimed, than could be met by existing agencies. It was apparent also that a library school in Portland would have good facilities for practice work both in municipal and county service, though in other types of libraries the city is somewhat deficient.

On the other hand, certain conditions distinctly unfavorable to a library school had to be taken into account. Among those was the lack of a strong type of leadership throughout the Portland library, and especially among the heads of departments upon whom would have to rest the chief responsibility for the success of the school. The trustees had recently elected to succeed Miss Isom, Miss Anne Mulheron, a young woman who had served in the Portland system about a year as the head of the school department. Miss Mulheron is an estimable young woman and may make a successful administrator. Many librarians who know her are confident that she will prove her capacity for so important an administrative position. Nevertheless, I felt that she is essentially an untried person without special equipment for directing the work of a library school. Even if Miss Mulheron had a strong staff of lieutenants in the library to assist her in conducting a school (which she has not as a matter of fact), and even if every other condition were favorable, it would seem to me but ordinary prudence to postpone plans for a library school until Miss Mulheron has demonstrated her ability to keep the administration of the library up to the standards set by Miss Isom. For even though the school itself should not be directly under the librarian, as has been proposed, the success of the school would depend in no small degree on the character of the service in the public library.

The person already selected to be the head of the proposed library school is Miss Ethel R. Sawyer, at present in charge of the training class. I was not at all favorably impressed with Miss Sawyer, even for her present responsibilities. Her office was the most cluttered-up and unbusiness-like place I have ever seen in any library or library school. The condition of her desk and office seemed to me to characterize her general mental and professional equipment. I cannot believe that she is a proper person to be placed in charge of, or even to teach in, a library school, where orderliness and business methods should constantly be inculcated, not only by precept, but by example, on the part of every officer and instructor with whom the student comes in contact.

A further and perhaps still more fundamental objection to Miss Sawyer for the head of a library school is her lack of general educational equipment and professional experience. While she may be competent to conduct a class for the training of clerical workers on the library staff, she could not by any possibility furnish the professional inspiration and breadth of view so essential for the successful professional worker. She had prepared for me a budget and an outline of the curriculum of the proposed school. The curriculum showed no real grasp of the training problem, while the budget disclosed the weakness of the project, allowing $500 for advertising and publicity, for example, and only $300 for books. If the need for a school is as great as represented, there would be no need to spend money to advertise for students. In my judgment, the library school of which Miss Sawyer was made director would inevitably be a failure. In my judgment also, a librarian and a board of trustees who have in mind a type of library school of which she would be a worthy head do not have a proper conception of standards of professional education. Naturally I hesitate to say this in writing, but feel it my duty to do so.

The heads of departments of the Portland public library, upon whom the proposed school would have to depend for a considerable part of the instruction, have not the general and professional training or wide experience which should be sought for in library school instructors. This fact is freely admitted by a competent observer with whom I consulted, a person who is at the same time very anxious to have a library school in Oregon.

A school established in Portland under present conditions and according to present plans would be staffed entirely by women. This is not a fatal objection, to be sure; some existing and worthy schools are in exactly that position, but it is a question whether we should have more of them. Library service is in need of able and well trained men, but young men will hesitate to enter library schools where all the instructors and most of the students are women.

Finally, to establish a library school in the Portland public library would violate what I believe to be a sound principle of encouraging the development of professional library schools in the universities. The State University of Oregon is not located at Portland, but at Eugene, 122 miles away. There is no thought of locating the library school at Eugene, but if the University is to have a school at Portland, the advantages of university control will be considerably diminished. The State University can furnish no financial support for a library school, as it has already pointed out to the Portland public library.

Having received an intimation, I judge, that my report might not be favorable to establishing a school under the public library, the librarian and trustees have sought an affiliation with the State University. The latest plan, according to my information, is to establish the school, by the aid of funds secured from the Carnegie Corporation, in conjunction with the School of Social Service, a department of the State University located in Portland. This relation would have a certain appropriateness and value in emphasizing the social service aspects of public library work, but it does not seem to me a satisfactory university relationship for a first-class professional library school. Miss Sawyer seems to me to have an ill-defined and hazy idea that a Portland library school could make a distinct contribution by emphasizing "social service."

A library school of the usual type located in Portland would find it exceedingly difficult to recruit a class of even a dozen students with the general education necessary for librarianship. Already there are four library schools in the Coast states, three of them approximating proper standards of admission and instruction. These schools can easily accommodate all who are seeking training. The difficulty is not to find a school for the students but to find students for the school. When the available schools are filled to capacity, it would then seem to be much wiser to enlarge and strengthen them than to establish more schools.

The principal obstacle in the way of following this obviously desirable course in most of the western states is the fact that each state aims to be educationally self-sufficient. Through its own state university it expects not only to provide general education for all its citizens, but to train for all the principal professions practiced in the state. State pride creates a strong preference for its own professional schools, even though in a larger and richer adjoining state professional schools of highest grade are open to non-residents at very moderate fees. Oregon people are strongly imbued with the idea that they must have their own library school. Apparently, they would prefer to rely on a weak school in Portland than a strong one in Seattle or Berkeley or in any state east of the Pacific Coast. This element of false state pride is a fact that probably cannot be eliminated, but it would seem to me unwise for the Corporation to foster it by giving Oregon its own school. A score of other states would be able to present claims as strong in many respects as Oregon's. It would seem to me much wiser to select strategically located schools and enable them to serve more than one state, devising ways, if possible, to counteract the pernicious idea that each state must have its own professional library school.

Conditions may change so that at some future time a library school could properly be established in Portland, even with financial assistance from the Carnegie Corporation. I cannot recommend giving aid to any library school project which does not appear certain to establish higher standards and attract a larger number of students than does any existing school. It might be wise, also, in aiding any public institution, municipal or state, to establish a library school to require the institution to pledge a reasonable share of the total budget out of public funds. If this were done, public library boards would not be so eager to maintain professional schools for the general benefit of the country.

CHAPTER 22

LIBRARY SERVICE FOR SMALL TOWNS AND RURAL DISTRICTS

Even though it does not seem advisable to start a library school in Portland at present, my study of the situation throughout the country, and particularly on the Pacific Coast, leads me to think that the Corporation might by spending a little money in Oregon do something much more worth while for the development of library service in small towns and rural communities and for the training of librarians to be of service under such conditions than by encouraging the establishment of another library school on the Pacific Coast at the present time.

I have in mind the aiding of some plan for the promotion of the county library idea. Oregon and California have in recent years made a splendid use of the county library system for reaching every individual, even in sparsely settled districts, and giving him approximately the same access to books and printed matter that he could have in the best city libraries.

Briefly, the situation in most of the country is about as follows: In the larger cities public libraries supported, as a rule, by public appropriations furnish for the serious and determined student some facilities for serious study or reading in fields that interest him for vocational or other reasons. By means of inter-library loans the intelligent and wideawake librarian can supplement his own resources by borrowing from other libraries. Very much remains to be done in this way of increasing public library support and improving the skill of the professional library worker and administrator so that the individual who does not live in or near a large city can realize the full benefits of access to books. In the smaller towns and cities the librarian and staff are in general less skilled in meeting the needs of the public and the library less adequately supported than in the large cities. As we pass to smaller and smaller towns the situation grows rapidly worse so that we find in the average community of less than ten thousand population a library which at best merely purchases a small number of books, often unwisely selected, and in a purely routine way performs the clerical process of permitting individuals to borrow what they happen to find on the shelves.

Salaries paid to librarians in small libraries seldom make it possible to secure a person of sufficient general or professional education to appreciate the opportunity of the library as an educational agency of first importance. The book resources of the small library itself are poor in quality and inadequate in quantity. The librarian does not know how to improve it, how to draw on other agencies when his own fails, or how, in other words, to furnish a library service. At best he gives only a clerical service. It is not strange, therefore, that small public libraries serve their communities mainly by providing reading for recreational purposes. The person who reads solely for recreation is in the habit of being content with anything that happens to be at hand. The inadequacy and inefficiency of a library used mainly for recreational purposes may not become apparent until it is called upon to serve its community by providing sources of information on practical affairs of life. Skilled direction should be provided even for recreational reading, but for any library to serve vocational and practical everyday bread and butter needs, skill and intelligence on the part of the librarian are absolutely indispensable.

It is the lack of broad education and skill and experience in making print serve the practical needs of life that now condemn all libraries to some extent, but the small library almost always, to a position in every community far below that which it could and should occupy.

Those who live outside of the smaller towns have for the most part no access to books at all. Just as I am reading over these paragraphs written several months earlier, I receive a letter from the director of the Extension Division of the University of Oklahoma, dated October 5, 1921, which gives point to what I am saying about the need for help in developing a rural library service. The writer says in part:

> The library destitution in this state is one of the most marked and deplorable aspects of its civic and cultural life. Up to a few months ago the Library Commission was severely impoverished. The last legislature, however, which skimped and cramped almost every other educational and public enterprise and interest, did remarkably well by the Library Commission, so that their program is considerably expanded just now, and they can operate on a much more aggressive scale for at least the biennium through which the present appropriation makes provision.
>
> The secretary of the commission tells me that half the counties have no libraries at all, and that there are about 130 in the entire state. The county in which I chance at this moment to be writing is one of the largest in the state, in square miles, and has a population of nearly 20,000 and is destitute of many of the civic and cultural institutions which progressive civilization is now disposed to consider essential. There is one high school, in the county seat, which is creditable up to the standards set by the old conventional program. The oncoming generation is being cared for much better, however, than is the adult life. ...
>
> There are shadows quite as deep as such lights are high. And one of the deepest of the shadows is the absence of libraries, and the lack of appreciation in the adult population of what a library is for, and is capable of being made in the community life. I have recently visited two communities maintaining neat and meagerly stocked Carnegie libraries, and the individuals in charge were following their routine with marked devotion and even some enthusiasm, but neither had professional training, and their own horizon was limited to the ideas which they had "picked up." The Commission itself scarcely aspires to go beyond the superficial six weeks course, even where librarians of that attainment can be secured.
>
> In the whole community movement we are preaching the doctrine of libraries, and now that the Commission has enlarged resources, the movement ought to show marked progress in the state during the next few years.

The progressive deterioration of rural communities is probably due as much to the lack of opportunity to bring to bear on problems of country life the experience and information available in print as to inadequate education. If the rural school does nothing more than teach children how to read; that is, if it can only give a fair degree of facility in getting ideas and information from the printed page, an adequate and adaptable library service can achieve wonders in putting the man who lives in the open country on a plane with the city dweller.

By means of the county system a library service as good as the best to be found in any city can be provided for every individual in a territory covering thousands of square miles. Moreover, by reason of good roads, telephones, and parcel post, this can be done almost as economically as in populous centers.

In library circles there is much talk of county libraries, but little understanding even among professional library workers of precisely what the county system proposed to accomplish and how it functions. Virtually nothing of value has been written about county libraries; no serious effort has been made to bring the idea to library trustees and the community leaders in states where it could be applied with very great advantage. I would suggest, therefore, that the Corporation could perform a notable service by following a plan something like this: First, cause a careful study to be made of the county library system as it operates in California and Oregon and wherever else anything of importance has been done. A report of semi-popular character which would deserve and secure wide publicity would be of great value. Not only would it popularize the idea but it would be useful in library schools in setting before students the present status of this branch of library service.

Having made such a study and report, the Corporation might well follow it up by fostering demonstration units. The idea is to select typical counties which already have a successful county system and make of them models, experimental plants, for the sole purpose of promoting county library work throughout the country. In object and method the model county library would be somewhat analogous to the agricultural experiment station or the model school. The aim should be to give the counties selected the best possible library service without expending more money than they could be expected eventually to spend for that service from their own resources, to try out various methods and report fully and continuously on every phase of the work.

Such model units would serve a very useful function in providing suitable places for observation and practice for those students in library schools taking special training for service in county systems. Indeed this function alone would justify the expenditure necessary to establish one or more such units within reach of library schools which are called upon to train for county library service. It is my opinion that money and effort put into some plan of this kind would be more fruitful in promoting library service in small towns and rural communities than larger amounts spent in establishing additional library schools.

CHAPTER 23

THE RIVERSIDE LIBRARY SERVICE SCHOOL

Though I had not been informed that the Riverside Library School was seeking endowment from the Carnegie Corporation, I inferred that such was the case. Consequently I made a special effort during my brief visit to California to understand the significance of the Riverside School well enough to make recommendations. In addition to visiting the school and talking with the leading librarians of the state about it, I have since conferred with many other librarians who knew Mr. Daniels or were acquainted with the Riverside School.

As a result I was prepared to recommend some financial assistance when the news of Mr. Daniels' death reached me. That, in my opinion, puts a very different aspect on the question. With Mr. Daniels gone I cannot recommend endowment or other financial support. To do so would be quite inconsistent with the whole tenor of my general report. With Mr. Daniels alive and working in Riverside I considered his inspiration and genius sufficient ground for making an exception to sound policy to the extent, not of endowing the school, but of granting a temporary subsidy. Now I can see no ground at all for deviating from what I consider the proper principles to be followed for all library schools.

In a few paragraphs I will briefly sum up my original findings in regard to the Riverside School. I visited Riverside and, in common with every one else who crosses Mr. Daniels' threshold, I was captivated by his genius and struck with admiration for the large place he had made for himself and his library in the community and in the affection of a host of friends in Riverside. Of the school itself there was little tangible evidence. What I saw going on was not much more than apprentice, or a "learn by doing" method, but yet I left Riverside feeling that a year spent in that environment, no matter what the character of the formal instruction, would be excellent preparation for service in small town and rural libraries.

In other parts of the state I tried to learn what leading librarians thought of the school and how its graduates stood the test in competition with graduates of other schools. In Los Angeles I found my library friends non-commital, unwilling, apparently, to express any opinion because they could not speak favorably. The librarian of Stanford University voluntarily talked of the Riverside School. He explained that university students thinking of entering library work often came to him for advice as to what school they should attend, frequently asking about the Riverside School because it is better known than any other. This question, he said, often places him in an embarrassing position because, while he does not consider it a first-class school and would prefer to have Stanford graduates choose a better school, he dislikes to say anything against Mr. Daniels. I inferred that perhaps Mr. Clark's attitude might be due in part to some personal disapproval of Mr. Daniels.

Personal dislike of Mr. Daniels I found everywhere, from Los Angeles to Seattle. Many were willing to grant his ability and genius, his gift of publicity and his local success in Riverside, but everywhere he was bitterly condemned for his antagonistic attitude toward every progressive measure the state library association sought to promote. In the East, also, I was surprised to find how many people regarded him with dislike or derision.

Mr. H. L. Leupp, the librarian of the State University and Mr. Milton R. Ferguson, the state librarian, and Mr. E. R. Perry, librarian of the Los Angeles Public Library, all seemed to appreciate Mr. Daniels' good qualities and to be without personal bias. Mr. Leupp, and his colleagues, did not consider that the Riverside School has had a strong staff, nor did they think it gets a good class of students or does thorough work. They evidently would not recommend the Riverside School to university students or be willing to accept graduates of the school for their own staff. At the same time Mr. Leupp was willing to grant that Riverside might do good work in training a certain class of students for service in small libraries.

Mr. Ferguson's attitude was similar to Mr. Leupp's. He thinks of the Riverside School, not as a complete library school, but as consisting of two short courses with a long period of apprentice work between and this is indeed the opinion of most, if not all, of the other library schools. Mr. Ferguson pointed out that graduates of Riverside who have gone to the state library have shown a lack of thorough training and after a brief experience confessed that they were mistaken in thinking they had adequate preparation.

As the state librarian, Mr. Ferguson is head of the county library system of California. I therefore sought his opinion of the Riverside School as a training ground for county library service. Mr. Daniels was ambitious to occupy that field more definitely. I found that while Mr. Ferguson appreciates the value to the student of the example set by the Riverside Library as to the place a public library may fill in a city, he does not consider the Riverside School a proper agency for training county Librarians. This involves one of the points over which Mr. Daniels has quarrelled most bitterly with his fellow-librarians, namely, the contract versus the direct county library system. The Riverside County Library is operated under the contract system, that is to say, the county contracts with Mr. Daniels' library for a service to the whole county. Three other counties in the state are organized on this plan, all the rest having a county library separate and independent of the large municipal libraries within their limits. Without professing to be an authority on county library organization, I must say that in theory the contract system seems to me to be preferred. The fact remains, however, that the state official at the head of the county system disapproves it and claims that it is unsatisfactory and is giving way throughout the state. In view of this attitude, naturally one could hardly look forward to making the Riverside School an important training center for the training of county librarians for service in California.

It is necessary also to consider the fact that California already has two other library schools, one in the State University at Berkeley and the other at Los Angeles, conducted by the Los Angeles Public Library. Even the state of California, with its remarkable interest in libraries, does not require three schools. In my judgment, Los Angeles is the best of the three and has the best location. As we have remarked at least once before, a library, like a medical school, must be located where the clinical and laboratory facilities are found. Riverside has nothing at hand except one small public library and a number of smaller county stations or branches. Moreover, I have constantly maintained that library schools conducted by public libraries should be regarded as temporary expedients. There seems to be no more reason for training librarians in the Riverside Public Library than for training teachers for the public schools of the state in the Riverside schools. The city could not afford to do that and the state would not permit it.

In my judgment, every consideration of broad, permanent policy weighed against trying to develop an important school at Riverside. There still remained, however, the personality and contagious enthusiasm of Mr.

Daniels, combined with the fact that he already had a school which, thanks to his natural gift for publicity, was well advertised, and into which he was putting and would continue to put a large share of his energy. While I could not recommend a permanent endowment, I was constrained to recommend an annual subsidy as long as Mr. Daniels was able to bestow upon it his personal attention and inspiration. He had already acquired a building for the school and I felt - I think he also felt - he greatly needed a competent assistant to take charge of the school under his direction. It would, I think, have been not unwise for the Corporation to offer Mr. Daniels $5,000 a year for the next five years, with the understanding that it might be continued from year to year beyond that period if conditions warranted it.

For the reasons I have already given, it seemed to me that permanent endowment would have been unwise. There is the further reason, also, that such endowment would have created a very bad impression on the other library schools and most of the librarians of the country. To have singled out for permanent endowment the weakest, most unfortunately located and least necessary school in a state, a school highly unpopular with librarians and state officials, would have been unfortunate. It would have sharpened the antagonism within the state and done little to promote the best interests of the library movement in California or elsewhere. Mr. Daniels was an insurgent, always spectacular and always flouting every suggestion of professional or educational standards. To most forward-looking librarians an endowment for Mr. Daniels' school would have seemed like approval of his attacks on certification of librarians and his studied disregard of the aims and purposes of the Association of American Library Schools.

A small, temporary subsidy, however, to enable him to employ a principal for the school and given on condition that he qualify for and seek admission to the Association, would have met with little criticism and perhaps with approval.

With Mr. Daniels removed from the Riverside situation I can see no reason whatever for even the temporary subsidy. No one can take his place. The property acquired for the school can be sold or used for library purposes as the local library board may determine. I would not put the training of professional librarians into the hands of any public library board. Their function is to conduct a public library. They may properly train local people for minor positions, but the professional education of librarians should not be a voluntary and self-imposed task of any small town library board. In my judgment the Riverside Library Service School should now be given up and all the library interests of the state centered on the two strategically located schools at Los Angeles and Berkeley.

If the Carnegie Corporation is inclined to give any assistance to library training in California, there is just now a splendid opportunity to put the state school on its feet and bring it into cooperative relations with the Los Angeles School. Two years ago the library school which had been conducted by the state library at Sacramento for several years was given up in favor of a school to be organized in the State University at Berkeley. Both the present and former state librarian believed that the state's library school should be a part of the university. Mr. Ferguson gladly gave up his school when it seemed that the university was in a position to organize and develop a school. For two years it was conducted by the university library without a special appropriation. It was expected that this year (1920) the legislature would appropriate $6,000 for the school, which has excellent quarters in the university library, but the demand for the severest economy in state expenditures caused the item to be eliminated. The University library cannot spare the funds from its own appropriations, consequently the school is in danger of being abandoned.

There is no lack of students or of need for the trained librarians. However, the library interests of the state are not well enough organized to impress their needs upon the legislature. Some form of temporary subsidy to get a university school well established would seem to me well worth consideration. If the Corporation, for example, were to offer the University $10,000 next year, provided the legislature would appropriate $5,000 and each year increase its share while the share of the Corporation diminishes and then ceases, a long step in advance might be taken.

Several special reasons may be pointed out for adopting this means of promoting library training. While it is recognized more and more that library schools should take their place in the universities along with other professional schools, the movement in that direction is slow and needs stimulus - a stimulus which could come from no better quarter than California. The University of Washington has a library school. The Wisconsin school has only a nominal university affiliation; it is really under the state library commission. Schools are being started in the University of Texas and in the University of Buffalo. Western Reserve University has long had a school endowed by Mr. Carnegie in 1904. But none of the university schools are adequately supported. Aid from the Carnegie Corporation that would result in proper support of a university library school by the great state of California would go far toward stimulating and guiding development in other states.

It is also possible that the value of this example could be greatly increased by bringing the Los Angeles Library School under the state school. The University of California already has a southern branch in Los Angeles. The Los Angeles Public Library would probably be glad to turn over its school to the university, if its proper support and administration were assured, perhaps providing suitable quarters for a time in the new public library building now being planned for immediate construction. The training of librarians, like the training of teachers, is a state rather than a city function.

California is known as the pioneer and leader in the county library movement - a movement rapidly growing in favor throughout the country as the best solution of the vexing problem of securing efficient service through the small public library and any service at all for the rural districts. California should even now be turning out trained leaders for service in other states, but of course she is under no obligation to serve the rest of the country. We have in another part of this report refused to recommend the establishment of a library school in Oregon, in spite of the fact that Oregon needs trained county librarians and there is at present no source of supply. She does not require enough county librarians to justify her in starting her own school. If there were a strong school in Berkeley making a special feature of county work, it would serve Oregon better than a weak school of her own.

It would be worth while in connection with the California state school to develop demonstration units of one or more county systems, for the specific purpose of cooperating with the library school. A comparatively small amount of money judiciously invested in a county library demonstration, which could be used as a laboratory for the University of California school, would make a unique and important contribution.

I am not attempting here to outline a plan for organizing and developing library training on the Coast; I merely make these suggestions as affording a possible method by which a comparatively small amount of money used to develop a state system will in the end accomplish far more, than if put into the Riverside School where it cannot call forth additional state or local support and can only serve to divide or weaken the forces needed for any real improvement of training facilities in the state.

CHAPTER 24

THE LIBRARY SCHOOL OF THE CARNEGIE LIBRARY OF ATLANTA

The Library School of the Carnegie Library of Atlanta seems to require separate and special treatment. This school was established in 1905 by a special donation from Mr. Carnegie. In the fifteen years from 1905 to 1920, Mr. Carnegie and the Carnegie Corporation gave to the school a total of $70,500. The question has been raised from time to time, when making the annual appropriation, as to whether money given to this school is producing an adequate return in training for librarianship and particularly whether it is filling the needs of the South for trained library workers. In order to gain first-hand knowledge of the school and reach some conclusion on these points, I visited Atlanta and inspected the school, conferring with the Director and others familiar with library conditions in Georgia and the South.

In the case of the Atlanta School there is no problem at all of too many schools for the area served. Its natural territory comprises eight states - Georgia, North Carolina, South Carolina, Florida, Alabama, Mississippi, Virginia, and possibly Tennessee. Library development throughout the South is in a very backward condition. There should be at least one school of some kind located in the South to train library workers for service in these states.

North Carolina has a state library commissions. Georgia has recently granted a small appropriation to a commission established many years ago. Though it has but two well organized public libraries, Florida is hoping to have a state commission. The other states lack an effective state agency. Library conditions in Georgia are apparently quite as good as those in any other part of the South, yet there are only thirty libraries supported in whole or in part by public funds in the whole state and of these only thirteen have a total income of $1000 or more. Twenty-three public libraries in the state occupy Carnegie buildings. No less than 103 counties are without any kind of a public library, and not more than 20 per cent of the white population has any access to books.

The library situation in Georgia and the South merely reflects general educational conditions. The proportion of literacy is low and the proportion of the population able to read effectively, either for pleasure or profit, is still lower. The South is becoming alive to the situation, however, and educational conditions may be expected to improve rapidly. Both state and privately supported institutions of higher education are springing into existence to develop a trained leadership that in a few decades should make itself felt.

Whatever the hopes for the future may be, one cannot overlook the fact that there is still a very limited demand throughout the South for broadly educated and professionally trained librarians. No better proof of this is needed than the fact that although the Carnegie Library School at Atlanta has been in operation for sixteen years, not a single graduate of the school is employed in any public library in Georgia, outside of the two largest cities - Atlanta and Savannah. The few graduates in charge of Georgia libraries before the war have now been forced out by the lack of funds for library support.

The number of students in the school may also be taken as an indication of general library conditions. The eight or nine southeastern states sent to the school only enough students to graduate a class of eight in 1921, or an average of one for each state. When one considers that some of these graduates will not continue in library work at all, while others will go into college libraries, the effect of the Atlanta library school on the library situation in the South is seen to be almost negligible.

Two fundamental questions are raised by a survey of the actual conditions: Does the South need a library school at all? And, if so, is the Atlanta school meeting the need as fully as possible?

In stating the case in favor of retaining the school, it is pointed out that very few southern girls can be expected to go to northern library schools. This is partly a matter of expense; to some extent also it is based on custom and tradition. Young women in the South, it is believed, will not readily go into library work unless they can get their training in the South. Moreover, it is not possible for the South to draw its library workers from the North. Salaries are now, and long will be, too low to make that possible and the South is convinced that workers from the North could not succeed because they would fail to understand the situation. Certainly it does appear that if the South is to have an adequate supply of trained library workers, the training must be provided in the South.

Assuming, then, that some training agency is needed in the South, is Atlanta and the Atlanta Public Library the place for it; and is the Atlanta Library School filling the present need?

Geographically, Atlanta has the advantage of a central location, easily accessible from all parts of the South. The Carnegie Library of Atlanta, with one or two possible exceptions, is the largest and best organized library south of Washington and east of the Mississippi. Laboratory facilities for library training are at present confined to the Carnegie Library of Atlanta, but with the development of Emory University, Agnes Scott College, and the State University of Georgia, at Athens, with its technology department in Atlanta, it seems probable that reasonably good library facilities of different types will be available in and from Atlanta.

It has been pointed out earlier in this report that there is already a tendency, which should be encouraged, to transfer the conduct of professional training from public libraries to educational institutions. Library development, however, has not reached that point in the South. Conditions at present are approximately in the same stage that Iowa, Wisconsin and other northern and western states were in fifteen or twenty years ago, when the library commissions, then recently established, began to conduct summer schools for the benefit of the small libraries which could not afford to employ a full-time, professionally trained librarian. Through summer schools and other methods of training in service those commissions raised standards of service. The South now needs efficient agencies for training in service. This need the Atlanta school does not supply. It does not attempt to give the untrained librarian in brief periods of residence, or without leaving her post at all, the kind and quantity of instruction she can take advantage of and apply at once in her own work. To get anything from the Atlanta school the library worker must be a graduate of a high school, must pass an examination which to even the best high school graduate is formidable, and must spend a year in Atlanta at an expense of at least $1000. With conditions as they are in the South today, this limits very seriously the usefulness of the school. Instead of functioning primarily as an agency for training in service, it seeks to be a professional library school, using the same methods and nominally maintaining the same standards as the professional schools in northern states which have many more and much larger libraries to serve.

On the basis of what I have been able to learn from various sources and from my brief survey of the work in Atlanta, I venture to express the opinion that the Atlanta school from the beginning has been guided too closely by the methods and standards of older library schools, instead of studying the needs of the South and then organizing to meet those specific needs.

in its effort to keep in good standing in the Association of American Library Schools, the Atlanta school may have missed the greater opportunity to be of service to the large number of small libraries in the South, which cannot derive much benefit from a school offering only a one-year professional course and maintaining a standard of admission which, though not high, is still high enough to keep out most or all of those who have charge of the public libraries in the smaller cities of the South.

In my judgment the Atlanta school is sacrificing its golden opportunity by trying to maintain the standards required by the Association of American Library Schools. It takes courage, independence, and initiative to disregard the opinions of one's professional associates and deliberately adopt a course which is likely to be interpreted as evidence of weakness and to result in loss of prestige. If it be true, however, as seems to me to be the case, that the South cannot at present supply the students for, or use the graduates of, a professional library school of the standards demanded in other parts of the country, then the Atlanta school should assume a different role. If the state universities of Georgia and of other southern states cannot at the present time meet the standards of the Association of American Universities, that does not mean that those universities are not doing good work and contributing much to the up-building of the South. It is better that they should reach a large number of people than to devote all their resources to doing those particular things which would give them formal recognition outside of the South.

The Atlanta Library School at best can only formally comply with the requirements of the Association of American Library Schools. It has not the laboratory facilities, the instructional staff or the student body to compete with the larger and stronger schools. It would not be advisable for a graduate of a southern college, desiring to enter professional library work, to go to the Atlanta school. It would be much better for her to spend a little more money, perhaps, and go to one of the larger and stronger schools in the North.

My recommendation is that the Atlanta school should take whatever measures are necessary to reach a much larger number of people who can derive some benefit from its instruction; that for the time being it should leave full professional training to other schools and devote itself to something more like extension instruction. Two things it could do and do well: (1) conduct a first rate training class for assistants in the Atlanta and other public libraries of the South and (2) short intensive courses for untrained librarians in charge of small public libraries.

The training class suggested would not differ greatly from the present library school. Entrance conditions should be made more flexible, the diploma of approved high schools being substituted for the present entrance examination. The course itself could readily be abbreviated in certain respects by paying less attention to the historical aspects of the different subjects and to advanced technique, and giving more time to supervised practice. More attention could well be devoted to community conditions and social and educational problems in the South. With such a modified course many more young women than at present could be prepared for library service in southern towns and cities.

As a second and very important part of the work of the re-organized school, I would recommend one short course, and possibly two, each year. A six weeks' course modeled on the best of the summer courses in other parts of the country would attract from all parts of the South librarians who cannot meet the entrance requirements or afford the time to complete a regular library school course. By skillful publicity and the cooperation of state authorities and trained librarians in the different states of the South, a class of at least twenty-five might be recruited each year. It would be desirable for the school to work out and be prepared to suggest to small public libraries a variety of plans for providing the money and taking care of their work to enable their librarians to go to Atlanta for the short course. For each of these short courses, at least one or two teachers and successful library workers should be brought from other parts of the country. If the short course were held in the winter, it would be comparatively easy to get workers from the North, whose presence would aid in recruiting large classes and whose instruction would be an inspiration and permanent influence in the South. Students in the long-term apprentice class would get a large part of their formal instruction in these short intensive courses, supplemented throughout the year by the staff of the Atlanta library.

For a long time to come even the larger libraries of the South will be unable to provide adequate training for their own assistants. They should, however, be glad of an opportunity to send the best of their untrained assistants to Atlanta for the short intensive course or the longer training course. This kind of cooperation is seriously limited or made impossible by the organization and methods of a school trying to keep step with professional library schools in parts of the country which are well supplied with summer schools and training courses in addition to the best of the library schools.

The professional library schools in the North and West are not training for service in libraries of the kind which prevail throughout the South. The head librarian and perhaps some heads of departments in such public libraries as those of Atlanta and Savannah should be graduates of professional library schools. Moreover, they should normally be college graduates, so that the Atlanta school, even as conducted at present, is not in a position to meet that need. It would be much better in every way for these strategic positions to be held by southern men and women who have gone North for their professional training.

It would be better for the South if the Carnegie Corporation, instead of keeping the Library School in Atlanta alive on its present basis, were to pay to the eight students the difference between the cost of going to Atlanta and to a northern library school. That difference would be very slight, so that used in this way the amount of money now given to the Atlanta school would enable at least twenty-five young women from the South to complete a course in a northern library school, where they would have far better opportunities for observing the best in library service. This may not be a practicable suggestion, but it emphasizes the need for a careful consideration of continued support of the Library School of the Carnegie Library of Atlanta as at present conducted.

The Atlanta Public Library would suffer by giving up the school, for the reason that without the additional salaries paid to its staff for instruction in the school, it could not secure and retain as good a personnel as it now has. Even with present salaries it cannot get good people from the North to go to Atlanta and stay for any length of time. Probably the best type of professional library worker for Atlanta and the larger cities of the South at the present time is a well educated southern woman who has taken library school training in the North.

The Carnegie Corporation might render a very important service by offering to young women in the southern states competitive scholarships in northern library schools. Holders of scholarships could be selected so as to arouse more interest in library work among the educated women of the South than the existing school at Atlanta can hope to do.

CHAPTER 25

OTHER LIBRARY SCHOOLS

Special attention has been given in preceding chapters to certain library schools which have received, or are seeking, assistance from the Carnegie Corporation. Three other schools in this class will be referred to briefly in this chapter - Western Reserve University, Carnegie Library School of Pittsburgh, and Simmons College. The primary need of every library school is better financial support. It is futile to call for higher standards and an extension of facilities until it is possible to pay salaries that will permit of larger staffs and a higher grade of instruction. Schools supported by state and municipal funds stand in need of larger incomes as much as those which are privately supported, but they are not likely to look to the Carnegie Corporation for permanent relief. In various indirect ways, however, as already pointed out, publicly supported schools will benefit by any assistance given to the better type of private schools.

The Western Reserve University Library School was started in 1904 with an endowment fund of $100,000 given by Mr. Carnegie. As invested at present, that fund yields an income of about $6,000. The balance of the total budget of the school in 1920, amounting to $9,360, was derived from the tuition fee of $100. Two-thirds of the total income is used to pay salaries of the teaching and administrative staff, leaving only $3,100 for all other purposes, such as supplies, printing, equipment, books, periodicals, traveling expenses, etc. In my judgment this school cannot adequately meet the needs of Cleveland and of Ohio for professionally trained librarians on its present income. There is great need for additional instructors and more adequate salaries. Larger quarters and better equipment are also a necessity before the school can increase its enrolment and place its instruction on a strictly professional basis.

The director of the school is paid a salary of $3,000 which compares favorably with salaries paid to the heads of certain other library schools. It should be recognized, however, that the director of this school is on a full-time basis and does not also hold an important administrative position as the head of some important library. When the present director retires, it will be impossible to fill the place with the type of person who should be selected for it. During the past ten years the director's salary has been increased from $2,000 to $3,000, but it should now be possible to pay not less than $5,000. The head instructor, the only full-time instructor besides the director, is paid only $1,920, which is but little more than the average initial salary of the graduates of the school. No other instructor is paid more than $500. Were it not for the excellent and largely unpaid cooperation of the staff of the Cleveland Public Library, this school would find it very difficult to maintain its present standards, which are apparently quite as satisfactory as those of other schools - the Pittsburgh School, for example, which has twice as large a budget and fewer students.

One of the fundamental requirements of the future professional library school is that it shall be organized as an integral part of a university of proper standing and ideals. The Western Reserve University School meets these conditions. The city of Cleveland, moreover, offers an excellent laboratory, particularly for the general first year of study in a professional library school. It is probably the enviable reputation of the Cleveland Public Library which brings many of the students to this school.

This is one of the library schools which should be able to take the lead in putting its work on a graduate basis. It is not much hampered by a strong, local demand for trained clerical workers. The Cleveland Public Library has its own training class for clerical and sub-professional assistants. There is need in Cleveland and that part of the country for a graduate professional school of the highest standards. Provided proper development can be assured thereby, money put into increased endowment for this school would do much to promote and improve library service generally.

In addition to raising its standards of instruction and requiring college graduation for admission, this or some other school in the Middle West should be in a position to offer a good, intensive short course in the summer for the untrained worker and perhaps also a summer school for library workers with good education who would like to take advantage of an opportunity to get a full library school course and receive the degree by taking courses in the summer. The University of Illinois is giving two separate summer schools of this character. There should be one such school in Ohio. If the Western Reserve University Library School does not shortly offer some such form of training in service, the State University or some other institution is likely to do so, with the unhappy result of adding another weak, struggling library school to those already in existence.

The Carnegie Library School of Pittsburgh offers a more difficult problem. From the time it was started in 1901 until 1918 it was not a general professional library school, but a school for training children's librarians. As the first school to occupy that field, and the only one until recently, it came to be well and favorably known. In 1918 a specialized course for school library work was announced, paralleling the specialized course for children's work, and the next year a general course was added. At the present time, therefore, the Pittsburgh school is attempting to combine general and specialized instruction within the one-year course. In the first semester a group of basic subjects common to the three courses is given to all the students. In the second semester they elect to go on with the general course, to take special training for work with children, or to prepare for school library work. Few students have so far elected the high school course or the general course. The school is still essentially a special school for the training of children's librarians and is so regarded throughout the country. Undoubtedly it is possible to develop the general course to a point where this school will rank with the other one-year professional schools. The question of whether it is desirable that this should be done in Pittsburgh is not an easy one to answer.

Since 1916 the library school has nominally been a department of the Institute of Technology, instead of a part of the Carnegie Library of Pittsburgh. This connection with the Institute, however, does not appear to give the library school the university relationship considered in this report to be necessary for the proper development of a professional library school. The director of the Carnegie Library of Pittsburgh still serves as the director of the Library School. The school continues to be housed in the library. It does not appear that the faculty or administrative officers of the Institute have any interest or voice in the management of the Library School.

If an effort is to be made to put this school on a worthy professional basis, several changes should be introduced. In the first place, it should be provided with adequate and suitable quarters outside of the Carnegie Library building, though within easy reach of it. The directorship of the library and the school should be separated and an educator of wide experience in professional library work placed in charge of the school, responsible to the Trustees of the Institute. It might be well also for the Trustees to associate with themselves in the conduct of the school an advisory board composed of the leading library workers and educators of Pennsylvania, and perhaps of other states. The feeling is strong among librarians in the eastern part of Pennsylvania that the Pittsburgh school means nothing to them, that they should have their own school, probably in Philadelphia. There may actually be some question as to whether even one high grade library school is needed in Pennsylvania at the present time. Certainly there is no need for two. The Pittsburgh school should exert itself at once to function as a professional school for the entire state and in doing this a large degree of independence of the Carnegie Library of Pittsburgh will be of assistance.

If, also, the Pittsburgh school is to be developed as a strong, professional school, it should plan to raise its entrance requirements to graduate standing. This ought not to be very difficult. Forty-two per cent of the class of 1921 were college graduates. Thirty per cent of the 397 graduates have a college degree. Plans should be made to base the specialized work now given in the second semester on one full year of general professional study.

To the impartial observer it does not seem to be true, as the catalogue of the school asserts, that "Pittsburgh offers unusual advantages as a location for a library school." The central department of the Carnegie Library has some excellent features, but aside from that, Pittsburgh is markedly deficient as regards a variety of types of well organized and active libraries. There are no special libraries to speak of, either professional or commercial. Neither the University of Pittsburgh nor the Carnegie Institute has a library which is at all adequate for laboratory purposes. A library school in Pittsburgh must, therefore, depend mainly on the Public Library for field work. Even the public library is weak in personnel and backward in developing a popular library service. In all the essential conditions for building up a strong professional school Pittsburgh is not to

be compared with Cleveland, in my judgment. I regret the more that this is
my conclusion, because I am a graduate of Western Reserve University and it
may appear to some one that I am influenced by that relationship. I have endeavored, however, to interpret the evidence impartially and I am confident
that any competent investigator would reach the same conclusion.

The Carnegie Library needs a good training school to select and prepare local people for service on its own staff in clerical and sub-professional positions. Having the library school at hand, the temptation is great to
try the impossible thing of making it function at the same time as a professional school and a training class. It may be feasible to put the training class
under the direction of the library school, but the essentially different
functions and methods of the two should be kept clearly in view.

As this report was nearing completion it was learned that some special
reference to the Simmons College School of Library Science might be in order.
Since Simmons is in several respects unique among the fifteen schools covered
in a general way in this report, it may be worth while to refer to it briefly
here. A brief statement of the facts in regard to the school is given in
Appendix I.

As pointed out elsewhere, a number of degree-conferring institutions
give the baccalaureate for three years of college study and one year of work
in a library school. In Simmons, however, the general college study and the
vocational training are combined in a most intimate fashion. The college *is*
the library school; or perhaps one would better say the library school *is*
the college - when combined with the six or seven other schools which together
actually constitute the college. In other institutions combining library and
college studies, students spend their three years in classes with students
most of whom are giving four years of collegiate study for the degree. The
library studies for which one year's college credit are given are taken in

a separate school, either a part of the same or some independent and cooperating institution. In Simmons the student begins her four-year course in a library school. A little of the vocational instruction she gets in the first and second year, more in the third and still more in the fourth.

This is a very definite plan which may or may not be better than those of other schools. Personally, I question the advisability of so combining the vocational studies and the general college course. In my judgment the professional librarian should have had a well-rounded four-year college course before taking up his vocational study. I doubt whether college study combined with technical subjects and aimed from the first toward the vocational goal has the same cultural, developmental and formative value that should come from an equal period of study in a strong liberal arts college. If it is necessary for the librarian to get along with less than a full college course, I would prefer to have him complete three years of liberal studies entirely outside the vocational atmosphere and then take a fourth year of intensive training in a professional library school, though, as pointed out elsewhere, I believe that the first-class professional library school should require the college degree for entrance.

At a certain stage in the development of library standards it is quite possible that the Simmons method may represent a step in advance. The girl who takes four years in the Simmons College Library School is better equipped than one who goes from the high school to take a one-year library school course. When other library schools are presently placed on a graduate basis, however, it is the Simmons graduate who will have the inferior equipment. Moreover, the Simmons method does not make it feasible to follow other schools in requiring the college degree for admission. It does not offer a four-year course in liberal arts. Unless, therefore, it gives up its four-year program and confines its library school to the one-year program which is followed by graduates of other colleges, Simmons cannot reach the standards of the best library schools at present - standards which should soon be adopted by all professional schools.

The Simmons Library School is undoubtedly doing good work. It has a strong faculty and the great advantage of being located in Boston, which is one of the best locations in the country for a library school. The library of the college itself, however, is relatively undeveloped and there is some question also as to whether the Simmons library school students are able to derive much benefit from the many excellent libraries in Boston.

In any well conceived plan for the organization of professional library training in this country, one strong library school should be located in or near Boston. One such school should be adequate for New England, and that one school should be connected with the university most likely to insist on the highest standards and able to offer to library school students instruction in a wide range of subjects to fit for specialized library service. Moreover, the one strong library school in the New England states should not only be open to men, but should be of such a character that it would attract able men into the library profession. While it is true that from half a dozen of the schools no men have ever graduated, the reason is that their work has not been of such a character that it appeals to men. Simmons, however, is the only school from which men are automatically excluded.

Library schools, it is true, have not developed according to any logical program and it is far from my thought to suggest that Simmons College should not have a library school. It does seem to me, however, that if the Carnegie Corporation undertakes to promote professional library training it should throw its support to institutions which in respect to their location, organization, and general relations naturally have a place in a well planned program. Consideration should also be given to the need of checking the feminization of library work as a profession. Men as well as women should be in training not only for administrative positions, but for the kinds of library work which require special mastery of technique and extensive book knowledge.

APPENDIX I

General Information in Regard to the Fifteen
Library Schools Studied in this Report.
(Arranged by Date of Founding)

NEW YORK STATE LIBRARY SCHOOL, Albany, N.Y.
    James I. Wyer, Jr., Director.

This was the first library school to be established. It was founded by Melvil Dewey in 1887 as the Columbia College School of Library Economy, New York City. In 1889 it was removed to the New York State Library and is now a separate division of the University of the State of New York (State Education Department) closely affiliated with the State Library, the director of the State Library being also director of the Library School. The school is supported as a part of the State Library by state appropriations.

PRATT INSTITUTE SCHOOL OF LIBRARY SCIENCE, Brooklyn, N.Y.
    Edward F. Stevens, Director; Josephine Adams Rathbone, Vice-Director.

Pratt Institute was opened in October, 1887. Three years later a class in library methods was started for the purpose of training library assistants, instruction being given by members of the staff of the Institute library. In 1895 the training class was organized as a regular library school with its own faculty. Since 1911 the librarian of the Pratt Institute Free Library has also acted as director of the school.

UNIVERSITY OF ILLINOIS LIBRARY SCHOOL, Urbana, Ill.
    P. L. Windsor, Director.

This school was established in 1893 as the Armour Institute Library School, a department of the Armour Institute of Technology, Chicago. The original one-year course was extended in 1894 to two years. In 1897 the school was transferred to the University of Illinois with a part of its faculty, its students, and its technical equipment. The director of the University library is also director of the library school. Funds for its support are provided by the University.

CARNEGIE LIBRARY SCHOOL, Pittsburgh, Pa.
John H. Leste, Director; Nina C. Brotherton, Principal.

To provide trained assistants for service in the children's reading rooms, which were than a new phase of library work, a training class for children's librarians was formed in the Carnegie Library of Pittsburgh in October, 1900. In response to a demand for trained workers from other libraries a Training School for Children's Librarians was organized in 1901. In 1916 the Training School became a department of the Carnegie Institute and its name was changed to Carnegie Library School. While most of the students are still enrolled in the special course for children's librarians, the school is now considered a general professional library school, a course for school library work having been added in 1917 and a course in general library work in 1918. From 1903 to 1916 Mr. Andrew Carnegie contributed to the support of the school. Since 1916 it has been supported by funds from the Carnegie Institute, an institution endowed by Mr. Carnegie for educational purposes.

SIMMONS COLLEGE SCHOOL OF LIBRARY SCIENCE, Boston, Mass.
June R. Donnelly, Director.

Simmons College was opened in 1902 as a vocational college for women. It was the desire of its founder to establish an institution that would give instruction in "art, science, and industry best calculated to enable the scholars to acquire an independent livelihood." The library school is one of eight departments of the college, the others being household economics, secretarial studies, general science, social work, industrial teaching, education for store service, and public health nursing. The School of Library Science offers two courses - the four-year course leading to the degree of Bachelor of Science and a one-year course for graduates of other colleges and women who have had at least three years of academic study elsewhere.

LIBRARY SCHOOL OF WESTERN RESERVE UNIVERSITY, Cleveland, Ohio.
    Alice L. Tyler, Director.

This school was established in 1904 by the aid of an endowment of $100,000 given by Mr. Carnegie. Instruction and field work are carried on in close cooperation with the Cleveland Public Library. A special department of library work with children was added in 1920 in continuation of courses given by the Cleveland Public Library since 1909. The College for Women of Western Reserve University gives full credit toward the bachelor's degree for a year's work in the Library School.

LIBRARY SCHOOL, CARNEGIE LIBRARY OF ATLANTA, Atlanta, Ga.
    Tommie Dora Barker, Director.

The Southern Library School was established in 1905 in the Carnegie Library of Atlanta by a gift from Mr. Carnegie sufficient to carry it on for an experimental period of three years. Since 1908 Mr. Carnegie and the Carnegie Corporation have made an annual grant of $4,500 a year. In 1907 the present name was adopted. The director is also librarian of the Carnegie Library of Atlanta. The management of the school is vested in the administration committee of the Carnegie Library of Atlanta.

LIBRARY SCHOOL OF THE UNIVERSITY OF WISCONSIN, Madison, Wis.
    Clarence B. Lester, Director; Mary Emogene Hazeltine, Preceptor (Principal).

This school is an outgrowth of the Wisconsin Summer School of Library Science conducted by the Free Library Commission from 1895 to 1905. In 1906 the course was lengthened to one year and the name changed to Wisconsin Library School. An act of the legislature in 1909 authorized the regents of the University of Wisconsin to cooperate in the maintenance of the school and designated the present name. Although nominally a part of the State University, the school is administered by the Free Library Commission. The director of the school is secretary of the Commission.

SYRACUSE UNIVERSITY LIBRARY SCHOOL, Syracuse, N.Y.
    Elizabeth G. Thorne, Director.

This school originated in a training class established in 1896 to provide assistants for the University Library. In 1908 a library school was established as a part of the College of Liberal Arts and empowered to confer degrees. Two courses are given. The so-called "degree course" consists of two years of technical library work, for which at least two years of college work are required. The certificate course, to which high school graduates are admitted, also consists of two years of technical work and twelve semester hours in the College of Liberal Arts. The director of the school is the librarian of the University.

LIBRARY SCHOOL OF THE NEW YORK PUBLIC LIBRARY, New York City.
    Ernest J. Reece, Principal.

A school for general professional training was opened in the New York Public Library in 1911, supported by a grant from Mr. Carnegie of $15,000 a year for five years and since continued from year to year by the Carnegie Corporation, being increased to $20,000 in 1921. Besides the regular one-year course a program of advanced studies is offered to graduates of schools belonging to the Association of American Library Schools. Beginning in 1920 "open courses" have been offered to experienced library workers.

LIBRARY SCHOOL, UNIVERSITY OF WASHINGTON, Seattle, Wash.
    William E. Henry, Director.

Beginning in 1911 the University of Washington gave formal training in librarianship through a department of instruction in Library Economy. In February, 1917, a library school was created. The director of the school is also librarian of the University library.

RIVERSIDE LIBRARY SERVICE SCHOOL, Riverside, Cal.

The origin of this school is explained by the late director, Mr. Joseph F. Daniels, as follows: "During the summer of 1910 a few students, together with the staff of the Riverside Public Library, began a study of the day's work in order to improve the service and to determine the policy and direction of the institution. During the spring of 1913 the need of a summer school was made plain by the frequent calls for such instruction. The cost of a school served by a faculty of experience and reputation seemed prohibitive, but with the training class as a nucleus, a beginning was made and the short courses have since been held, summer and winter." The expenses of the school are met by students' fees.

THE LIBRARY SCHOOL OF THE LOS ANGELES PUBLIC LIBRARY, Los Angeles, Cal.
    Marion L. Horton, Principal.

This school is an outgrowth of a course of training for library workers conducted by the Los Angeles Public Library from 1891 to 1914. In 1914 the training class system was organized into a one-year professional library school. It is supported by public library funds.

THE ST. LOUIS LIBRARY SCHOOL, St. Louis, Mo.
    Arthur E. Bostwick, Director; Mrs. Harriet P. Sawyer, Principal.

The St. Louis Library School, a department of the St. Louis Public Library was established in 1917, as an enlargement and extension of the training class of the St. Louis Public Library begun in 1910. It is supported from funds of the St. Louis Public Library. The director is librarian of the St. Louis Public Library.

UNIVERSITY OF CALIFORNIA, COURSES IN LIBRARY SCIENCE, Berkeley, Cal.
    Harold L. Leupp, Librarian.

Courses in library science in the State University were extended in 1919 to cover approximately the scope of the one-year professional library schools. Because it was considered that the University was the best place for the state supported library school, the California State Library School, established by the State Library in 1913, has now been given up. The library courses are given by members of the staff of the University Library and other libraries in the vicinity. It is hoped that the legislature will soon make a special appropriation for the support of a complete library school.

APPENDIX II

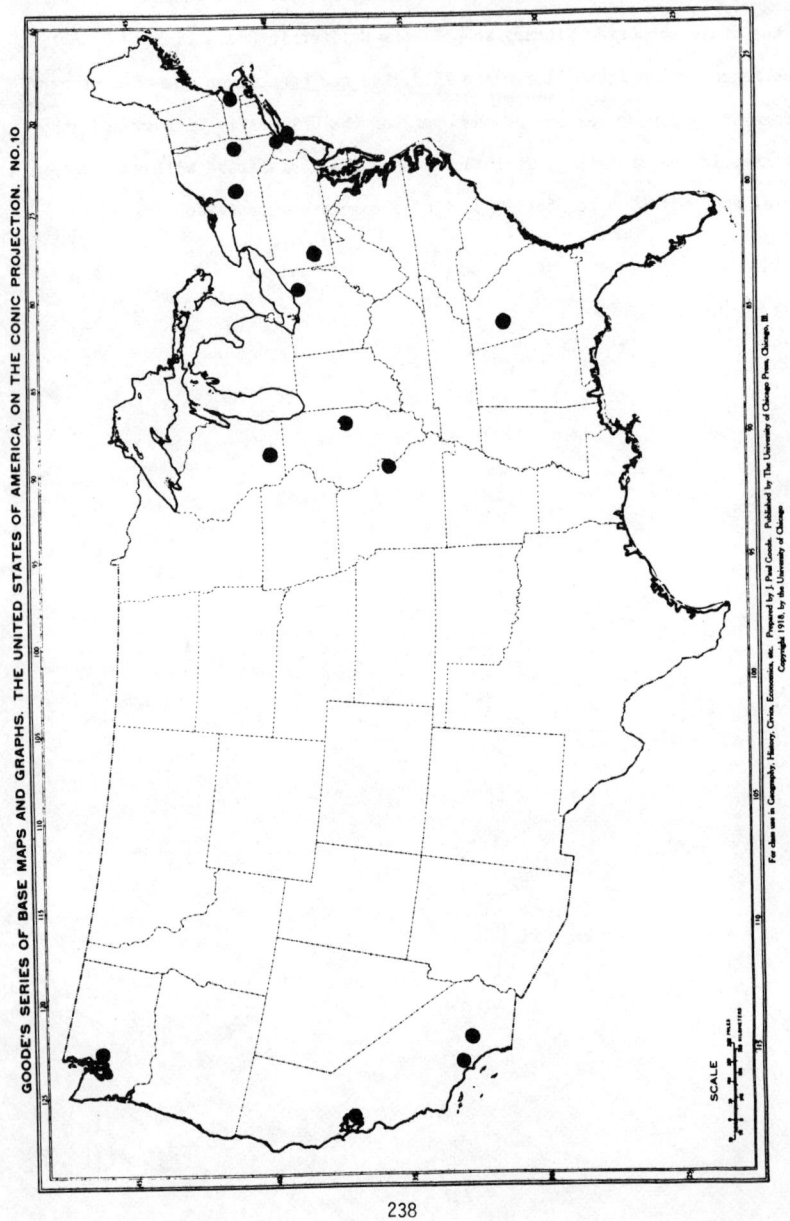

MAP SHOWING LOCATION OF LIBRARY SCHOOLS.

APPENDIX III

A. SPECIMEN ENTRANCE EXAMINATION QUESTIONS,
LIBRARY SCHOOL OF THE NEW YORK PUBLIC LIBRARY

History

Answer question 2 and seven others.

1. To what nations are we indebted for the fundamental principles of our knowledge of any ten of the following:

Algebra	Gem-cutting	Printing
Arithmetical notation	Government	Road making
Architecture	Law	Sculpture
Astronomy	Music	Textile making
Building	Physics	Theology
	Pottery	

2. a. Discuss in about 300 words the causes for the fall of Rome;
    or,
   b. Give in about 300 words an account of the feudal system;
    or,
   c. In about 300 words give the causes and consequences of the French revolution.

3. What was the Holy Roman Empire?

4. Give the names of five persons connected with the Renaissance, explaining briefly the part played by each.

5. Locate five of the following, giving briefly their historical associations:

Anjou	Helvetia	San Juan Hill
Byzantium	Iona	Tours
Carthage	Jamestown	Tyre
Gaul	Runnymede	

6. Who were any five of the following:

Albigenses	Covenanters	Jacobites
Benedictines	Fenians	Know-nothings
Carbonari	Guelphs	Populists

7. Give briefly the historical significance of five of the following:

Alexander the Great	John C. Fremont	John Marshall
Simon Bolivar	Giuseppe Garibaldi	Carl Schurz
Edmund Burke	John Huss	John Wycliffe
John C. Calhoun	Niccolo Machiavelli	

8. a. Give a brief sketch of the history of the German Empire between 1870 and 1914;
       or,
   b. Discuss briefly the unification of Italy.

9. a. Give the causes and results of the Russo-Japanese war;
       or,
   b. What were the causes of the separation of Norway and Sweden?

10. Name three danger points in connection with its foreign relations that the United States has passed without resorting to war.

11. Write a brief account of one of the following:
    Louisiana purchase
    Missouri compromise
    Northwest territory

Current Events

Answer question 1 and five others, of which one must be either 4, 5, 6, or 7.

1. Name your home town, or that in which you have chiefly lived for the past twelve months. Give five matters of current interest which in that time and in that place engaged the thought or energies of any considerable number of its citizens.

2. a. Name ten organizations which work for the social welfare of the American people;
       or,
   b. Name five such organizations and speak of the program or the work of one of them in the past twelve months, or as advertised for the coming months.

3. Name ten men who have had public mention as possible presidential candidates, and give the party of each.

4. Name five persons immediately concerned with Irish, Italian, or Russian affairs, and state briefly their connection.

5. Describe two of the following:

    American legion
    Committee of 48
    Interchurch world movement
    National education association
    Non-partisan league

6. What is the present status of the League of Nations? Name 15 states which are members of the League. Explain briefly the Council, the Assembly, the Secretariat.

7. Where are the principal oil-fields of the world? By whom are they owned? Explain the relation of oil to recent, present, and possible future events.

8. With what do you associate any five of the following:
> Gabriele d'Annunzio Henry Morgenthau
> Lady Astor Glenn E. Plumb
> Paul Deschanel San Remo
> Morris Hillquit William S. Sims
> Alvarado Obregon Arthur Townley

9. Through what periodicals or by what means do you personally keep in touch with current events?

General Information

Answer question 1 and four others.

1. Explain the allusions in any five of the following quotations:

> Talk to him of Jacob's ladder, and he would ask the number of the steps. - Jerrold.
>
> Through the sad heart of Ruth, when, sick for home, She stood in tears amid the alien corn. - Keats.
>
> The Meccas of the mind. - Balleck.
>
> The Niobe of Nations. Byron.
>
> 'Tis Apollo comes leading His choir, the Nine. - Arnold.
>
> Doubting Thomases at the convention. - Newspaper headline.
>
> Was this the face that launched a thousand ships, And burnt the topless towers of Ilium? - Marlowe.
>
> Earth proudly wears the Parthenon, As the best gem upon her zone. - Emerson.

2. Characterize briefly two of the following, giving a somewhat longer account of a third:

> Jenny Lind Fritz Kreisler
> Stephen C. Foster Edward A. McDowell
> Johannes Brahms

3. Characterize briefly five of the following:

> Fra Angelico J.A.M. Whistler
> John S. Copley Ralph A. Blakelock
> El Greco Edwin A. Abbey
> Francis Seymour Haden

4. Characterize in a single phrase (e.g., English poet, American painter) ten of the following:

> Christopher Wren Augustus St. Gaudens

        George Grey Barnard   John Stuart Mill
        Talcott Williams   Herbert Putnam
        Junius Brutus Booth   Sir William Osler
        Orville Wright   Thomas H. Husley
        Augustin Daly   Joseph Chamberlain
        Charles A. Dana

5. Give an account of the development during the 20th century of a subject in science or economics in which you are interested.

6. Locate ten of the following:

        Belfast   Yukon   Santiago
        Durazzo   Hebrides   Johannesburg
        Fiume   Honolulu   Rio de Janeiro
        Congo   Vancouver   Versailles

Literature

Answer five questions.

1. a. Name five well-known translations of Greek or Roman classics;
   or
  b. Tell the story of one of the Greek or Roman classics.

2. Supply the missing name in five of the following:
      --- and Beatrice;   --- and Fanny Brawns;   --- and Laura;
      --- and Highland Mary;   --- and Stella;   Abelard and ---;
      Mary Wollstonecraft and ---.

3. a. Give a brief account of the modern literary development of any country other than the United States and England, illustrating by some specific titles;
   or
  b. Name five living dramatists, three of whom are continental writers, and give a list of the chief works of any one.

4. Discuss in about 300 words the literary work of any one of the following writers:

        Dante   Hugo
        Goethe   Ibsen

5. Characterize briefly (e.g., American novelist and poet) ten of the following:

        Joseph Conrad   W.W. Gibson   John Masefield
        St. John Ervine   Joseph Hergesheimer Graham Wallas
        Robert Frost   A. B. Housman   William Butler Yeats
        John Galsworthy   Vachel Lindsay   Archibald Marshall
                          Amy Lowell

6. a. What were the chief characteristics and who were the leading writers of the Victorian period of English literature;
   or
  b. Discuss any similar group of writers in whom you are especially interested.

7. Give source of five of these quotations:
    a. The world is too much with us; late and soon,
        Getting and spending, we lay waste our powers.

    b. The light shineth in the darkness, and the darkness
        comprehendeth it not.

    c. A sorrow's crown of sorrow is remembering happier things.

    d. Oh to be in England
        Now that April's there.

    e. I saw the spires of Oxford as I was passing by,
        The gray spires of Oxford, against the pearl gray sky.

    f. Or like stout Cortez when with eagle eyes
        He stared at the Pacific, and all his men
        Looked at each other with a wild surmise.
        Silent, upon a peak in Darien.

    g. Or ever the silver cord be loosed, or the golden bowl be broken,
        or the pitcher be broken at the fountain, or the wheel broken
        at the cistern.

8. If you were to choose the first ten books to be printed in the new type for blind readers, what ones would you choose, and why?

B. TYPICAL ENTRANCE EXAMINATION QUESTIONS, VARIOUS SCHOOLS

History

What leagues of states or nations have existed at various times prior to the Great War? Give the object of each.

State briefly the event connected with each of the following dates: 480 B.C., 451 A.D., 476 A.D., 1066 A.D., 1688 A.D.

What Mediterranean races shaped the 20th century conception of the arts, law, religion, mathematics and philosophy?

Show how the monastic orders benefited western Europe in other than religious matters.

Trace the development of the Mediterranean civilization from the earliest known history down to the Roman Empire.

Give an outline history of the 19th century in Europe, showing the principal changes that took place in the government and territorial possessions of England, France, Germany, and Italy.

Discuss the relations that existed between church and state in Europe during the Middle Ages. What great ideas underlay the conception of the Holy Roman Empire?

What were some of the immediate political results of the Protestant reformation?

What peoples of Europe are Celtic in origin? What are Teutonic? Which Slavic? Which Turanian? How does their origin affect their political sympathies and relations?

What progress toward constitutional government has been made among Asiatic countries in recent times? Write about half a page concerning one of those countries.

Give a brief history of the political parties in the United States showing the issues that led to the formation of each, naming their leaders and mentioning as many as you can of the presidents elected by each party.

Discuss the causes and results of the Wars of the Roses.

Give the origin of the "blood and iron" policy of Germany and the outstanding men who laid the foundation of the present German Empire.

Literature

Around what social questions were the following novels written?

    Alton Locke   Nicholas Nickleby
    Uncle Tom's Cabin Daniel Deronda
       Hard Cash

In what books do the following characters appear? Answer 10.

    Tiny Tim   Ben Gunn
    Maggie Tulliver Mrs. Proudie
    Bottom   Gloriana
    Bathsheba Everdeen Nora Helmer
    Beatrix Fairfax Arthur Dimmesdale
    John Ridd   Jeanie Deans

Who wrote the following and when were they written?

    Don Quixote   Quentin Durward
    Tom Jones   Pendennis
    Paradise Lost Old Wives' Tales
    The Divine Comedy Idylls of the King
    Barchester Towers Pride and Prejudice
    Great Expectations Pilgrim's Progress
    Canterbury Tales Stones of Venice

Give author and title and briefly characterize one important work in the literature of each of the following countries:

    Norway   Spain
    Russia   India
    Italy

Name some of the men identified with each of the following literary groups:

> English Lake poets
> Pre-Raphaelites
> Transcendentalists
> Augustan age of English literature
> French romanticists
> Restoration dramatists
> Scandinavian dramatists
> Roman poets

What is an epic? What are the three great epics of classical literature? Give concerning one of these (a) Author and language in which written; (b) Historical foundation; (c) Theme; (d) Some of the qualities that determine its rank in literature.

Plan the chapter heads for a book to be called Literary Landmarks of America. What localities would have to be included and what names are associated with each?

What are some of your literary heresies; i.e., authors whom you enjoy reading but whose works do not rank with standard literature? Write a brief defense of one of them.

Who wrote (answer ten):

> Montcalm and Wolfe
> Emma
> The Wandering Jew
> Literature and Dogma
> The Blessed Damozel
> Jerusalem Delivered
> The Life of the Bee
> Lycidas
> Antigone
> Modern Painters
> Woman and Labor
> On the Heights

Discuss briefly the poetry movement of the present day.

What is meant by ten of the following terms: epic; stilted verse; miracle plays, conventional verse; genuine pathos; monolog; anthology; sagas; poetic license; psychological development; same thesis; plot, sustained interest; character delineation; realism; romanticism.

What is meant by ten of the following: Lake poets, Transcendentalists; Song of Roland, Nibelungenlied; Victorian age; Nature poets; Naturalists; Romance literatures; Celtic revival; Saxon influence; Renaissance; Mediaeval literature; Arthurian legends; Beowulf; Bede.

General Information

With what do you associate the following:

> Bayreuth festival
> Credit mobilier
> Empirical
> Mandatory
> Non-partisan league
> Program music
> Psychoanalysis
> Spartacans
> Tanagra
> Tara's Hall

Characterize briefly ten of the following persons, locating each by country and by century:

> Wolsey
> Cato
> Xerxes
> James Bryce
> Garibaldi
> Alexander Hamilton
> Thomas a Becket
> Noah Webster
> Henry David Thoreau
>
> Sobieski
> Robespierre
> Carmen Sylva
> Auguste Rodin
> Henry Davison
> Henri Petain
> William James
> Phillips Brooks
> Rabindranath Tagore

Explain what is comprised in the following subjects (answer eight):

> Chemical technology
> Numismatics
> Child psychology
> Impressionism
> Sanitary engineering
> Counterpoint
> Physiological chemistry
>
> Meteorology
> Psychotherapy
> Bibliography
> Archaeology
> Economic geology
> Pedagogy
> Aesthetics

Name the painter or sculptor of the following, and tell, when possible, the whereabouts (answer eight):

> The Laocoon
> The Man with the Hoe
> The Descent from the Cross
> The Horse Fair
> Napoleon at St. Helena
>
> The Greek Slave
> Die Heilige Hacht
> Beatrice Cenci
> Mona Lisa
> Venus de Milo

What are the favorable results hoped for from (answer five):

> City planning?
> Community pageants?
> Rural credits?
> Conservation of water power
>
> Presidential primaries?
> Indeterminate sentence?
> Self government in schools?
> Restricted Immigration?

Write about a page on any one of the following subjects: Adamson law; Russian revolution of 1917; The situation as to Home Rule in Ireland; Recent movements in public education; French revolution; The Crusades.

APPENDIX IV

Paper entitled "Some Present-Day Aspects of Library Training," containing original proposal for national certification board.

The original report included at this point the following article reprinted from Library Journal:

"Some Present-Day Aspects of Library Training," Library Journal, v. 45, September 1919: 562-568

APPENDIX V

REPORT OF THE SPECIAL A. L. A. COMMITTEE ON CERTIFICATION, STANDARDIZATION, AND LIBRARY TRAINING, 1920

***

The Committee is convinced that the establishment of a board confined chiefly to giving professional certificates based on examinations, library experience or the possession of library school diplomas or certificates might obstruct rather than promote professional standards. Any board whose purpose is to raise professional standards should have a wider scope. Examinations should be incidental, not fundamental in the board's activities. In its attempts to promote better professional status for librarians through established standards for professional training or experience, such a board should investigate and evaluate all agencies for training in library methods and should correlate their work into a coherent and comprehensive system which should furnish the greatest practicable opportunity to the greatest number of library workers. It should recommend the establishment of new training agencies as needed and should establish grades of library service and provide for suitable credentials based on training and experience.

This will imply active cooperation with other organized agencies. The A. L. A. Committee on Library Training and the Professional Training Section consider various phases of library training. The Committee on Standardization of Libraries and Certification of Librarians appointed by the Council of the A. L. A. has already made valuable suggestions on its specific subject. The Association of American Library Schools has done constructive work in its own field. The League of Library Commissions largely determines the trend of summer library schools. The Special Library Association has devoted considerable time to discussing suitable training for its types of library work. The Secondary Education and Library Departments of the National Education Association are very influential in determining the future of training for school librarians.

All these, and other organizations, are needed to act with any board of library standardization and certification. They cannot well perform the centralized functions properly belonging to such a board. There are other ways in which they can assist. Many potential phases of library training are as yet quite undeveloped, or only partially developed. Among these, correspondence courses conducted by a central responsible agency, with instructional or regional centres in which short courses and practical work in residence, to supplement the correspondence courses, could be given; the temporary exchange (for purposes of practice) of library assistants; fixing standards for training classes and more definite determination of the place of normal-school courses and college courses in bibliography in the general scheme of library training. Suitable correlation of these agencies would make it possible for any ambitious librarian (however small her library or remote her town or village) to obtain a fair amount of systematic training at a minimum of time and expense.

The establishment of a reasonable basis of credit would require the evaluation of both experience and training and would ensure substantial justice to the ambitious librarian unable to attend a lengthy course in a training class or library school. It would make it easier for such library worker to continue her professional studies in a library school or other recognized training agency in case an opportunity to attend the class or school should arise. It might also enable the library schools to improve their courses by eliminating much elementary routine work and instruction which are now necessarily included in the courses.

Certification necessarily implies some standard of experience and training on which credits may be based, hence standardization in its broad sense is implied in the creation of any board such as is here indicated. In view of the existing committee of the A. L. A. on Standardization, which has been making a study of this subject, this special committee makes no definite suggestions on standardization but assumes that the Board will utilize the results of such investigation. This Committee wishes to emphasize the advisory function of such a board and to point to the fact that it need in no way infringe on any rights or initiative of state library boards, commissions or associations. It would, on the other hand, undoubtedly often be of service to them in obtaining needed state legislation.

The same is true of any registration or employment bureau which the A. L. A. or other responsible body may establish. By taking a broad view of the field the board would issue credentials based on quality of training and experience rather than on mere length of service (irrespective of its type or value) or on the mere possession or non-possession of a school certificate. Such credentials would be of the greatest value to any agency for recommending workers for library vacancies and would help remove any misunderstandings and distinctions based merely on attendance or non-attendance at library schools or training classes.

The make-up of such a board presents difficulties. To be representative it must include varied leading types of library work. It must not be so large as to be unwieldy. Since its functions are advisory and legislative, it must detail its executive work to an executive staff. Its success will therefore largely depend on financial support sufficient to obtain the services of a competent executive staff, preferably at A. L. A. headquarters.

The Committee recommends the creation of a board of nine members, five to be elected by the Council of the American Library Association, one of whom shall represent a public library with a training class, one a small public library, and one a college or reference library. The four other members shall be elected by the Council upon nomination by each of the following organizations: the Association of American Library Schools, the League of Library Commissions, the National Education Association, and the Special Libraries Association. In regard to the fifth member to be elected by the Council, the Committee is divided. The majority prefer to leave the library connection of this member unassigned in order to give a wider range of choice. To provide continuity of policy and definite terms of service two of the members elected by the Council should be elected each year at the annual meeting of the A. L. A. for a term of two years. The fifth member elected by the Council and the four members elected on nomination of the library organizations named above should be elected for a term of five years each, one being elected each year at the annual meeting of the A. L. A. This will, after four years, result in the election of three new members annually. It will ensure continuity of policy, while permitting enough change of membership to prevent undue conservatism. At the organization of the board the members shall draw lots to determine their terms of office (one year, two years, etc.) required to put the two-year and five-year terms as outlined, into effect.

The Committee believes that constitutional provision should be made for such a board. In view of the delay necessarily involved in such action and the immediate need of some such body, it further recommends that the Executive Board appoint a committee such as is outlined above for the immediate consideration of such subjects as may properly be brought before it and to serve until a permanent board is authorized. To give additional standing and authority to such a board it is advisable to consider also its incorporation under state or federal charter.

To summarize, the board could serve the purpose which similar boards in other professions, such as the American Medical Association, the national and state bar associations, etc., are serving. It could help give the public some fairly concrete idea of the character and value of library work by approving practical standards of library work based on real library conditions. It could improve the status of library workers by recognizing through credentials the services of those whose work or training enabled them to meet successfully the standards required for good library work. Through improvement in the quality of library training agencies and through multiplying opportunities for using these agencies it could virtually eliminate the need of any library worker's being deprived of at least some measure of professional training. It could act, not as an autocracy aiming at arbitrary uniformity or equally arbitrary distinction, but it could stand back of any honest attempt to improve the quality of library service as far as such improvement would be possible under local conditions.

The following specific recommendations are presented:

1. That a National Board of Certification for Librarians be established by the American Library Association and that permanent provision for such a board be incorporated in the constitution of the Association.

2. That this Board shall investigate all existing agencies for teaching library subjects and methods, shall evaluate their work for purposes of certification, shall seek to correlate these agencies into an organized system and to that end shall recommend such new agencies as seem to it desirable and shall establish grades of library service with appropriate certificates. It shall actively cooperate with any official bureau of information or registration established by any of the professional organizations electing or nominating members of the board.

3. That the creation of such a board shall have for one of its purposes the stimulation, through state and local library commissions or associations, of the improvement of library service and the professional status of library workers. The board shall render these organizations all possible assistance in any such action as is contemplated by them.

4. That, pending constitutional provision for such a board, the Executive Board of the American Library Association be instructed to appoint

a special committee of nine members to be constituted substantially as outlined in the foregoing report.

5. That adequate financial support for this board be provided from funds procured through the Enlarged Program campaign or otherwise.

                        Frank K. Walter, Chairman.

                        Alice S. Tyler.

                        Adeline B. Zachert.

                        A. S. Root.

                        C. C. Williamson.

APPENDIX VI

REPORT OF A. L. A. COMMITTEE ON NATIONAL CERTIFICATION, 1921

<u>Contents</u>: National Certification, 1919-1921 - Fundamental Principles Involved - A Warning - Voluntary versus Compulsory Methods - Responsibility Rests on Certification Board - Advisory Committees Suggested - Plan of Certification Tentatively Suggested - Outline of Tentative Scheme - General Explanation of Plan - Special Certificates - Certificates for Unlimited Term Recommended - Sub-professional Certificates - Application to Librarians now in Service - Certification Will Aid in Recruiting - Board not Concerned with Salaries - Relation to A. L. A. Employment Service - Composition of Certification Board - Comparison with British System - Recommendations.

National Certification, 1919-1921

A plan for a national certification system presented to the Association in very general outline at the Asbury Park Conference in 1919 was informally approved at that time and referred to the Council. Subsequently it was considered by the committee in charge and embodied in the Enlarged Program. Although it later became necessary to abandon the major part of that Program, the certification proposal has survived as the one feature aiming at the advancement of the library profession which must not be abandoned but carried forward at all hazards. In spite of the general approval it has won and some impatience to see it put into effect, your committee considers it advisable in a matter of such far-reaching importance to proceed deliberately. Last year the plan was carefully considered by a special committee appointed by the Executive Board. The report of this committee recommending the establishment of a National Board of Certification for Librarians was adopted at the Colorado Springs conference and forms the basis of the study which has been given to the subject by the present committee.

Fundamental Principles Involved

The proposed national certification plan is based fundamentally on the principle that it is not only the right but the duty of the American Library Association to formulate standards of fitness for professional library work; and this principle carries with it as an inevitable corollary the right and duty of the Association to cause to be created, and even to contribute to the financial support of, some properly constituted body for accrediting training institutions which maintain the standards of instruction deemed necessary for efficient and progressive library service.

The principle of accrediting educational institutions, through voluntary organizations, both academic and professional, is well established. Tremendous advances in medical education, for example, have resulted from the application of this principle. By its action a year ago, the American Library Association put itself definitely on record in favor of national certification and the use of the accrediting device to secure professional progress and progressive efficiency in library service. It is a notable step the Association has already taken, but we still have before us the more difficult practical task of financing and organizing the Certification Board. Until that body is actually at work little can be done to remedy the conditions which have so long made library work the most underesteemed and underpaid of all public services.

A Warning

A word of warning may be in order here. Efforts will no doubt be made to discredit the idea of a national certification system and accredited training agencies, backed by the American Library Association. Honest differences of opinion will naturally arise in working out the details, but no discussion of matters of detail can be allowed to obscure the object we have at heart or place permanent obstruction in the path of progress. We must be on our guard to distinguish between attacks born of selfish and unworthy motives and the sincere questionings of those whose judgment may differ from our own.

Voluntary versus Compulsory Methods

The situation in the library profession demands that emphasis be laid at this time on voluntary rather than compulsory methods. The need for compulsory standards of fitness cannot be as readily demonstrated to the layman as in such professions as medicine or law where danger to life and health or loss of property are the direct and manifest result of incompetence. Other professions under similar circumstances have found it expedient to use voluntary methods. It is to be hoped that legislation will eventually embody any workable system of standards evolved, but legislation which precedes the creation of such standards is likely to result in more evil than good.

The voluntary system proposed can be applied at once to the entire staff and not merely to the head librarians as contemplated in pending legislation. It can also be adopted by individual libraries in states which, as a whole, will long be backward in library development. Communities too small to work out systems of service for themselves will find it easy to adopt the national standards. In some cases state-wide legislation applicable to all cities is impossible because of an extreme form of home rule charters.

Perhaps the principal advantage of the national voluntary system lies in its second feature - coordination and accrediting of training agencies. Following the modern system of certification for teachers, it may be assumed that it will be found desirable to certify without examination the graduates of approved training schools. In teacher training the state is traditionally a self-sufficient unit, and can properly be so because of the large number of teachers required. The number of professional library workers, on the other hand, is so much smaller that many states cannot be expected to support adequately their own professional library school. They will necessarily recruit workers, particularly for specialized types of work, from schools located in other states, but how futile it would be for each of the forty-eight states to make its own examination and accredited list of the twelve or fifteen, or more, library schools in all parts of the country and how confusing to the schools to be subject to the separate and inexpert scrutiny of forty-eight states, to find themselves accredited perhaps by some states and not by others. The only sensible thing is evidently to provide one central accrediting agency.

The feeling is widespread that for some time to come many people must be kept in library work who have not gone through a long period of training and apprenticeship. If this view is well founded, it points to the wisdom of starting with a voluntary rather than a compulsory system. When the state of

Wisconsin recently passed a law requiring high schools to employ librarians with a certain minimum of technical training, it was found that comparatively few persons could qualify. Something of the same sort would undoubtedly occur today in nearly every state if standards that mean anything were to be made applicable at once to any except the head librarians in the larger cities. After the voluntary system has been in operation a few years, its standards can gradually be made compulsory as local conditions permit. The time may come when national standards will be enforced everywhere by local and state authorities under the sanction of law. This may mean either enlarged or diminished functions for the National Certification Board; just which, is a matter that need not concern us now. It is possible, however, when the time comes that every state shall have its own library certification board as every state now has its accountancy board, that the National Board for the Certification of Librarians may be called upon, as the American Institute of Accountants is now, to prepare questions for the state examiners and to grade the examination papers, under a cooperative arrangement with the state boards, thus securing uniformity among the states and expert service for the state authorities.

It may be argued that it is not the duty of library workers to concern themselves especially with standards of library service; that it is the public which is affected by poor and inadequate service and that it is to the public, therefore, that we should look for the initiative. This attitude, though not uncommon, shows a complete lack of acquaintance with the experience of other professions in establishing standards. As a rule, the need of a minimum standard of qualifications for the practice of any profession has been recognized clearly by the leading members of that profession long before the general public has reached the point of demanding it. It is to be expected that capable and conscientious workers will themselves see the result of an incompetent and inadequately equipped personnel before it becomes evident to the laymen. In medicine, law, teaching, accounting, engineering, dentistry, pharmacy, and so on, the initiative in fixing and advancing salaries has been taken by the far-seeing and public spirited members. Standards may be secured and maintained by law in some professions almost from the beginning, while in others it is necessary for a long period to rely on the voluntary action of the professional group. In medicine, law, dentistry, and in general in those professions in which the danger to the public from inadequately trained and incompetent practitioners is easily demonstrated, certain minimum standards are usually embodied in state law without difficulty. On the other hand, professions in which the danger to life, health, or property resulting from incompetence, either relative or absolute, does not make a popular appeal, proper standards may have to be secured and maintained for a long period by the voluntary action of professional organizations. A good illustration of this is found in the case of architecture. Voluntary action has been almost the sole reliance up to the present time. A few states are now passing architects' licensing laws but for a long time to come the only standards in many states will be those maintained by the profession itself.

Responsibility Rests on the Certification Board

The proposed National Board will be responsible for working out the details of the certification and accrediting system. It must be made up of the ablest and most experienced members of the profession, whose minds will be open to all helpful suggestions and who will go about their important work with the single purpose of doing the constructive and helpful thing. The Board will not pass back to the Association the responsibility for making decisions in matters of detail. We must expect to delegate to it the task of devising and administering a certification system. We shall judge it by its fruit. We must give it time and then if it fails to accomplish satisfactory results, our remedy is, first, constructive criticism and, finally, change of personnel brought about by the methods provided in advance.

Advisory Committees Suggested

Qualifications for professional library work are essentially the same in every part of the country. Some communities in each state maintain a higher standard than others, but no geographical divisions, whether bounded by state lines or measured in larger units, are marked off as distinctly different from the rest of the country. This is particularly fortunate in many ways and in particular because it simplifies the task of the National Certification Board. While it is entirely practicable, therefore, to set up standards for the entire country, it may well be found advisable for the Certification Board to organize advisory committees in various sections of the country to assist in the application of those standards. In the opinion of the present committee, one of the earliest tasks of the Certification Board should be the formulation of a plan for advisory committees so constituted as to be representative of the best professional ideals and practice of the states. Upon such advisory committees the Board should rely for much of the information on which to base its judgments in all cases requiring first-hand knowledge of conditions. In backward parts of the country satisfactory advisory committees might represent a group of two or more states in the beginning. The utility of a system of properly constituted local advisory committees is apparent. They would keep the National Board closely in touch with local conditions in all parts of the country, would serve to bring the work of the Board to the attention of state and local associations, and would be of the greatest assistance in securing the adoption of national standards by state and local authorities.

Plan of Certification Tentatively Suggested

Little further progress can be made until funds are available to carry on the activities of the Board. The necessary detailed work involved in the preliminary investigations and determinations is far too onerous and momentous to be put upon any body of busy and over-worked librarians. The conduct of its business after policies and procedures have been established will require close and constant attention. It is impossible to launch the scheme without funds. The principal items of expense will be the salaries of an executive and the necessary clerical staff, money to pay the necessary traveling expenses of members of the unpaid board, and general office expenses. Until an annual income of at least $10,000 is in sight, it would, in the opinion of your committee, be unwise to proceed with the organization of the National Board of Certification for Librarians.

In the meantime, it may be profitable to examine the project from as many angles as possible. This committee would not presume to prepare a detailed plan for the use of the future Certification Board. There can be no objection, however, to suggesting the outlines of a tentative plan merely for the purpose of giving a clearer understanding of the implications and possibilities of the principles already adopted. Though the Board, when organized, may not see fit to be guided by suggestions offered here, they may contribute to the clarity of our thinking, and even help in finding financial support.

It is in this spirit that your committee wishes to submit for discussion a tentative scheme of certification illustrative of what the Board may eventually adopt. The plan here proposed embraces four classes of certificates, the three upper classes being of professional and the fourth of sub-professional or clerical grade. In the following discussion the professional classes will be considered first.

<u>Outline of Tentative Scheme</u>

CLASS I.

    E d u c a t i o n: Same as for Classes II and III.

    Experience: Notably successful experience of at least ten years in library administration or in professional library work requiring special technical skill and involving considerable responsibility.

    T y p e s o f p o s i t i o n s t o b e f i l l e d b y h o l d e r s o f C l a s s I c e r t i f i c a t e s: Chief librarian, and occasionally assistant librarians, of large libraries - municipal, state, university, college, endowed libraries, etc.; head of department in large libraries, where position requires special technical qualifications, or broad knowledge of library work, with supervisory or administrative responsibilities; directors of library schools and the notably successful professors and instructors in library schools.

CLASS II.
Grade A.

Education: (1) Graduation from approved college, with reading knowledge of at least one modern language other than English; and (2) not less than one year's successful study in an approved library school with recommendation of school faculty.

Experience: Not less than five years' successful experience after taking library school course, except that one year of approved specialized or advanced study may be substituted for two years of the experience required for Class II certificate.

Grade B.

Education: (1) Not less than one year of successful study in approved college, or the equivalent, including reading knowledge of at least one modern language other than English; (2) one year's study in approved library school with recommendation of school's faculty; or passing of examination in library economy and such other tests as may be prescribed by Certification Board.

Experience: Ten years' successful experience, less one year for each full year of study (beyond the first year) in an approved college and for one year of study in an approved library school.

Types of Positions: Head of public libraries in smaller cities, smaller state libraries, less important college and university libraries; assistant librarians in such libraries; heads of departments in libraries of all sizes; branch librarians; reference librarians; librarians of important school libraries; heads of important special libraries; teachers in library schools.

CLASS III.
Grade A.

Education: (1) Graduation from approved college, with reading knowledge of at least one modern language other than English; and (2) not less than one year's successful study in approved library school with recommendation of school.

Experience: None required

Grade B.

Education: (1) Not less than one year of successful study in approved college, or equivalent, including reading knowledge of at least one modern language; and (2) one year's successful study in approved library school and recommendation of school faculty; or, passing of examination in library economy and such other tests as may be prescribed by Certification Board.

Experience: None required.

Types of Positions: Professional assistants in all departments; heads of small libraries; heads of minor departments; branch librarians of smaller branches.

CLASS IV.
Grade A.

Education: Four year course in approved high school; instruction in approved training class or other approved training agency, as may be required by the Certification Board.

Experience: None.

Grade B.

Education: Four year high school course, or equivalent to be determined by the Certification Board; and passing of examination in library technique and such other tests as may be prescribed by the Certification Board.

Experience: At least one year of approved library work.

General Explanation of Plan

The distinction between the three classes of professional certificates is based primarily on successful experience, professional achievement and demonstrated fitness for some branch of professional library work. A full college course or its equivalent is the presumed minimum of general education desirable for these three classes, after a reasonable period has elapsed in which to adjust library schools and library service to the higher standards now clearly demanded in our library work of professional grade. For the present the system proposed offers opportunity for entrance to professional classes to those who have less than a full college course, as well as for exceptional persons who have had no formal education at all but who are able to demonstrate capacity for achieving success in professional library work. At every point, however, an effort is made to offer some slight premium in favor of college and university education. One of the underlying purposes of the scheme here suggested is to employ the certification system for the purpose of raising the standard of general education in library work without doing injustice to those now in service or in training.

Within Class II and Class III two subdivisions or grades are provided. In Class III these two grades, A and B, are designed to differentiate between those who enter with full approved preparation, and those whose general and technical preparation is sub-standard though still acceptable if followed by successful professional service. In Class II also the two grades are designed to recognize the difference between standard preparation and something less, and by so doing to stimulate, even though slightly, an effort to secure a standard type of training.

Advancement from Class III to Class II and from Class II to Class I should probably not be automatic. Mere length of service should not qualify for the higher certificate. The Board should require some definite test of success. In some way it would have to make sure that length of service alone would not result in advancement from class to class. College graduates with approved general library school training would enter Class III automatically on the recommendation of the library school. Library school graduates offering less than a full college course would also enter Class III but would not be eligible to advancement to Class II in as short a time as those who enter with a college degree. Into Class III, Grade B, persons with no college study and no library school training could enter if they satisfy the Board that they possess the equivalent of one year's college study and prove by passing examinations set by the Board that they have the practical equivalent of a one year's course in an approved professional library school.

The way is thus intentionally left open for any capable and ambitious person to enter the national certification system and advance to the highest class side by side with the college graduate who has also a library school training. It would normally take the untrained person a little longer to reach the top and the standards of the Board should insure that the person who enters by the examination method is quite the equal in professional outlook and equipment to those who enter in the normal way through college and library school. With some such system in effect every available method of training in service would be in demand. The Board would probably be called upon to prepare syllabi in the subjects in which examinations would be held. Lack of opportunity to attend a library school would not completely bar from professional certificate any person adapted to library work, possessed of fair ability and determined to succeed.

It will be the task of the National Certification Board to formulate rules and regulations defining the terms used and making the tests as simple and objective as possible without destroying the value of the graded system of certificates or doing substantial injustice to any class of library workers. No system can be made entirely automatic. Something will always have to be left to the judgment of the Certification Board and its advisory committees.

Special Certificates

In addition to these three classes of general professional certificates, a group of special certificates should be provided for. In the beginning these should probably be at least equal in rank to Class II certificates and call for special qualifications in addition to those required for general professional certificate of Class II. Comparatively few of these may be needed, but with increasing specialization in library service, the list of special certificates will have to be extended. Among the special

certificates which will probably be found desirable from the beginning, the
Board may issue one which will stand for special skill in cataloguing. Such
a certificate should carry with it a guaranty of thorough general and technical training, with special training in cataloguing and a period of successful work long enough to demonstrate ability to give satisfactory service in
positions of responsibility requiring exceptional skill. Other special certificates should stand for similar special ability and success. Certificates
for high school work, children's work, and business library work are types
that readily suggest themselves as among the first to be used. It should not
be inferred that these special certificates would be considered a prerequisite
for special work in a special field. Even the head cataloguer in a large
library might have only a Class II general certificate while the rest of the
cataloguing staff might be found in general Classes II, III, or IV. Nevertheless, the worker who is ambitious to reach the front ranks of his special
branch of work will naturally strive to earn the special certificate as soon
as possible.

Certificate for Unlimited Term Recommended

It will be observed that differentiation between certificates of
higher and lower rank is not based on the length of time for which they are
valid. That is the method employed in practically all of the state systems
thus far proposed and seems to have been taken over bodily from teacher certification. Without raising the question as to whether this is the best
method to be adopted for compulsory state certification for librarians, the
committee wishes to point out the advantages for a voluntary certification
system of establishing classes each of which is, in effect, a life certificate except for such provision as may well be made for revocation for cause.
Let us assume that the National Certification Board were to follow the limited term plan and grant, let us say, three year and five year certificates.

At the end of the period the holder may not apply for renewal. Technically he has automatically dropped out and no longer holds the national certificate. The Board must, therefore, renew his certificate without his request or follow him up and urge him to apply for renewal or qualify for a certificate of higher rank. Either of these alternatives would be contrary to the spirit of the proposed system and, which is more important, would require a large amount of routine and clerical work in keeping up the records of the Board. If the system has to be supported to any large extent by fees, perhaps the limited term plan with small renewal fees would recommend itself for revenue purposes, but it may be questioned whether the income from this source would do much more than meet the additional expense involved. It would seem to the committee much better to make the initial fee to each class somewhat larger and avoid the difficulty of periodical renewals.

Sub-professional Certificate

In addition to the three general professional classes and the various special certificates of professional rank, a Class IV, or sub-professional, certificate is provided in this suggested scheme. This Class IV is not to be considered as an entrance door to the professional classes. A few of the best clerical workers in this group will undoubtedly qualify for the professional classes but there should be no presumption or a normal line of promotion from Class IV to Class III. Workers to be certified in Class IV are indispensable in any well organized library but the general education and technical training required are very different from the requirements of the professional classes. As this assertion may seem to run counter to current theory and practice, some further explanation of the various reasons for such a Class IV certificate may be offered here.

Library service of nearly every type involves a large amount of purely clerical or routine work which can be distinguished with no great difficulty from professional service. This clerical work is unlike most of the so-called clerical work in other kinds of public service or private business. Nevertheless it has all the characteristics of clerical occupations. Moreover, it requires both intelligence and training, just as the clerical work in a business organization requires the training of the bookkeeper, stenographer, and general office worker. It does not require either a college education or a professional library school training. The general confusion of the professional and clerical grades of service is one of the conspicuous defects of library organization at the present time, and this confusion tends to be carried over into the work of training agencies.

The Class IV certificate is provided, therefore, to give conspicuous recognition to the distinction between the professional and clerical types of library work, and to make it clear that both types are essential, that both require special, though not the same, qualifications, education, and training. A few examples from other vocations will help to make the distinction clearer. Hospitals require both doctors and nurses. It would be difficult to say that one is more important than the other for both are necessary; but their education and training, while similar in some respects, are so different on the whole that they are never confused. A comparison of the mechanical engineer and the mechanic, the architect and the draftsman, the banker and the bank clerk in varying ways offer a useful analogy to the situation which actually exists though not sufficiently well recognized in library service. A sound certification system should recognize the difference and build upon it.

Class IV, then, will make evident to all the difference between the two types of trained library workers. No little harm is being done at the present time by the vague and uncertain meaning attached to the term "trained librarians." A person with a very limited education and a training class type of instruction is, of course, a "trained worker" though not capable of filling positions requiring professional outlook and skill. The certification system should make this difference perfectly clear. The smallest independent libraries probably cannot command the service of a professionally trained librarian and where this is the case the trustees and community should be conscious of the fact. The larger towns and cities whose librarians fall in Class IV or below will recognize at once that their library service is below standard.

The plan of giving the trained clerical worker a recognized place in the certification scheme should have the effect of making that the minimum qualification which will satisfy even the smallest library, without also making it the final goal. Any community with the least local pride and interest in its library will want a librarian who is able to qualify for the lowest certificate recognized by the National Board, while healthy rivalry between communities will lead each to desire a librarian of professional grade. Communities should not be too severely condemned for their contentment with inferior library service. The ordinary layman member of a board of trustees, having little or no knowledge of any library except his own, cannot be expected to pass on the technical qualifications of the librarian.

The Class IV certificate will also serve a useful purpose in enabling the Board to standardize training classes, summer schools, and other agencies engaged in training for the sub-professional services. The product of approved training classes, and other agencies of the same grade would be granted a Class IV certificate without examination in the same way that it is proposed to give Class III certificates to graduates of approved professional library schools.

Application to Librarians Now in Service

The suggestions sketched above look upon the national certification system as a going concern, - a condition that probably cannot be reached inside of two or three years. After the general plan has been worked out and adopted, the Board will be confronted with two problems requiring much constructive imagination and no small amount of tact and judgment. The first is the problem of classifying and certifying librarians now in service and bringing them into the system. The second is the classification and accrediting of training agencies, since entrance to the system will from the start be partly through the library schools.

It should be clearly understood that the system proposed is designed primarily to apply to those entering library service in the future, yet it is desirable from the very first to bring in at least the larger part of workers now in service. Nothing else is so certain to insure the success of the plan. As the system is purely voluntary, it will be the task of the Board to create an interest and a desire to participate in it. It is not opposition but indifference that the Board will have to contend with in the beginning.

Obviously the standards designed for future entrants cannot be applied literally to the existing body of workers. It would seem that the procedure of the Board should be somewhat as follows: A system of certification having been formulated and adopted, it will be given wide publicity and carefully explained. Each library worker will be able at once to form a pretty accurate estimate of the place in the scheme to which he is entitled by his present work and responsibilities. He will then make application to the Board for the certificate to which he considers himself entitled, or will simply apply for certificate, leaving the matter of class entirely to the judgment of the Board. The blanks provided would ordinarily give the Board the information necessary to pass on the application; in doubtful cases it would seek the assistance of properly constituted advisory committees.

No applicant now in service would be subjected to examination other than the statement of facts submitted in making formal application for certification. Examinations come into play only in dealing with future entrants who cannot offer the required credentials from approved institutions of general and technical education. Promotion from Class to Class for those now in service who apply for certificate within a reasonable period should be based wholly on professional growth and success, all formal and technical requirements being waived. Each worker should be accepted on the basis of what he is now doing and not made to suffer any disadvantage for lack of formal technical training. This is all that anyone can ask. The whole system when once established should go far toward wiping out the present more or less artificial distinctions between those who get their training by experience and those who arrive via the schools.

Certification Will Aid in Recruiting

It may appear that the setting up of the certification system, with higher standards for future entrants to professional positions, will have a tendency to increase still further the shortage of competent workers. A moment's reflection will show, however, that such is not likely to be the result. Libraries will have exactly the same workers they had before. Some of them may not be certificated and some may not have as high a professional certificate as may be desirable for the position held, but no organization is any worse off than it was before. The difference is that under the certification system each library knows exactly where it stands. For a time it may have to get on with a larger proportion of workers of sub-professional rank than it should, but the system gives a definite goal towards which to work.

In the long run the fixing of standards, by fostering professional spirit and increasing efficiency, will raise salaries and attract more and better recruits which improved and enlarged training agencies will bring into the certification system and relieve the existing shortage of competent workers. There will always be a shortage of trained and competent workers in any profession which offers, as library work now does, a haven of refuge for those who cannot meet the standards required by other professions. According to the well known Gresham's law, bad money drives good money out of circulation. A similar law operates in any profession in which the untrained and incompetent are allowed to set the standards of service and compensation.

Board not Concerned with Salaries

It is probable that in the course of time each class of certificate will come to stand for a definite range of salaries. A Class III certificate, for example, might stand for a salary of $1,500 to $2,400; a Class II for $2,000 to $4,000; and Class I, $3,000 and upwards. Salaries for the different classes of certificate holders would necessarily overlap and the range for each would have to be quite extensive to allow for differences in local conditions. Standardization of salaries to correspond with standard grades of professional rank is no part of the present proposal and will not come within the scope of the duties or powers of the National Board.

Relation to A. L. A. Employment Service

It is evident, however, that there should grow up at once an intimate relation between the Certification Board and the A. L. A. employment service. The records of the Board in regard to each certificated member will be far more complete than the employment service can hope to bring together for its own use. Even if it were possible financially for the employment office to duplicate the personnel records which the Certification Board will necessarily accumulate, there are other obstacles which could not be readily overcome. Though the files of the Certification Board would be considered confidential, it should be possible for the A. L. A. employment service to make proper use of them and in this way render a service to library workers and administrators which would be invaluable.

Composition of Certification Board

The committee believes that the composition and organization of the Certification Board merits some further thought. The committee reporting last year recommended the creation of a board of nine members, five to be elected by the Council of the American Library Association, one representing a public library with a training class, one a small public library, one a state or federal library, one a college or reference library, and one with library relations not specified. The four other members were to be elected by the Council upon nomination by each of the following organizations: The Association of American Library Schools, the League of Library Commissions, the National Education Association, and the Special Libraries Association.

After thorough consideration the present committee endorses this plan in principle, but raises the question as to whether it would not be advisable to bring in also a representative of institutions primarily engaged in the work of professional education in general. Many of the library schools are now more or less closely affiliated with universities, and the tendency is clearly in that direction. If library work and training are to be put on a par with other professions, the presence of a representative of the American Association of Universities or the National Association of State Universities might prove to be of very great assistance. To make room for such a member in a board of nine, it has been suggested that the League of Library Commissions might be omitted, since the interests represented by the commissions are fully cared for by other members of the Board. The problem is to secure in the membership of the Board a proper representation of all the library and educational interests which will come within the influence of its activities. The exact form of organization is not of primary importance, however, because its constitution or articles of incorporation will naturally provide a workable method of changing its composition and machinery to conform to changing needs and conditions.

The present committee also wishes to call special attention to the importance of a suggestion made by last year's committee in regard to incorporation of the Certification Board. It is clearly essential that such a body should have a high degree of independence and not be subject to the exigencies of Association politics or endangered by such a drive as might readily be engineered by a small but active and discontented element. It must be able to maintain a consistent policy and program over a long period of years. The Board should also be in a position to deal without fear or favor with all present and future library organizations as well as with all other professional and educational organizations having any interest in standards of library service and training. A board incorporated by Congress or one of the states, with a membership constituted in some such way as recommended by last year's committee, would be sufficiently amenable to the real opinions and desires of the library profession. The American Library Association by appointing a majority of its members will have adequate control over its activities and as an independent incorporated body, its dignity and authority would be insured.

Comparison with British System

The national certification system will secure for American librarianship the advantages, without the disadvantages, which the British Library Association derives from its scheme of examinations and certificates, coupled with its system of classified membership. Roughly speaking, the three classes of certificate holders in our proposed plan would correspond to the fellows, members, and student members of the British Association. The British system of association dues also gives a hint as to a method for financing the work of our National Board. Fellows pay dues of L2 2s a year, and members L1 11s a year, while student members pay only 10s 6d. It would seem to be quite fair and entirely practicable to assess holders of Class I certificates $10 a year, Class II $5 a year, Class III $2 a year, and Class IV $1. Such a scale of annual fees in addition to examination and entrance fees would go far toward meeting the expenses of the Certification Board after the first few years.

Some such scale of dues would correspond approximately to salaries received and be much fairer than the low flat rate which is the only practicable method under present conditions of A. L. A. membership. The committee makes no recommendation on this point but offers the suggestion for consideration.

Recommendation

In view of the fact that no practicable means of financing the activities of a Certification Board are yet in sight and it is therefore unwise and inexpedient to proceed at once with the organization of the Board, your committee recommends that the Executive Board be empowered to appoint another temporary committee whose duties shall be to give the subject continuous consideration in general and especially (1) to seek financial support, (2) to prepare articles of incorporation, and (3) to proceed immediately with the incorporation and organization of a Certification Board whenever funds are available to carry on its work with a reasonable assurance of permanency.

Respectfully submitted

C.C. Williamson, Chairman.

James F. Hosic.

Dorsey W. Hyde, Jr.

Cornelia Marvin.

Everett R. Perry.

Josephine Adams Rathbone.

Julia A. Robinson.

Azariah S. Root.

LOCATION OF LIBRARY SCHOOLS IN 1921

TRAINING FOR LIBRARY SERVICE

A REPORT PREPARED FOR
THE CARNEGIE CORPORATION OF NEW YORK

BY

CHARLES C. WILLIAMSON

NEW YORK
1923

D. B. UPDIKE · THE MERRYMOUNT PRESS · BOSTON

TABLE OF CONTENTS

	PAGE
FOREWORD	v
INTRODUCTION	vii

CHAPTER

		PAGE
I.	TYPES OF LIBRARY WORK AND TRAINING	3
II.	THE LIBRARY SCHOOL CURRICULUM	12
III.	ENTRANCE REQUIREMENTS	26
IV.	THE TEACHING STAFF	34
V.	METHODS OF INSTRUCTION	40
VI.	TEXT-BOOKS	48
VII.	FIELD WORK	53
VIII.	JOINT COURSES, ACADEMIC CREDIT, DEGREES, AND ACADEMIC STATUS	69
IX.	FINANCIAL AND OTHER STATISTICS	72
X.	THE RELATION OF SALARIES TO THE IMPROVEMENT OF LIBRARY SCHOOLS	83
XI.	THE PROFESSIONAL LIBRARY SCHOOL AND THE UNIVERSITY	86
XII.	ADVANCED OR SPECIALIZED STUDY	91
XIII.	PLACEMENT OF LIBRARY SCHOOL GRADUATES	103
XIV.	RECRUITING FOR THE LIBRARY PROFESSION	107
XV.	TRAINING IN SERVICE	110
XVI.	CORRESPONDENCE INSTRUCTION	114
XVII.	STANDARDIZATION AND CERTIFICATION	121
XVIII.	THE PROBLEM OF THE SMALL LIBRARY	130
XIX.	SUMMARY OF FINDINGS AND RECOMMENDATIONS	136

APPENDIX

		PAGE
§ I.	GENERAL INFORMATION CONCERNING THE FIFTEEN SCHOOLS STUDIED IN THIS REPORT	149
§ II.	ENTRANCE EXAMINATION QUESTIONS OF LIBRARY SCHOOLS	152
	A. Specimen Questions, New York Public Library School	152
	B. Typical Questions, Various Schools	155
INDEX		159

LIST OF STATISTICAL TABLES

	PAGE
Number of Hours of Class-room Instruction given by Eleven Library Schools in the Major and More Important Minor Subjects in the Curriculum	22
General Education, Technical Training, and Library Experience of Library School Instructors in 1920–21, including only those giving Courses of at least Ten Class-room Hours	35
Library School Budgets: Totals for All Purposes and Amounts of Salaries at Various Periods	72
Salaries of the Directors, Principals, and Leading Instructors of Library Schools in 1921	73
Student Fees in 1921	74
Library School Statistics: Maximum Capacity and Registration in 1920–21; Average Initial Salaries of Graduates in 1914 and 1921	75
General Statistics of Graduates of Library Schools	78
Salaries of Graduates of Five Representative Library Schools in 1921	81

FOREWORD

THE study on which the following report is based was undertaken in accordance with a resolution of the trustees of the Carnegie Corporation of New York passed on March 28, 1919, and Dr. Charles C. Williamson, then Head of the Division of Economics and Sociology at the New York Public Library and now Director of Information Service of the Rockefeller Foundation, was invited to undertake the enquiry. An advisory committee consisting of Dr. Herbert Putnam, Librarian of Congress, Dr. James H. Kirkland, Chancellor of Vanderbilt University, and Dr. Wilson Farrand, Principal of Newark Academy, was appointed to coöperate in the study and to review the report. The verdict of these gentlemen was most favorable: they reported that the publication of the study "would, in the judgment of the committee, be highly desirable."

The subject of training for library service, while possessing an intrinsic importance that is as yet but little appreciated in this country, is of such dimensions as to lend itself well to the unitary and comprehensive treatment which follows. All of the library schools in the United States were visited and carefully examined; the most expert opinions on the problem were analyzed and compared; and, finally, the use made of the product of these schools, together with the need and demand for more and better training, was subjected to as thorough a statistical study as the available material permitted.

As a whole, therefore, the problem is one which a single, inclusive study of this character may do much to illuminate; and it is believed that Dr. Williamson's report will prove to be of decisive value in clarifying a situation which was not so difficult as it was neglected.

HENRY S. PRITCHETT,
Acting President.

June 1, 1923.

INTRODUCTION

THE primary purpose in preparing the following report was to present existing conditions in this country with respect to training for library work in such a way that the educator and the layman interested in educational problems might be able to form a true conception of the steps that should be taken to improve this phase of the library situation.

The author has been obliged to limit the scope of his study to the so-called professional schools. He has treated only incidentally training classes, summer schools, and other types of library training agency. An effort has been made to discover and to point out the strong and weak points in the organization of these library schools and in the training which they offer. Many of the defects disclosed could be remedied by the schools themselves; others are due to extreme poverty and can be remedied only by increased income.

All of the schools were visited and their organization and methods studied during the academic year 1920–21. The report therefore describes conditions as they existed at that period.

A brief historical sketch of each of the schools will be found in Appendix I. All but two of them, the Riverside Library Service School and the University of California library courses, were considered approved or accredited schools—that is, they had been admitted to membership in the Association of American Library Schools, an organization described in some detail in the chapter on standardization. Other schools are in the process of development: the University of Texas and the University of Buffalo, for example, have organized courses of instruction for which recognition as professional library schools may ultimately be sought; in Portland (Oregon) and in certain other cities plans for the organization of schools are also being considered.

TRAINING FOR LIBRARY SERVICE

CHAPTER I
TYPES OF LIBRARY WORK AND TRAINING

THIS chapter enters into a general discussion of the appropriate education, general and vocational, for different types of library work. Much use is made throughout the following pages of the words "professional" and "clerical." Before entering upon any systematic description or critical discussion of vocational training for library work, it is desirable to make as clear as possible the meaning which will henceforth be attached to these terms. As the word "professional" is used in these pages, it is not synonymous with vocational, tho that has been customary in library literature. Nor is the word "clerical," as used here, confined to that part of the work in a library which is essentially the same as the so-called clerical labor carried on in business and other organizations. Much of the necessary work in a library is peculiar to libraries, yet it is distinctly of clerical grade. Those who do this work, however, have not been called clerks but have been placed with all other library workers in one vocational group of "librarians."

For clear thinking on the subject of training for library service it is necessary to understand the different kinds of work which must go on in a library. In this report we recognize two distinct types which, for want of better terms, we call "professional" and "clerical." Each of these types or phases of library work demands general and vocational education of a particular character. The distinction between the two is only vaguely understood and seldom applied in library organization and practice. It therefore seems desirable to dwell upon it at some length before proceeding to an examination of the library schools and other training agencies. While in one sense this is an introductory or preliminary chapter, it will be apparent that it is also a summary of some of the most important conclusions of the whole study.

In library work of nearly every kind efficiency requires careful attention to a large amount of detail. The supreme importance of attention to detail in records and the necessity for skill and accuracy in routine operations have apparently been allowed to obscure somewhat the real nature of professional library work and the kind of training required to fit for the highest type of success. Library schools originated at a time when methods of handling the detailed record work of libraries were being worked out with scientific care and precision. The difficulty of supplying libraries with assistants who were skilled in handling such detail and possessed of enough general understanding of the significance and importance of care and accuracy seems to have led the first schools to shape their curricula to meet the needs of the time, which was natural and desirable. The unfortunate result is that an attempt has been made ever since, more or less unconsciously, to give to manual labor of a purely clerical and routine nature the dignity and importance of professional work. This has made and continues to make library work unattractive and distasteful to men and women with the proper educational and general equipment for successful service in types of work which are of real professional character.

A shortage of persons fitted for the higher grades of library work has been felt for some time, and will no doubt continue to be felt until some differentiation is recognized by library administrators in the organization of library staffs between duties of clerical and routine character and those requiring professional outlook and attainments. A "trained" worker in a library may be of either one or the other type, but at present it is commonly assumed that all "trained" workers are of the same general grade. There are many kinds of work in any library which can be performed just as well (perhaps better) by a young woman with a high school education and a little appropriate instruction and experience as by a college graduate with the best library school training that can be devised.

Two main types of training for library work are required. The first is the broad, general education represented at its minimum by a full college course which has included certain important subjects, plus at least one year's graduate study in a library school properly organized to give a thorough preparation for the kind of service referred to in this volume as "professional." The second type calls for a general education represented approximately by a four-year high school course, followed by a course of instruction designed to give a good understanding of the mechanics and routine operations of a library, together with sufficient instruction and practice to ensure proficiency and skill in one or more kinds of the clerical and routine work which we may call "sub-professional" or "clerical."

Library administrators appear to be making little or no effort to keep these two types of work distinct; or, if they do recognize such grades of work, they assume that the clerical worker will in the course of time, and solely by continued experience in clerical work, develop capacity for the higher or professional grades. Occasionally this has occurred in the case of exceptional individuals; but the assumption that the difference between the clerical and professional worker is length of experience only is unfortunate, and has much to do with the low state of library service and the absurdly low salaries offered for even important positions of professional character.

Since the library administrator does not organize his staff in such a way as to make clear the qualifications needed for different types of work, the library schools have not been under the necessity of making the distinction; and many of them have not done so. They have admitted to the same classes students who by no possible chance could give acceptable service of any except the clerical type along with those well qualified to enter the highest grade of professional work. Exactly the same instruction has been given to both groups. In other words, the schools have been trying and are still trying to train clerical workers and professional workers in the same classes and in the same way. The results could not possibly be satisfactory, and they have not been. The time has now come to apply the remedy for this fundamental defect. The situation calls for a proper organization of library service and the provision of separate facilities for training each class of worker.

Graduation from an accredited college after four years of study leading to the bachelor's degree should now be recognized as the minimum of general education needed for successful professional library work of any kind. Much of the record-keeping and routine in libraries of all kinds can be carried on very well by persons who have less than this amount of general education and even by those who have had only a high school course. For the sake of the library profession and to elevate the standards of library service, some distinction between professional and sub-professional or clerical grades of library work is essential.

College education is now required of the high school teacher in practically every part of the country. How can the public library, even in the smallest town, be expected to serve intelligently the needs of all classes if the librarian is not at least as well equipped as the high school teacher? The librarian, indeed, if he is to live up to his opportunities, should be the intellectual peer of the high school principal, the superintendent of schools, the minister, the editor, and all other educated persons upon whom the community depends for leadership.

The need of training for librarianship, even for the smallest libraries, is almost universally recognized; but the mistake is often made of assuming that the training needed is confined to matters of library technique and clerical routine. It is true that to be successful a librarian must understand library methods, but no amount of training in library technique can make a successful librarian of a person who lacks a good general education. The most essential part of training for librarianship is the general education that is ordinarily secured nowadays through a college course. Some knowledge of foreign languages and literature, history, sociology, economics, government, psychology and the natural sciences, every librarian worthy of the name must have. Moreover, he must know more than the average college graduate about the literature and sources of information in all the principal fields of interest, and have at his command the bibliographical tools and devices for unlocking the printed sources of information on any subject. It goes without saying that the high school student cannot do this. If he could, a college education would cease to be important as background and preparation for any profession. The time required for the specific training for librarianship is comparatively short—usually but one year—because the most important part of the equipment is general education and a knowledge of men and books which can be acquired in a variety of ways but which is most likely to be found in those who have completed a college course.

A person with the intellectual and general equipment for librarianship can ordinarily get in one year from a properly organized library school the general technical training needed for any type of professional library work. In order to do the highest grade of work, however, and to make rapid progress in any specialized line, the student should have an opportunity for special study, not immediately following the year of general technical study, but after at least one year of professional library work.

No amount of study in a library school can fit for successful library service the individual who lacks the fundamental educational equipment. On the other hand, many persons having the necessary education and native fitness and capacity have taken it up with complete success in spite of a lack of technical training. It is far easier for an intelligent educated person interested in books and people to make a success of library work than it is for one having all the technique the library school can give him, but lacking in general intellectual and cultural background.

Some discussion has been occasioned in library circles by the fact that many of the most successful librarians are without library school training. The question has been raised as to whether a library school course is helpful; whether, indeed, it may not be an actual hindrance to the highest success in types of librarianship requiring initiative, originality, resourcefulness, and large administrative capacity. Two possible conclusions are indicated: in the first place, it should be perceived more clearly that the least important part of the librarian's equipment is that which the library school gives him, and that therefore a high standard of general education should be required for admission to the professional school; secondly, it is probable that the schools should so adjust their methods of teaching and the content of their curricula that students with adequate education and capacity will not find that in the process of acquiring a knowledge of library technique they are in danger of missing the broad professional outlook, and of suffering a certain deadening of initiative and imagination which is likely to result from an excessive attention to minute detail.

Library technique should be presented to men and women, properly educated for professional library work, from the point of view of principles and policies. Too often, even in the best of schools, such subjects as cataloguing and classification have been taught as if the student had no mind. "Do it this way and don't ask why," has frequently represented the instructor's attitude. Granting that such a method may legitimately be used in dealing with a class of apprentices, it is ridiculous when applied to college graduates who suppose they are being educated for a profession and in a professional spirit.

To the library school of a graduate and truly professional character we should look for the workers needed to fill all positions requiring extensive and accurate book knowledge, skill in organization and administration, and expert technical knowledge in many special lines. Being professional schools, these institutions will in no case aim to train specifically for any one library staff.

To another type of library school, illustrated by the "training classes" conducted by the larger libraries, we must look for trained clerical workers. The subjects covered by the two kinds of training agency will to a certain extent be the same. Clerical or sub-professional workers will need instruction in cataloguing, in classification, in all kinds of record-keeping topics,— including filing, indexing, alphabeting,—and in typewriting. They can be taught such things as the nature and uses of subject headings, not with the idea that they will be responsible for the subject heading work in any important library, but that they may be more intelligent and efficient within their own range of duties. For this type of training a large amount of drill and practical work will necessarily accompany the class-room instruction. On the completion of such a course an intelligent person with a high school education should be able to give efficient service, especially in the library in which and for which he has been especially trained. It should not be possible to say of him, as library administrators now often say of library school graduates, that he has been taught a great many things and has hazy ideas about library work in general but cannot do any kind of work acceptably well.

Some of the so-called library schools at the present time are not equipped to do more than give a good thorough training for clerical workers. Under certain conditions that is the most important thing that can be done; and the school which neglects to do it well, in an attempt to achieve the impossible and give a professional training with inadequate resources and ill-prepared students, is doing the cause of library service more harm than good.

In the last analysis every library will have to make its own decision as to what positions on its staff require professional training. The number and proportion of such positions will be determined by the size and character of the library as well as by the money available for the payment of salaries. A reference library will require a larger proportion of professional librarians than a circulating library of the traditional type. The large library system will require a smaller proportion, tho perhaps a higher grade, of professionally trained librarians than the small library, for the reason that the greater specialization made possible in the large organization permits the professional worker to supplement and supervise the work of a larger number of workers of clerical grade.

The mere recognition of this principle will do much to solve the training problem. In the first place, it will considerably reduce the number of people that the professional library schools will be called upon to turn out. Assuming, as has apparently been done by some library executives, that practically the entire body of library workers, even down to pages, should have a full library school training, the impossible task would fall upon the library schools of training all library workers by means of one general type of curriculum. At the present moment the demand for trained workers, which is alleged to be far in excess of the supply, is in reality not solely a demand for fully equipped and professionally trained workers, but for both types. When this fact is recognized, professional library work will make a far stronger appeal to college men and women as a career, not only because the professional type of work will be more attractive in itself, but also because it will make possible more adequate salaries. The confusion of clerical and professional work tends inevitably to keep salaries down to the level of the clerical grade. No matter what the financial resources of an institution, it is not justified in paying clerical workers much, if any, more than those of equal education and experience receive in commercial and other competing fields of work. In many cases the law of supply and demand will make it possible to maintain efficient clerical staffs at salaries even lower than those offered by commercial and private employers.

Until the distinction between clerical and professional workers is sharply made and adhered to the demand for adequate salaries for the professional group will prove ineffective because they will be economically impossible. A careful appraisal of the duties actually performed by many workers for whom professional salaries are demanded will show that they are often in large part clerical and not worthy of higher remuneration. Until library work is so organized that professional workers devote all their time and energy to professional tasks,— tasks which workers with less adequate general and technical equipment cannot perform without permanent damage to library service,— it is not worth while to expect librarians to be paid on a professional basis. When library work is so organized and is adequately remunerated library schools able to offer professional training of high character will not need to worry about the difficulty of securing enough students to fill their classes, nor will librarians have cause to bemoan the dearth of trained assistants.

The inherent attractions of professional library work will never fail to produce the necessary supply of workers when working conditions and salaries are properly adjusted. Neither will the call for trained clerical workers go unanswered when the type of worker and the type of training required are clearly defined. At no time during the last three years would the library schools have had any great difficulty in filling their classes with a good grade of high school graduate who, with proper training, would have made excellent clerical workers. Some of the library schools conducted by public libraries should confine themselves to this task and let their libraries look to the professional schools for the other type of trained worker.

Some of the stronger library schools may find it possible and desirable to offer both types of training, in separate classes of course, and perhaps to some extent by a separate corps of instructors. In general, however, workers of the clerical grade can and will be trained for the larger libraries by their own training classes. Any library finding it necessary to add to its clerical staff as many as ten new members a year is likely to find it wise to maintain a training class. With one competent person in charge of the class and doing most of the teaching, aided as required by other professionally trained members of the staff, a library can provide its own clerical workers more economically and quite as efficiently as if it should attempt to conduct a library school.

To such a program some library executives will make the objection that they wish their entire staff to have full professional training. This is at best a counsel of perfection, tho in reality it probably reveals a lack of understanding of the principles of economical and efficient administration. If it is true that the high school graduate is not fitted for the professional work, it is also true that the college graduate will not give the best service in strictly clerical positions. If a person with college education is satisfied to spend his time, or any considerable part of it, on tasks the high school graduate can perform equally well, he will probably give no better service than the latter and will actually be inferior and likely to be dissatisfied with his position and remuneration.

Small libraries will find it somewhat more difficult than large ones to provide a properly trained personnel. For professional workers they will of course look to the library schools, but a supply of trained workers of the clerical grade will not be so readily secured. Requiring too few persons of this grade to warrant the expense of conducting a training class, they will have to resort to some other agency for competent clerical assistants. The most available but least desirable source will be apprenticeship. Young women residing in the community will be taken on the staff and expected gradually to learn the work by doing it under direction. In some cases this may prove fairly satisfactory. The amount of instruction that can be injected into such apprenticeship will necessarily depend on the size of the professional staff and the time and teaching ability available for the task.

In many cases it should be possible for smaller libraries to make arrangements with larger ones within easy reach to train their clerical

TYPES OF LIBRARY WORK AND TRAINING

assistants. There would seem to be no good reason why the training class of a large library should not accept students from libraries in smaller adjacent towns and cities, charging a proper fee, to be paid not by the student, perhaps, but by the library benefited. In other situations a group of smaller libraries in the same neighborhood may conduct a training class coöperatively. Still other small libraries may find a solution of the problem by sending their assistants to attend short courses and summer schools conducted for that purpose by state commissions, universities, etc. Some help in the training of clerical assistants may also be expected from properly conducted correspondence courses.

Whatever the method employed for recruiting clerical workers, it is of the greatest importance not to overlook the fact that training is necessary for the best results. Without the trained clerical assistant the professional worker will be overburdened with responsibilities for detail from which he should be free in any properly organized library. A certification system should recognize the grade of clerical assistant and admit to that grade only those whose general education and library training meet the standards provided. Under a certification system which makes the essential distinction between professional and clerical grades, there will be little or no danger that individuals qualified for clerical work will be able to pass themselves off for the higher grade. There will be no reason, therefore, why accredited and standard training classes cannot, if they choose, accept for training students not under appointment or pledged to accept appointment on the library's own staff at the end of the period of training. In such a case it would be proper, of course, to charge a reasonable fee for the course.

CHAPTER II

THE LIBRARY SCHOOL CURRICULUM

IN order to make as clear as possible to the general reader the scope and content of library school curricula, the following brief descriptions of courses have been compiled from the current issues of the announcements or catalogues of the leading schools. These statements are not designed to be a complete outline of the courses given in any one school; they constitute rather a composite summary of the descriptive statements which seem best adapted to convey a fair idea of the subjects in which it is deemed necessary for the professionally trained librarian to receive instruction in the schools.

It may at first seem to the reader that we are introducing here a mass of detailed information which should have been relegated to an appendix. This matter is deliberately brought in at this point, however, in order to give at the outset a good idea of the scope and content of the library school curriculum. It serves also, it is believed, to give point to the contention made throughout this report that professional library training should be based on a broad, general education. The different courses are arranged in the order of the average amount of time given to them in the class-room schedules of the eleven schools which reported on this point. Each paragraph under a subject is taken from the statement of a different school.

Cataloguing

"The course includes lectures, recitations, and practice work in dictionary cataloguing and alphabeting. Each lesson is followed by an exercise in actual cataloguing, the books used being selected to furnish illustrative examples of the rules given in class. The exercises are revised from sample cards and corrections discussed in class. The corrected cards are converted into sample dictionary catalogues, which are indexed to bring out examples of rules. The A. L. A. rules mimeographed on cards for convenience in study and reference are followed with minor modifications."

"A study of mechanical devices and supplies used in cataloguing; methods of duplicating cards; problems in ordering cataloguing supplies."

"Practice is given in alphabeting and in the ordering, handling, and use of Library of Congress printed cards. . . . Each student keeps the revised cards for about 200 books, correctly arranged and furnished with guides, as a sample catalogue for future help.

THE LIBRARY SCHOOL CURRICULUM 13

Additional lectures are given on cataloguing of children's books, cataloguer's reference books, supplies, cataloguing of foreign books, music scores, and maps. Lectures and practice in the use of fuller collation and imprint are given. . . ."

Book Selection

"Designed to familiarize, so far as possible, with books and writers, their scope, qualities and respective values in certain leading classes of literature, and with sources and aids in book selection in these classes; to define and analyze the principles underlying discriminating selection of books for library use; and to cultivate the power of judging books according to their value and suitability for different types of readers and libraries."

"(a) Principles of book selection in Biography, History, Travel, Sociology, Nature and Popular Science, and Religion; study of standard and current aids and book reviewing publications; study and practice in annotation and evaluation; exercises in compilation of special lists; study of editions and series desirable for library use. (b) Survey and analysis of modern fiction (in English), covering principles of critical judgment, aids and guides, and study and practice in annotation, for modern fiction, historical fiction, foreign fiction in English translation, 'borderland' fiction, short stories, fiction of the current year."

"Translation of the works of the leading French novelists are read and reported upon, followed by a survey of representative novelists of Spain, Italy, Germany, Scandinavia, and Russia. Recent poetry, the short-story, and modern drama are studied. . . . The class examines about forty new books each month, and attention is given to current publications by reading and checking the issues of the Publishers' Weekly. The large amount of reading required in this course may be expected to encroach upon the time which a student usually gives to general reading."

"Aims to cultivate further the power of judging books as to their value and adaptability to various types of libraries and people. Practical problems in the selection of translations of the classics and foreign fiction, series, editions, quick selection of new books, etc. Reading of selected modern novelists, dramatists and poets is required and problems of selection in these fields discussed. Facility in estimating books is developed further through the writing of book-notes and reviews. The economical spending of book funds is taught through the checking of second-hand, remainder and other bargain catalogues of American and English dealers."

"After considering the qualities of a good edition, the various editions of the standard authors are studied, and those best suited to library use are recommended."

"The evaluation and selection of periodicals for library use are considered briefly."

Reference Work

"A study of the standard works of reference, general and special encyclopedias, dictionaries, annuals, indexes to periodicals, ready reference manuals of every kind, special bibliographies, and the more important newspapers and periodicals. Works of similar scope are compared, and the limitations of each pointed out. Lists of questions made up from practical experience are given, and the method of finding the answers discussed in the class. Problems in selection of reference books, especially for the small library, are assigned and talked over. The aim of this course is not only to promote familiarity with a considerable number of well-known reference works, but also to give the student some idea of the method in the handling of books, to familiarize him with the use of indexes, tables of contents, and varying forms of arrangement, and, finally, to suggest some method of comparison and evaluation."

"Lectures and problems from the standpoint of college and university libraries, large reference libraries or departments. Principal topics: interlibrary coördination and coöperation in reference work; organization of reference material; law libraries and law books; care and use of manuscripts; medical libraries; patents publications; legislative reference; local history and genealogy; publications of learned societies; dissertations; indexes to foreign periodicals; trade and professional journals."

Classification

"The Dewey Decimal classification is used as the basis for a thorough consideration of the subject matter of books, with a view to their arrangement on the shelves, both of the large and small library. Lectures are given also on the Cutter Expansive and the Library of Congress classifications."

". . . Practical work in classifying selected lists of books, considering the various requirements of large, small and special libraries; brief history of classification; comparison of the principal systems; use of the Cutter-Sanborn tables for assigning book numbers."

"The importance of adapting classification to the need of special localities and types of libraries is emphasized through the discussion of specific books. Methods of simplification, especially in biography and literature, are taught. The study of book numbers is included in this course."

THE LIBRARY SCHOOL CURRICULUM 15

Administration

"This course includes the administration of large libraries, the administration of small libraries, and a short course in business methods.... In the consideration of the administration of small libraries, practical details of management and the adaptation of methods to the needs of a small library are emphasized. The principal topics are: library finance; statistics and reports; relation of librarian to trustees; the staff and the reading public; the place of the library in the community; coöperation, publicity, and extension of the use of the library."

"Library legislation."

"Work of a library organizer; office systems; accounts and bookkeeping; business correspondence."

"Forms and supplies."

"An analytical study of reports and statistics in their vital relation to the practical work of the library, including the graphic presentation of these."

"Methods of bringing public and library together. Outside publicity, including reaching the business men, newspaper publicity, miscellaneous printed matter and its distribution, placards, car cards, movie slides, outside bulletin boards, window displays and exhibits; and inside publicity, including lectures, exhibits, book displays, and bulletins."

"Methods and problems of city extension by means of branch libraries, deposit stations and smaller agencies; rural extension, including county and township systems and the book automobile; state traveling libraries and other work of library commissions."

Library Work with Children

"This course aims to give the principles of library work with children, and comprises a series of lectures on management and training of children; equipment of a children's room; books for little children; books for younger children; how to judge fiction for boys and girls; historical stories; boys' reading; girls' reading; program of a children's department."

"Book selection for children; administration and equipment of children's rooms; library work with schools and playgrounds; coöperation with other educational and social agencies."

"Principles underlying the art of story-telling, applied to the selection, adaptation and oral presentation of stories. Students electing this course will tell stories in the playground and other branches of the library."

"History of children's literature. The purpose of the course is to trace the development of children's literature in England and America and to study the forces which affected it and determined its characteristics at different periods. Beginning with the time of Aldhelm and Bede, typical books of each period are discussed, the chap-books, old-fashioned books for children, and facsimile reprints in the Library School collection being used for study and comparative purposes."

Current Events

"As an aid to the student in following the affairs of the day, attention is given to the events chronicled from time to time in the daily newspapers and in the weekly and monthly periodicals."

"Round table devoted to the review of important current activities and events, designed to give practice in the use of periodicals and to develop judgment of the value of the material presented."

"Survey of the history of general American periodicals, also the best in special subjects, as Science, Fine Arts, and Education; English and widely-known continental magazines."

Public Documents

"A study of the publications of the United States Government, with a consideration of state and municipal documents, as illustrated by the publications of the state of ─────. . . . The Executive Departments, Congress, and other government offices are considered as sources of information for libraries. The printing and distribution of documents, their indexes, and their use in reference work are taken up. Emphasis is laid upon the documents of most value to the small library."

Subject Headings

"Principles of subject indexing as applied to the dictionary catalogue are discussed and the relation and correlation of subjects are studied both in relation to the entry of books in the catalogue and to the arrangement of books on the shelves."

"Assigning subject headings on the basis of the A. L. A. List of Subject Headings and the Library of Congress lists."

"In studying subject headings, analytics, cross references, and the headings assigned specific books by the students are discussed. The A. L. A. subject headings is checked by each student."

THE LIBRARY SCHOOL CURRICULUM 17

Subject Bibliography

"The best and most available bibliographies and selected lists in various departments are considered as to their authority, date, content, arrangement, merits, defects, and adaptation to different uses. Special topics, such as the scope, utility and limitations of bibliography are also treated. For graduation each student submits a selected and annotated bibliography that tests the ability to collect, arrange, and definitely to evaluate the literature of the subject chosen. Methods of work, authorities used, and results obtained are examined and criticised. A study is made of the organization and work of those societies and institutions of America and Europe which are interested in the stimulation of bibliographical movements, in the perfecting and unifying of bibliographical methods, and the production of bibliographical material. Special attention is given to coöperative undertakings and international bibliography."

History of Libraries

"History of European libraries, early and present; American library movement; library associations and library periodicals; great American libraries and their specialties; American library biography."

"Development, characteristics and tendencies of the American library movement; different types of libraries; library associations, national and state; library commissions and their work; library training."

". . . Origin, materials and development of writing; origin and spread of printing; methods of book illustration; history of bookbinding."

"Book illustration, title-pages, printers' marks, and famous printers and presses."

Fiction

(See Book Selection.)

Lending Systems

"Discussion of the principles underlying the relations of the library to the public brought about by the loan of books, and the character of the service to be rendered; a study of the various necessary and desirable records connected with this work, representative loan systems suitable for various types of libraries, and rules, regulations, and practices incidental to the service."

"History and principles of charging systems, with detailed study of Browne, Newark and Columbia University charging systems.

Circulation of periodicals, music, pictures and books for foreigners. Besides loan work routine the following topics are discussed: access to shelves, rent collections, book disinfection; distribution through branches, stations, schools and home libraries, interlibrary loans."

"Registration, infectious diseases *vs.* library books, fines, reserves, renewals, rules for lending, pay collections, training of staff, and apprentice classes."

"Consideration of the business principles which should underlie routine and of the social principles which should govern relations with borrowers forms the basis of the course."

Trade Bibliography

"Historical development, national book-trade bibliographies of Europe; English and American book-trade bibliography, general, national, and special; related bibliographical aids, important catalogues, and special bibliographies."

"Aims to give . . . a working knowledge of about thirty-five American, English, and foreign trade publications which are of constant use to libraries in their dealings with book-sellers and publishers and in the acquisition of books in general."

Binding and Repair

"Lectures treat of materials, processes, and methods of binding; practice is given in judging materials and workmanship as to strength, durability, appearance, and cost. Students become familiar with all processes by inspecting books in various stages of binding, and by visiting binderies. The necessary technical routine and the preparation of serials, pamphlets, and books for binding and re-binding are also considered. Mending is taught by practical work and demonstration."

"Publishers', and re-inforced bindings, and history of the art of bookbinding (with slides)."

"Practice in mending; in preparing books and periodicals; in giving specifications for binding of a varied assortment of books; in estimating wearing qualities of different editions."

"Mechanical processes necessary in preparing books for circulation, mounting pictures and clippings, binding pamphlets, magazine covers, etc."

Order Work

"The subjects included in this course are book-buying, discounts, ordering books, checking and entering bills, the accession book and

THE LIBRARY SCHOOL CURRICULUM

its substitutes, the shelf list, serials and continuations, exchanges, gifts, duplicates, pamphlets, clippings, the history of copyright and the copyright law."

"Importations; second-hand auction purchases."

Printing and Publishing

"Lectures discussing the features of a printed book, such as the parts of a book, type pages, illustrations and color printing, the printing of books from plates, etc., are given to cultivate an appreciation for well made books. Further, the characteristics of the best known American publishers and their works are discussed to familiarize the students with the standards of publishing and the value of imprint."

"Lectures and practice aim to give the student the information most needed in preparing the simplest library publications. Includes the preparation of copy, mechanical editing, routine and processes of printing, correction of proof, library stationery and blanks and forms, and examination of library reports and bulletins as to waste and economy, types, indentions, etc."

School Libraries

"The value and place of the high school library; types; relations to the public library; selection of books and periodicals; modifications in classification, cataloguing and other records; charging systems; aids in reference work; the administration and use of the school library; special problems of the school librarian; making and use of a clipping and picture collection; the vertical file; lessons on the use of books; vocational guidance; special features such as lantern slides, stereographs and music records."

"Previous pedagogic training or teaching experience is desirable for this course."

"The work of the school and teachers' department, deposit stations in the schools, educational theories and books are discussed in order to give an intelligent understanding of the possibilities of coöperation with teachers."

Library Buildings

"Methods of planning and equipping library buildings, with discussion of the form and arrangement of rooms for various library departments and calculation of book capacity."

"Shelving, lighting, furniture and fittings, decorations, equipment for social service purposes."

"Principles are illustrated by lantern slides and photographs showing plans of library buildings."

Community Relations

"Study of library work and possibilities of a definite city or other community. The topography, population, political, financial, industrial and other social conditions will be considered in their relation to actual and potential library work in the community."

"Designed to give the student a knowledge of the library's relation to the community as a whole and of the various agencies for industrial, social and civic betterment with which it may coöperate."

"Municipal and government activities and problems, methods of working with local organizations, neighborhood survey, etc."

Shelf Work

"This course includes practice in assigning book numbers by the Cutter-Sanborn author tables; lectures on the shelf-list, showing its value for inventory and statistical purposes; methods for checking continuations and government documents, and caring for pamphlets, pictures, slides, etc."

"Book supports, shelf labels and other appliances; preservation and arrangement of pamphlets; inventory; shelf-listing. Model shelf-lists are made both on cards and on sheets."

Languages

"Technical French and German. A study of an extensive list of German and French book titles, customary abbreviations, etc."

Accessioning

"The condensed and loose-leaf accession books are used, and other systems of keeping accession records and of withdrawing books from the library are taught. The mechanical preparation of books for the shelves is included."

Indexing

"Marking matter for indexing; choice of headings; form of citation; verification; filing; full and brief indexing; periodical indexes; indexing documents; correlation of entries; cross references; editing for print; form of printing; labor-saving methods and devices."

Notes and Samples

"Each student is required to submit for inspection a collection of material on the various phases of library work. This collection includes books and pamphlets on library economy, bibliographies and reading lists, library periodicals, publications of individual libraries, blanks and forms used in library administration and the problems, notes and other required work of the regular courses. No certificates or diplomas are awarded to students who do not present well-selected and well-arranged collections of reasonable size."

Special Libraries

"Information regarding the important and rapidly growing work of industrial, commercial, financial, and other special libraries, by visiting librarians, and experience in such libraries."

Books for the Blind

"Lectures are given on library work for the blind, the history of types for the blind, books, magazines, games, writing appliances and music, and other subjects of interest to the blind."

Altho no less than twenty-five distinct courses are recognized in the curricula of the library schools, about half of the student's time is devoted to four subjects—cataloguing, book selection, reference work, and classification. These four subjects may well be called the heart of the curriculum, for altho the actual time devoted to any one of them varies greatly from school to school, these are the subjects on which all the schools lay primary emphasis.

The table on page 22 shows the number of class-room hours devoted to the major and most of the minor subjects in the curricula of the eleven schools from which reports were received. Differences of terminology and the variety of groupings and combinations of subjects encountered make it impossible to arrive at strictly accurate averages or to compare one school with another at every point. The table serves, however, to indicate the remarkable variations in the time given by different schools to even the major subjects. Cataloguing, for example, gets 105 class-room hours in one school and only 35 in another, the average for the eleven schools being 60. One school devotes 76 hours to book selection and another only 27. Time allotted to reference work varies from 69 to 30 hours. Classification claims 47 hours in one school and only 20 in another. In the minor subjects variations are naturally still more pronounced.

NUMBER OF HOURS OF CLASS-ROOM INSTRUCTION
GIVEN BY ELEVEN LIBRARY SCHOOLS IN THE MAJOR AND MORE IMPORTANT MINOR SUBJECTS IN THE CURRICULUM

Subjects	School[1]											Average for eleven schools reporting
	1	2	3	4	5	6	7	8	9	10	11	
Cataloguing	44	57	105	90	57	45	35	66a	43	61	61	60
Book Selection	57	60	27	60	36	52	50	60	76	45	32	50
Reference Work	53	47	44	60	30	50	30	44	36	69	60	48
Classification	42	47	44	25	35	30	20	33b	28	32	33	34
Administration	76	25	20	18	36	37	20	40	27	17	34	32
Children's Work	15	6	18	30	9	18	35	12	c	27	24	18
Current Events	15	c	35	c	18	c	15	c	30	24	32	15
Public Documents	13	12	10	25	10	15	10	16	12	11	20	14
Subject Headings	30	17	15	20	10d	e	10	e	e	19	30	14
Subject Bibliography	f	30	6	g	13	10	12	10	26	32	f	13
History of Libraries	3	30	14	32	10	2	10	5	10	8	8	12
Fiction	6	gh	25	5	gh	10h	10h	24	gh	16	32	12
Lending Systems	6	10	5	7	6	19	10	8	13	16	18	11
Trade Bibliography	10	17	4	30	7	10	8	gi	6i	16	f	10
Binding and Repair	7	12	7	9	10	10	23	5	4	6	12	10
Printing & Publishing	13	10	8	9	2	5	18	c	5	9	6	8
Order Work	4	9	6	6	5	5	5	16	12	8	3	7
School Libraries	2	26	1	g	6	1	20	gj	c	j	2	5
Library Buildings	4	9	4	6	k	6	3	3	8	5	6	5
Filing	2	l	8	6	4	1	10	g	10	2	4	4
Community Relations	g	g	3	g	g	9	15	g	10	8	g	4
Shelf Work	2	7	9	3e	2	2	3i	d	8	2	2	4
Languages	m	m	23	m	m	m	m	m	m	m	20	4
Accessioning	3	2	3	g	4	8	2	i	i	2	2	3
Indexing	3	9	5	g	3	1	g	g	n	c	3	2
Inventory	1	o	o	o	p	1	1o	g	o	2	1	1

a. Includes shelf listing.
b. Includes subject headings.
c. Not given.
d. Included in cataloguing.
e. Included in classification.
f. Included in reference work.
g. Not segregated.
h. Included in book selection.
i. Included in order work.
j. Included in children's work.
k. Included in library administration.
l. Included in indexing or cataloguing.
m. Required for entrance.
n. Included in filing.
o. Included in shelf work.
p. Included in accessioning.

Several conclusions of possible significance may be drawn from these facts. Obviously there is no agreement among the schools as to the relative importance of the different subjects in the curriculum. The amount of time given to a subject seems to depend on the personal opinion or desires of the instructor or the principal. While considerable interest has been manifested in discussions as to what should constitute the minimum essential instruction in cataloguing, apparently no effort has been made by the Association of American Library Schools to arrive at minimum standards for the course in cataloguing. Complaint is common that the curriculum is overcrowded, while important new subjects are clamor-

[1] Numbers replace names of schools.

THE LIBRARY SCHOOL CURRICULUM

ing for admission. The school that succeeds in giving its students the essentials of cataloguing in thirty-five hours, while others require two or three times that length of time, can take up other subjects that may be more important for the general professional course. Teaching skill, as well as equipment and methods, is an important factor in determining the amount of time to be given to a subject.

While it manifestly would not be desirable to bring about strict uniformity in the content of the various courses in the curriculum, there does seem to be need for a certain degree of standardization of both the major and minor courses given in the first year of professional library school study. Nomenclature should be standardized and standard courses worked out and officially adopted by the proper professional body. The term "book selection" means far different things in different schools, and terms used in presenting the subject do not have at all the same meaning everywhere. The situation is similar in other parts of the curriculum. It is impossible to tell what instruction a student has had in book selection from the mere fact that he had a course in that subject in an accredited library school. The fundamental courses in library schools, as in schools of law and engineering, should all have the same scope. To bring this about should be one of the important duties of the certification board recommended elsewhere in this report. Before such a board can accredit a library school for the certification of its graduates, it must satisfy itself that standard courses are given. Development of training in service for library workers through other agencies than library schools will require the formulation of minimum standards as to the scope and the content of courses which are to be accepted for certification purposes.

The library school curriculum has passed through something of an evolution, and it is quite likely to undergo even greater changes in the future. The schools at first confined their attention largely to technical library subjects, such as cataloguing and classification. Later, cultural and other studies were introduced to make good any deficiencies in the student's education. The present tendency is to eliminate the general cultural and informational courses from the library school curriculum, requiring for admission everything of that nature considered essential for successful library work. Courses in literature are still given in some schools, but usually in a limited way as a part of the subject of book selection. A "fiction seminar," or special course in the study of fiction, is now given in about half of the schools. Where this is considered important, it is not looked upon as a cultural subject but rather as a part of the technical equipment of the library worker, needed equally by those who have and those who have not had adequate college courses in literature. There is no doubt that such a course is valuable for the librarian who is called upon to select and purchase fiction for his library and to guide the reading of its patrons. The point that seems to be overlooked, however, is that for similar reasons the library school student needs instruction in the literature of scientific, technical, business, social, economic, and political subjects. Instruction in such subjects is even more important than in pure literature, since the standard library reference books and current guides for book selection in fiction and pure literature are more numerous and of higher quality than in scientific and practical subjects in general. Neglect of these large new fields of interest by the reading public may be due in part to the one-sided character of the library school curriculum. Too much attention is still paid by the library schools to pure literature, both in their entrance requirements and in their curricula. The traditional view of the library as the workshop and playground of the literary and leisure classes persists, tho social and economic subjects are now competing for first place in the interests of book selection experts.

It is impossible, within the library school curriculum, to give instruction in the wide range of subjects which must claim the attention of the professional librarian. To be equipped for his work, he must enter upon this professional training with nothing less than a good all-round college education. Many library schools still consider it desirable to give a course in current events in order to create an intelligent interest in the more important subjects that engage the attention of the reading public. For the most part, however, these are the schools that require only a high school education for admission. Schools with higher standards of education look upon the teaching of current events as they would upon a course in elementary economics or general history —necessary, of course, for the skilled librarian, but a prerequisite to and not a part of, library school training.

The library school curriculum as it stands represents in the main the current demands of the librarians who employ the graduates and the experience of the graduates themselves. Most library school teachers and principals are keenly alert to discover any new topic of interest to librarians or any new development in the library world in order to bring them into the curriculum. One school has an active advisory committee of three graduates to which the question of changes that may be desirable in the curriculum is regularly put. Another school circularizes its graduates periodically to get suggestions for new courses or new topics to be introduced. Everywhere library school officials have an ear to the ground for any evidence of dissatisfaction with what the schools are teaching. This attitude, however, does not make for radical changes in the curriculum. Rather it results in excessive conservatism and conformity to custom and tradition. The suggestions that come back to the schools are only echoes of what they have been doing.

No school has ever attempted or is now prepared to disregard what has been done in the past and make a thorough, scientific analysis of what training for professional library work should be and build its curriculum upon its findings, instead of following tradition and imitating others. A more aggressive leadership is needed. Those who are interested in promoting training for library work should see to it that men and women of energy and initiative are brought into the schools. Some of the pioneers in the library school movement were of this type and they have left their mark.

It would be ungracious to criticize the schools for not doing more to put library service on a higher plane. Within the limits of their pitifully small resources they have probably done all that can fairly be asked of them. Not, therefore, as a criticism but as encouragement to push on to better things, it should be pointed out to the library schools that an opportunity is theirs to wield a potent influence in bringing about a new library movement. Some of the epoch-making advances just ahead in the library world are discussed elsewhere in this report. Standards of service are to be worked out; a certification system inaugurated; methods of training in service for library workers devised, including an effective system of correspondence instruction; and county libraries and library extension promoted to the point where "books for everybody" will be a reality. In university, research, and other types of library, equally rich opportunities await the advent of leaders with vision and enthusiasm to set new standards of service. It is to the library schools that we should be able to turn for inspiration and guidance; but it must be confessed that trained leadership of the quality now demanded is not likely to be produced by the present curriculum and personnel of the professional schools.

CHAPTER III
ENTRANCE REQUIREMENTS

WITHIN certain limits it is probably true, as Mr. E. A. Bostwick, librarian of the St. Louis Public Library, says, that the greatest service of the library schools is in selecting people fitted for library work.[1] Certainly schools cannot turn out a satisfactory product with only one year of instruction unless the students selected have the necessary education and special aptitude. All the schools pay special attention to the selection of their students, but the methods employed seem to warrant careful scrutiny and possibly considerable revision. Little or no effort seems to have been made to utilize modern vocational and psychological tests. Except as to age of applicants admitted, there is little agreement as to what entrance requirements should be.

As a rule, applicants must be at least twenty-one years of age and not over thirty-five. Two or three schools put the lower limit at twenty years, while one specifies thirty and another forty years as the age beyond which a person should not attempt to enter library work through the schools. Tho persons above thirty-five are seldom rigidly excluded, they are strongly advised against taking the course unless they have been continuously engaged in similar intellectual pursuits. Persons over thirty-five are said to find the work difficult and to be at a decided disadvantage in securing positions.

A four-year college course is required for admission to only two schools, the New York State Library School and the University of Illinois Library School. The Los Angeles and the Carnegie Library Schools require a college degree only for the special course in high school library work. Even the college course is not considered sufficient by the better schools unless it has included two foreign languages. "A knowledge of foreign languages is always necessary," says the New York State Library School, "and each additional language with which the student is acquainted is a direct professional asset." The "best preparation for general library work is a college course which includes a rather wide range of subjects." Most of the schools recognize the value of a college education but do not find it practicable to require it for admission. In the Los Angeles school, "two years of college will ordinarily be required. Four years of college is strongly advised and is

[1] *Proceedings of the American Library Association*, 1912, p. 155.

essential for school library work." The Wisconsin catalogue states that "the importance of a four years' college course as an educational equipment for library work cannot be too strongly emphasized."

Admission to all the schools, except the New York State and the University of Illinois, is by examination, altho applicants having degrees from approved colleges are accepted without examination in practically all others, with the reservation by some that the college course must have included a broad training and modern languages. In all cases applicants for examination are required to have had four years of high school or its equivalent. The examinations of all the schools cover about the same range of subjects—history, literature, general information, current events, and one or more modern languages. The purpose and scope of these examinations are well expressed in the following statement from the circular of the New York Public Library School:

"'The entrance examination is designed to test the candidate's qualifications for professional library training, and particularly to determine whether he possesses the habits of mind and the fundamental knowledge essential to the proper performance of his duties as a librarian. It involves answering questions on history, current events, general information, and literature, together with translation of French and of one other modern foreign language, preferably German, the choice of which is subject to approval by the Faculty. The questions, while allowing fair range of choice, assume reasonable familiarity with the main facts and names of literary and general history; and as regards the present, an intelligent interest in local, national, and international affairs."

Typical lists of examination questions are given in an appendix to this report. To the ordinary educated person, and even to the experienced library worker who has been out of school or college for a few years, the questions asked in many entrance examinations may seem too difficult and varied, especially in history and literature. But the examinations follow practically the same lines each year, so that a candidate in possession of a series of questions from the different schools can form a pretty close estimate of what he must do to pass. It does not appear to be the practice to mark the papers rigidly or to hold to any definite passing mark, the theory being that the examiners can learn what they need to know about the candidate whether he answers the questions correctly or not.

Two possible criticisms may be made of these examinations. If the questions are used primarily as mental tests, they are very crude and unscientific. Far better tests could be devised for selecting persons with the general information and personal qualities requisite for library work—tests, too, which would not appear so formidable that many excellent persons would be deterred by the fear of failure and disgrace from attempting to enter a library school. On the other hand, the kind of examination commonly used cannot be considered as an adequate means of testing the candidate's general education and information: they cover too narrow a range of subjects and in too superficial a way.

Languages and general information are of fundamental importance for all professional library work. But special knowledge of literature and history is not as important for many kinds of library work as is acquaintance with social and applied sciences. As an educational preparation for library work nothing has been discovered which can take the place of a thorough college course of varied content. The University of Illinois and certain other schools suggest in some detail a program of college studies which should be followed in preparation for library work. A high school graduate may often pass the type of entrance examination given by the library schools as readily as the college graduate. Nevertheless, the college graduate of equal native ability has a breadth of view and an ability to attack new problems and master them which are very important for the professional library worker, but which are seldom found in one whose education has not been continued beyond the high school.

It is not meant to imply that every college graduate is fitted for library work. It may well be that even when the college degree is required some properly constructed selective test should also be applied. The point that should not be lost sight of is that a high school education does not fit any one for professional library service, and that no entrance examinations can be devised that will serve as a substitute for four years of college education.

Entrance examinations are usually held in June, tho several of the library schools which admit by examination also hold another in the fall. By the coöperation of local libraries, candidates who live too far from the school may take the tests in or near their own home town. Since the examinations of all the schools using that method cover approximately the same range of subjects and hold to about the same minimum standards of education, the desirability of uniform examinations or a single examination for all the schools suggests itself. Some of the schools have felt the need for such a system. It is increasingly difficult to prepare examinations without repeating questions previously asked by some school. A uniform system would put all candidates on the same basis, and make it unnecessary for a student to take the examination of two schools or more so that if he fails to pass for one he may still enter another. Some school authorities believe a higher grade of student would be secured by uniform tests. If scientific and approved tests are to be employed, it is particularly desirable to have them worked out coöperatively. The uniform college entrance examinations need only be cited to show the advantage and possibilities of such a system. A student who passes the general examination could select the school he prefers to attend, while the school itself would be free to accept or reject those who pass the general examination.

As matters stand at present, however, there is little likelihood that separate examinations by the schools will be abandoned. Some of the schools take a seemingly unwarranted pride in their own particular questions; others find it advantageous to use flexible standards in rating the papers of applicants. The heads of some schools state that they seek a particular type of student and for that reason could not dispense with their own examinations. The latter objection would be more convincing if some clear description of the special type of student sought were given. Should the national certification board, recommended elsewhere in this report, become a reality, it may be possible to work out uniform admission tests that will satisfy all parties. For the time being, local conditions, jealousies, and rivalries stand squarely in the way of this as of many other desirable improvements.

Perhaps the most mooted feature of the entrance requirements of library schools is actual experience in library work. The views of those who insist on the desirability of such previous experience are well expressed in this statement, which appears in the catalogue of the Library School of the University of Wisconsin:

"It is desired that as many as possible shall come to the school with library experience. Practical work in a good library for a year or more, in addition to the educational and literary attainments, is the best preparation for the year's work in the school. It tests the candidate's aptitude for library work, gives a knowledge of library terms, and familiarity with library processes, and makes a student more eager for, and appreciative of, what the library school has to offer. . . . While it has not seemed wise as yet to establish an absolutely rigid requirement of library work extending over a definite period, still this preliminary library experience is considered so important that applicants without it are strongly advised to spend much more than the required several months in apprentice work before entering the school."

The New York State Library School also considers previous experience so desirable that "all admitted students without such experience are strongly urged to spend as much time as practicable in voluntary or other staff service in their local libraries or elsewhere before entering school." "Some library experience," it is further stated in the latest catalogue, "will in all probability be an entrance requirement in the near future."

On the other hand, several of the most important library schools do not even recommend previous experience. They consider that employment in libraries of inferior standards, unsupervised and unrelated to the student's actual need of preparation for school work, is very likely to prove a serious handicap.

There is no doubt, however, that the wholly inexperienced student does need an orientation in the library business before being plunged into the maze of technicalities of the professional library course. He needs to become familiar with the ordinary library tools and terminology and to get some insight into the aims and methods of library service. This orientation is accomplished by several schools through a preliminary period of practice work for inexperienced students just before the opening of the regular school year, usually in the library with which the school is connected. This preliminary practice ordinarily covers two weeks.

It is not clear that this short practice period is always so organized and supervised as to accomplish efficiently the desirable or necessary orientation. It would seem that, if this is as important as many authorities believe it to be, special pains should be taken to give the student as good an introduction as possible through lectures, reading, inspections, and individual conferences. It is to be feared that at present so much is left to chance in this preliminary course that it is of doubtful value.

Many of the schools have much to say about the "personality" qualifications for admission. Several of the circulars announce that in considering applications for admission personal qualifications and natural aptitudes for library work are taken into consideration. The usual method of applying this personality test is an interview with the head of the school. The following quotation from the circular of one of the schools illustrates the stress laid upon "personality" and the "interview."

> "Personal qualities and a more or less discriminating sense of literary values are, however, essential considerations. It follows, therefore, that an interview . . . is an important entrance requirement. Despite the expenditure of time and money involved by such an interview, it is insisted upon, except under unusual conditions."

Undoubtedly it is very important to give much weight to personal qualifications and natural aptitudes. It is impossible, however, to put much confidence in the personality tests as now applied. In the first place, no attempt has been made to determine scientifically what personal qualities are essential: it seems to be assumed that library work is of a homogeneous character, and that consequently the same personality tests can be applied to all who desire to enter library service. It may be questioned whether there is any such thing as "library work" in general. There are many kinds of library work; and if there are any special capacities and aptitudes which make for success, they must be considered in relation to each distinct type of work. It will probably be found that any qualities which are necessary for library work in general are just those qualities required for success in most other professions.

The first thing for the library schools to do is to define the qualities that they seek in candidates. The next thing is to give more assurance that they are able through a brief interview conducted by one person to detect the presence or absence of those qualities with sufficient exactness to justify giving weight to the result. The impressionistic method of the interview seems likely to reflect the personality of the interviewer as much as that of the interviewed. If it were possible to arrange independent interviews by several competent persons the results could be accepted with much greater confidence.

The personality test as conducted at present may actually be responsible in part for the acute shortage of competent library workers. Those who apply the "personality" test have their own background of experience and acquaintance with types of library and library work. Their undefined ideal personality seems likely to embody the qualities they would seek for the kinds of library work they know best. By eliminating all others in the selective process, school officials may unconsciously deprive libraries of many excellent workers in special positions. The impressionistic, or interview, method cannot disclose temperamental defects. These come to light later; and every school has among its graduates persons who constitute perpetual "problems" for the school principal assuming, as most of them do, a large measure of responsibility for keeping every graduate employed and contented.

Much can be said in favor of simplifying entrance requirements by specifying a full college course for all students in professional library schools and at least a high school course for admission to training classes. If desired, the school can call for the applicant's college record and accept only those whose work is of high grade. If classes must be further limited, other tests can be applied to applicants; but any effort to base selection on personal qualities and aptitudes for library work should be discouraged until such qualities and aptitudes are carefully and clearly defined and more accurate methods of detecting them are worked out by vocational psychologists. It does not appear that up to this time any of the library school authorities have approached their problem in the scientific spirit or made any use of scientific methods.

Before leaving the general topic of admission requirements, some reference may be made to certain minor features. The earlier schools concerned themselves largely with training in the technique, and even the mechanics, of library work. With the lapse of time a differentiation, not clearly recognized, however, has taken place between the broader or professional type of training and the training necessary for those who are to do the actual clerical work of record-keeping, etc. The development of library work as a profession has been hampered by the tendency on the part of the public to look upon it as wholly clerical in nature. The library schools and the actual organization of libraries have not only done little to remove this handicap but have even done much unconsciously to perpetuate it. Some of the library schools still require students to acquire the vertical or library handwriting, while nearly all of them lay great stress on skilful use of the typewriter. Several schools require the ability to operate a typewriter with fair accuracy and speed before admission; others permit students to make good the deficiency during the year's course, often providing machines for practice.

There is much to be said, of course, in favor of ability to operate a typewriter as a part of the general equipment of any educated person. Any intellectual worker is likely to derive considerable advantage from the ability to make skilful use of the typewriter, but it is not clear why such skill should be required as part of the professional librarian's equipment any more than of that of the teacher, the engineer, or the business man. The typewriter is far more indispensable in every business office than it is in the average library, yet the professional schools of business do not make typewriting an essential part of their course. That is left to the schools for training the clerical staffs required in business offices. The same general relations should obtain between the library training class and the professional library school. It is not surprising to find that able and ambitious college men and women hesitate to look to library work as a professional career when assured by the catalogues of the so-called professional training schools that "a ready ability to use the typewriter is an important part of a modern librarian's equipment" and is "necessary in almost any library position."

CHAPTER IV
THE TEACHING STAFF

A DETAILED analysis of the training and experience of members of the teaching staffs of twelve of the library schools seems to indicate a quite definite lack of fitness of a large proportion of them for giving instruction of high professional character to students with college or university education. The table on the following page tells the whole story. About half (48 per cent) of the instructors giving ten lectures or more during the year 1921 were not college graduates. Many, it is true, had had a partial college course, while others had carried their studies somewhat beyond the high school in educational institutions of some kind.

It should not be inferred that a college degree is considered an absolutely indispensable part of the equipment of the library school instructor. Certainly some of the most successful teachers now on the staffs of the library schools are without the college degree. The bachelor's degree, however, is in general a fair measure of an individual's intellectual equipment and has come to be regarded as the minimum essential for all kinds of teaching above the elementary school. In no part of this country would instruction in a well-organized high school be considered acceptable if half of the teachers were not college graduates.

Library school instruction, moreover, should rank not with high school but with college instruction. In respect to college faculties, the best opinion is even more insistent on full college education, and in the better institutions an advanced degree is usually a *sine qua non* for instructors. It does not seem probable that a few small library schools will get better results from a teaching staff of which 48 per cent. are without the bachelor's degree than would a college. No self-respecting college would attempt it. Some of the protagonists of things as they are attempt to justify the existing condition by belittling the value of a college education and arguing that some instructors are better without it than others ever will be with it.

As a matter of fact, the present situation is due almost entirely to economic necessities and inadequate standards. College graduates of fair ability are not attracted by the salaries library schools offer. Consequently library schools have to recruit their staffs from a group which is not eligible for attractive positions in other fields. If proper salaries

GENERAL EDUCATION, TECHNICAL TRAINING, AND LIBRARY EXPERIENCE OF LIBRARY SCHOOL INSTRUCTORS IN 1920-21

INCLUDING ONLY THOSE GIVING COURSES OF AT LEAST TEN CLASS-ROOM HOURS

School number[1]	No. of instructors	No. of college graduates	No. of library school graduates	No. teaching in same library school from which graduated	No. having previous teaching experience	No. having teacher's training	Experience in library work of value in teaching	
							Good	Apparently inadequate
1	6	2	6	1	2	1	5	1
2	17	11	16	13	0	0	10	7
3	5	1	5	4	0	0	4	1
4	5	3	4	1	2	0	4	1
5	9	5	5	2	2	0	7	2
6	8	5	6	3	3	1	5	3
7	9	6	8	6	3	2	7	2
8	11	5	7	2	1	1	9	2
9	5	4	3	0	3	2	4	1
10	9	4	8	4	1	0	7	2
11	8	4	5	0	3	0	3	5
12	8	2	8	6	0	0	3	5
Total	100	52	81	42	20	7	68	32

[1] See note 1, page 22.

were paid in all library schools and the best instructors possible were secured, it would not be long before at least 90 per cent. would have college training.

Most library schools also retain something of the flavor of apprenticeship training, in which beginners are put into the hands of those who have not yet risen to the higher ranks but who have become proficient in some part of their craft. If the library schools hope to take rank with other professional schools of the higher grade, they must accept the existing academic standards for all teaching above the elementary schools. Throughout this report it has been emphasized that professional library work requires a college education. College graduates going into library service should not be asked to take their professional training under a group of instructors one-half of whom are without the college viewpoint.

The library schools have been more careful, in recruiting their staffs, to secure instructors with technical training than those with general education: while only 52 per cent. of the instructors are college graduates, 81 per cent. have completed some kind of course in a library school. It is significant also that 42 per cent. are teaching in the same school in which they took their own library training. Certain schools, by choice or necessity, select nearly all instructors from their own graduates. The obvious disadvantages of this practice are an inevitable inbreeding and a certain imperviousness to new ideas or methods.

It is not at all surprising that among library school instructors special skill in teaching is not conspicuous. Only 7 per cent. of the instructors have had any kind of training in the science or art of teaching. It seems safe to assume that none at all has had the slightest instruction in the methodology of the teaching of library subjects. In recent years the growth of vocational education has drawn attention to the need of special teacher training for each of the many subjects to be taught. The need of preparation for teachers of agriculture, for example, seems to be well recognized. A recent report of the United States Bureau of Education does not regard the work of a state agricultural college as *bona fide* "unless the curriculum includes at least a two-hour course in special methods of teaching agriculture and at least one three-hour course in either psychology or education." Is that an unreasonable standard? Is special preparation for his work any more important for the teacher of agriculture than for the teacher of library theory and practice?

THE TEACHING STAFF

Only 20 per cent. of library school teachers bring to the library school any experience in teaching. The outstanding successes on the faculties are found almost entirely within this 20 per cent. who had behind them good teaching experience in school or college before taking up library school instruction.

Opinions may differ as to the desirability of requiring actual experience in library work as a qualification for teaching the various subjects in the curriculum of the library school. Some teachers lacking extensive experience in any kind of professional library work may prove more satisfactory than others whose experience has been excellent but who lack teaching ability. Granted a scholarly attitude of mind, a thorough knowledge of the subject-matter, an interesting personality, and ability to teach, an instructor's work must benefit very greatly from a considerable period of somewhat varied experience in library work. Long experience alone, however, is no evidence of qualification for library school teaching.

An examination of available information as to the practical library experience of these one hundred instructors indicates that a little over two-thirds (68) have held library positions of such a character for such a period and with sufficient bearing on subjects taught as to make it possible to describe their experience as "good." The experience of thirty-two of the instructors, on the other hand, must be characterized as "apparently inadequate." This is not surprising, however, in view of the very low salaries paid. A man or woman with fair qualifications for teaching and good experience can ordinarily command a much larger salary than is available in library schools.

Almost without exception library school principals complain of the extreme difficulty they experience in securing new teachers. Low salaries are probably at the root of the problem. On the surface, however, it does not seem to be primarily a question of salaries. A strong disinclination toward teaching pervades the library profession, largely as the result, perhaps, of the fact that so many librarians were formerly teachers who have found library work more congenial, if not more remunerative. A further difficulty in finding persons to fill the comparatively few positions on library school faculties is the fact that of those who are inclined to teach not many are qualified. Few of those who possess the necessary professional knowledge and experience have either the essential personal qualifications or the training and experience required for successful teaching.

Concerted effort should be directed toward raising the quality of instruction in the library schools. Tho an increase in salaries will not of itself bring relief, other measures are likely to be of no avail so long as salaries remain at anything like the present level. A teaching position on a library school faculty must in some way be made to carry at least as much professional prestige as the higher administrative posts in public libraries. It must be made possible for men and women of the highest quality, who are good teachers, to find a permanently satisfactory career in library school instruction. The schools themselves must be put on a higher professional basis and an opportunity offered to instructors, through longer vacations and freedom from excessive drudgery and overloaded schedules, to make contributions to the scholarly or practical sides of library work.

Library school teaching may be less attractive than college teaching because of the comparative lack of freedom as to the content both of the curriculum as a whole and of the individual courses. The tendency has existed from the beginning for library schools to be more or less dominated by a single personality. The ideas and ideals of that personality, consciously or unconsciously, mold the content of the courses and even determine the methods of instruction. Most school principals are conscious of exercising control only to the extent required to prevent overlapping of courses and direct conflict as to rules and practices taught in the schools. As a matter of fact, actual control probably goes much farther — so far, indeed, that little scope is left for the originality and enthusiasm of the gifted teacher.

In a one-year course this is almost inevitable. The time is so short for covering the wide range of topics with which an acquaintance is considered essential that the curriculum must be very closely planned and organized. In the curriculum of any professional school the necessity for covering a specified range of subjects is likely to seem more compelling than in a college of liberal arts. In library schools particular effort seems to be made to give the student a cursory acquaintance with every kind of library work and every problem he is likely to meet. This tends to reduce the teaching to routine and to make the work unattractive to the genuine teacher, to whom it seems more important to give the student a professional attitude toward his work, to awaken his enthusiasm, and to develop his power of attacking problems, than to hurry him through a prescribed list of topics.

For apprenticeship and training classes a minute control of the con-

THE TEACHING STAFF

tent of the course and the rules taught may be quite proper. For the professional library school it is at least an open question as to whether better results would not follow from a greater use of the project method, with less lecturing and a much less strict adherence to syllabi which years of use have made well-nigh exhaustive on every subject.

We could profitably cease to expect the library schools to send out graduates crammed with information about every conceivable subject, from incunabula to color-band filing, and demand, rather, men and women of liberal education, well grounded in the fundamentals of library practice and ideals, familiar with the librarian's tools, and resourceful in attacking and solving problems as they arise. Instead of suppressing differences in the views of library school instructors, it would be well to encourage them to emphasize their own opinions and points of view. Otherwise students, having little incentive to think problems through and form their own opinions, take them ready made from the instructor who teaches what the principal has decided to be the official policy of the school.

CHAPTER V
METHODS OF INSTRUCTION

THE lecture method predominates in all library school instruction, altho the better the school the fewer the lectures and the larger the use of other methods. In catalogue descriptions of courses, lectures are usually said to be supplemented by readings, problems, recitations, seminars, class discussion, class practice, quizzes, or individual conferences with students. While the proportion of lectures and other forms of instruction necessarily varies somewhat, depending on the nature of the subject, the size of the class, etc., nevertheless, most of the library schools apparently place an excessive dependence on the lecture. This is frankly admitted by most of the library school authorities, who agree that, in general, the best schools and the best teachers make the least use of the lecture.

Altho it is freely conceded that the lecture method is overworked, it is claimed that the worst abuses have now disappeared, and that further improvement is scarcely possible under existing conditions. This problem is not peculiar to library schools. In all higher and professional instruction the lecture has proved to be the line of least resistance for the poorly prepared, overworked, or unskilled teacher. Yet even the skilled teacher in the library school finds a measure of justification for much lecturing. Inadequate preparation of a part of the students in a class seems to put a natural limit on the effectiveness of other methods. Library school classes which include college graduates with excellent library experience and students having only a high school education and no acquaintance with libraries drive even the best teachers to an excessive use of the "pouring in" method. None of the schools are large enough to permit of a classification or grading of students on the basis of education and experience.

As the curriculum has developed, it contains subjects of somewhat minor importance to which only a few hours of instruction can be given. The necessary orientation, for which the lecture is probably the best method, requires so much of the time allotted for the subject that, in order to cover the ground in the little time that is left, the instructor persuades himself that he must lecture continuously. While a conscious effort on the part of the administrative and teaching staff to

METHODS OF INSTRUCTION

economize the students' time is entirely praiseworthy, it is doubtful whether the desired result can best be reached by emphasizing the lecture method. The general use of mimeographed syllabi represents a vast improvement over the old lecture system. Yet one still finds occasionally that library school students are required to write into their notes verbatim the language of the instructor. The need of better text-books and manuals to save the students' and the teachers' time and to improve the efficiency of library school teaching is so acute that it will be discussed in more detail in another chapter.

It must also be made clear, in fairness to the library schools, that methods of instruction of which more use might advantageously be made are out of the question because of the heavy demand they would make on the instructor's time in the holding of individual conferences and the reading and revision of written work. It is particularly important, not only in teaching all of the so-called "record work," but also in such courses as book selection and reference, to require the student to express himself in writing. In the professional school this should not be allowed to degenerate into a mere drill in routine processes for the sake of acquiring skill and speed but should be used judiciously to ensure rapid and firm grasp of principles involved. One of the results of the common failure to distinguish between professional library training and the training for routine and clerical work is that library schools which should be conducted on a professional plane do not stop at giving their students a grasp on principles and methods but are deadening their initiative and enthusiasm by drilling them in the routine processes of hand work and the memorizing of rules and classes. The professional library schools have need to be on their guard against overemphasizing skill in clerical technique: there is danger that by forcing upon their students a perfection in detail, they will stifle the indispensable qualities of enthusiasm, imagination, and initiative.

The wholly legitimate and desirable use of written work is limited in the library schools to-day by lack of proper assistance for the instructors. Each school has one or more "revisers," who assist the instructors in reading and correcting written work. Not much improvement can be made in library school instruction until money is available to employ a sufficient number of competent revisers to free the instructor from the detailed work which now takes time that should be devoted to study and research, and contacts with practical library work and with his colleagues in the profession. In important scientific schools laboratory assistants may outnumber the teaching staff itself, but poverty has all but denied such aids to library schools.

We cannot refrain at this point from noting that what has just been said about the nature of instruction in library subjects shows it to be peculiarly adapted to the correspondence method. Even in the residence schools, where student and teacher can meet and talk, the best instruction in many courses is carried on by means of written communication between them. Correspondence instruction as a method of "training in service" is fully discussed in a later chapter.

One of the curious results of low standards for both instructors and students and of lack of contact of many schools with institutions of learning is the incongruous adaptation of the methods and terminology of the university. One who, being accustomed to think of the seminar as a group of students engaged in original research under the guidance of a scholar and investigator, comes upon the "seminar" of high school students engaged in acquiring a modicum of elementary information on book selection or some other subject in the curriculum under a teacher without college training or experience in research, can understand a certain reluctance on the part of university faculties to accord library schools the recognition to which their field of work and general relations to intellectual pursuits abundantly entitle them. It is fortunate, however, that the schools do take themselves with the utmost seriousness, and by dint of patient and devoted, if not brilliant, effort do achieve results which are surprisingly large when measured by their resources in personnel and equipment. Better teaching equipment, higher standards of education and experience on the part of the teaching staff, and more attention to methods of instruction, are obvious needs of all the library schools, tho, of course, in varying degrees.

On no question in the administration of the library schools is there a wider diversity of opinion than on the use of part-time as against full-time instructors. As library schools have virtually all developed in close connection with some public or university library, their direction and most of the teaching have usually been in the hands of the members of the library staff. Certain schools have separated the school staff from the library staff and are convinced that no other plan is practicable. Other schools, on the contrary, have no full-time instructors at all and seem equally confident as to the superiority of that method. Most of the schools have one or more persons giving full time to instruction, a larger or smaller share of the teaching being done, as a rule, by members of some library staff in the vicinity. The certainty that the principal of each school will be found defending its own practice suggests that library schools have acquired the convenient habit of making a virtue of necessity.

There can be no doubt that the part-time and full-time systems have each their peculiar advantages as well as disadvantages: that under one set of conditions the balance may be in favor of part-time instruction, while under other conditions full-time service may give the best results. For the most part, the actual practice of the schools is not determined by theory but by finances. Schools in a financial position to employ a corps of full-time instructors do so.

The great advantage claimed for part-time instruction, and usually the only advantage mentioned by its advocates, is the opportunity through constant contact with actual library work to keep abreast of library progress. It is alleged that the full-time instructor is in danger of becoming an impractical theorist and even a formalist or reactionist. The claim is made in some schools that under the part-time system a better type of person is secured for both sides of the work than either school or library alone could hope to secure. Unfortunately, the results of actual experience under the two systems are far from conclusive. The two schools which give a two-year course and require a college degree for admission pursue diametrically opposite policies. The University of Illinois Library School has a separate faculty, believing that the greater part of any professional course should be in the hands of instructors giving full time to the work, and that it is difficult to secure persons who can give first-class service on both the library staff and the school staff. The New York State Library School, on the other hand, depends for its instruction almost entirely on the staff of the state library and holds that any other method would be far less satisfactory.

Serious disadvantages inhere in the part-time method. The instructor has no continuous contact with the student and is not so freely available for consultation and informal discussion. Part-time instructors are not likely to view their teaching in a broadly professional spirit nor take a deep interest in educational problems. In any such division of work, one part or the other, or both, are almost certain to suffer.

Not many of those whose opinions have been sought fail to recognize the need of at least one or two full-time instructors to look after details of organization and administration and to give the technical and major courses—cataloguing, classification, and perhaps book selection. The part-time instructor in such subjects as cataloguing and classification is in too great danger of teaching the methods he uses in his own library. For training schools that is possibly acceptable, but for strictly professional instruction a broadly comparative and detached point of view is essential. Many of the minor subjects in the curriculum can well be taught by librarians fresh from their professional duties.

Perhaps it would not be altogether fair, under present conditions, to use as a basis for ranking the schools the proportion of the teaching staff giving full time to the school. That, however, is coming to be a practical method of appraising other kinds of professional schools and must sooner or later be applied also to the library schools. This is, in a sense, inevitable, because the part-time instructor is usually a result of an attempt to conduct a school with insufficient funds. The school with an adequate income, other conditions being the same, will be the best, for it will employ the best instructors, who will give all their time to their school work.

It appears from all the available evidence that a library school of high professional rank should be large enough and provided with sufficient funds to require the full-time services of at least four instructors to give the major courses, particularly the so-called technical courses. Being conscious of the dangers pointed out as inherent in full-time service, the individual instructor should, with the coöperation of the school, make the necessary plans to get the requisite contact with actual library work and problems by vacation service on library staffs, by making library surveys, by sabbatical years, etc.

The special or visiting lecturer, even more than the part-time instructor, is an outstanding characteristic of nearly all library schools, tho in some cases the difference between special lecturer and part-time instructor is not very clear. Ordinarily the special lecturer gives only one or two lectures. He may be either a resident or non-resident specialist who is brought in from year to year to supplement the regular instruction in some definite way. The special lecture of the right type is considered quite essential in the conduct of many of the minor courses, but satisfactory lecturers are difficult to secure.

Sometimes a course, such as library administration, is made to consist largely of these special lectures, the instructor's part being to correlate and supplement them as best he can. In theory the special lecturer, like the part-time instructor, is supposed to bring to the class-room the practical point of view and to help in making a vital contact between theoretical instruction and actual library work.

Certain special lectures, usually classified as inspirational, may have little or no direct relation to the work of instruction; while others are conceded to be neither instructional nor inspirational but are considered to have value in introducing the students to the leading personalities in the library profession. In the latter group are found library administrators who are invited to talk to students solely for placement purposes.

The best authorities confess that the special lecture feature of library school instruction has been overworked. In consequence, in recent years the better schools have greatly limited or virtually abandoned the number of such lectures. When put to the test, they have been found to have very little either of informational or inspirational value. This is particularly true of the single lecture. The value of special lectures is said to increase with the number given by one individual on the same general topic. It has been found difficult to correlate single lectures, even when they are excellent in themselves; but too often they have been entirely disappointing. Speakers classed as specialists frequently fail to develop their subject as desired. One library school principal, admitting the futility of special lectures, holds that they do, nevertheless, have a good effect by giving the students more respect for and confidence in their regular instructors!

For some schools the expense involved constitutes the principal objection to the special lectures. Casual lecturers, usually librarians of professional standing who happen to be at the school or in the vicinity and are asked to talk to a class, ordinarily are not paid, but as a rule the special and visiting lecturers receive an honorarium of from $5 to $25, traveling expenses also being paid, at least for the single lecture.

To reduce the item of traveling expense and yet secure desirable lecturers from a considerable distance, the library schools in the eastern states have coöperated informally in arranging lecture circuits. The principal of one of the schools is designated each year to arrange a schedule for one or more lecturers, usually of the inspirational type. Traveling expenses which would make one lecture or two prohibitive for a single school bear less heavily when shared by three or four schools. The difficulties of finding lecturers acceptable to several schools and of arranging satisfactory schedules tend to confine the lecture circuit system, even in the east, to rather narrow limits. In the central and far west, distances are so great that it is seldom feasible for even two schools to coöperate on a single lecture.

A more ambitious plan of coöperation among library schools proposed from time to time combines to some extent the system of part-time instructor and visiting lecturer. It seems desirable that many of the minor subjects in the library school curriculum should be taught by specialists. Local specialists not being available, and the work covering only a few weeks each year, so that a full-time member of the faculty is out of the question, it is natural to suggest that a person who combines the required special knowledge or experience and teaching ability should be engaged to go from school to school repeating a short intensive course. In theory it would be possible in this way for each school to enjoy the best instruction. Too often the minor subjects have to be presented by some local librarian not especially qualified or by some regular member of the school staff who is not a specialist in the subject and is already overburdened with the range of subjects he is expected to teach.

In a very limited way coöperative effort of this kind has been employed. The Los Angeles School and the Riverside School, for example, both employ Mr. W. Elmo Reavis, of Los Angeles, to teach bookbinding. Perhaps the two other schools on the Pacific Coast would benefit by engaging the same excellent teacher. Serious difficulties, however, at once arise. Mr. Reavis might find that his business would not permit a month's absence in Berkeley and another in Seattle. It might not be practicable to give up his business and spend his entire time going from school to school. To most persons such an occupation would be distasteful, and there is some question as to whether the quality of a teacher's work would be maintained through even a short period of such teaching. Again, there is the difficulty, at times insuperable, of the inflexible schedules of individual schools. On account of the time lost between courses and the extra travel and living expenses, the cost to each school of securing such specialists might prove prohibitive with their present budgets. Similar difficulties also stand in the way of exchange of instructors, even for short intensive courses, tho undoubtedly much benefit would result from such exchanges if they could be arranged.

Such considerations may perhaps render any extensive scheme of coöperative instruction impracticable at the present time; but as the schools raise their standards and undertake more specialization they will probably be forced to seek opportunities to coöperate in this way. With fewer and larger schools and more adequate budgets, it may also become possible to do many things which, under present conditions, seem impossible, however desirable in theory.

CHAPTER VI
TEXT-BOOKS

THE efficiency of library schools and other training agencies would be greatly increased by satisfactory teaching aids, particularly text-books. For the most part, the volumes which students are required to buy, such as the American Library Association *Catalog Rules*, the *Decimal Classification*, the American Library Association *List of Subject Headings*, and Kroeger's *Guide to Reference Books*, are not text-books at all but manuals of practice and reference books for the practising librarian. The library student must, of course, learn to use these tools of the trade, just as the engineering student must learn to use engineering handbooks, books of formulae, tables of logarithms, and many other aids to computation; but while familiarity with such tools, an understanding of their purpose, and some skill in their use is indispensable, an engineering school could hardly use them as text-books in courses devoted to mastering the principles of any branch of engineering.

The emphasis given here to the lack of text-books should not be construed as a recommendation that library school instruction be conducted by the text-book method, the teacher assigning "lessons" and hearing recitations. Perhaps that obsolete method, however, has as much to commend it as the extreme form of the lecture system under which the instructor attempts by the class-room lecture to give the student all the information he is supposed to need. Most of the subjects taught in the library school involve the presentation of much detailed information. In bibliographical and technical subjects, such as cataloguing and other record work, much importance attaches to the precise form in which the facts are written or printed. In many of the fundamental subjects, also, free use should be made of illustration in the way of reproduction of forms and records, photographs, plans, etc. Much of the content of the curriculum needs, like the subject of architecture, to be presented to the eye, so that ordinary lectures are a peculiarly inappropriate method. The student needs to have placed before him an unusually large amount of printed matter, much of it prepared especially for instructional purposes.

Two types of printed matter are needed, the text-book and the treatise: the first designed particularly for the student in training and the

TEXT-BOOKS 49

second more of the nature of an encyclopedic compilation of practice and procedure, methods and policies, adapted to the needs of both the beginner and the experienced library worker. From the pedagogical standpoint, virtually no text-books are available for the library schools and other training agencies. The efficiency of all types of library training agencies would be incalculably increased by well-written manuals presenting a reasonably complete exposition of the theory and practice of the various subjects, with enough concrete description and illustration to fix the principles and the main facts in the student's mind, the whole presented in such form and arrangement as to lead the student into the subject by the easiest path, and onward through its more difficult phases in the shortest time with the least effort on his part.

Every library school instructor has now to utilize some unsatisfactory substitute for the kind of teaching tools that should be available. In the hands of the skilful teacher the A. L. A. *Catalog Rules* and the *Decimal Classification* are better than no text-books at all, but without a teacher few students, however serious and capable, could make much progress with them. One of the chief difficulties that must be met and overcome in establishing the system of correspondence instruction recommended in this study is the lack of proper text-books. When such volumes do become available they will mean much to the untrained, isolated worker everywhere.

Some teachers attempt to make up for the lack of text-books by preparing reading lists of the best available material on the topic, in the form of periodical articles, reports, papers, etc. On many important subjects, however, useful literature is not only inadequate but scattered and inaccessible. The attempt to use it results in such waste of the student's time that some schools have abandoned required readings altogether.

The lack of text-books has resulted in a very extensive use of syllabi in mimeographed form, prepared by each instructor for his own courses and revised from time to time. These syllabi, containing outlines of lectures, bibliographical matter, definitions, etc., are indeed a great step forward from the time when the student learned everything by means of lectures. Important points, definitions, and much detail regarded as important were dictated to the class slowly enough to enable the student to write it out precisely in longhand. Notebooks slowly and laboriously compiled in this way the student was taught to regard as indispensable, not only for the purpose of his school work, but also for guidance in dealing with problems to be met later in his active library work — a kind of *vade mecum* or cyclopedia of library practice.

Adequate handbooks and treatises covering many phases of library administration and practice would relieve the schools of the necessity that seems now to confront them of presenting to their students a systematic and comparative description of library practice and procedure largely through lectures. The lack of a suitable professional literature of a cyclopedic nature seems to have a tendency to force the library schools to develop their lecture courses in that direction. The effort to cover the subject comprehensively and completely to the last degree tends to obscure principles and policies by the very mass of detail, and to substitute the acquisition of facts for an understanding of their significance. If accessible and authoritative treatises were available, it would be easier to put professional instruction on a higher plane: the instructor would be relieved of the feeling of responsibility for systematically presenting every detail of the subject. This would also relieve the curriculum from extreme pressure and make it possible to devote more time to accumulating information on subjects which cannot easily be worked up from printed sources whenever the need arises.

It was apparently the need for something of this kind that prompted the publication of the A. L. A. *Manual of Library Economy*. This "manual" consists of some thirty-two chapters by different authors, all but three of which have appeared as preprints, these three being still in course of preparation. Eight of these chapters deal with types of libraries, eighteen with problems of organization and administration, and six with special forms of library work. Some of these preprints are used for instructional purposes in the schools, but all of them are inadequate both as text-books and as manuals of practice. They are too brief and sketchy. A volume instead of a pamphlet should be prepared on each important subject treated.

If text-books and systematic treatises are so much needed, why are they not forthcoming? One reason is, perhaps, the comparatively small demand. The financial return does not promise to be sufficient to stimulate either their preparation or publication. The experience of the A. L. A. Publishing Board indicates, however, that such publications can be made to yield a small profit, tho of course not enough adequately to compensate the author. The preparation of such works should not have to wait upon a financial stimulus. Professional interest and service should be sufficient, and doubtless would be, save for the fact that comparatively few librarians have either the capacity or the time for authorship. In education, engineering, medicine, law, accounting, and many other professions, technical treatises and text-books multiply, regardless of slender financial returns to the authors.

We must look to the leading experts in the library profession and, above all, to the instructors in the library schools to produce an adequate and worthy professional literature. Library schools must be able to pay salaries that will secure for their instructional staffs the leaders in the profession, who not only can teach but who can contribute to library progress by producing useful and much needed publications. This will help to give the library schools the prestige in university faculties which they now lack, and will aid in drawing a better class of student to the schools.

A very important contribution could without doubt be made at this time to the improvement of instruction in library schools by a comparatively small amount of money used to stimulate the preparation of text-books and manuals adapted to instructional purposes. On the faculties of the library schools are a few men and women who have been hoping for years to have an opportunity to put into shape for publication the results of their study and experience in special fields. Teaching schedules are heavy, however, and not many library schools can afford to give their instructors sabbatical years. There should be available for a period of years a sum of money large enough to pay the salary, and perhaps an allowance for traveling expenses, of one library school instructor on leave of absence each year for the specific purpose of enabling him to complete for publication a work which, when published, will be useful to the schools and to the library profession generally. Such a prize or fellowship should be made competitive and awarded by a properly constituted committee instructed to select the person who has in hand the piece of work most needed by the schools and so near completion that it can be finished within the year. The A. L. A. Publishing Board (endowed by Mr. Carnegie) would doubtless find it profitable to publish any book written under these conditions. The stimulating effect of this would not be confined to the prize winner of the year, but would extend to all who might hope by hard work to win it in some future year and would therefore begin at once to lay their plans with that in view. The entire effect on the teaching in the library schools should be good. Such a "fellowship" might be offered for a period of five years in the beginning. Toward the end of that period it would be easy to determine whether it should be continued or modified or abandoned. If the certification board recommended in this report should be organized, that would be an ideal body to entrust with the responsibility for awarding the fellowship.

CHAPTER VII

FIELD WORK

ALL library schools supplement their class-room instruction given in the form of lectures, readings, discussions, problems, seminars, etc., by bringing students into contact in one way or another with some phase of actual library work. The methods of accomplishing this differ very considerably, but the methods are no more divergent than the terminology. The Association of American Library Schools has made some effort to standardize the terminology, with the result that "practical work," as distinguished from "practice work," is now the accepted term for describing the activities supposed to be carried on by the student under actual library conditions. In some cases this is done under the supervision of representatives of the school, while in others practical work means actual library work done altogether outside of the supervision of the school. "Practice work" thus comes to mean class practice, or the work done by the student either in preparation for or following and definitely related to the class-room exercises. In cataloguing, classification, book selection, and other courses there is ample opportunity for class practice, that is, for work not done under actual conditions but in accordance with assignments made by the instructor and later corrected or revised. "Field work" in some schools has exactly the same meaning as "practical work." In general, however, the term tends to be used to describe that part of the practical work which is done in a library other than that with which the school is connected, and frequently seems to be restricted to work in libraries at some distance from the school. But the terminology is not settled, some schools — Wisconsin, for instance — using the terms "practice," "field practice," and "practical work," interchangeably. Certain schools use the term "laboratory work," with the idea, apparently, that such a simile tends to put their field work on a more scientific basis or on a little higher plane. As a matter of fact, the class practice, such as can well be carried on apart from any actual operating library, bears to library instruction the same relation that laboratory work does to instruction in the natural sciences. Class practice is therefore as appropriately labeled "laboratory work" as is the field work.

In the course of his instruction the student should come into close contact with actual library work of many kinds. In doing this through his field work he may actually serve as a member of a library staff, or he may be present merely as an observer working out problems assigned by his instructor. If in the instructor's opinion he can carry on his observations better, can get a better insight into the problem assigned and do it in a shorter time by working as a member of a library staff, there can be no objection to that plan. But there must be many points in a professional library course at which the student can gain far more through a very short period of purposive observation than through a long period of actual service on a library staff. This will be elaborated in subsequent pages.

Every library school recognizes to some extent the desirability of supplementing its theoretical instruction by contact with or active participation in some kind of actual library work. It does not appear, however, in the published or oral statements made on behalf of the schools, that there is anywhere a very clear understanding of the underlying pedagogical principles involved. Certain schools seem to proceed upon the assumption that the class-room instruction itself may be expected to make of some of the students, at least, skilled librarians, and that the field work is designed merely to demonstrate their skill or reveal their lack of it. "It is necessary and important," says the catalogue statement of one school, " that students be brought into contact with actual library conditions and their ability tested."

Other schools proceed on the theory that field work is merely a means of clinching the class-room instruction by giving a better understanding of theory and principles and a firmer grasp on the essential facts. This view is expressed by the statement of one school that its field work is designed to give " an opportunity for the demonstration of the principles presented through class instruction." Another school bases the need of field work on both the test-of-ability and the aid-to-instruction theories. Its brief period of supervised "practice" " serves not only to test the ability of students when confronted with actual conditions, but also makes clear much of the class work."

Most of the schools give no explanation of their reason for devoting from an eighth to a quarter of the year to field work; perhaps there is no reason why they should. But several of the best schools do attempt to explain the basis for their procedure, and these explanations seem to show clearly that in so far as the program of the library schools is based on any conscious philosophy, it relies almost entirely on formal instruction. In theory field work is merely an adjunct to, or one phase of, formal instruction.

FIELD WORK

In one or two cases, however, the casual use of the word "experience" in reference to field work suggests the possibility that some of those in charge of schools may be thinking of such work as a means of acquiring skill of some kind. One school, while clinging to the idea that its "practice" work "enables the student to test the theories discussed in the class-room," actually goes on to make a fair statement of the way in which at least the beginnings of skill in library work may be acquired by supervised practice. Explaining the purpose of its field work, the Library School of the University of Wisconsin says that by means of it students "acquire poise and confidence in meeting and serving the public, and ascertain for themselves how library work reaches out to all interests in a community, and becomes a vital element in its life." This is the nearest approach that has been found in any of the printed matter issued by the library schools to a recognition of the fact that skill in the performance of any kind of library work must be wrought out by actually doing the work.

The amount of field work included in the one-year library school course would seem to have no scientifically determined basis. It actually varies in the different schools from a total of four weeks in one school to approximately twelve weeks in another, counting a week as forty hours. No better illustration can be found of the complete lack of carefully determined standards for the library school course. Some schools find that the best results can be secured by four weeks of practical work, while others find it desirable to extend the period to twelve weeks and to reduce correspondingly the amount of class instruction. It does not seem possible that both methods can be equally sound, yet it would doubtless be difficult by comparing the work of students trained under the two methods to say which is more effective. The reason for the difficulty is that so many other factors are present in the final result. Not only are the ability and previous experience of the student to be considered, but the amount and character of class-room instruction and, in the matter of the field work itself, the efficiency with which it is adapted to the needs of the particular student and the amount and character of the supervision that he receives.

The amount of field work varies greatly; but the point in the course at which it is introduced is subject to an even greater variation. The two main types are: (1) the "blocked," or full-time "practice," usually in the months of February or March, or both; and (2) an equal or larger amount scattered irregularly throughout the year or with a given number of hours per week. The first is illustrated by the library schools of the New York Public Library and of the University of Wisconsin, and the second by the University of Washington. Various combinations of these two methods, along with still other devices, are found, as the following tabular statement shows:

FIELD WORK: ITS AMOUNT AND POSITION IN LIBRARY SCHOOL CURRICULA

New York Public Library	Four weeks' "blocked practice," in February, usually in two assignments
New York State Library	Fifty hours during year in State Library and local libraries; "blocked practice" during March, outside of Albany
Pratt Institute	Throughout year; outside field work during spring vacation
Simmons College	Two weeks in March; two weeks in summer vacation between junior and senior years
Western Reserve University	One hundred hours, distributed throughout the year; eighty-one hours of "blocked" field work latter part of second semester
University of Wisconsin	Eight weeks of field work, February and March
University of Illinois	One month of field work
Los Angeles Public Library	One week in the months of November, February, and March; and the month of June
University of Washington	Six hours a week for five quarters for undergraduates; twelve hours a week for thirty weeks for graduate students
St. Louis Library School	Three hours a week throughout the year; four weeks in February
Carnegie Library, Atlanta	Three hundred sixty-six hours distributed throughout the year
Carnegie Library School, Pittsburgh	Three hundred forty-eight hours scattered throughout year, with two weeks "blocked practice" in February

The wide variation in methods followed grows partly out of theoretical and partly out of practical considerations. Those in charge of some schools believe that the results for the student are better if he is allowed

FIELD WORK

to concentrate on his class-room work for the first semester, and then to give all his time to field work for a month or two, coming back to the class-room again for the rest of the year, except for occasional observational assignments. Other schools proceed to scatter field work throughout the year on the theory that the assignments can be so correlated with class instruction that students will benefit by having their theoretical and practical work on each subject at about the same time. No effort seems to have been made to weigh the merits of these two diametrically opposed methods by careful experimentation or scientific procedure. It seems very doubtful whether it can ever be possible for any school to arrange schedules of instruction in such a manner that students will actually have their practical and theoretical work on every subject at the same time. Most schools would certainly find it quite impossible. It may also be somewhat easier in a small library to give a large amount of practical work to many students if their assignments are scattered throughout the year. Where practice students are not relied upon to supplement the regular staff, and especially in the larger libraries, "blocked practice" is doubtless more convenient. It would seem that, on the whole, the time at which the field work is given has been determined with reference to the convenience of the practice library or of the school rather than from any consideration of educational theory.

Particular enquiry was directed to the methods of making assignments for field practice. The results are disappointing. No clear-cut and well-defined objective was discovered. Among the points considered was the method of determining to what type of library and to what particular library a given student should be sent for his outside practical work, or "field" work. Shall the student be placed in the kind of work in which he is already interested, which may be taken to mean his probable future work, and perhaps the kind of work in which he already has some degree of skill? On this point two very widely divergent theories emerge. Certain schools assert that assignments are based on the needs of the student, which would necessitate placing him in a type of work in which he is not especially interested, but in which his class work shows he needs to strengthen his equipment, in order to go out with a well-rounded training and general acquaintance with professional library work. Another group of schools pursues the opposite policy and places the student for field practice in that particular type of library in which he is most interested and to which he looks forward for permanent service. The latter usually leave the choice of a library for field work to the student's own initiative; unless his choice is obviously unwise, it is approved. In a few cases an effort is made to divide the practice period and follow both methods. The earlier part of the field work would thus be devoted to strengthening some weak point, and the later to some line of work in which the student is already well equipped.

Schools that provide a large amount of "practical" work in one library—usually the one with which they are connected—and a relatively short period of "field" work in outside libraries make more or less effort to distribute the former work among all the principal types of service. Thus the Pratt Institute School of Library Science devotes to practical work in the cataloguing, circulating, and reference departments about one hundred hours each, sixty-six hours in the children's department, and twenty-one hours in the reading-room. The outside work or field work can then be chosen with reference to the student's future work, if that is known; and if not, with reference to his interests and preferences.

Still another basis of selecting a location for field work disregards both the student's needs and preferences, and strives to place him under the supervision of particular persons. This may be sound philosophy and a safe policy to follow, if superior individuals can be found who have the time to devote to practice students. Unless the standards for this personal basis of choice are very clearly defined and strictly adhered to, there is grave danger that it will do harm. It would be easy, for instance, for a school to assume that any field work must be good for its students if done under its own graduates, no matter what the type of library.

The fundamental purpose of field experience should determine the method of making assignments. If the purpose is to acquire skill, then future work and present interests should be the determining factor. If grasp of principles and better understanding of subjects taught is the purpose, then the practical work, if it cannot cover all subjects, should be selected to represent the branches in which the student has not shown proficiency. For example, if his class work in cataloguing has been weak and uncertain, he should be put into cataloguing for the field practice. If the aim is to try him out, to see whether his success in actual work is what could be anticipated from class-room work, then the type of field work does not greatly matter, and nearly everything depends on the skill of the supervisor and the kind of report made to the school officials.

FIELD WORK

Field practice in a one-year professional course as a means of acquiring skill should be left out of consideration. Grasp of principles and a clear understanding of subjects taught are the objects of class-room instruction. If only students of first-class ability and maturity are admitted to the schools and then if the instruction is of high quality, the student should be able, by the aid of systematic and detailed observation in contact with actual library work under the instructor's supervision, to get sufficient grasp of the principles of every phase of professional work. A prolonged period of field practice should not be necessary as a test of the student's general capacity. The faculty should be able, by means of class-room exercises and the so-called class practice, to gain adequate insight into the student's ability. If it cannot be acquired in this way, certainly the chances are small that it will be acquired by means of the so-called practical work.

If a long period of field practice under actual library conditions is not necessary or desirable as a part of the first year's professional instruction, neither should much time be given to it as a means of helping the student to find the type of work he desires to take up. In the first place it may be that his mind is already quite made up on that point; but even if it is not, he is very likely to find the first openings in other and quite different fields. As the "practical" or field work is usually managed, the student would not have sufficient opportunity to make an adequate experiment in all the different possible lines. Furthermore, as to the student's actual choice, the testimony of school principals seems to show that this does not after all result from the field work, but rather from his general range of interests and tastes, aided most by the impressions gained from tours of inspection to various libraries.

From the report forms furnished by the schools for the use of librarians who supervise practice work it may be inferred that one important object of the field practice is to secure information about the student which will be useful in placement. This purpose is nowhere avowed in print and is suggested only by inference in oral statements and in the report blanks alluded to. It may be an open question whether the school is justified in taking very much of the student's time to discover, if possible, some of his personal qualities which may have a part, even tho a very important part, in determining his professional success. Even if it does nothing else, the year's study must lay broad and deep the foundations of knowledge, ensure grasp of principles, impart an appreciation of the ideals of library service, and develop a professional attitude toward the work. It seems impossible to escape the conclusion that the school cannot be expected in one year to do all this and find time for the prolonged practice necessary to produce a skilled professional librarian.

And is the school justified in taking much of the student's time to gain information to be used principally for placement purposes? So long as the schools feel called upon to give so much attention to this phase of their work, undoubtedly all the information they can get about the student from the reports of supervisors of practice is valuable. But there are at least two large questions involved here: the first is whether the schools are not assuming too much responsibility for the placing of the student, especially in view of the fact that they cannot pretend to turn out skilled workers; the other point of doubt relates to the fullness and reliability of any information concerning the student's capacity and fitness for library work which is contained in reports on his field work.

Does the use of the field practice for placement purposes justify the time devoted to it? Much depends on: (1) the skill used in putting the student into an environment which will elicit the desired information about him; and (2) the skill of the supervisor in taking the student through those experiences which will furnish an adequate and reliable test of his capacities and in reporting on them. The latter requires on the part of the supervisor a full and sympathetic understanding of the aims and methods of the school, a fairly intimate acquaintance with the student's previous training and experience, and, above all, plenty of time to devote to the student under his supervision. As these conditions are seldom or never fulfilled, it becomes necessary to question the value of field practice as a means of gaining information needed for placement purposes. Still other considerations point in the same direction. Not only do the reports of supervisors fall short in quality, but they are inadequate also in point of quantity. Reports are based on brief contact with a student who is not, and cannot be, given an opportunity to take responsibility, and who, with a feeling of being on trial, does not do himself justice.

It may well be urged that the task of the school is simply and solely to give the student instruction, inspiration, and stimulus, and not to assume responsibility for any other element of his success. As it is, the schools seem to feel responsibility for (1) selecting only students who are certain to succeed; (2) giving instruction; (3) analyzing character, ability, and special aptitudes of students in order to place them successfully at the end of the year's study or remedy mistakes as soon thereafter as possible; and (4) developing a degree of skill, in several lines of library work, so that the student can enter upon the practical duties of almost any type of position offered at the close of the course. In the discussion of entrance requirements we have already expressed doubt as to the success of the selective process as now carried on. The primary and fundamental responsibility which the school cannot escape, and by which it must be judged, is its work of instruction. It probably should assume less responsibility for placement and disclaim any pretence of being able in the one-year general course to add to instruction the experience necessary to produce skilled library workers. The best thing the school can do for the student and for the library profession is to devote itself to instruction and to drop students who do not show the mental capacity to maintain a high standard. The professional library school should not permit itself to be turned aside from its main purpose to experiment with the student and plan for launching him on his professional career. It will do well to confine itself to selecting students of the highest ability and broad education, free from obvious defects of character or health, and then give them the best possible instruction, making the work of so high a grade that differences in capacity will appear in records of scholarships. The student's school record and the judgment of instructors, added to his own preferences and desires, should be the basis for recommendations to employers.

Many schools take particular pains to emphasize the fact that students are sent into libraries to work as members of the staff under *actual* library conditions. Practice work should not be *actual* library work under normal conditions. Actual library work is not carried on for the benefit of the staff or to give instruction to students. Of course an intelligent member of the staff gradually acquires information and skill in some kind of work, but that is purely incidental to a vast amount of routine work; and some very intelligent people work all their lives in a good library without getting a professional outlook. The thing to be avoided ordinarily is putting the student to work under *actual* conditions. He should not even be treated as a new member of the staff. His work must be planned and supervised, not with reference to his present or future usefulness to that organization, but solely with a view to giving him an opportunity to observe and learn at first hand as rapidly as possible everything he needs in order to possess a broad grasp of the whole range of library problems. If his work is properly organized, it is not done under actual conditions; it then closely resembles class practice in purpose and method. To treat the library school student as a member of the active staff is to exploit him, or, at best, to waste his time.

Field work carried on by the student as a member of a library staff is in most cases wasteful of his time and unsatisfactory because it does not give him an opportunity to observe minutely, critically, and comparatively all phases of the work of a completely organized library unit. It is assumed that, no matter what he is doing, he is gaining experience which will help him when he takes a position; whereas his future work may be very different, and even if it is not, it may be so unlike in detail that what he has acquired by practice may be no help at all but an actual hindrance.

Student practice is in general poorly supervised and inadequately analyzed and reported to the schools. To give the best and largest results, field work needs as competent guidance as class work. Comparatively few head librarians or heads of divisions and departments have the time, the desire, the knowledge, or the skill to supervise the student's field work. The ideal supervisor must be a real teacher, a skilled library worker, fully informed as to the other work of the school, and well acquainted with the student's attainments and needs. Such supervisors are so rare that it would seem as if the schools must needs keep the supervision of the field work pretty much in their own hands. This is quite practicable where the instructors are members of the practice library staff and can also supervise the field work. This dual function puts more responsibility on the instructor and requires more of him in the way of all-round practical ability.

If, however, field work must be supervised by some one not a member of the school staff, the school must see to it that the supervising librarian is qualified for the task, has the time to give to it, and is possessed of the essential facts about the student. Some schools pay considerable attention to this; others very little. The librarian selected to supervise a student's field work should be given a full account of his previous education and experience, his work and record in the school, his strong and weak points, etc. Certain schools do this with some degree of care. The instructor talks with the students, either as a class or individually, about their field work, and then writes more or less

FIELD WORK

fully to the outside supervisor. This is all helpful and good so far as it goes. Supervisors usually report, either by means of a blank form or by letter. The chief use made of these reports, as pointed out above, seems to be to gain information for placement purposes. They add comparatively little to what the instructors already know as to the student's ability and habits of work.

There is no doubt that the long period of field work during which classes are entirely suspended gives some relief to overworked instructional staffs. The poverty of the schools, however, should not be translated into poverty of professional equipment on the part of the student. The year's study is none too long to lay well the foundations for professional work. The curriculum is crowded and other important subjects are pressing for recognition. It is exceedingly important, therefore, that the student should not put more time than necessary into his field work, that it be so organized and supervised that he will gain from it the maximum concrete information and breadth of view and resourcefulness. If more instructors are necessary, they should be forthcoming. If a more competent director of field work is needed, school authorities should press for the necessary funds. If satisfactory supervisors of field work not connected with the school can be found, they should be paid for their services. It is not reasonable to expect librarians to devote themselves to students without compensation. The service that can be rendered by even the best student in the course of his field work in a properly conducted library is not adequate compensation for the attention that should be given to him. To try to balance the account in this way is certain to result in improper exploitation of the student. Only one school, so far as enquiry has shown, pays the outside supervisors anything for guiding the students' field work, and even in this one case the pay allowed is wholly inadequate.

One of the weakest points in the "practical" or field work is the common failure to require adequate reporting from students. Even in some of the best schools students doing field work make no reports at all or no regular reports. In some cases the instructor later discusses the work with the student; but this is evidently not a satisfactory substitute for frequent, regular, and careful written and oral reports by the student. It would seem to be self-evident that nothing should be left undone to induce the student in the field to think about what he is doing and to relate it to what he has learned in the lecture and class-room. The mere spending of a certain number of hours a day in a library for a definite period carries no assurance that the student is deriving adequate benefit from his experiences. He should not be sent to any post except for a definite purpose. He should be told what he is expected to get, and should make as definite a report as on any assignment in his course.

This would require a different system and higher standards for supervision of practice work. As a matter of fact, the field work should probably be planned by the various instructors, each one laying out a program as definitely related to the instruction given in his own courses as is the so-called class practice. This is necessary if the field work is to be regarded as a supplement or aid to instruction. Too much is now left to chance in definitely relating field work to instruction. If observation is to clinch class instruction, the two must be very closely correlated.

The time that can be devoted to supervised practical work in the course of one year's study is entirely too short to produce skilled library workers. The most important thing—the really essential thing—is to give the student during the one year as thorough a grounding as possible in the principles underlying library practice and methods. There is not enough time to give him the background of facts and principles which are essential for the highest skill and also to make it possible for him actually to acquire some degree of skill in the only way it can be acquired, namely, by doing actual library work, preferably, at least in the beginning, under the supervision of a skilled worker. The schools should not hesitate to admit that they cannot turn out skilled workers, and should attempt to give only such instruction as will make the acquisition of skill speedy and certain. With this clear understanding, the schools may properly continue to include in their one-year general course a small amount of so-called "practical" work, solely as a means of increasing the efficiency of class-room instruction, and not at all with an idea of producing skilled library workers. In the best sense, the average graduate of a one-year course in a library school is not a trained librarian; he should have had the best of instruction, but he should not be expected to have acquired special skill.

A large amount of field practice in a general professional course of one year is open to serious question on several counts. The primary purpose of the school is to lay a broad basis for skill in some type of professional work, not to develop that skill, and certainly not to impart skill in the routine processes which belong to the clerical grades of library service. The latter is a very important consideration. It is the function of the training class to give the student skill in the performance of the duties of some particular position in a particular library. The relatively small amount of instruction which accompanies the practice is not calculated to give any professional equipment, but to make the acquisition of skill in routine clerical work easier and more certain. One instructor with the aid of members of a library staff can give all the instruction required by a training class. Professional library work should be organized on a very different basis. The large part which the practical work has hitherto played in the professional course is additional evidence that no clear distinction has yet been made between professional training and clerical training.

The place for the field practice as a means of imparting skill in professional grades of library work is not in the one-year general course, but in a second year devoted to advanced study in some special field. This is the real counterpart of the extensive practice which necessarily forms a large part of the training-class work. The years immediately following the general professional course, together with a second year of specialized study, correspond to the medical student's interneship. The four-year course in medicine is not interrupted by short interneships or periods of practical work. Throughout the period of instruction, and particularly toward the end, the student is brought close to practical work by laboratory and clinic and given full opportunity for observation under the guidance of the instructor, but there is no thought of turning him loose to "practice" under the actual conditions that will confront him after he has his degree and is licensed to practice.

It will be said, of course, that a student who has not done much practice work will be a mere theorist, without practical knowledge and unable to do anything well. It is a *little* theory that is the dangerous thing. The present system of field practice does not sufficiently clinch and check up theories learned from lectures and reading, but it does seriously interfere with thorough instruction. Thorough comparative study, carried on under the supervision of competent instructors and conforming to a high standard, will be the best safeguard the school can have against turning out half-baked theorists. The present system of field work in the one-year course certainly gives no such assurance.

The proposal to do away to a large extent with the so-called practical work as a part of the first year's study does not mean that a successful library school can be conducted apart from good library facilities. On the contrary, it assumes the widest possible range of libraries and library service of high standards for observation purposes. Training-class work can be conducted in a single library, and even in a very small library; but professional training requires a wide acquaintance with library methods and organization, to be acquired only by systematic observation and reporting under the guidance of a skilled instructor. In passing, it ought to be said that a supervisor of field work should be the most experienced and practical library worker on the staff of the school, and at the same time a trained teacher. The failure to recognize the fundamental difference between professional training and the sub-professional type of training is nowhere more apparent than in the assumption that adequate professional education can be given in a small isolated library, however excellent that library may be of its kind. No worthy professional school can be conducted out of easy reach of many libraries of different types and sizes, maintaining high standards of organization and service.

An important feature of the program of several of the older and best known library schools is the annual library "visit," or tour of observation and inspection, made by the entire class and lasting a week or more. The classes of the New York State Library School, accompanied by some member of the faculty, spend about ten days visiting, in one year the leading libraries of Washington, Philadelphia, and New York and vicinity, and in the alternate year the libraries of Boston, Springfield, Worcester, and Providence. Pratt Institute, the New York Public Library, the Carnegie Library School of Pittsburgh, and the University of Illinois Library School make similar class trips each spring. Other schools, not able for one reason or another to provide for such expensive trips, seek to accomplish the same result by means of one-day visits to nearby cities, while still others are able to extend their observations no further than to libraries in their immediate locality.

There is no question that these extended trips are of very great value, if not absolutely essential, for professional training. The school authorities in every case report that students return from such trips enthusiastic about what they have seen, and enter into the class work with keener interest and greater appreciation. Students thus have an opportunity to become acquainted with different types of libraries, to appreciate the needs which give rise to them, and to observe their methods of operation. Many students have a very limited acquaintance with large library systems and the more important kinds of special libraries. On the basis of the observations made on these trips, they are sometimes able to decide definitely what line of library work they wish to enter. Another very practical end not lost sight of by the school authorities is the introduction of students to leading workers in the profession and even to prospective employers. Various other advantages accrue from these trips, in the nature of by-products, perhaps. Thus, one school finds the annual trips help to keep the school instruction abreast of library progress, while another finds that the instructor in charge of the excursion is able to acquire an intimate acquaintance with the students such as could be got in no other way.

These trips are not designed to be mere pleasure junkets. The students are held responsible in one way or another for showing definite additions to their professional knowledge and outlook. In some cases topics for report are assigned in advance to each student. Other schools organize the class into various committees, each being responsible for reports on special topics, and after their return the presentation of reports may be followed by discussion and quizzes. On the whole, the aim is very much the same as that of the so-called "practical" work—to reinforce and illustrate class instruction, to fix important facts and ideas in the student's mind, and to instil in him the habit of taking a comparative view of methods and procedure.

Some schools do not differentiate trips of inspection and observation from field work. In the University of Wisconsin there are no library visits apart from the field work, but the libraries studied are reported on in great detail, following a standardized, elaborate outline.

Schools which, because of their location or other unfavorable conditions, cannot make the class trips for observation are still able to realize a large part of their advantages by means of planned visits by individual students to libraries within easy reach. While something of the enthusiasm and inspiration which comes from the extended class trip is likely to be lost, the student stands to gain, on the other hand, by the more leisurely inspection and more detailed reports made possible.

If our conclusion as to the real object of the field work is valid, it is not participation in actual library work so much as directed and supervised observation that is to be sought. This is also the purpose of all kinds of library "visits" and inspection trips. Any course designed to provide a thorough professional training should include both the extensive observation afforded by the brief trips to other cities and the intensive observation which must be secured in local libraries. Whether the extensive or intensive observation should come first is largely a pedagogical question. Tentatively, it may be assumed that the local and intensive observation, related somewhat closely to the class instruction, should precede. With this as a background the student will go on the extended trips with seeing eyes. The outline of points to be covered in the more rapid surveys will have been fixed in his mind by his detailed comparative studies in local libraries.

CHAPTER VIII
JOINT COURSES, ACADEMIC CREDIT, DEGREES, AND ACADEMIC STATUS

A CONSIDERABLE proportion of the fifty per cent. of library school graduates who have the college degree did not take a four-year college course and then the library school course, but took both in four years, receiving college credit for the library courses. About two-thirds of the graduates of the Simmons College School of Library Science have taken the library training as a part of the general college course. In the University of Washington and the University of California the library school admits students who have completed the junior year in the undergraduate college. After spending his senior year in the library school, the student gets his bachelor's degree. In the University of Wisconsin and Western Reserve University the library schools receive a few students from the arts colleges under a joint course arrangement which enables the student to receive both degrees in four years. In some instances colleges in the same locality with the library school, tho not parts of the same institution, have arranged similar joint courses. Thus Occidental College in Los Angeles gives the A.B. degree for three years of work in the college and one in the Los Angeles Public Library School. A similar arrangement has recently been made by the Carnegie Library School with the Carnegie Institute of Technology and the University of Pittsburgh.

Graduates of any accredited library school may be permitted, in individual cases, to offer certain library courses for the bachelor's degree; but college faculties are not always willing to give full academic credit, particularly for technical courses. In the University of Illinois, for example, college credit is given for the courses in the history of libraries, reference work, and sometimes book selection. A representative of the faculty of one college which has refused to consider a joint course with the library school of the same university explained that his college had certain standards of scholarship for its own faculty which the library school did not maintain; and that since it did not attempt itself to instruct seniors and freshmen in the same classes, it did not care to credit seniors for library school work taken with a class a majority of whose members had had no college study at all. While this position may seem ultra-conservative, it is undoubtedly reasonable and exposes a real danger that the joint courses may seriously weaken the college course.

One of the fundamental viewpoints of this report is that professional library work requires a college education or its full equivalent. Three years of college study, however, are better than two, and two are better than none. In so far as the joint courses have been a means of improving the general education of library school students, they can be endorsed. Certain library schools have frankly sought to effect joint course arrangements with neighboring colleges with the hope of getting more students and raising the general level of their preparation. Even the joint course, however, should be considered a temporary expedient. Every professional library school should make definite plans to pass on to a strictly graduate basis.

The joint course plan as described above, in which three years of college work are followed by one year devoted exclusively to library school study, is to be preferred to the Simmons College plan, in which the library courses are spread throughout the four years. While comparatively little of the vocational work in Simmons is given before the junior year, it would seem much better to postpone all vocational courses until the senior year, and better still, until after the bachelor's degree has been received.

Only seven, or less than half, of the library schools recognized in this study have the power to confer degrees or are connected with degree-conferring institutions. Students in the schools which cannot confer degrees usually receive a certificate on satisfactorily completing the one-year course, and a diploma at the end of the two-year course. The degrees conferred for work in library schools are B.L.S. (Bachelor of Library Science), B.S. (Bachelor of Science), A.B. (Bachelor of Arts), B.L.E. (Bachelor of Library Economy), and M.L.S. (Master of Library Science).

A committee of the Association of American Library Schools has recently considered the subject of professional degrees for library courses. In its report it is recommended that the B.L.S. degree be recognized as the professional degree to be conferred on the completion of a course of two years of professional and technical study, for admission to which a four-year college course is required. This has been the practice in the past. The New York State Library School and the University of Illinois are the only schools that have given the B.L.S. degree (with the exception of two by Syracuse University). The B.L.E. degree formerly conferred by the University of Washington and Syracuse University as a professional first degree on the completion of one or two years of study has been dropped, as recommended by the committee. It was also recommended that the degree of M.L.S. be conferred whenever the character of work done in library schools which are on a graduate basis meets the requirements usually set for graduate work leading to a master's degree. Seven M.L.S. degrees have been conferred by the New York State Library School and one by Simmons College.

Approval of the Association is given to the general practice of conferring the degree of A.B., or B.S., either with or without the addition of "in Library Science," on the completion of one year of professional and technical study, when that year forms a part of a four-year college course, or one year of such study in addition to four years of undergraduate college work. The B.S. degree has been conferred in this way by Western Reserve University and Simmons College, and the A.B. by the University of Illinois, the University of Washington, and the University of Wisconsin.

In library schools affiliated with a municipal or state library and not organized as a part of a university, all members of the teaching staff have the rank of instructor, regardless of salary, length of service, or experience. This fact may, perhaps, have had some influence in keeping all salaries low. If different grades of teaching service were recognized, it is possible that the higher grades would command larger salaries. In schools organized as an integral part of a university, members of the faculty in most cases have the same grades and salaries as in other departments or schools. The head of the university library school usually has the rank of professor. In certain cases the rank of assistant professor is found, but with few exceptions every one on the staff, except the director, ranks as an instructor and has only the salary of an instructor.

Every existing university library school is a negligible part of the institution, often unnoticed or looked down upon by the other faculties and especially by departments in which research is emphasized. The causes for this lack of prestige seem to be the smallness of the library school, the brevity of the course, the predominance of women in both faculty and student body, the preponderance of teachers having only the rank of instructor, and the total lack of anything recognized as productive scholarship. All of these conditions are remediable and will tend to disappear as the standards of the library profession are gradually raised, increasing the size and importance of the professional schools.

CHAPTER IX
FINANCIAL AND OTHER STATISTICS

ONLY ten of the library schools were in a position to give any information in response to a request for the total amounts of their budgets for 1920–21. And of the ten schools included in the following table only two, apparently, pretend that the figures give anything more than a rough approximation of the total cost of operation. Two or three schools only have independent budgets, the others being operated as an integral part of a library or an educational institution. Probably in no case do the figures include any charge for heat, light, janitor service, etc.

LIBRARY SCHOOL BUDGETS
TOTALS FOR ALL PURPOSES AND AMOUNTS OF SALARIES AT VARIOUS PERIODS

School Number[1]	1910–11 Total	Salaries	1915–16 Total	Salaries	1920–21 Total	Salaries
1	$15,133a	$9,322a	$16,604	$11,878	$21,500	$14,885
2	7,000b	4,828b	7,500b	4,936b	19,048	15,120
3	12,602c	7,830	11,506c	7,525	15,309c	11,930
4			11,181	10,066	11,540	10,590
5	8,050	4,950	8,970	5,520	9,360	6,260
6					7,190c	4,290
7	4,764	3,976a	5,145	4,300	6,650	5,850
8				2,390	5,553d	5,895
9	4,500	2,939	4,500	2,950	4,500	3,455
10			2,050	1,410e	3,350	2,730e

a. For 1911–12.
b. Represent part of budget only; balance not segregated from library budget.
c. Approximate only—based on estimates.
d. For 1919–20.
e. Not including service of library staff.

The extreme poverty of most of the library schools is clearly revealed by this table. The sum total of the budgets of the fifteen schools probably does not exceed $150,000. The budgets for 1920–21, compared with those of ten years and five years earlier, reveal a comparatively static condition. The schools are evidently not keeping pace with the growing needs of the libraries of the country. The total budget of any one of the library schools, with the exception of three or four, does not exceed the salary of the head librarian of the public library in the larger

[1] See note 1, page 22.

cities, or the salary of the superintendent of schools in many cities of less than 100,000 population. It is small wonder, in light of the figures as to salaries of principals and leading instructors shown in the following table, that service on library school faculties does not make a strong appeal to successful and ambitious librarians and educators.

SALARIES
OF THE DIRECTORS, PRINCIPALS, AND LEADING INSTRUCTORS OF LIBRARY SCHOOLS, IN 1921

School Number[1]	Director	Principal or Vice-Director	Best Paid Instructor
1	$5,500a	$3,200	$2,000
2	b	2,500	2,000
3	4,500a	2,700	2,400
4	8,000a	3,000	2,180
5	4,000	c	2,530
6	3,000	c	1,920
7	2,550	c	2,100
8	b	2,500	2,100
9	c	3,300	2,200
10	4,400	c	3,500d
11	c	1,920	1,800
12	9,000d	2,280	1,500
13	b	c	1,800

a. Salaries thus marked are derived from more than one source — in some cases from both public and private funds.
b. Information not available.
c. No position with this title.
d. Salary as librarian of the city public library.

The Western Reserve University School is the only one that has its own endowment. The Library School of the New York Public Library and the Library School of the Carnegie Library of Atlanta receive annual grants from the Carnegie Corporation. The schools in Pratt Institute, Simmons College, and Syracuse University are supported in the same way as other departments of those institutions. In the state universities of Illinois, Washington, and California, the library school is carried in the budget of the university library. Similarly, the New York State Library School has no financial status apart from the State Library. In Wisconsin the library school is carried in the budget of the Free Library Commission. In Riverside, Los Angeles, and St. Louis, public library appropriations are used to supplement the income from tuition fees.

[1] See note 1, page 22.

Tuition fees in all the schools are very moderate, in keeping with library salaries in general. The Simmons College fee of $200 a year is the highest of any school, while the Atlanta school has no tuition fee. Tuition and other fees of twelve of the schools are shown in the following statement:

STUDENT FEES IN 1921

New York State	$100 for two years; $150 for non-residents
New York Public Library	$45 for first year for residents of New York City or those living within commuting distance; $75 for others in first year; $25 for second year
Pratt Institute	$100 a year (one-year course). $5 registration
University of Illinois	No tuition fee. $50 a year incidental fee (two-year course). $10 matriculation fee; $10 diploma fee
Simmons College	$200 a year (four-year course and one-year course)
Western Reserve University	$100 a year (one-year course). $5 registration
Carnegie Library, Atlanta	No tuition fee. $5 registration
University of Wisconsin	$50 a year (one-year course) for residents of Wisconsin; $100 for non-residents. $5 registration
Carnegie Library School, Pittsburgh	$100 a year (one-year course). $5 matriculation
Los Angeles Public Library	$50 a year (one-year course) for residents of Los Angeles County; $75 for others. $5 matriculation
St. Louis Library School	No tuition fee for residents of St. Louis; $45 a year (one-year course) for residents of Missouri outside of St. Louis; $75 for residents of other states
Syracuse University	$120 a year (two-year course). $5 matriculation; $6 university infirmary; $8 athletic fee

Light is thrown upon the question of a need for more library schools by the fact that the fifteen schools examined are being utilized to only about 60 per cent. of their total capacity. These fifteen schools reported a total maximum capacity of 612 students enrolled at one time. This includes three schools in which some students take a second year's work, so that if all the schools were filled to their capacity, the number finishing the course each year would be somewhat less than 600. The total number of students enrolled in these schools in 1920–21 was approximately 370, or 60 per cent. of their combined maximum capacity. The

LIBRARY SCHOOL STATISTICS

SHOWING MAXIMUM CAPACITY AND REGISTRATION IN 1920–21; AVERAGE INITIAL SALARIES OF GRADUATES IN 1914 AND 1921

Name of School	No. of students school could accommodate	Students enrolled in 1920–21	No. completing course in 1921	Average initial salary of graduates		
				1914	1921	Per cent. of increase
New York State	75	35	26	$922a	$1,728	87.4
Pratt Institute	30	26	24	764	1,413	84.9
University of Illinois	42	34	25b	1,200	1,585	32.1
Simmons College	60	30	18	683	1,233	80.3
University of Wisconsin	40	26	25	780	1,394	78.7
Carnegie Library School, Pittsburgh	50	27	21	720	1,320	83.3
Western Reserve University	30	22	28	1,260	1,580	25.4
New York Public Library	60	36	26	776	1,412	82.0
Library School, Atlanta	25	8	8	600	1,200	100.0
Los Angeles Public Library	30	27	25	720	1,190	65.3
University of Washington	20	12	12	780	1,200	53.8
St. Louis Library School	40	17	16	c	943	
University of California	30	30	21	c	1,250	
Riverside	30	15	15de	900	1,200	33.3
Syracuse d	50	26	14e	f	f	
Total	612	371	304			

a. For 1915.
b. Only seven of these completing the two-year course.
c. School not yet established.
d. Does not include "short course" students.
e. Approximate.
f. No report received.

estimate of maximum capacity for each school is based on the physical equipment, size of rooms, desks available, etc. In a few instances the present staff of instructors would not be adequate to care for all the students the plant would accommodate. Additional instructors or assistants to instructors, usually known as revisers, would have to be added to the staff of certain schools if they were to receive as many students as their rooms and equipment make possible.

Assuming that the existing schools are properly distributed geographically, there seems to be no reasonable doubt that the most efficient and economical way to increase the number of persons in training for professional librarianship is to fill the schools already in operation to something like their full capacity, rather than to establish new schools with meagre financial support and small enrolment.

No attempt has been made to estimate the number of new library workers with professional training that are required by libraries of all kinds each year. When it is considered that a certain proportion of the graduates of these fifteen schools enter and remain in clerical positions, for which the appropriate training is that afforded by the training class rather than by the library school, it seems altogether probable that if most of the schools were to put their work on a strictly professional basis and fill up their classes, they would be able to turn out all the librarians needed for some time to come.

In most communities the need is not for a professional library school, but for a training class designed to take graduates of the local high schools who possess the requisite personal qualifications and fit them in a comparatively short time for the various grades of clerical work that play so large a part in the operation of all libraries. No institution for professional training is likely to maintain adequate standards if it is mainly engaged in fitting residents of the same community to fill a local need.

Approximately 304 students completed in 1921 a course of one or two years in the fifteen library schools, which is about the average number of graduates of the same schools in the last few years. Reports of enrolment for the year 1921–22 indicate a considerable increase over 1920–21.

The total number of graduates of all the schools from their beginning, not including summer school and short-course students, is approximately 5000. Of this number only 276, or between 5 and 6 per cent., were men. Nearly half the schools have never had any men students

FINANCIAL AND OTHER STATISTICS

at all. Over 60 per cent. of all the men trained for library work by the library schools studied at the New York State Library School, while of the 183 men still engaged in library work 122, or 67 per cent., are graduates of that school. This is a very significant fact in view of the need for attracting more men into library work. If we are to judge by the statistics, college men prefer a school of the highest standards which comes most nearly to meeting the requirements of a professional school organized on a graduate basis.

The statistics of graduates still engaged in library work have no special significance. One would expect to find that a fairly large proportion of all the graduates of the older schools have died or taken up other work. The figures show that 62 per cent. of the graduates of all schools are still actively engaged in some kind of library work. Of all the schools established ten years or more ago, the New York Public Library School makes the best showing, with nearly 78 per cent. of all its graduates still in the ranks. The women make a better showing in this respect than the men, not only in the New York Public Library School, but also in the two other schools which have had an appreciable number of men graduates.

The rather high proportion of women graduates who marry and leave the profession seems to be matched by the greater tendency of men to take up other work, due perhaps to the wider range of opportunities open to men in administrative and other intellectual pursuits at larger salaries than have been customary in library work. Taking all the schools together, and including the most recent classes, about 22 per cent. of all women graduates have married, very few of them continuing in library work after marriage. The percentage differs materially among the different schools, being the lowest for the University of California and the highest for Simmons College. (*See table, page 78.*)

Unfavorable comment has been made at times on the seemingly large proportion of women graduates of library schools who marry. The question has been raised as to whether vocational training not utilized is a good investment either for the individual or society. A fair interpretation of the statistics presented here seems to leave little ground for criticism of library school graduates on this score. In the first place, as the figures show, men graduates drop out of the profession in about the same proportion as women. If statistics were available, it would probably be found that women trained for teaching and other professions marry in even larger proportion than those trained for librarian-

GENERAL STATISTICS OF GRADUATES OF LIBRARY SCHOOLS, 1921

Name of School	Year established	Total No. of graduates, including class of 1921	Average No. graduates per year	Men graduated No.	Men graduated % of Total	Graduates still in library work Men No.	Graduates still in library work Men %	Graduates still in library work Women No.	Graduates still in library work Women %	Women graduates who have married No.	Women graduates who have married %	Graduates having a college degree No.	Graduates having a college degree %	College graduates in class of 1921 No.	College graduates in class of 1921 %
New York State	1887	902a	27	176a	19.5	122	69.3	387	53.3	140	19.2	692	76.7	26	100.0
Pratt Institute	1890	677	22	24	3.5	16	66.6	437	66.9	145	22.2	83	12.2	8	33.3
University of Illinois	1893	671a	24	40	5.9	21	52.5	330	52.3	168	26.6	480b	71.5	5	100.0
Carnegie, Pittsburgh	1901	397	20	0	0.0	0	0.0	234	58.9	109	27.5	119	29.9	9	42.8
Simmons College	1902	429	27	0	0.0	0	0.0	263	61.3	125	29.1	429	100.0	18	100.0
Western Reserve University	1904	339	19	5	1.4	4	80.0	217	64.9	64	19.1	88	25.9	5	17.8
Carnegie Library, Atlanta	1905	150	9	0	0.0	0	0.0	89	59.3	38	25.3	6	4.0	1	12.5
University of Wisconsin	1906	424	28	6	1.4	2	33.3	275	65.7	78	18.6	155c	36.5	6	24.0
New York Public Library	1911	333	33	22	6.6	15	68.1	244	78.4	48	15.4	109	32.7	14	53.8
University of Washington	1912	113	12	1	.8	1	100.0	83	74.1	27	24.1	113	100.0	12	100.0
Los Angeles Public Library	1914	130	18	2	1.5	2	100.0	76	59.3	13	10.1	41	31.5	13	52.0
St. Louis Library School	1917	59	15	0	0.0	0	0.0	42	75.9	8	13.5	7	11.8	3	18.7
University of California	1919	40	20	0	0.0	0	0.0	37	92.5	1	2.5	40	100.0	21	100.0
Riverside (Public) Library	1913	d													
Syracuse University	1908	e													
Total		4,664		276	5.9	183	66.3	2,714	61.8	964	21.9	2,362	50.6	141	46.3

a. Approximate number of students completing at least one year's work.
b. Estimated.
c. 54 of the 155 took the joint course in the University and the Library School.
d. Data furnished inadequate.
e. No report received.

ship. It is also claimed, and with some plausibility, that library school training is excellent preparation for the duties of homemaking and the social responsibilities of married women. Certainly it would be a mistake to assume that a woman librarian who marries is lost to the cause of library progress. Not only has she in most cases given a longer or shorter period of service in return for her training, but as a responsible citizen, perhaps as a member of the board of trustees of her local library, the ex-librarian may be able to do more to improve library service than she could as an active member of a library staff.

While therefore we may conclude that library schools cannot justly be criticized on the ground that too many of their women graduates marry and are lost to the service, it may still be in order in comparing the standing of the different schools to assume that those whose graduates remain in the profession in the largest proportion have succeeded best either in the selection of students with the special qualifications needed or in imparting to them the kind of training and inspiration which holds them in the ranks of the profession.

Throughout this report stress has been laid on the view that for professional library work, as distinguished from the more mechanical, routine, or clerical aspect of the operation of libraries, a college education should be a prerequisite. Two of the best schools do require a college degree for admission, while three undertake to give both the bachelor's degree and the library school degree for a course of four years' study which combines three years of college and one year of library instruction. In several of the schools which admit high school graduates on examination, the classes have a fair proportion of college graduates. Over one-half of the 1921 class in the New York Public Library and in the Los Angeles Public Library schools entered with the college degree. The proportion of students who enter the schools with a college education is steadily increasing. It should not be difficult within a reasonable length of time to make the bachelor's degree an entrance condition for all professional library schools. Schools which are called upon to train for sub-professional grades of service will naturally continue to accept students with only a high school diploma.

Constant reference has been made to the low salaries paid to library workers. Accurate statistics of the salaries of graduates of all the library schools are not available. For five representative schools, however, complete and fairly comparable data have been secured and are shown here in graphic form. The subsequent summary table shows that

DISTRIBUTION OF SALARIES IN 1921
OF GRADUATES OF FIVE REPRESENTATIVE LIBRARY SCHOOLS

Bars indicate number of persons in each salary group

Figure 1
An Eastern School
34% of graduates receive less than $1500

Salary	Number
Under $1200	8
$1200 to $1499	81
$1500 to $1999	(longest bar, off-scale)
$2000 to $2499	29
$2500 and over	7

Figure 2
A Western School
28% of graduates receive less than $1500

Salary	Number
Up to $1200	5
$1200 to $1299	10
$1300 to $1399	5
$1400 to $1499	12
$1500 to $1599	15
$1600 to $1699	16
$1700 to $1799	6
$1800 to $1899	15
$1900 to $1999	7
$2000 to $2099	5
$2100 to $2199	8
$2200 to $2299	3
$2300 to $2399	2
$2400 to $2499	3
$2500 and over	2

Figure 4
School having a fairly typical salary distribution
47% of graduates receive less than $1500

Salary	Number
0 to $1200	34
$1200 to $1299	35
$1300 to $1399	25
$1400 to $1499	28
$1500 to $1599	38
$1600 to $1699	23
$1700 to $1799	14
$1800 to $1899	20
$1900 to $1999	10
$2000 and over	30

Figure 3
One of the Smaller Schools
50% of graduates receive not more than $1500

Salary	Number
Up to $1200	10
$1201 to $1500	27
$1501 to $1800	21
$1801 to $1900	11
$1901 and over	4

Figure 5
One of the Oldest Schools
46% of graduates receive less than $1500

Salary	Number
Up to $1200	38
$1200 to $1299	29
$1300 to $1399	30
$1400 to $1499	31
$1500 to $1599	41
$1600 to $1699	19
$1700 to $1799	13
$1800 to $1899	18
$1900 to $1999	7
$2000 to $2099	14
$2100 to $2199	7
$2200 to $2299	4
$2300 to $2399	4
$2400 to $2499	9
$2500 and over	17

FINANCIAL AND OTHER STATISTICS 81

over 40 per cent. of all the graduates of the five schools now engaged in library work earn less than $1500 a year. Only 15 per cent. receive as much as $2000, while only 3.6 per cent are holding positions that command as much as $2500 a year. These figures are all based on recent reports and include the general increases occasioned by war conditions. One of the five schools is among the oldest and largest, while none of them has sent out less than ten graduating classes. Salaries of past graduates, however, have not increased since 1914 as rapidly as the average initial salaries reported by the schools. On account of the careful attention given by the schools to the placement of their graduates, the initial salaries shown in a preceding table may be accepted as accurate.

SALARIES OF GRADUATES OF FIVE REPRESENTATIVE SCHOOLS
IN 1921

School Number[1]	No. of graduates reported on	Salaries					
		Below $1500		$2000 or more		$2500 or more	
		No.	%	No.	%	No.	%
1	257	89	34.6	36	14.0	7	2.7
2	114	32	28.1	23	20.2	2	1.8
3	73	37 a	50.0	3	4.1	0	0.0
4	257	122	47.5	30	11.7	9	3.5
5	280	128	45.7	55	19.6	17	6.1
Total	981	408	41.6	147	15.0	35	3.6

a. Includes those receiving $1500.

In 1914 the unweighted average of the initial salaries of graduates of the twelve schools reporting on this point was $842, or about $70 a month. In 1921, with fourteen schools reporting, it had risen to $1332, an increase of 58 per cent. This increase reflects the shortage of library workers during and immediately following the war period. No similar increase has taken place in library salaries generally. The figures merely show that new and inexperienced workers have been taken into library staffs at beginning salaries approaching, if not exceeding, salaries paid to experienced workers already employed who are not in a position to demand the compensation the newcomer can command.

The actual salaries paid to some 5000 library school graduates, who may be called the élite of the library workers, numbering in all prob-

[1] See note 1, page 22.

ably 15,000, suggest that perhaps library work is not a profession but rather a minor intellectual and clerical occupation. Doubt is cast by these figures on the insistent assertion that there is an acute shortage of librarians. The average increase of initial salaries from 1914 to 1921 of 58 per cent. does indeed indicate a relative shortage during that period; but present salaries do not seem to show a condition that justifies the increase in the number of library schools and of trained workers advocated by some library administrators.

Improvement in library service is more likely to result from a limitation of the product of professional library schools, accompanied by a higher standard of general and professional education, until such time as salaries paid make it economically possible for library work to compete with other professions in attracting men and women of first class ability and qualities of intellectual and community leadership. In other words, not more library schools or larger classes, but a better grade of student and higher standards of instruction are the fundamental needs in professional training for librarianship at the present time.

CHAPTER X

THE RELATION OF SALARIES TO THE IMPROVEMENT OF LIBRARY SCHOOLS

A FUNDAMENTAL cause of any shortage of trained and competent library workers is the fact that salaries paid in nearly every grade and type of library service are lower than in other lines of work requiring equal ability and education. Until recently, graduates of library schools took their first positions at an average salary of $70 a month. Changes brought about by war conditions have caused some improvement. At present graduates are being placed in their first positions at an average salary of about $1332 a year, but this is considerably less than a college graduate with one year of postgraduate study is offered in high school teaching.

The low initial salary, however, is not so great a deterrent to the capable and ambitious man or woman who finds the work otherwise attractive as the slowness of promotion, the small and uncertain salary increases, and the very meagre income which can reasonably be expected even after a long period of service. The lawyer and the physician may earn less in the first year or two after leaving the professional school than the librarian; but in the older professions a person of ability, industry, and good training is almost certain of a good income in a few years, and for those whose professional success is marked, an income many times that of the successful librarian is assured.

It is quite possible that library personnel would be improved if initial salaries were lower and ultimate salaries higher. Men and women of mediocre ability are induced to take up library work by the fair initial salaries offered and then never leave it, but remain in the ranks to be promoted slowly to the higher positions as the abler workers pass on to more lucrative and attractive occupations. In this respect library work is not unlike teaching. "The beginning salary for the teacher," says one educational authority,[1] "is sufficient to hold, sometimes permanently, the teacher who is really a failure, and the upper salary is not sufficient to hold in the profession those teachers who show the greater worth. It thus happens that the professions of law and medicine usually cast off their failures while the teaching profession often casts off its successes."

Comparatively few library positions pay over $5000, and until re-

[1] J. L. Creech, "Why do Men turn from Teaching?" *Educational Administration and Supervision*, October, 1920, v. 6, p. 391.

cently the list of those paying as much as $4000 would not have been a very long one; and this, too, for those who have spent a lifetime in the service. Such salaries as these, moreover, are paid only in administrative positions. It is not surprising, therefore, that those seeking a career have come to look upon library work with disfavor—as a field which, whatever other attractions it may offer, does not promise more than a bare subsistence.

So long as library work as a profession suffers this handicap, library schools will be obliged to give relatively short courses, admit all applicants except the obviously unfit, and be content to remain small. A university devoting its resources to vocational or professional training may well hesitate to provide training facilities for a very small group whose services are not likely to be valued as highly, on an average, as many kinds of unskilled manual labor. It is really surprising that more institutions have not abolished their library schools either on account of the small demand for graduates or because of the low salaries paid.

The Drexel Institute, in 1914, did discontinue its library school largely on the ground that the demand for its graduates was too slight and salaries were too small to justify any further expenditure on it.[1] On account of the small enrolment the per capita cost of the library school students was discovered to be the highest in any department of the Institute. From the time of its organization in 1892 to its discontinuance in 1914, 317 students were graduated (only two of them men), or an average of less than fifteen per year. Nor was there any prospect of being able to increase the enrolment materially, especially since the Institute was designed to be primarily a school for Philadelphia. For some years before 1914 the number of students had been limited to twenty, but the average number from Philadelphia was less than four per annum.

A study of the salary and employment situation in Philadelphia also suggested the discontinuance of the school. On this point Dr. Hollis Godfrey, the President of the Institute, reported as follows:

"We found in comparing the number of positions and salaries in a selected group of Philadelphia libraries, that there are one hundred and twenty holding positions in selected libraries, drawing from $216 to $600 per annum; thirty-one drawing from $600 to $720 per annum; twenty-seven drawing $900 per annum; and twelve drawing over $900. In five years all the general libraries in

[1] Since this report was completed the Drexel Institute Library School has been revived by the new President of the Institute, Dr. K. G. Matheson.

Philadelphia took direct from the Library School seven graduates. Total notices on file of vacancies in libraries of the United States for the past five years at salaries of $600 and over, were one hundred and sixty-six. It should be remembered, of course, that this employment field is for young women graduates, but it must be equally remembered that this is the record for five years. On the basis of the facts shown above, the board decided that the Library School should be given up."

The considerations which led to giving up the Drexel Institute Library School might almost equally well be used to urge the discontinuance of all library schools. Enrolment everywhere is small, per capita cost of training high, and salaries paid to graduates are uniformly lower than in any other field of work. No one, however, who has the slightest appreciation of the importance of trained library service would suggest giving up all the library schools. On the contrary, the situation points to the opposite conclusion. The schools should be strengthened in every way, enrolment multiplied, standards of fitness for library work raised, and salaries increased to a point that will lead college men and women to look upon library work as a desirable career.

Elevation of professional standards and improvement of salaries will have to go hand in hand. Neither is likely to come about until the teaching staffs of the library schools can command the best talent in the profession. They will then take a somewhat broader view of their function and be able to make their work appeal to the best type of college man and woman. Both the salary and training situations can best be attacked through some system of certification for librarians and an efficient method of accrediting training agencies. The system which seems to the writer most likely to accomplish the best results is outlined in a chapter on standardization and certification.

CHAPTER XI

THE PROFESSIONAL LIBRARY SCHOOL AND THE UNIVERSITY

A LIBRARY school conducted by a public library, primarily to supply the need for trained workers on its own staff, must necessarily labor under many serious disadvantages in endeavoring to offer a thorough professional education. In the first place, every library important enough to have its own professional school will need also to conduct a training class. The attempt to combine the two is fatal to both. But the objections to the public library professional school go much deeper. No library is organized for the purpose of providing general professional education. Its object is to furnish library service. But if it could be shown that the most practical way to secure professionally trained librarians is through the service institution, of course any more or less theoretical objection would be waived. Such, however, does not appear to be the case.

There is a fundamental contradiction in the very idea of a *professional* training to fit for service on the staff of any one institution. If the general training is actually professional in character, it cannot be molded even the slightest to the peculiar conditions of a particular institution. The only legitimate way in which a library supporting a professional school can gain a special benefit from the supply of trained workers created is by paying them as much or more than is offered by other employers. If it is prepared to do this, it can get trained workers at any time without going to the trouble and expense of conducting its own school. The trustees of at least one library which conducts a library school are said to be disappointed that so many of the graduates go to other libraries. The head of any truly professional school will endeavor to place its graduates as widely as possible and at as high salaries as possible. A fundamental conflict arises, therefore, in the conduct of a library school by a public library unless the library authorities, understanding the situation thoroughly, declare that it is their intention to use public money—appropriated for local library service—to conduct a professional library school in the interest of all libraries, and not for the special benefit of their own institution. They should be prepared to see every graduate of the school find employment elsewhere, if service in other libraries should for any reason prove more attractive.

As a matter of fact, it is not probable that any library board would undertake to conduct a library school if such schools were held up to adequate standards. The expense would be so great that they would at once see its impropriety, not only from an educational viewpoint, but also from the viewpoint of their own trusteeship and responsibility to local taxpayers. A training class for clerical workers is amply justified, even in comparatively small libraries, and under the existing standards of library schools the difference in expense of conducting a training class and a library school is so slight that a library board can readily justify the additional cost, because of the added prestige that the training class gets if it is known as a library school. When proper standards for professional schools are insisted upon, the financial burden thus put upon public libraries that have schools will lead to their abandonment, or to their seeking outside support, or to their affiliation with some of those educational institutions organized and supported for the purpose of providing professional education of whatever kind the public welfare demands. The training of professional librarians should cease to be the self-imposed task of municipal library boards and be turned over to the universities. There should be no more reason for expecting or permitting the public library of one city to train librarians for a whole state or for the whole country than for allowing the public schools of that city to use municipal revenues to train teachers for the whole state. The state would not permit the latter as a matter of educational policy; and any taxpayer would seem, on the face of it, to have a clear case against a municipal library board which uses money appropriated for public library service to support a professional library school of the type which should prevail.

Let us assume, however, that the public library is able to conduct its school by means of funds which can be legitimately used for the purpose. The question then becomes one of general educational policy and the answer is perhaps not quite so clear. If the public library can adequately support a professional library school, we need only enquire as to whether it can, for the money put into it, secure as good results as if the school were conducted under other auspices.

The question of general educational policy involves a consideration of the adequacy of the teaching staff and general facilities, the relative ease of attracting well-educated men and women as students, and the actual results attained in the long run under different types of school. Looking at the matter in the light of broad educational policy, it would seem to require a very exceptional situation in library work to justify a plan that has not proved satisfactory in the case of any other profession. Medical schools conducted as adjuncts to medical practice or hospital service have proved to be inferior and have been supplanted almost completely by schools organized within universities. The situation is similar in regard to all the other professions. In no other case does the need of an institution for professional services on a large scale justify it in attempting to assume the entire responsibility for offering professional training in that field. The school system of a large city may train its own elementary teachers, but no city attempts to train teachers specifically for its high schools or for administrative positions in educational service. Universities, state and endowed, can and do maintain colleges of education of the highest professional grade. The principles and general methods of organizing professional education are fundamentally the same for all the professions for which a higher education is commonly required. University boards and university officials are better fitted to supervise professional education for library work than are public library boards. University authorities are dealing all the time with educational problems — with problems of professional education. Their experience and breadth of view ought to give them a decided advantage over a library board whose main business is of a very different character and to whom a small library school as the sole responsibility in the field of professional education must either be treated as of little importance or become unduly burdensome.

As to the maintenance of proper standards in the teaching staff, the advantage would again seem to lie with the university school. It should be stated at once that existing library schools not connected with universities have some instructors who would take high standing on any university faculty. Final judgment, however, cannot rest on individual cases. We are approaching a time when the professional library school must be a graduate school. The regular instructors must themselves have college training, as well as special training and experience in their own fields at least equal to that required in the teaching staff of the best professional schools. Can this be realized in the public library type of school? Granted more adequate financial support, perhaps it can, but it does not seem probable. University authorities are more likely to insist on the graduate school standard than are public library authorities. Putting the members of the instructional staff on a graduate basis does not mean making all of them full-time "academic theorists";

it does mean that, in addition to the necessary first-hand knowledge of library technique and methods, they shall be possessed of the general education and personality necessary to fit them to instruct college men and women.

College men and women of the type needed in library work will not tolerate the standards of instruction found too often in existing library schools. The instructor who is wholly competent to train clerical workers may fail completely to attain the standards of professional training. The school that does not satisfy the needs of college men and women should not be allowed to rank as a professional school, for students in professional schools must be recruited from the colleges. This is an additional and very important reason for believing that the university type of school is to be preferred. In the colleges and universities are found the men and women who will later occupy positions of leadership. Many of them are looking forward to a permanently satisfactory career, the gateway to which they will naturally seek in the professional schools maintained by their own or other universities. Able college men and women are more likely to enter the library schools in universities than those in public libraries. The university school seems to offer entrance to the whole field of library work; the public library school to the public library field alone. Tho this is not necessarily the case, it must seem so to the student looking at it from the outside.

In respect to the variety of types of library work and highly developed library systems, adequate support and excellence of administration, the advantages are decidedly in favor of the public library. Merely as a laboratory, the public library is usually superior to the university library. It should be assumed, however, that any library school of professional grade will make the fullest possible use of the best laboratory facilities available. A university medical school utilizes the best hospital facilities within reach through some form of coöperation or affiliation. Naturally a university library school would do the same. A good university library school in close proximity to excellent libraries of all the principal types would offer an ideal opportunity for the best professional training.

It is true that the library school will be one of the smallest departments of a university and thus suffer some disadvantage, but it should not be much smaller, even under present conditions, than certain other and well-recognized departments. The normal distribution of students in a university with a total enrolment of 10,000 students has been estimated as follows: Arts and sciences, 2500; graduate school, 500; medicine, 200; law, 200; dentistry, 200; pharmacy, 200; various lines of engineering, 1800; agriculture, 1500; veterinary medicine, 150; commerce and business, 1200; education, 1000; journalism, 200; library science, 50; landscape architecture, 50; architecture and design, 150; music, 100.[1]

---

[1] President R. M. Hughes, of Miami University, Oxford, Ohio, in *Proceedings of North Central Association of Colleges and Secondary Schools*, 1920, pp. 78-89.

CHAPTER XII
ADVANCED OR SPECIALIZED STUDY

TO bring about a reasonable degree of efficiency in library service, adequate provision must be made for specialized training. A glance at the personnel specifications for any of the larger libraries is sufficient to show how diversified and specialized library work has now become. While library service has been growing more and more highly specialized, and will doubtless continue to do so, the training afforded by the library schools has for the most part remained general. It is approximately accurate to say that the aim of the library schools at present is to fit every student to take up any branch of library work which may offer an opening when he has finished his one-year course.

In most of the leading professions specialization in practice is promptly followed by a corresponding specialization in professional education. In engineering, for example, specialization in industry long ago forced engineering schools to provide specialized courses. Speaking of this feature of engineering education, Dr. Charles R. Mann says: "Formerly the choice lay among civil, mechanical, and mining engineering; now the selection must be made from aeronautical, agricultural, architectural, automobile, bridge, cement, ceramic, chemical, civil, construction, electrical, heating, highway, hydraulic, industrial, lighting, marine, mechanical, metallurgical, mill, mining, railway, sanitary, steam, textile, telephone, topographical engineering, and engineering administration."[1] Library work, to be sure, has not become so highly specialized as engineering—owing in part to the fact that modern library service is a comparatively recent development, and in part also, perhaps, to the fact that the library being, as a rule, a branch of the public service, has not benefited by the stimulus toward increased efficiency through specialization which comes from commercial competition.

The schools explain their failure to provide specialized training partly on the ground that there is insufficient demand for it, while librarians reply that there is a potential demand which would become actual if the schools were equipped to turn out well-trained specialists. The truth seems to lie somewhere between the two positions. Libraries have too often expected the schools to turn out in one year assistants who

---

[1] *A Study of Engineering Education*, by Charles Riborg Mann. 1918. 139 pages. Bulletin Number Eleven, the Carnegie Foundation for the Advancement of Teaching.

can readily fill any position in any kind of library. Largely for financial reasons the schools have been unable to expand their work beyond the general one-year course; but had they been able to do so, the low salaries paid even to skilled specialists in library work, together with the lack of recognized standards of fitness for special work, would have kept the number seeking special training so small that the schools would scarcely have been justified in offering specialized curricula.

A point has now been reached, however, where there is apparently sufficient demand to make it feasible to provide specialized professional training. The rapid expansion of public and private libraries, the development of many types of special library, and a keen interest at the present time in higher standards of service, put a responsibility on the professional training schools of which they are becoming aware, but which as yet they have taken no adequate steps to meet. Specialized curricula have been offered so far by accredited library schools in only two or three instances, the best examples being the courses in children's library work given by the Carnegie Library School of Pittsburgh and Western Reserve University Library School, and a course in legislative reference work by the University of Wisconsin Library School.

It might be said that a certain kind of specialization has been attained by the two-year schools — New York State and the University of Illinois. Since these two schools admit only college graduates and give a two-year course, it is possible for them to cover more thoroughly all the subjects in the curriculum. As a consequence graduates of these two schools have become especially prominent in the administrative and scholarly aspects of library work. In point of fact, however, these two-year schools do not offer specialized study. Aside from a very few elective courses in the second year, they cover in the two years essentially the same range of subjects taken up by the one-year schools. The work is naturally somewhat more thorough, certain second-year courses being properly described as "advanced," but it is nevertheless essentially accurate to say that they attempt, like the one-year schools, to prepare students equally well for all kinds of library work.

Recently the growing demand for workers with specialized training has led some of the schools to deviate slightly from their general program in the direction of specialization. Special and visiting lecturers have briefly described their specialized work; the students have inspected some of the more notable examples of special library and have even been permitted to do their field work in very specialized lines. It

ADVANCED OR SPECIALIZED STUDY

would be a misfortune, however, if either students or school authorities were to be misled into believing that this slight look into specialties constitutes specialized professional training. These lectures on special libraries and a certain amount of field work in libraries of these types are not only legitimate but quite essential features of a general professional course. Specialized training is a very different thing, and is not to be secured by listening to a few lectures followed by a brief tour of inspection. The specialist is not a beginner but an expert, a master of the history, theory, technique, and practical problems of his field.

Library school authorities very generally take the ground that no specialization is possible within the one-year course, and undoubtedly this is sound policy. Nothing less than one year's instruction is sufficient to provide a broad foundation for professional work of any kind. The primary function of every library school must be to provide this general all-round training, and it does not appear that this can be done in less than one full academic year. Two or three schools, indeed, offer a second year's work of general character, while other schools have looked forward to adding a second year of the same kind; but it has always been difficult, and seems now to be increasingly difficult, to hold students for this second year of general instruction. Apparently, fewer students still would remain for the senior year if two years' work were not required for the desired degree. Many students, moreover, would apparently be willing to forego the degree if the work of the junior year represented in itself a well-rounded introduction to library work.

The opinion of experienced library workers is very decidedly against the two-year general course. It is believed that it would be much better for the two-year schools to give in one year all the essentials of a general professional course and then offer a second year of specialized, advanced work. There has been a feeling that it is unnecessary, and even a waste of time, to spend two years acquiring the fundamental training. Students who have taken two years for the general course show no marked superiority over those who take both years in one or those who have had their training in the better one-year schools. It is probable that any difference which may be pointed out will be due to the higher educational standard for admission to the two-year schools. Statistics compiled by the University of Illinois show that 152 women students who took the second year's work are earning $89 a year more on the average than 110 women who stopped at the end of the first year. Nine men who took the two years' work are earning $619 more on the average than eight who took only one year. These figures do not prove, however, that the second year's study was worth while, even from the standpoint of earning power. The best students were probably encouraged to return for the second year and get the degree, the poorer students being allowed or persuaded to drop out at the end of one year. The surprising thing is that the difference between the earnings of the two groups is not greater.

Few well-informed librarians have any doubt that a second year of training is needed for those who look forward to responsible positions in professional library work. The opinion is very widely held, however, that while the first year of study should be general and basic, the second should be definitely and even minutely specialized in the field in which the student is to take up his work. The actual demand for a year of specialized training has now become strong enough to make it imperative for the schools to give some heed to it.

Probably the most important group for which specialized training should be provided at once are the school librarians, and particularly the high school librarians. In states that have the best educational standards the high school librarian must have the qualifications of a high school teacher—which means a college degree with special training in education and some graduate study—in addition to a certain amount of professional library training. A college education and one year's study in a library school do not give adequate preparation for high school librarianship. A second year of special preparation is coming to be essential, the course to consist of three elements: (1) special study of high school library problems, supplementing and adapting the general course; (2) special study and training in educational subjects: history of education, educational psychology, and the high school curriculum; (3) extensive field practice, consisting of quite long periods devoted to actual service in well-organized high school libraries under the close supervision and direction of able and experienced high school librarians. At the end of this second year's work the student would be much better equipped to organize and administer a high school library than he can be at the end of the second year's work in one of the two-year schools at the present time. A graduate of the full course in either the New York State or University of Illinois School has spent more time than is necessary on various subjects which are highly important for other kinds of library work but of little or no value in a high school library. He will probably have taken only a brief elective course of rather general character on school libraries and will have had a limited amount of "practice" in high school libraries. No opportunity will have been offered for the training in education which is indispensable for acceptable and efficient service as a high school librarian.

For other types of library service requiring special preparation, the present library school facilities are even less adequate than they are for the high school library. Leading librarians in the college and university group have for several years been outspoken in their criticism of the failure of the library schools to provide adequate or appropriate training for special reference and research work of a scholarly character. A prominent university librarian writes:

> "The best reference people I have met in my own experience are not library school graduates but university-trained people who have somehow gone into library work. I recognize, however, the extraordinary value of the addition to their other equipment of the training afforded by library schools, and I am always seeking persons who have had that training for our staff. In looking for people to take charge of our graduate reading rooms, however, I have given other considerations foremost place and have made a known scholarly attainment the basis of selection. I would rather have such people with an imperfect knowledge of library technique, than the best trained technician who lacks university training and some graduate study.
>
> "It seems to me that the requisite thing is some such sort of scholastic library work as was given for so many years at Göttingen by Dziatzko. Such work could be done at Harvard, Yale, Princeton, Michigan, Chicago, perhaps at Minnesota and Cornell; but I am absolutely certain that no one of the librarians or chief assistants at those institutions can find the time, under the pressure of their work as now arranged, to give such instruction."

While the demand for this type of training has not been as clearly defined as for high school work and other special fields, it would seem to call for a second year of study carefully planned with reference to the special needs of college and university libraries referred to in the statement just quoted.

The need for specialized training for library work with children has long been recognized and fairly well provided for in the Carnegie Library School and, more recently, in Western Reserve University. Under the plan of organization proposed in this report, specialized training for professional work with children would be given as a second year of library school study, consisting of some technical library courses, with much attention to literature for children, thorough courses in education, child psychology, and the relations of the library to the public school, accompanied by much field work and practice under expert supervision.

Another important branch of library service which calls for at least one full year of specialized study and training is cataloguing and classification, combined with several closely related divisions of library organization and service. Advanced courses in technical cataloguing and the principles of classification, with a large amount of field work, giving opportunity for comparative study and responsible service under skilled supervision, would afford thorough preparation for positions as chief cataloguers and senior assistants in the cataloguing and classification divisions.

Special preparation for order work could be combined with the cataloguing and classification, or with advanced training for reference work. The actual grouping of subjects for the year of specialized work in book selection, order work, cataloguing, classification, and reference will require careful consideration. Our purpose here is merely to suggest in broad outline some of the types of specialized curricula.

Courses in library administration should be provided among the first. Objection is often made to training for administrative positions on the ground that administrators are born, not made. The same can probably be said with almost equal truth of cataloguers, reference librarians, children's librarians, etc. Even the person endowed with a gift for administrative work needs a broad basis of technical knowledge and special familiarity with the problems with which he is concerned. In the general one-year course there is no opportunity to take up many subjects with which heads of libraries, large and small, must deal. Such subjects as personnel management, the general principles of organization and management, applied psychology, government, and finance should be introduced in this course. Graduate schools of business administration and experiments in training for various types of executive positions show conclusively that training for executive work is practicable.

There is abundant material for a year's work in preparation for executive positions, not only as heads of library systems large and small, but as branch librarians, chiefs of division, assistant librarians, college and university librarians, etc. It is not proposed to make executives, but to take those who have already shown some capacity for administrative functions and give them instruction and training that will help them to develop their capacity. The futility of trying to teach administration in the general course might be admitted without weakening the case for advanced training for those who have already shown some ability in that direction.

County and rural library service, which may include secretaries of library commissions, state organizers, etc., promises in the near future to call for a large number of workers with special training. The development of county library systems is already being seriously retarded by the lack of properly qualified leaders and organizers.

Some library school favorably located should develop a special course for the training of persons who are to teach library subjects not only in library schools, but in training classes, summer schools, normal schools, colleges, etc. The inadequate equipment of library school instructors has been referred to in a preceding chapter. At the present time those who find themselves called upon to teach library subjects have nowhere to look for help, but must struggle along by means of their own unguided experience. Even one short course in principles of library school teaching would greatly improve the situation. Unfortunately, the salaries paid to instructors in library schools and training schools are so low that they can scarcely be expected to spend much time or money on special training. Experience with a so-called "normal course" offered by Pratt Institute School of Library Science a decade ago is sometimes cited as evidence that there is no demand for such a course. Better salaries, however, and higher standards of qualification for teaching positions should make it possible for some school in a strategic position to develop a course of such practical value that it could be given in alternate years, if not every year.

A very large field for specialized training is afforded by the business library. While the opinion is still held in some quarters that the worker with a thorough general training can make the necessary adaptations for the business library field, it is clear from the extent to which business library subjects are being introduced in the one-year courses that considerable demand has arisen for special training. It is equally clear that it is impossible to furnish the indispensable general professional training and also any adequate special training for business library work in a one-year course. A second year of specialized work appears to offer the only satisfactory solution. Such a course should be organized as soon as possible in at least one school, and in a school so located as to offer excellent opportunity for field work and to command the services of competent instructors of wide practical experience.

A year of specialized training supplementing the general course will eventually be called for in various other special fields. Courses in public documents, with statistics and sociology, in chemistry, fine arts, technology, law, medicine, and agriculture, are among the possibilities for the immediate future. The two-year schools cannot make this radical change in the character of their second year's work a moment too soon. For the one-year schools the necessary adjustment is simpler. Those which are able to secure sufficient financial support, and are so located that they can command adequate opportunities for field work and secure the services of experienced and superior instructors, can offer specialized courses whenever there is a demand for them.

To provide the kind of specialized training proposed here, it will also be necessary in most cases for the library school to be located in the vicinity of other educational institutions whose coöperation will be indispensable. Thus, for the specialized course for high school librarians, the instruction in education and pedagogy must be sought in a teachers' college or department of education of a university. Tho not quite so necessary, it would be highly advantageous to have the coöperation of a school of education in the training of children's librarians. For business library training, college courses or, better still, courses in a school of business administration should be combined with the special instruction in library technique and the field work. A special course in library administration would require the coöperation of college or university faculties. In fact, the lines of specialized work which any library school can offer will depend very largely on the facilities in the same locality for giving instruction in subjects required in the specialized course, but which cannot be given properly by the library school itself without unreasonable expense. No advanced work should be undertaken where excellent facilities for supervised field work do not exist, or where it is difficult to secure the part-time services of superior instructors.

Advanced special work of the character here proposed should not as a rule follow immediately the first year of general study. Exception might be made in the case of mature students who have had very remarkable experience before entering the school. Exception might possibly be made also for students who have specialized to an unusual degree in the subject-matter of the proposed library specialization. It is generally agreed that the second year's work will be taken with far greater profit after the student has spent at least one year in library work. This preliminary experience gives, what there is no time for in the first year of school work, a period of actual service long enough for the student to acquire some degree of skill and long enough to enable him to decide in what branch of service he wishes to specialize. Moreover, this period of practical work between the general and special courses should serve to eliminate the less competent, for no one should be accepted for the year of specialized study who has not made a very good record in actual service.

One very important result of this actual experience will be that the student will run no great risk of fitting himself for a special line of work in which later he finds no satisfactory opening for employment. One of the strongest reasons advanced by school officials for not attempting to give specialized courses at present is that very few students know what special kinds of work will be available when they have finished their course. A student who has been in actual work for at least one year would hardly return for a second year of study without having some very definite assurance of a position awaiting him at its completion. Often he will be able to secure leave of absence from some post to which he expects to return better equipped for efficient service and promotion as a result of the additional year of study. Library administrators will gradually come to require such advanced training for all of the most important positions in the professional service. Special training should also receive recognition in certification schemes.

It seems altogether probable that advanced study of the kind and quality here proposed would at once attract enough students to make the plan practicable. Less than half of the students in the junior classes of the two-year schools return for the senior year. Fewer still would return if the junior year's work constituted in itself a complete and well-rounded course. To get a good general course, many students now feel compelled to take the senior year, tho students who leave at the end of the junior year find good positions awaiting them and usually "make good." Officials of the two-year schools fear that no students would come back for a second year's work if all were forced to spend at least one year in practical work. And this would probably be so in the case of the existing second year of a general nature. A second year of advanced study of very practical and specialized character, however, once its value is demonstrated, should draw a reasonable number of students, not only from the first year classes of the same institution, but also from the graduates of other schools.

Under present conditions the senior classes of the two-year schools are recruited almost entirely from the junior classes in the same schools. Very few graduates of the one-year schools take the senior year either at New York State or the University of Illinois. This may be due to some extent to a conviction existing in certain of the schools that in their one-year course they cover the general essentials of library training as well as the two-year schools do, and that their graduates would therefore find the second year's work largely repetition and not worth the time and expense. Apparently little effort has been made, except in the second year so far developed at the Library School of the New York Public Library, to arrange the curricula of the two-year schools so that the second year would make a special appeal to graduates of the one-year schools. Moreover, the two-year schools require college graduation for admission and this in itself necessarily excludes most of the graduates of the other schools.

When all professional schools are put on a graduate basis and the work of the first year is organized as a thoroughly well-rounded and complete general course, graduates from all the schools should naturally expect to take a second year of special training wherever accredited courses are offered in the special fields they desire to enter. Graduates from all the schools might go to Western Reserve for children's work, to the New York Public Library for a special business library course, to Wisconsin for legislative reference, to the University of California for a county library course, and so on. Several schools should offer a year of special training for high school libraries.

Courses in all of the principal special fields of library work should be offered by at least one school, and that the one best equipped to give them by reason of strong teaching staff, presence of coöperating faculties, and exceptional opportunities for field work. Probably no one school should be expected to develop courses in all the specialties, but all should be offered somewhere. In developing its proper specialties each school will naturally be guided largely by its own local demand. The pressure of this local demand, on the other hand, should not be permitted to force specialization too far into the year of general professional instruction.

Such courses need not be given every year, if the number seeking them does not warrant it. They might well be offered only every third year.

ADVANCED OR SPECIALIZED STUDY 101

If definitely announced and made known to all potential applicants, those who desire a special course could make their plans one, two, or even three years ahead, and arrange for leave of absence from their posts. It might be found practicable and desirable to plan all second-year courses so that they could be taken one-half at a time.

The number of students enrolling for this type of specialized training would not usually be large enough to require formal lecture courses by the library school faculty. The instruction in library subjects would therefore be given largely by readings, problems, discussions, and individual conferences with the instructors in charge. Instruction in related subjects would ordinarily be given through the regular courses in coöperating institutions. Field work should occupy a large part of the student's time and be very carefully planned and supervised by practical experts in the special field. As in the general course, the field work should include a large amount of planned observation and reporting; but unlike the method recommended for the general course, it should also include much actual work carried on under the direction and criticism of a competent expert. In a course of this kind, the acquisition of skill is a definite objective. While skill in any kind of library work is not to be expected or sought as a primary result of the first year's study, a high degree of skill in the chosen work must be the main objective of the year of specialized training.

If organized on some such plan as here suggested, the cost of specialized training for library service, while greater perhaps than for the general work, should not be excessive. The task of organizing and directing the work would rest on the principal or some competent member of the school staff, but would not require the full time of one person until the number of courses offered and the enrolment reached considerable proportions. The specialists giving the instruction in library subjects and directing the field work should be properly compensated for their service; otherwise it will not, as a rule, be efficient. Instruction given by coöperating institutions would not entail great expense for the library school. The ordinary fees for such courses would have to be added to the library school fee, or the regular library school fees shared with the coöperating institution.

On any other plan of operation the expense of a year of first-class specialized training is now prohibitive and will indeed remain prohibitive for a long time to come. Elaborate plans have been proposed for a post-graduate library school with a full corps of well-paid instructors and an expensive physical equipment. Eventually it may be desirable to develop a school of this character. It is clear, however, that the next step must be worked out at a minimum expense by utilizing fully the resources of the stronger professional schools in coöperation with other educational institutions in the same vicinity, using the services of competent specialists on the part-time plan and effecting a more thorough utilization of opportunities for field work.

It is possible that some specialized training of the character described above could be given *in absentia* by an institution properly equipped for it. Such study might not be acceptable for a degree, but might, if properly safeguarded, receive some recognition in a certification system. The subject of training in service by correspondence methods is discussed in a later chapter.

CHAPTER XIII

PLACEMENT OF LIBRARY SCHOOL GRADUATES

LIBRARY schools undertake not only to select and train those who are to become our professional librarians but they also serve their students and graduates, as well as library boards and administrators, in the capacity of employment agencies. Almost every library school regards this phase of its work as of great importance — so important that the active head of the institution usually gives it his personal attention and in not a few cases appears to give it a considerable part of his time, particularly at certain seasons of the year. While in their published statements the schools usually disclaim responsibility for placing their graduates, they nevertheless feel that responsibility keenly.

It is commonly estimated that from 90 to 95 per cent. of the graduates are placed initially by school officers. In the last three or four years, however, there has been no difficulty in finding places either for members of the graduating class or for older graduates. Much effort, on the other hand, has been expended by the schools in trying to find among their graduates persons capable of filling the available positions.

Most of the schools keep in very close touch with their graduates and former students. Through correspondence, regular reports, and various other means principals usually know pretty nearly what salary each one is receiving and whether he is contented or desirous of making a change. All this involves considerable correspondence and, especially in the case of the older schools, a large amount of such record work as any efficient employment agency requires.

Several factors have apparently contributed toward making the placement function so prominent in the conduct of all library schools, particularly of the older ones. In the first place, there has been no other agency to which employers could look for library workers. Commercial agencies have not developed as they have for teachers. Little use has been made of advertising in professional journals, and in any case that method has very decided limitations. An unwritten but rather widely observed code of professional ethics forbids one library to "steal" employees from another. That is to say, subordinate members of a library staff often have only such opportunities to move to another library as the head librarian approves. To a certain extent the library schools bow to this code, yet in the interest of their graduates who are in danger of getting "pocketed," they do not hesitate to open the doors of opportunity for promotion to better positions. Library administrators generally turn to the schools when seeking assistants. Practically speaking, they have been the only source of information about professionally trained workers. Even those librarians who have been most skeptical of the value of library school training turn regularly to the schools for aid in recruiting their staffs.

The very success of the schools as general employment agencies and counselors for their graduates has resulted in a certain prejudice on the part of not a few library administrators against employing the library school product. No sooner has the school-trained assistant learned his duties, they say, and become fairly efficient, than his school finds another position for him at an increased salary. To employ library school graduates, therefore, is to have a constant succession of beginners. For this reason they prefer to train their own assistants and enjoy some assurance of being able to retain them after they have become proficient.

The proper answer of the library school to this indictment is of course evident. Any library can retain a competent assistant by paying him what he is worth. Certainly, library salaries do not indicate that there has been any objectionable "profiteering." School officials, however, are conscious of the criticism they incur in paving the way to promotion for their graduates, and try to keep in mind the interests of employers as well as of their students. It is quite common for school principals to discourage their graduates from changing positions oftener than every two years.

The library schools have also been in a position to give good service as employment agencies because of the intimate knowledge they possess of their graduates. Useful information has been assembled in the first instance in the process of selecting candidates for admission. Classes in all the schools are so small that the principal and members of the faculty come to know each student somewhat intimately and are able to follow his professional career. They are therefore in a position to supplement the school records by personal knowledge of the special capacities and defects of each graduate, and are thus able to make recommendations with a high degree of intelligence and discrimination.

The lack of any generally recognized standards and tests of professional fitness tends to put the employment of library assistants on the sole basis of personal choice, and thus the recommendation of the library school principal is naturally sought. The placement function of the library schools would be much less conspicuous if public library staffs were more generally recruited by civil service methods in which examinations, records of experience, and various practical tests formed the gateway to competitive appointment. As library employees, however, are generally the personal choice of the librarian or the choice of the library board, great dependence—perhaps undue dependence—comes to be placed on the recommendation of the library school. The school, indeed, is sometimes looked upon as a substitute for the state and municipal civil service machinery through which other positions in the public service are usually filled. We cannot discuss here the interesting problem of the soundness of the principle of combining in one agency the functions of training for a technical branch of the public service and the testing and approving of that training as a basis for appointment to office.

It is perhaps a cause for regret that conditions in the library field have made the library schools almost the sole form of employment agency. The primary function of a library school is not, of course, to find or fill positions, but to fit its students for a high type of professional service. Not a few librarians, however, who lack library school training and fail to appreciate its value, are tempted to look upon the school as an expensive kind of employment agency. A group of non-school librarians has recently organized a Library Workers' Association with the avowed and primary purpose of providing for its members an employment service, which is designed to open up to them avenues of professional advancement now enjoyed only by the protégés of the library schools. Unfortunately, many of these non-school library workers seem to believe that their chief handicap is not a lack of professional training, but the lack of an *alma mater* ever watchful for opportunities to promote the personal and professional interests of her sons and daughters.

It would be unfair to leave the impression that library schools are unique in the attention they give to the placement of their graduates. Certain teacher training institutions have acquired a wide reputation for success in putting their graduates into important administrative positions in the public schools. It may not be out of place, however, to suggest that the library schools need to be on their guard against an excess of zeal in this entirely legitimate activity. A safe policy to follow is that set forth in the following statement from the head of one of the best of the schools:

"We do not initiate the correspondence in respect to a vacancy. Our regular practice is to answer those letters that come to us asking for candidates, by recommending one or two or three of our students who appear to us to be qualified to fill the position, and in most instances our correspondence ends with that letter, unless the librarian, or library board member, or student, writes for further information. To probably 15 or 20 per cent of the requests during the past year we have replied that we had no one to recommend, though most of the time one or two of our former students were on our lists as needing places. We try not to recommend people unless they fit into the particular place for which we are asked to suggest candidates. Two or three times during the past year I have recommended librarians who never had any connection with this school because I thought they were better prepared for the job than any of our own students who were available."

The latter part of this statement refers to a criticism frequently directed at the library schools for an alleged tendency to recommend one of their own graduates and vigorously push his candidacy even tho he is not especially qualified for the post, which might be better filled by some one whose school has not heard of the vacancy or is less aggressive in its placement policy. It would doubtless be easy to exaggerate the extent of undesirable practices of this sort. Library boards and library administrators, also, must share some of the blame, because they open the way for such abuses by their uncritical and indiscriminating use of recommendations.

It has long been hoped that the American Library Association might develop an employment service for employers and trained and untrained employees, and relieve the library schools to a large extent of this somewhat burdensome function. The prospect is not bright, however, for an efficient central agency. The American Library Association is without funds to organize it properly, even assuming that it might later become self-supporting. It is questionable also whether the country is not too large to be served by a single centralized employment office.

The projected national certification system with its regional agencies, discussed fully in a later chapter, would seem to go far toward solving the problem of securing full and dependable information about all professional librarians. Even if it should not be practicable for the certification board itself to provide an employment service, its coöperation might ensure the success of a service conducted in the office of the American Library Association.

CHAPTER XIV
RECRUITING FOR THE LIBRARY PROFESSION

IT is a matter of no little urgency that professional library work be disentangled forthwith from the skilful use of hands in the mechanical operations that play so large a rôle in every active and useful library. Until this is done, library work will not make a strong appeal to the better type of college man and woman. The almost complete absence of men in library school classes is not to be explained solely by the fact that salaries are low and on the assumption that college men are all looking primarily for opportunities to make money. Largely because it is generally looked upon as clerical, library work has come to be known as "women's work." Men generally, and women to a large extent, do not think of it as offering a desirable professional career. The so-called "recruiting problem," brought about by the acute shortage of competent library workers, will not be solved until library service does offer to well-educated men and women as desirable a career as other learned professions.

The library schools have heretofore assumed too large a share of the responsibility for recruiting library workers. Part of this error has doubtless been due to their deep professional interest, but in part also, no doubt, to the necessity for keeping their classes filled, since an important share of the income of nearly all the schools is derived from student fees. The willingness of the schools to serve as the chief recruiting agents should not be allowed to obscure the fact that the responsibility for keeping up the supply of competent workers rests upon the profession at large. Not only is it somewhat undignified for the schools to be pressing upon college men and women the desirability of taking up library work, but they are not in a position to do it effectively. They are, in the first place, open to the suspicion of "drumming up trade." Moreover, library school instructors are seldom forceful and convincing speakers. Most of them are women, which tends to confirm the impression that library work is a feminine vocation; many of them are not college trained, and for that reason cannot meet the college student on his own level; and most important of all, the picture of library work given by library school instructors tends to be theoretical: they do not always speak as active participants in the many interesting and worth while types of library service. College and university officials have referred to the harm done to the recruiting cause by the representatives sometimes sent out by the library schools.

In choosing their occupation young people probably are influenced more by what they see than by what they are told about any vocation. What they ordinarily see in the life of any library worker does not tend to magnify the importance of the work in their minds. This is particularly true of the staff of the college library, which is likely to be the only library the college student knows anything at all about. In too many cases the college librarian is an overworked, underpaid individual, ranking socially and academically below the teaching staff, and in no sense a subject for emulation by the ambitious student. Even where the head librarian's position is not inferior to that of the teacher, the rank and file of the library staff do not occupy an enviable status. Even at its best the college library represents a special type of library work of limited appeal. From it the student would get little idea of the human interest and opportunities for public service inherent in public and other kinds of library work. Unfortunately, the usual vocational advisers of college students are not in a position to overcome this natural handicap suffered by library work. Deans and professors themselves are often ignorant of the rich opportunity for service in the library field; they are much better equipped to discuss with students the opportunities in law, medicine, engineering, and other professions, and even in business.

Having in mind this problem of bringing into the schools a somewhat higher grade and a larger number of students, the library school principals were asked what their observation showed to be the chief factor in bringing students to the school. Almost without exception the answer was, "Our own graduates." Sometimes mere proximity, the reputation of the library system used for practice work, the friends of the teachers, etc., determine which school is selected.

In the writer's judgment, the organization and curriculum of the library schools should be modified to any extent that may be necessary to make them the gateways to professional library work for college men and women. The circularizing of college students and the sending of speakers to talk to students will effect little. In the qualifications of the teaching staff, the content of the curriculum, and the methods of teaching, the schools must be brought to the level of graduate schools. More and more, too, it will probably be found that library schools run by public libraries will not attract the best college students. As pointed out elsewhere, the place for the professional library school is in the university which is so located as to command adequate opportunities for field work. Large public libraries will continue to maintain training classes for the sub-professional grades of the service. When professional education of librarians has gone where all other professional education is going—to the university—a long step will have been taken toward a solution of the recruiting problem.

Library schools lack altogether the aid which may be derived from scholarships and fellowships in stimulating the interest of desirable candidates for admission. In some schools tuition is free or merely nominal. As a rule, however, the tuition fee is a substantial amount. If these schools had the funds to provide a few scholarships, to be awarded on the basis of merit in such a way as to help bring into the classes promising men and women who would not otherwise train for library work, the result would be very beneficial.

In addition to scholarships to cover tuition fees, it is the general opinion of the library school officials that great benefits would be derived from a few scholarships or fellowships which would cover not only tuition fees but most of the other necessary expenses of a year's resident study in a professional library school. Library schools connected with the universities especially feel the need of such aid to enable them to compete with graduate schools, which draw some of the best students into teaching and other lines of work by offering inducements of this kind.

Most of the older schools have small loan funds provided by the alumni for the use of needy students. These funds seem to be wisely administered and very useful. They are comparatively small, however, and the loans that can be made seldom cover more than tuition fees. As the money borrowed is always paid back, such funds increase slowly.

In most schools there is little or no opportunity for needy students to meet a part of their expenses by paid labor of any kind. School work is definitely planned to occupy all their time and they are discouraged from making an effort to earn anything during the school year. Two or three schools, however, do permit students to take half-time work or less, thus completing a year's study in two years or more while serving on some library staff, usually that of the library with which the school is connected. In general this practice is looked upon with disfavor, tho it is difficult to see why there should be any objection to it if it enables capable workers to secure professional training who would otherwise have to forego it.

CHAPTER XV
TRAINING IN SERVICE

TOO little attention has been paid among librarians to the possibilities of professional improvement of workers while in service. In this respect perhaps less has been done in the larger than in the smaller public libraries. The assumption has become firmly fixed that there are only two ways for an individual to reach the upper ranks of the profession—through the traditional type of library school and through the tedious process of learning by experience. Even for the graduate of the library school there is a noticeable lack both of incentive and opportunity for continued intellectual and professional growth and improvement. To some extent this could be corrected by the development of specialized, advanced work in library schools. Little can be expected, however, from merely offering the opportunity unless at the same time sufficient incentive is created.

The main reason for lack of incentive is the failure on the part of libraries to adopt a properly graded scheme of service with definite standards of educational and professional attainments for each grade. It has not been made sufficiently clear that mere length of service does not fit one for the higher and more responsible positions. Very few libraries have any kind of system of efficiency ratings, and it is safe to say that not one has developed a rating system comparable to those commonly used for grading teachers. The narrow salary limits and very small increments also place too slight a premium on superior ability and success. Whether the library worker enters the service without preliminary training or through the library school, after he is once in the system conditions are not such as to make him feel that his advancement requires continued systematic study and growing efficiency. To some extent the lack of standards of personal qualifications on the part of library workers rests back upon the lack of standards for the service which a community should expect of the library as a whole. Only a few progressive libraries have made a beginning in the work of standardization and classification of personnel. The system of certification advocated in this report should be a very great aid in supplying the stimulus to improvement in service which is now generally wanting.

One of the main objects of the state library commissions has been to provide a little much needed training for untrained and too often uneducated persons actually in charge of small public libraries. In fulfilling this function use has been made of traveling representatives, often called "organizers"; library institutes, modeled to some extent on teachers' institutes; and summer schools. In regard to the work of organizers as a means of giving training in service, little need be said. While under any properly organized state system of libraries inspectors are needed to visit the libraries frequently and offer suggestions and criticisms, it would be financially impossible at present to assign organizers to all libraries having an untrained librarian for a long enough period to make the instruction effective. If the untrained librarian had the proper education and cultural background, an adequate staff of organizers might do effective work; or if advantage could be taken of a well-organized system of correspondence instruction, the visits of the state organizer might become more fruitful.

The organizer working single-handed with the individual librarian can do so little that a system of local institutes and round tables has developed in some states. The general method and purpose of the institute and round table are well stated by Miss Plummer, who says:[1]

"The institute was tried first and consisted of two or three meetings at some town or village containing a library. One of the meetings was usually open to the public and intended to arouse public interest in the welfare and development of the local library. Librarians from neighboring towns and villages were invited, papers were read, discussions encouraged, and a question box was a usual feature. Usually an official of the library commission, of the state library, or of the state association had charge; the local librarian was chairman of a committee on local arrangements, and a number of trained or experienced librarians assisted with the program. The chief value of the institute was a method of propaganda rather than of instruction, since the best effect was usually through the public session and the making of professional acquaintances outside the meetings. The librarians most in need of help often felt timid and constrained in the meetings and got most of their practical assistance from the individual conversations between sessions. These facts pointed the way to the round table. This is a gathering of librarians living in towns and villages not far apart to whom is sent at their request some one capable of giving help in their daily problems and difficulties. At least two sessions are held at one of the libraries concerned, and attention is concentrated on the immediate expressed needs of these libraries. It is much easier to se-

[1] *Training for Librarianship*, by Mary W. Plummer, revised by Frank K. Walter, Chicago, A. L. A. Publishing Board, 1920.

cure such expression under these circumstances than in the institute meetings. The older type of institute has largely given way to the round table, under whatever name it may be conducted. In New York state a definite state program for the institutes is planned and the state divided into definite districts where the general program is given. At the same time a large force of volunteer conductors insures so much latitude in the form of the meeting and the treatment of the subject as to make each meeting practically local in its application. In states with library commissions the regular conduct of round tables is a common, recognized duty of the state organizer."

The need of the institute and round table to remove some of the handicaps of the untrained librarian will pass with the coming of county libraries and a trained service, to be brought about by certification and higher standards. Professional conferences — local, state, and national — will necessarily continue to have a very large usefulness for the interchange of ideas and information and the fostering of professional interests and ideals. Untrained library workers as a rule do not attend professional meetings. With the elimination of the untrained worker and the consequent improvement in service and salaries, professional organizations will increase in strength and power for service. These organizations can do and have done much good, but their activities have been narrowly limited by the lack of financial resources. All such organizations depend almost entirely on the dues of individual members, which must be kept very low to correspond with library salaries. Libraries, being supported almost entirely by public or institutional funds, cannot well contribute financially to the support of the activities of professional library organizations, however important the work they may be able to do. The most that public libraries can do is to grant their employees, without loss of pay, the time required to visit other libraries, attend professional conferences, and do a reasonable amount of professional committee work. The possible activities of professional library organizations, whether local, state, or national, offer a fruitful opportunity for private philanthropy. A comparatively small amount of money supplementary to the contributions which library workers generally make from their own meagre salaries would accomplish large results in strengthening and supplementing the labor of love which librarians are everywhere giving to their organized efforts.

Training in service in most of its phases is of the nature of a makeshift, a substitute for something better which, for the time being, is impossible or impracticable. The agencies and methods employed necessarily change with the conditions which give rise to them. This is true not only of the types of training just referred to, but also of the best known and most commonly used agencies: the summer school, the training class, and apprentice instruction. One method of training in service, of which virtually no use has yet been made, is so promising for the future that it will be discussed fully in the following chapter.

CHAPTER XVI
CORRESPONDENCE INSTRUCTION

NOTHING better illustrates the general backwardness in the development of library service and technical training for it than the almost complete failure to make use of the correspondence method of instruction. Commercial correspondence schools long since proved the feasibility of such instruction. It was then adopted and improved by great endowed and state-supported institutions, and has now developed to an extent unrealized by those who have not had occasion to follow educational developments rather closely.

The United States Bureau of Education reports correspondence work conducted by 73 non-commercial institutions in 39 states and the District of Columbia, 61 of these being state supported and 12 privately endowed. Both the commercial and non-commercial schools offer correspondence instruction in a great variety of vocational subjects, tho with some minor exceptions nothing has appeared for library work. In view of the great dearth of trained workers this is all the more surprising and calls for some explanation.

Apparently the principal reasons for this condition are general unprogressiveness, which may be regarded as either a cause or a result of low salaries; an attitude of prejudice or suspicion toward correspondence study; and a lack of standards in library service and of incentives to increased efficiency. The difference between what a library assistant can earn with and without the kind of instruction and training that would be possible by correspondence has been too slight to bring the commercial school into the field. The endowed institution also has not taken it up because of the comparatively small demand. The lack of demand in turn can be traced in part to the general absence of graded systems of service in which promotion is based on competitive tests of skill and efficiency, and in part, perhaps, to an attitude of prejudice toward correspondence study on the part of librarians. Librarians are essentially conservative. Long overworked and underpaid, submerged in routine duties and free from a strong public demand for efficiency, librarians as a whole have not themselves been innovators.

It is not necessary here to describe the methods or set forth the possibilities and advantages of correspondence study. This has already been so well done that we need only cite the conclusions of competent investigators to prove the desirability of making some attempt to apply correspondence instruction to the library field. In the conclusion of his report on "Correspondence Study in Universities and Colleges," Dr. Arthur J. Klein says:

"Inexpensive methods of quickly reproducing written material in considerable quantity have, in combination with cheap and rapid mail service, enabled correspondence teaching to be carried on extensively and effectively. But more important than these external devices are the pioneer study and practice of the method by the proprietary correspondence schools and the universities and colleges supported by public funds. Their work has developed the technique of the method and shown the extent and effectiveness of the service that can be rendered. The experimental state in the development of the general method has now been passed and the results obtained are now available to serve as a basis for the application of the method upon a more extensive and serviceable scale."

As to the general method of correspondence study, Dr. Klein says:

"The essential characteristic of correspondence study is not the fact that it is instruction by mail; that is in many cases merely incidental. The correspondence method has been tried in resident instruction with results which indicate that the ordinary methods of class instruction may in some degree be displaced profitably by further application of the correspondence method. Indeed, the correspondence method has always been used in resident instruction in certain subjects and in many cases no other method is possible. English composition, for instance, cannot be taught in any other way than by correspondence-study methods.

"It is not, then the intervention of the postal system which gives to correspondence study its virtue. The method of instruction is the essential thing. It may or may not be applied through the mails. The chief characteristics of the method are constant efforts by the student and correction by the teacher. As ordinarily applied in correspondence study, the method consists of the assignment by the instructor of definitely planned work, the writing out by the student of the results of his work, the correction and criticism by the instructor of the written lessons, and the suggestion and assistance upon points where the student needs such special help. The student is tested on the whole of every lesson. He not only recites the entire lesson, but reduces it to writing, so that any error may be detected and corrected. The criticism by the instructor is also clearly and definitely written. No slipshod or evasive work, no bluffing is possible for student or for instructor. The hard grind which such methods require from students is such an ever-present fact, so much a part of correspondence study and so seldom found in class work, that this method of working is more truly than postal transmission the essential feature of correspondence study."

In view of the extensive use now being made of correspondence instruction in vocational subjects, the heads of library schools and many librarians were asked to state what subjects taught in library schools could not also be taught by correspondence, what difficulties would be encountered, and whether they would be in favor of having such instruction tried out under proper conditions. No one was found willing to assert that there is any subject in the curriculum which cannot be taught by correspondence, provided the student has access to books. Organized collections of books are indeed the indispensable laboratory for much of the instruction in library methods and problems. Some study of value could doubtless be carried on with the aid of comparatively few books, and provision might even be made by the teaching institutions for lending these. In few, if any, of the library school courses is class discussion an indispensable element. Tho of unquestioned value, the advantages of class-room work are likely to be largely or wholly offset by specific advantages of the correspondence method.

Some of the difficulties assumed by librarians to be inherent in correspondence instruction merely reflect a lack of familiarity with what has already been accomplished in perfecting the methods used. Other difficulties are real and would have to be faced and solved. The very serious need for text-books and teaching material in the library schools has been pointed out in a preceding chapter. Successful correspondence instruction would necessitate some attention to the pedagogy of the subjects taught and would require the preparation of text-books and other teaching material. This difficulty, however, instead of being an argument against correspondence instruction is really an argument in its favor. Instruction in library schools and training classes would be greatly benefited by the improved methods and tools which would have to be produced for correspondence study.

The difficulty of providing satisfactory opportunity for field work for correspondence students is referred to, but this objection seems to arise in part from a failure to appreciate the conditions under which correspondence study would ordinarily be undertaken. Students would usually be actually engaged in library work; if found desirable, enrolment could be limited to those so engaged. This would give a skilful instructor ample opportunity to see that the student relates his study to his work. In certain courses opportunities for field work and observation might be limited for the person employed in a small, isolated library. But so are they limited, and very narrowly limited, for students in several of the existing library schools. If there were any courses in which the student could derive no profit from the kind of field work available to him, he could be refused enrolment. For the student who is aiming to cover the whole ground of a full professional training, such courses could be reserved for the brief period of resident study which it would probably be desirable to require for any professional certificate or academic credit.

In libraries everywhere, large and small, workers are to be found who lack technical training and are unable, for financial or other reasons, to leave their work and attend a library school. Training classes and summer schools will not meet their need, even assuming that those are within their reach. With the proper encouragement from library boards and administrators, workers of this kind might enroll for correspondence study in large numbers and derive great benefit from it. For some the benefit would take the form of a broadening of vision so as to include other phases of work than that in which they are actually engaged; for others the benefit would lie in a deeper knowledge of the principles and technique of their own particular work. For workers of ability and broad education, correspondence study might very well be made an acceptable substitute for library school training.

It is indeed the possibility of substituting correspondence study for a library school course that constitutes the objection which some school authorities make to it. They fear that standards of training and service will be lowered. Experience in other fields does not seem to lend support to this fear. The popular prejudice against correspondence study would likely be sufficient to prevent the person with that training from displacing one with better, or even inferior, training acquired in a library school. In other words, a person who has acquired his training through a correspondence course would necessarily have to possess a better equipment than a library school graduate to get the same recognition. It is to be expected also that the best of those who attempt to get some instruction by correspondence will sooner or later find a way to take some resident study. A well-managed correspondence course is likely to pick out and bring into the schools persons well adapted for library work who might otherwise not get to the library school at all.

In so far as correspondence study aids those already in service to be more efficient, it would also tend to raise rather than lower standards. The institution conducting correspondence instruction could exercise any desired amount of control by requiring high standards of preliminary education and fitness, particularly from those who wish their study to count toward a professional certificate or school certificate or diploma. It is not apparent that instruction of a high grade given by correspondence is in any greater danger of lowering standards than are summer schools, short courses, institutes, etc. This also disposes of another difficulty foreseen by some in the alleged inability to choose students with sufficient care. It is believed that the correspondence institution could select its students as carefully and efficiently as any other. However, unless very serious dangers actually appear, it would seem wise to put the instruction in many courses at the disposal of all applicants who show that they can do the work successfully. The proposed system of national certification would prevent the wholly unfit from masquerading under false pretences.

The principals of library schools without exception have expressed a desire to see correspondence instruction in library subjects tried, if it can be done under proper conditions. None of the schools is in a position at present to furnish these proper conditions. In the first place, none of them has the financial resources to undertake new activities. Correspondence instruction, if attempted, should be by the best obtainable teachers—those who are specially qualified for the task and who would enter upon it with enthusiasm. They should also be well paid for their work. Such instruction could not succeed if expected to be self-supporting. No worthy professional education of any kind can be wholly supported from students' fees. Library schools are all endowed or subsidized or supported by public appropriations. Correspondence students should be required to pay substantial fees, but a large part of the cost of instruction should be met from some other source. To ensure the highest degree of economy and efficiency, correspondence instruction should be offered, for the present at all events, by only one institution, and that one selected or created with a view to furnishing the most favorable conditions possible.

Actual experience in teaching library subjects by correspondence is too limited to be of real significance, yet the little experience that can be cited does, on the whole, confirm the conclusion reached on other grounds that this method has large possibilities and should be given a fair trial. The University of Chicago has for many years offered through its correspondence study department a course of twenty-four lessons on "Technical Methods of Library Science," designed to furnish an elementary training in practical library work for those who are unable to attend a library school. While the announcements state that students should have as preparation for the course at least two years of college education or its equivalent, students are accepted who have only a high school course. The tuition and matriculation fees amount to $24, or $1 a lesson. The books required cost $10 or $12 more. At present the average enrolment is about fifteen active students. Most of these are engaged in some kind of library work, some of them being teachers who have to care for school libraries. The instructor in charge of the course states that many of the students get a great deal out of it, short as it is, and confined almost exclusively to the mere routine or mechanical phases of library work. It seems quite clear that if this course were considerably expanded and enriched it would have a wide appeal. So long as the student has to pay the full cost of the instructors' time and the overhead charges, it will not be possible to do thorough work and assist the student to apply his instruction in such a way as to give him the equivalent of practice or field work. Better text-books, better teaching methods, and many specialized courses are needed. Instruction of this sort requires endowment or subsidy quite as much as does resident study.

The California State Library is giving correspondence instruction in cataloguing, the number of students reported in January, 1921, being twenty-six. It was estimated that about half of these were doing good work and deriving substantial benefit from the course. The instructor in charge feels keenly the need of proper text-books and teaching material. To meet the requirement of a Wisconsin law, every high school in that state must have a teacher-librarian who has had a minimum of library training in addition to the qualifications of a teacher. The supply of teachers with the required amount of library training was found to be so small that the Extension Division of the State University was called upon to provide the necessary instruction by correspondence. Between 250 and 300 students were enrolled in 1920. Those who had previously had a little library experience or knew something about books and libraries are reported to have done well in the course, while those to whom the whole subject was new got very little out of it. It is also reported that a course on reference books and their use is offered through the correspondence study department of the University Extension Division of the University of Missouri.

One of the most interesting possibilities in the use of correspondence study is its application to graduate, specialized study of the character recommended in an earlier chapter. Dr. Klein predicts that "the practice of permitting graduate students to secure credit by correspondence will undergo a great development during the next few years." Several western universities permit candidates for the master's degree to take a part of their work by correspondence, while the University of Chicago permits candidates for the doctor's degree to "substitute correspondence study for resident work upon approval in advance of the head of the department in which the work lies."

CHAPTER XVII

STANDARDIZATION AND CERTIFICATION

AT every point in our survey of library schools and other training agencies, the need for higher standards, for standards of any kind, indeed, has been the outstanding conclusion. Practicable methods of formulating standards and putting them into practice must therefore be sought.

So far as the library schools are concerned, it would seem that the need might be met by the Association of American Library Schools which was organized in 1915 with a constitution under which the ten charter members agreed to maintain the following standards: (1) a four-year high school course, or its equivalent, for admission; (2) a course of at least thirty-four weeks of technical instruction in preparation for general professional library work; and (3) not less than two full-time instructors with at least two instructors who are graduates of a library school having such standards. In 1918 an outline of the information to be submitted by schools applying for admission was drawn up, but no change has been made in the formal standards. A two-thirds vote of all members of the Association is required for the admission of new schools. Los Angeles was admitted in 1918, the University of Washington in 1920, and St. Louis in 1921. Of the fifteen schools reported upon in this study only two—Riverside and the University of California—are not members of the Association at present.

It is provided in the constitution that any school failing to maintain the Association's standards may be dropped from membership by a two-thirds vote, subject to reinstatement at any time on proof that requirements are being complied with. It scarcely seems possible that any institution willing to call itself a professional library school could fail to meet the extremely simple standards fixed by the Association, yet it has been suspected that compliance on the part of certain schools has been no more than nominal, at least. Having once organized without applying proper standards to its charter members, the Association is now helpless either to enforce the existing inadequate requirements or to make necessary advances. Motives of self-interest and personal relationships effectively block any attempt to enforce its standards, except perhaps in their application to new schools; and unpleasant feelings are easily aroused by demanding of applicants for admission standards not being maintained by charter members. If there is to be any effective supervision over the standards of library schools, it must come from outside the Association. This is the opinion of the best library school authorities familiar with the situation and anxious to see standards raised.

If the Association of American Library Schools is not the proper agency for formulating and applying standards for library schools, what kind of body should take its place? No satisfactory answer can be given to this question if considered solely from the side of the professional schools. Their standards are low partly because standards of library service are low. It would be futile to expect any great and sudden improvement in professional training without at the same time doing something to create a demand for improved service. True, the converse could be alleged, namely, that it is not worth while to demand higher standards of service because workers with the capacity and training are not to be had. Standards of service and standards of training are indeed inseparable. In this chapter, therefore, an effort is made to discover where we should begin and what steps should be taken to put professional library training and service on a more efficient basis.

The amazingly low standards of professional fitness of library workers have been pointed out from time to time. Librarians have much to say about themselves as educators and intellectual leaders in their communities—an enviable position which they might occupy if they were alive to their opportunity. Intellectual leadership requires broad knowledge and training. Are library workers qualified for leadership? A committee of the Minnesota Library Association recently reported that outside of the Twin Cities and Duluth only nine librarians of public libraries in the state have a college education, tho there are 104 public libraries and 237 high schools. The situation in most other states is not much, if any, better. What can be expected in the way of intellectual leadership from librarians who have less education than high school teachers? Discouragement over the situation is in no way relieved by the fact that many of these uneducated workers are known as "trained" librarians. Through library schools, short courses, and summer schools they have acquired some smattering of library methods and technique. In many cases they are doubtless able to manage their libraries with efficiency in matters of routine. The clerical work, in other words, may be well done, but that alone does not give a public library the prestige of an educational force in the community.

STANDARDIZATION AND CERTIFICATION

It is unnecessary to enter at length at this point into a discussion of the effect which low standards of professional fitness have on a library's standing and influence in a community. The facts are becoming clear to the leaders in library work. The remedy proposed by the Minnesota Library Association is two-fold: (1) improved opportunities for training; and (2) certification of librarians. These are the measures to which the forward-looking library forces are rapidly turning. In some ten other states certification proposals have recently been under discussion and some slight experiments are being made. The interest of library workers is keen, tho it must be admitted that the public is as yet indifferent. Librarians are ready and waiting expectantly for the creation of an effective system of certification.

It must come as something of a shock to the intelligent layman to discover that for professional library work there are no recognized standards of fitness, by which is meant not only that there are no standards required by law for library workers who serve the public at public expense, but even that the organized library profession has formulated no minimum standards of training and equipment for library workers of any class or grade. Here and there a single library has developed a "scheme of service" with some definite standards of education, training, and experience for each grade and position. Such standards are both voluntary and local, however, and can therefore be ignored or abandoned at any time.

The formulation and wide acceptance of standards of fitness is clearly the next step in improving library service. Complaint is ever heard of low salaries and inadequate appropriations. Without question, salaries of library workers are unusually low and libraries inadequately supported; but there can also be no question that this condition will continue as long as library work stands alone among the professions without recognized standards of qualification for efficient service.

Some system of certification is everywhere in force for public school teachers. The reasons for certification of teachers need not be reviewed here. Many of them, if not all, apply with equal force to library workers. Wherever the incompetent are allowed to compete with the competent, the former will win when competition is waged on a salary basis, as it so conspicuously is in public library service. Men and women of education and ability have no desire to train for a pseudo-profession without standards, or for work in which a newcomer without education, training, or experience is often accorded the same standing and recognition as the person with the best training obtainable and long and successful experience.

It may be argued that library workers are not called upon to concern themselves about standards of library service: that it is the public which is affected by poor and inadequate service, and that it is to the public, therefore, that we should look for the initiative. This attitude, tho not uncommon, shows a complete lack of acquaintance with the way wholesome standards have been established for other professions. As a rule, the need of a minimum standard of qualification for the practice of any profession has been recognized clearly by its leading members long before the general public reached the point of demanding it. It is to be expected that the capable and conscientious workers themselves will see the result of incompetency and inadequate equipment before it becomes evident to the layman. In medicine, law, teaching, accounting, engineering, dentistry, pharmacy, and so on, the initiative in fixing and advancing standards has been taken by far-seeing and public-spirited practitioners.

Standards may be secured and maintained by law in some professions almost from the beginning, while in others it will be necessary to rely for a long period on the voluntary action of the professional groups. In medicine, law, dentistry, nursing, and in general in those professions in which the danger to the public of inadequately trained and incompetent practitioners is easily demonstrated, certain minimum standards are usually embodied without difficulty in state law. On the other hand, in professions in which the danger to life, health, or property resulting from incompetency, either relative or absolute, does not make a strong, popular appeal, proper standards may have to be secured and maintained for an extended period by the voluntary action of professional organizations. A good illustration of this is found in the case of architecture. Voluntary action has long been the sole reliance for fixing proper standards. A few states are now passing architects' licensing laws, but for a long time to come the only standards in many states will be those maintained by the profession itself.

It is not uncommon or undesirable to have minimum standards of fitness embodied both in law and in the rules of voluntary professional bodies. This method is well illustrated by accountancy. While every state has its accountancy board or corresponding authority for passing on the qualifications of public accountants, membership in the American Institute of Accountants is open only to those who meet certain professional qualifications prescribed by the Association itself. Neither the American Library Association nor any of the other organizations of library workers, unless exception be made of the American Library Institute, are, strictly speaking, professional bodies, nor could they well be so long as there are no recognized standards of qualification for a professional librarian. The American Library Association admits to full membership every person, whether engaged in library work or not, who shows enough interest in it to pay the small annual dues. The same is true of the state library associations. Under these conditions it is obvious that library service as a profession is not only without standards, but lacks even the machinery for creating standards.

Starting with conditions as they are, various methods of procedure are possible. The American Library Association might (1) create within its own membership a selected group or class who meet prescribed qualifications (to be determined by examination or otherwise) or (2) it might create or foster some agency for formulating and applying standards in a voluntary way to all library workers, whether members of the Association or not. For many reasons the latter seems to be the more desirable course.

A third method by which librarians themselves might elect to begin the work of building up professional standards is through legislation. An examination of the experience of other professions and some understanding of the present situation in the library field make it quite clear that this is not the line of effort that is likely to produce the best results in the long run, or any result at all in the near future. In the first place, library work certainly belongs in that group, along with architecture and engineering, in which it is most difficult to bring home to the general public the necessity for making high standards of personal fitness compulsory by law. That may come later, but in the meantime and while the public is being educated to appreciate that the librarian, no less than the teacher or the doctor, must be competent, standards will need to be formulated and applied voluntarily. No other method of educating the public to demand a high standard of personal service will be so effective as the simple expedient of creating such standards by the voluntary action of the profession itself.

The idea of certification for library workers is necessarily not new. Teacher certification and the licensing of practitioners of many other professions have inevitably suggested it many times. As a practical matter, however, certification of librarians has but very recently been given serious consideration. For several years the American Library Association has had a committee on standardization and certification, its duties being undefined and its activities limited to brief reports on the general feasibility and desirability of certification of librarians and the formulation of minimum standards of library service.

Under the influence of teacher certification, it was but natural that compulsory standards should be widely adopted first for high school librarians. To California, often regarded as the most progressive of all the states in library as in educational matters in general, apparently belongs the honor of taking the first step in compulsory certification. In enacting the county free library law of 1909, the paramount importance of securing a high degree of fitness in the heads of county library systems led to the creation of a board of library examiners "to pass upon the qualifications of all persons desiring to become county librarians." This certification provision for county librarians was followed by a law requiring all high school librarians to have a special certificate similar to that of a high school teacher. A recent Wisconsin law required every high school in the state to employ a teacher-librarian, which means a person who has the general qualifications of a high school teacher, plus library training equivalent to a four-credit college course.

Aside from a few relatively unimportant beginnings, nothing at all has been done in the way of voluntary or compulsory certification. In a loose sense, library school diplomas and certificates have stood for a kind of elementary certificate of fitness, but many of the best known librarians and a large proportion of most library staffs have not had library school credentials. The schools, too, have differed widely in regard to their standards of admission and training. Moreover, the certificate of a library school can bear no evidence as to success after leaving the school. Library school credentials, therefore, cannot take the place of a general system of certification.

Library workers throughout the country are taking a deep interest in certification as a means of improving library service by raising the standards of qualification and improving the status and salaries of library workers. This interest has been stimulated to an appreciable extent by a plan for national certification first presented to the American Library Association in June, 1919. This proposal was received with unusual interest and manifest approval, and was referred to the Executive Board for early consideration. Along with all other proposals for

STANDARDIZATION AND CERTIFICATION

enlarging the scope of the Association's activities, the project of a national certification board was presently placed in the hands of the Committee on Enlarged Program, and after examination and discussion was adopted and given a prominent place in the so-called Enlarged Program. Because of the widespread interest in the plan and an evident desire to have it worked out in more detail and better understood by the Association, the Executive Board appointed a committee "to consider the subject of certification, standardization, and training, and report to the annual conference of 1920." The significant features of the committee report are the recommendation for the establishment of a National Board of Certification for Librarians, a specific plan for the composition of a board representing all the library interests of the country, and a suggestion for its incorporation under state or federal charter. It is further recommended

> "That this Board shall investigate all existing agencies for teaching library subjects and methods, shall evaluate their work for purposes of certification, shall seek to correlate these agencies into an organized system and to that end shall recommend such new agencies as seem to it desirable and shall establish grades of library service with appropriate certificates. . . .
> "That the creation of such a board shall have for one of its purposes the stimulation, through state and local library commissions or associations, of the improvement of library service and the professional status of library workers."

Pending the necessary constitutional provision, a special committee, constituted substantially as outlined for the proposed board, was recommended and later appointed. This committee confined its activities to a closer study of the composition of the national certification board and a general survey of its duties and functions. Until funds are in hand to carry on its work, it is useless to create the board. No detailed plan for its work can be adopted in advance of its organization and independent study of the problem.

To summarize the present status of the movement for certification of librarians and standardization of library schools, it may be said that while a few sporadic efforts are being made to secure certification laws, voluntary action seems more likely to be widely effective under present conditions. A plan for voluntary national certification has, therefore, been worked out in the last two years. To put the plan into operation, funds will be needed. After the preliminary work is completed and the system well established, it may become at least partially self-supporting by a system of fees for examinations and certificates. In the meantime, a few progressive states are going ahead with plans for compulsory certification for the heads of public libraries. Between these local efforts, even where they are successful, and the plans for national certification, there is no conflict. As was pointed out in the original proposal, very little effective legislation can be expected for a long time; and to guide such legislation as can be secured, it is most desirable that the library profession should formulate minimum standards of service. The few legislative proposals now under consideration present a bewildering variety of requirements and methods, which is to be expected in the absence of any semblance of recognized professional standards. Once such standards are set up, it is reasonable to anticipate that state schemes will conform to them so far as practicable.

In one respect the library profession at this moment is in a peculiarly fortunate situation. In many other professions—such as teaching and medicine—state or local legislation developed in a haphazard fashion; and it has proved to be exceedingly difficult to bring about a reasonable degree of uniformity. By the creation of a national board of standards at the very beginning of the movement for state certification legislation, the library systems of the various states can be relieved of troublesome variations and complexities.

In earlier paragraphs of this chapter some general reasons were advanced for voluntary action by professional organizations. At this point it may be well to advert to some of the more specific reasons for believing that the situation in the library profession demands that emphasis be laid at this time on voluntary rather than compulsory methods. The voluntary system proposed can be applied at once to the entire staff—and not merely the head librarian, as contemplated in all pending legislation. It can also be adopted by individual libraries in states that will as a whole long be backward in library development. Communities too small to work out systems of service for themselves will find it easy to adopt the national standards. In some cases state-wide legislation, applicable to all cities, is impossible because of an extreme form of home rule charter.

Perhaps the principal advantage of the national voluntary system lies in its second feature, the coördination and accrediting of training agencies. Following the modern system of certification for teachers, it may be assumed that it will be found desirable to certify without examination the graduates of approved training schools. In teacher training the state is traditionally a self-sufficient unit and can properly be so because of the large number of teachers required. The number of professional library workers, on the other hand, is so much smaller that few states can expect to rely mainly on their own library schools. They will necessarily recruit workers, particularly for specialized types of service, from schools located in other states. But how futile it would be for each of the forty-eight states to make its own independent examination and accredited list of the twelve or fifteen or more library schools in all parts of the country, and how confusing for the schools to be subject to the separate and often inexpert scrutiny of forty-eight states, to find themselves accredited perhaps by some states and not by others. Evidently the only sensible thing is to provide one central accrediting agency.

A more detailed statement in regard to the functions and duties of the National Certification Board, including tentative suggestions for a system of certificates that such a board might adopt, together with some explanation of the way the system would be inaugurated and applied, is to be found in the 1921 report of the temporary A. L. A. certification committee.[1] As an addition to its primary function, or rather as an important phase of that function, the certification board would exercise a degree of supervision over the library schools and other training agencies. To a certain extent it would take the place of the Association of American Library Schools, which, as has been pointed out, cannot be relied upon to become an effective instrument for enforcing minimum standards on the part of library schools. The power of the board to withhold the national professional certificate from the graduates of an unaccredited school would make its rulings and decisions effective. The board should not stop, however, with merely formulating standards and inspecting and accrediting training agencies, and then certifying the output of accredited institutions or admitting to certificate by examination. It should also become a central agency for promoting professional training in the many ways that would be open to it. It should very soon occupy a place analogous to that of the Council on Medical Education of the American Medical Association.

---

[1] American Library Association, *Annual Report*, 1920-21, pages 78 ff.

CHAPTER XVIII
THE PROBLEM OF THE SMALL LIBRARY

THE problem of creating trained personnel for the small library cannot be separated from the improvement of library service in general. Free access to books for everybody requires a pooling of book resources and personal service in a way which has not yet been attained. The small library can no more be self-sufficient in personal service than in book resources. Even under the present system much can be done to help the service in small libraries by raising of standards generally. But the only permanent and effective method of attacking the problem of service in the small library is by creating a workable library system, and this requires the coöperation of all agencies interested in improving the service in all types of library.

Briefly, the situation in most of the country is about as follows: In the larger cities public libraries, supported, as a rule, by public appropriations, furnish for the capable and determined student some facilities for serious study or reading in fields that interest him for vocational or other reasons. By means of inter-library loans the intelligent and wideawake librarian may supplement his own resources by borrowing from other libraries. Very much remains to be done in the way of increasing public library support and improving the skill of the professional library worker and administrator so that the individual who does not live in or near a large city can realize the full benefits of access to books. In the smaller towns and cities the librarian and staff are in general less skilled in meeting the needs of the public and the library less adequately supported than in the large cities. As we pass to smaller and smaller towns the situation grows rapidly worse, so that we find in the average community of less than ten thousand population a library which at best merely purchases a small number of books, often unwisely selected, and in a purely routine way performs the clerical process of permitting individuals to borrow what they happen to find on the shelves.

Salaries paid to librarians in small libraries seldom make it possible to secure a person of sufficient general or professional education to appreciate the opportunity of the library as an educational agency of first importance. The book resources of the small library itself are poor in quality and inadequate in quantity. The librarian does not know how to improve them, how to draw on other agencies when his own fails, or how, in other words, to furnish library service. At best he gives only clerical service. It is not strange, therefore, that small public libraries serve their communities mainly by providing reading for recreational purposes. The person who reads solely for recreation is in the habit of being content with anything that happens to be at hand. The inadequacy and inefficiency of a library used mainly for recreational purposes may not become apparent until it is called upon to serve its community by providing sources of information on practical affairs of life. Skilled direction should be provided even for recreational reading; but for any library to serve vocational and practical every-day bread and butter needs, skill and intelligence on the part of the librarian are absolutely indispensable.

The librarian's lack of broad education and skill and experience in making print serve the practical needs of life now condemns all libraries to some extent, but the small library almost always, to a position in every community far below that which it could and should occupy.

The progressive deterioration of rural communities is probably due as much to the lack of opportunity to bring to bear on problems of country life the experience and information available in print as to inadequate education. If the rural school does nothing more than teach children how to read—that is, if it gives even a fair degree of facility in getting ideas and information from the printed page—an adequate and adaptable library service can achieve wonders in putting the man who lives in the open country on a plane with the city dweller.

By means of the county system a library service as good as the best to be found in any city can be provided for every individual in a territory covering thousands of square miles. Moreover, by reason of good roads, telephones, and parcel post, this can be done almost as economically as in populous centres.

In library circles there is much talk of county libraries, but little understanding, even among professional library workers, of precisely what the county system proposes to accomplish and how it functions. Virtually nothing of value has been written about county libraries; no serious effort has been made to bring the idea to library trustees and community leaders in states where it could be applied with very great advantage.

The high degree of transportability of printed matter and the constant improvement of transportation facilities mean that for practical purposes all that stands in the way of equal access to books is the lack of intelligence, education, training, and capacity for usefulness on the part of the librarian. It should not be assumed that those who live in the small community or in the open country are entitled only to a book service which consists of a purely mechanical exchange of books into whose selection and purchase little or no intelligence, understanding, and appreciation have entered. With the perfecting of library systems and the general improvement of standards of service, every man should be able to command the services of a skilled librarian.

Tho the problem of an adequately and properly trained service is far from being satisfactorily solved even in the large library, it is in small public libraries that the situation is on the whole most difficult. Yet the need for an intelligent and active library service is no less acute in small towns and rural districts than in the larger cities. Indeed, in many respects the small isolated community has the greater need and presents the richer opportunity. Quantitatively speaking, there is less need, of course, tho it is probable that in the average small town the proportion of the population able and willing to take advantage of a good library service is just as high as in the cities. And in the small community substitutes for what an active library can offer are less common than in the city. Bookstores and newstands do not exist, school libraries are undeveloped, lectures and the ordinary means of popular education are not so abundantly supplied.

In the relatively isolated condition of small towns and rural communities the library has its richest opportunity to coöperate with the schools, to provide for all ages the only adequate means of popular education, and to bring to bear on the economic and social problems of rural life the information and stimulus now available in abundance through a variety of printed matter. The poverty of the schools and the inadequacy of the teaching, instead of proving that books are not needed, only point to the very great need for the educated, professional librarian. The schools at best can only teach the individual to read; the library is the one public agency able to create the desire for reading throughout life and to give wise direction as to what to read. It is not sufficient to provide "something to read." The lower the average of education and the weaker the natural impulse to find in books healthful recreation, mental growth, and the broadening effect of stories of travel, biography, science, etc., the greater the opportunity for, the greater the need of the skilled and educated librarian.

A community of well-educated people may get on very well with an uneducated librarian, provided he possesses enough technique to purchase books selected by some one else and to manage the necessary records and routine clerical work. In the ordinary small town and rural community the uneducated librarian—who does not have a wide knowledge of books and human nature, who does not understand the manifold applications of science to our common life, who is not well informed and deeply interested in social and economic problems, who does not have a real understanding of the problems of community life and organization, who, in other words, has not the education or capacity for community leadership or the special training necessary to make leadership felt through a library service—can be of very little value. In any community in which the average person has enough education to get at the thought and information in the printed page, the librarian has an opportunity for service quite the equal of that possessed by the minister, the doctor, the teacher, or the editor.

It must not be assumed that the small town or rural library has less opportunity to be helpful to citizens in their vocational and business interests than the city library. Governments are spending millions of dollars in this country in scientific study of every phase of agriculture and rural economics. The results are published in both popular and scientific form, but fail to reach effectively the very persons for whom they are designed because an efficient distributing agency is lacking. A well-educated librarian, with professional training, can aid in the effective use of the wealth of agricultural literature. The clerical type of librarian can do nothing at all.

What can be done for communities too small or too poor to avail themselves of the services of a professionally trained librarian? There is but one satisfactory answer: make the library unit large enough, and efficient service is possible. This may be done through the county system. The same principle is involved in the consolidation of rural schools: districts too small to maintain good schools are combined. In no other way does it seem possible in this country to give to every citizen the fullest access to books, and intelligent direction in their uses.

But progress towards the county system is slow. What can be done while awaiting its development to make the service of existing small libraries more efficient without the danger of putting still farther off the time when "books for everybody" will be a reality?

Three distinct situations have to be dealt with: (1) The community that has a library and is large enough and wealthy enough to employ a professional librarian but does not do so, either because it does not know the value of efficient library service or because it thinks it has the best that is to be had; (2) the community that appreciates the value of a library, but is evidently too small to have an efficient, independent service; and (3) towns and rural districts without books or library service of any kind, and without any conscious need for them.

Until county systems develop, each of these problems requires special treatment. The first calls for education and above all standardization and certification. The expected aid from certification in this situation is discussed elsewhere. Improvement can be made only gradually. Certification may eliminate poor librarians, but it will not immediately produce good ones. Adequate salaries and better training facilities will in due time produce the type of librarian demanded. Such librarians will not stand in the way of county systems, but will be a very strong factor in their development.

Certification will not set aside economic law. Where adequate salaries cannot be paid, certification and a supply of professionally trained librarians will avail little. This is the condition which state library commissions have been hopefully attacking. Little libraries in the hands of uneducated and untrained, often unpaid, librarians offer as hopeless a situation as can be found in the whole range of social and educational problems. By such means as state supervision, state organizers, summer schools, and short courses for untrained librarians, the commissions have sought to improve conditions. Even tho the state commissions had adequate funds for their task—which none of them have—they would only be pouring water into a sieve. Fifty years of such effort would not suffice to effect appreciable improvement, except so far as it might lead to a change of system or to the employment of educated librarians, where the latter is possible.

Indeed, it is a serious question whether the superficial acquaintance with those parts of library technique which can be given to persons of limited education through summer schools and other means used by the commissions may not often prove to be a very real hindrance to the development of library service. In spite of the best intentions and ample warning, such a librarian is likely to consider himself as thereby fully equipped for his task, without knowing or being capable of knowing what his real opportunity is. The community so served is in still greater danger of mistaking what is at best an efficient routine library service for the service which could be given by an educated and professionally trained librarian. It is rare nowadays that any community thinks of the librarian as a person of education who possesses a knowledge of practical affairs which, combined with good judgment and a knowledge of books, makes him much more than an efficient book clerk.

Shall we, then, conclude that it were better to make no effort in behalf of the untrained and often uneducated librarian who, along with his community, is the victim of an inherently inefficient system? Let the answer be "no." While we are putting all our efforts into securing a better system, we can safely, if we understand what we are doing, employ all available means for getting the best results from the system under which we are working. So long as we must have uneducated and inadequately trained librarians and library assistants in small libraries, let us supplement their education and give them such technical instruction as they can be brought to seek through summer schools and every other agency. Only the best of the class will seek such help, and the danger of giving a false impression of what is being done and thus helping to entrench a system that must disappear, can be largely, if not wholly, avoided by the system of certification.

The program to be recommended, therefore, while we await the development of the county library system, is this: secure librarians with college education and professional training wherever that is economically possible; in the smaller places be satisfied for the time being with the best that can be had. If it is only possible to secure as librarian a person with high school education, give him the technical training necessary and a certificate of the clerical, sub-professional class. No library, and no community, will then be in danger of imagining that it has a professional service. No community, it is to be hoped, will look upon such a situation as more than temporary. The mere knowledge that its library service is sub-standard will prove a mighty stimulus to improvement. Other communities, for the most part of smaller size, will find themselves unable to reach even the sub-professional standard of service; but if they are doing the best they can do under the system, that is all that can be expected, and every means should be used to help them reach at least the lowest standard recognized in the certification system.

CHAPTER XIX
SUMMARY OF FINDINGS AND RECOMMENDATIONS

I. *Types of Library Work and Training*

EACH of the two general types of library work, which may be called "professional" and "clerical," demands general education of different grades and vocational training quite distinct in character and method. The difference between these two types of library work has not been kept clearly in view in library organization and administration, and they therefore tend to be confused in the work of the library schools.

2. Professional training calls for a broad, general education, represented at its minimum by a thorough college course of four years, plus at least one year of graduate study in a properly organized library school. For the clerical work of libraries, training may consist of a general education of high school grade, followed by a comparatively short period of instruction in library methods combined with sufficient practice to ensure proficiency and skill in clerical and routine work.

3. Library schools should confine themselves to training of the professional type. Training of the clerical type will be provided through the so-called training classes conducted by libraries.

II. *The Library School Curriculum*

1. There is little agreement among the schools as to the relative importance of the different subjects in the curriculum. About half the student's time is devoted to four subjects—cataloguing, book selection, reference work, and classification. But even to these major subjects some schools give two or three times as many hours of instruction as others do.

2. There is need for a certain degree of standardization of both major and minor courses given in the first year of professional library school study. With the adoption of certification systems and the development of various agencies for training in service it will be necessary to formulate minimum standards as to scope and content of courses.

3. To make standards dynamic rather than static they should be subjected to constant scrutiny by the schools themselves in the light of frequent reanalyses of the training necessary for the professional librarian. The content of the curriculum, in other words, and the meth-

FINDINGS AND RECOMMENDATIONS

ods of instruction, should be determined by first-hand acquaintance with the most progressive library service rather than by tradition and imitation.

4. A composite statement of the scope and content of the twenty-five or more distinct subjects included in the curricula of the library schools reveals (*a*) the difficulty of providing thorough instruction and training in the whole field of library work in one year, and (*b*) the necessity of a broad, general education of collegiate grade as a basis for library school instruction.

III. Entrance Requirements

1. Two library schools require for admission the completion of an approved college course of four years. A four-year high school course or its equivalent is the minimum in all other schools, admission being by examination, except for college graduates.

2. Examinations are crude and unscientific, if considered as mental tests; as a means of testing the candidate's general education, they cover too superficially too narrow a range of subjects. Languages are properly emphasized; but too much stress is laid on pure literature, history and the humanities in general.

3. Uniform entrance examinations for all the schools would have many advantages, but as matters stand at present are not likely to be adopted.

4. On the question of experience in library work as an entrance requirement, authoritative opinion and actual practice are at variance. The orientation needed by the student without adequate experience should be carefully planned.

5. Many library schools lay great emphasis on "personality tests," which represent an impressionistic method of very questionable value. It is believed that schools will do well to abandon personality tests and admit on evidence of education and ability to maintain a high standard of scholarship.

6. Among the minor entrance requirements ability to use the typewriter is common. This appears to be a relic of an earlier stage of training for library work and not an essential part of the professional librarian's equipment to-day. It is an actual hindrance to recruiting librarians among college men and women.

7. One of the most fundamental conclusions of this report is that professional library training should be based on a college education or

its full equivalent. Joint courses, in which the student completes a library school course and earns the bachelor's degree in four years, represent a higher standard than that maintained by most library schools at present, but should nevertheless be looked upon merely as a step toward placing library schools on a strictly graduate basis.

IV. *The Teaching Staff and Methods of Instruction*

1. Analysis of the training and experience of instructors in library schools indicates that many of them are not fitted to give instruction of high professional character to college graduates. The statistics show that:

(*a*) Only 52 per cent. of the members of the instructional staffs of the library schools in 1921 were college graduates;

(*b*) 42 per cent. were teaching in the same library school in which they received their own training;

(*c*) 93 per cent. of the instructors had no training in the science of teaching;

(*d*) 80 per cent. had no experience in teaching before joining the library school staff;

(*e*) 32 per cent. were without adequate experience in practical library work.

2. Concerted effort should be made to raise the quality of instruction in library schools by increasing salaries and making teaching positions more attractive in various ways to trained and experienced librarians of the highest ability.

3. The principal defects in the methods of instruction are:

(*a*) Excessive dependence on the lecture method, due in part to inadequate and uneven preparation of students;

(*b*) Lack of suitable text-books and teaching materials;

(*c*) Heavy demands on the instructor's time, resulting from a lack of clerical assistance; and

(*d*) The part-time system of instruction.

4. The part-time system of instruction, tho not without its advantages, is the direct result of attempting to conduct library schools with insufficient funds. The professional library school should have not less than four full-time instructors.

FINDINGS AND RECOMMENDATIONS

5. The special or visiting lecturer, giving only one or two lectures in each school, has been an outstanding characteristic of instruction in most library schools. While these special lectures have not been entirely satisfactory, need is felt for some scheme of coöperative instruction that will make it possible to have the minor subjects in the curriculum taught by specialists.

6. The efficiency of library school instruction is seriously impaired by the lack of suitable text-books and handbooks or treatises on various phases of library practice. To stimulate the production of professional literature of this kind, it is recommended that a sum of money should be provided in the form of an annual fellowship which would pay the salary and traveling expenses of one library school instructor on leave of absence from his post for the specific purpose of enabling him to complete for publication a work which when published will be of special use to library schools.

7. From four to twelve weeks, or from one-eighth to one-quarter of the school year, are devoted by the library schools to field work, usually known as "practical" work. Altho this represents a large part of the year's work, there seems to be no special interest on the part of the school authorities in the educational principles involved. The various assumptions underlying this part of the curriculum, so far as any are discernible, are:

(*a*) That the student during his period of work in the practice library is acquiring skill in his profession;
(*b*) That the period of field work is needed to reveal his ability or general capacity for library work;
(*c*) That it enables the student to discover the special kind of work he desires to enter;
(*d*) That it is useful in furnishing school officials the kind of information which they need in placing the student after graduation.

The conclusion reached after an examination of these points of view is that all are unsound or unimportant; that field work should be looked upon as that phase of formal instruction carried on by purposeful observation, supplementing class-room instruction; that, in other words, field work is merely one important method of instruction.

8. The field work of library schools is in general unsatisfactory and of very doubtful value to the student. The most obvious defects are:

(a) The point in the course at which field work is introduced seems to be determined by the convenience of the practice library or of the school, rather than by educational principles;

(b) Methods of making assignments are not guided by the thought of giving the student a broad basis of information and a grasp of principles, and holding him up to a high standard of scholarship;

(c) Student field work is in general poorly supervised and inadequately reported on, both by the students themselves and by the supervisors of field work;

(d) Service on a library staff under actual library conditions, instead of being the ideal method, is in reality one of the poorest methods, because at best it is a waste of time as a rule, and often represents an exploitation of the student;

(e) Too large a share of the student's time in the first year of professional study is given to the prevailing type of field work. A comparatively brief period of well-planned and skilfully supervised observation in approved libraries is recommended.

9. Opportunities for *extensive* observation are afforded by class "visits" to a large number of important libraries. The intensive observation recommended must usually be carried out in local libraries, hence the importance of having professional schools located in communities which offer the widest possible range of well-organized libraries of different types.

10. Library schools are placement as well as training agencies. The great importance which the placement function has assumed is due mainly to the fact that there have been no other agencies to which employers could turn for information about trained library workers.

V. *Library School Finances and Salaries*

1. The fundamental cause of many of the deficiencies noted in the work of the library schools can be traced to inadequate financial support. A study of the finances and financial administration of the library schools shows that:

(a) Only two or three schools have independent budgets and keep accurate records of the cost of operation;

(b) Only four schools had a total expenditure in 1920–21 of more than $10,000;

(c) The average salary of the best paid instructor in each school (not including the director) was about $2000;

(d) Salaries paid instructors are too low to attract well-trained, experienced library workers who are willing and able to teach;

(e) Judging from the comparatively static condition of their budgets, the library schools are not keeping pace with the needs of the libraries for trained service.

VI. The Need for More Library Schools and more Students in Training

1. Fundamentally the recruiting problem can be solved only by making library service as attractive and desirable a career for well-educated men and women as other learned professions. Library salaries are now too low to attract men or women of first-class ability and qualities of intellectual and community leadership. Statistics furnished by five representative library schools show that over 40 per cent. of their graduates earn less than $1500 a year; only 3.6 per cent. earn over $2500 a year.

2. It does not appear from salaries paid to educated and trained librarians that there is need for many new professional library schools or a great increase in the number of students. The primary need is for a better grade of student and higher standards of instruction.

3. Statistics for the fifteen schools examined show that the present enrolment represents only 60 per cent. of their total physical capacity. It is concluded, therefore, that the best way to increase the number of persons in training for professional librarianship is to fill existing schools rather than to establish new ones with the same meagre financial support and small enrolment.

4. Whatever responsibility the library schools have for the recruiting problem can best be met by:

(a) Maintaining the highest standards of professional education;

(b) Taking a leading part in the movement to put library service on a satisfactory economic and professional basis; and

(c) Coöperating with professional organizations and college and university authorities in presenting to college men and women the rich opportunities for service in the library field.

5. Fellowships and scholarships should be established in the best library schools to stimulate the interest of desirable candidates for admission and to enable the university library schools to compete with other graduate departments for the best students.

VII. The Library School and the University

1. One of the most important conclusions of this study is that the professional library school should be organized as a department of a university, along with other professional schools, rather than in public libraries, state or municipal. Schools now conducted by public libraries should either take the definite status of training classes or be transferred to university auspices in fact as well as in name. This conclusion is based on the following considerations:

   (*a*) The public library often attempts, with inevitable failure, to combine the training class and the professional school;
   (*b*) The public library is a service institution, not organized for the purpose of providing professional education;
   (*c*) Public library authorities should not be permitted to use public funds to conduct a professional library school: they would not do so, on account of the expense, if library schools maintained proper standards;
   (*d*) It is not sound public policy for a local municipal library to assume the task of training professional librarians;
   (*e*) It is easier for the university library school to establish and maintain proper standards;
   (*f*) The university school has a better opportunity to attract to the library profession men and women with college training.

2. Library schools are noticeably lacking in the prestige enjoyed by professional schools generally. The reasons for this condition seem to be:

   (*a*) The smallness of the library school;
   (*b*) The brevity of the course;
   (*c*) The predominance of women in the faculty and student body;
   (*d*) The preponderance of teachers having only the rank of instructor; and
   (*e*) The total lack of anything recognized as productive scholarship.

University library schools developed on the lines laid down in this report should gradually overcome these handicaps.

VIII. Specialized Study

1. While library service has been growing more and more highly specialized, the training provided by library schools has remained gen-

FINDINGS AND RECOMMENDATIONS

eral, partly because of insufficient demand for specialized training and partly because the schools have been financially unable to expand their work.

2. It is recommended that the first year of professional study continue to be general and basic; that the work of the second and following years be definitely and even minutely specialized.

3. The fields of professional library work for which specialized training should now be provided include school libraries, college and university libraries, library work with children, library administration, cataloguing and classification, county and rural library work, and business libraries. In various other fields there is a growing demand for specialized training.

4. In the organization of specialized training the following considerations are fundamental:

- (a) Between the year of general study and the period of special training at least one year of first-class library experience should be required.
- (b) The comparatively small demand for an advanced type of specialized training makes it necessary to work out a system at a minimum expense by utilizing the resources of the stronger professional schools, in coöperation with other educational institutions in the same vicinity, using the services of competent specialists on the part-time plan, and taking full advantage of opportunities for field work.
- (c) No one school should be expected to offer courses in all the specialties or to give highly specialized courses every year; in developing such courses each school will be guided mainly by the local demand and the character of the local coöperating agencies.
- (d) To develop the type of specialized training recommended, a library school must be so situated that it can coöperate with other educational institutions, such as schools of education, schools of business, etc.

IX. Training in Service

1. There is a conspicuous lack of both opportunity and incentive on the part of library workers, including library school graduates as well as others, to seek continued professional growth and improvement. The principal means of creating the proper incentive are to be found

in well-developed schemes of service, with proper efficiency ratings, and a comprehensive certification system.

2. Agencies for training in service have been confined to summer schools, training classes, apprentice classes, institutes, and meetings of professional organizations. Most of these are designed only for the subprofessional grades of service. For professional workers a new type of summer school and short intensive courses in library schools are needed. Correspondence study promises also to be of great value.

3. Virtually no use has yet been made of correspondence instruction as a method of training in service for library workers, altho it has reached a high degree of development in its application to many other cultural and vocational subjects.

4. Correspondence instruction in library subjects should be undertaken at once, provided it can be done under proper conditions, which means that:

    (*a*) The most competent instructors should be employed and special attention paid to methods of teaching and the preparation of suitable text-books;

    (*b*) Correspondence instruction should not be expected to be self-supporting;

    (*c*) Such instruction should not be attempted by all or many of the existing library schools, but preferably by one special institution, or perhaps coöperatively by a number of schools.

5. The difficulties and objections that can be pointed out do not seem to be at all serious. The general conclusion is that some way should be found as soon as possible to offer instruction of the highest grade by correspondence methods, under conditions which will ensure it a fair trial.

X. *Certification of Librarians and Standardization of Library Schools*

1. No generally recognized standards of fitness for library workers have been formulated. With minor exceptions, standards of training and fitness are nowhere fixed by law, even for librarians whose salaries are paid from public funds.

2. Library work belongs in that group of professions, along with architecture and engineering, in which the first step in formulating standards can best be taken through voluntary action by the profession itself. After the public has come to appreciate that the compe-

tency of the librarian, no less than that of the teacher and the doctor, must be guaranteed, it may be possible through legislation to supplement voluntary by compulsory methods.

3. A plan for a system of voluntary certification of librarians on a nation-wide scale has been worked out and is now under consideration by the American Library Association. Granted the right kind of leadership and adequate financial support during its formative period, this plan, which provides for a representative and responsible national certification board, could be inaugurated at once.

4. Among the most obvious advantages of the voluntary system of national certification are the following:

(a) It makes possible the establishing of generally recognized standards and uniform methods before state and local legislation has developed in a haphazard fashion, eventually making it necessary, tho exceedingly difficult, to reverse the process and bring about a reasonable degree of uniformity.

(b) On a voluntary basis standards can be applied at once to all grades of library personnel and not merely to head librarians, as contemplated in most pending legislation.

(c) Private libraries of many kinds, as well as individual public libraries in states which, on account of legal or other obstacles, will not have compulsory certification for a long time, can come under the national voluntary certification system at once.

5. Library schools and other training agencies are in need of a representative and authoritative body to assist them not only in formulating standards, but particularly in enforcing standards agreed upon. The Association of American Library Schools cannot be expected to perform this function. The proposed national certification board could serve also as a standardizing agency for library schools, having authority to enforce its decisions through its power of certifying without examination the graduates of approved schools. Besides its functions in the certification of librarians and accrediting of library schools, the board would naturally become an effective central agency for the promotion of all types of library training.

XI. The Problem of the Small Library

1. The improvement of library service in small towns and rural districts is not to be sought through stimulating the development of train-

ing agencies specifically adapted to the type of librarian and the economic situation represented by the average small public library. General improvement in standards of service, through certification of librarians, strengthening of professional library schools, and the training of leaders, will accomplish more in the long run for the small public library than the multiplication of library courses and training schools of the usual type.

2. A permanent solution of the problem also requires a change from a fundamentally unsound system of small isolated, independent libraries to a system in which the administrative unit is large enough to make it economically possible to command the services of an educated, professionally trained and skilled librarian. In most states this means the so-called county library system.

3. The main effort of all concerned should be directed toward the extension and improvement of the county library system. Tho there is danger that an inherently inefficient system may become further entrenched by the use of makeshift and inadequate remedies, it would be a mistake to conclude that therefore no effort should be made in behalf of the untrained and often uneducated librarian who, along with the community, is the victim of a bad system.

4. Awaiting the advent of the county library system, the following program should be adopted:

(*a*) Every community in which it is economically feasible should be stimulated to employ the educated, professionally trained skilled librarian.

(*b*) Communities unable to employ librarians of this professional grade and obliged temporarily to be content with inferior service should be assisted in all possible ways by state library departments and various methods of training in service.

APPENDIX

APPENDIX I
General Information in Regard to the Fifteen Library Schools Studied in this Report
Arranged by Date of Founding

New York State Library School, Albany, N. Y.
James I. Wyer, Jr., Director.

This was the first library school to be established. It was founded by Melvil Dewey in 1887 as the Columbia College School of Library Economy, New York City. In 1889 it was removed to the New York State Library and is now a separate division of the University of the State of New York (State Education Department) closely affiliated with the State Library, the director of the State Library being also director of the Library School. The school is supported as a part of the State Library by state appropriations.

Pratt Institute School of Library Science, Brooklyn, N. Y.
Edward F. Stevens, Director; Josephine Adams Rathbone, Vice-Director.

Pratt Institute was opened in October, 1887. Three years later a class in library methods was started for the purpose of training library assistants, instruction being given by members of the staff of the Institute library. In 1895 the training class was organized as a regular library school with its own faculty. Since 1911 the librarian of the Pratt Institute Free Library has also acted as director of the school.

University of Illinois Library School, Urbana, Ill.
P. L. Windsor, Director.

This school was established in 1893 as the Armour Institute Library School, a department of the Armour Institute of Technology, Chicago. The original one-year course was extended in 1894 to two years. In 1897 the school was transferred to the University of Illinois with a part of its faculty, its students, and its technical equipment. The director of the University library is also director of the library school. Funds for its support are provided by the University.

Carnegie Library School, Pittsburgh, Pa.
John H. Leete, Director; Nina C. Brotherton, Principal.

To provide trained assistants for service in the children's reading rooms, which were then a new phase of library work, a training class for children's librarians was formed in the Carnegie Library of Pittsburgh in October, 1900. In response to a demand for trained workers from other libraries a Training School for Children's Librarians was organized in 1901. In 1916 the Training School became a department of the Carnegie Institute and its name was changed to Carnegie Library School. While most of the students are still enrolled in the special course for children's librarians, the school is now considered a general professional library school, a course for school library work having been added in 1917 and a course in general library work in 1918. From 1903 to 1916 Mr. Andrew Carnegie contributed to the support of the school. Since 1916 it has been supported by funds from the Carnegie Institute, an institution endowed by Mr. Carnegie for educational purposes.

Simmons College School of Library Science, Boston, Mass.
June R. Donnelly, Director.

Simmons College was opened in 1902 as a vocational college for women. It was the desire of its founder to establish an institution that would give instruction in "art, science, and industry best calculated to enable the scholars to acquire an independent livelihood." The library school is one of eight departments of the college, the others being household economics, secretarial studies, general science, social work, industrial teaching, education for store service, and public health nursing. The School of Library Science offers two courses—the four-year course leading to the degree of Bachelor of Science and a one-year course for graduates of other colleges and women who have had at least three years of academic study elsewhere.

LIBRARY SCHOOL OF WESTERN RESERVE UNIVERSITY, Cleveland, Ohio.
Alice L. Tyler, Director.

This school was established in 1904 by the aid of an endowment of $100,000 given by Mr. Carnegie. Instruction and field work are carried on in close coöperation with the Cleveland Public Library. A special department of library work with children was added in 1920 in continuation of courses given by the Cleveland Public Library since 1909. The College for Women of Western Reserve University gives full credit toward the bachelor's degree for a year's work in the Library School.

LIBRARY SCHOOL, CARNEGIE LIBRARY OF ATLANTA, Atlanta, Ga.
Tommie Dora Barker, Director.

The Southern Library School was established in 1905 in the Carnegie Library of Atlanta by a gift from Mr. Carnegie sufficient to carry it on for an experimental period of three years. Since 1908 Mr. Carnegie and the Carnegie Corporation have made an annual grant of $4500 a year. In 1907 the present name was adopted. The director is also librarian of the Carnegie Library of Atlanta. The management of the school is vested in the administration committee of the Carnegie Library of Atlanta.

LIBRARY SCHOOL OF THE UNIVERSITY OF WISCONSIN, Madison, Wis.
Clarence B. Lester, Director; Mary Emogene Hazeltine, Preceptor (Principal).

This school is an outgrowth of the Wisconsin Summer School of Library Science conducted by the Free Library Commission from 1895 to 1905. In 1906 the course was lengthened to one year and the name changed to Wisconsin Library School. An act of the legislature in 1909 authorized the regents of the University of Wisconsin to coöperate in the maintenance of the school and designated the present name. Altho nominally a part of the State University, the school is administered by the Free Library Commission. The director of the school is Secretary of the Commission.

SYRACUSE UNIVERSITY LIBRARY SCHOOL, Syracuse, N.Y.
Elizabeth G. Thorne, Director.

This school originated in a training class established in 1896 to provide assistants for the University Library. In 1908 a library school was established as a part of the College of Liberal Arts and empowered to confer degrees. Two courses are given. The so-called "degree course" consists of two years of technical library work, for which at least two years of college work are required. The certificate course, to which high school graduates are admitted, also consists of two years of technical work and twelve semester hours in the College of Liberal Arts. The director of the school is the librarian of the University.

LIBRARY SCHOOL OF THE NEW YORK PUBLIC LIBRARY, New York City.
Ernest J. Reece, Principal.

A school for general professional training was opened in the New York Public Library in 1911, supported by a grant from Mr. Carnegie of $15,000 a year for five years and since continued from year to year by the Carnegie Corporation, being increased to $20,000 in 1921. Besides the regular one-year course a program of advanced studies is offered to graduates of schools belonging to the Association of American Library Schools. Beginning in 1920 "open courses" have been offered to experienced library workers.

APPENDIX 151

Library School, University of Washington, Seattle, Wash.
William E. Henry, Director.

Beginning in 1911 the University of Washington gave formal training in librarianship through a department of instruction in Library Economy. In February, 1917, a library school was created. The director of the school is also librarian of the University library.

Riverside Library Service School, Riverside, Calif.

The origin of this school is explained by the late director, Mr. Joseph F. Daniels, as follows: "During the summer of 1910 a few students, together with the staff of the Riverside Public Library, began a study of the day's work in order to improve the service and to determine the policy and direction of the institution. During the spring of 1913 the need of a summer school was made plain by the frequent calls for such instruction. The cost of a school served by a faculty of experience and reputation seemed prohibitive, but with the training class as a nucleus, a beginning was made and the short courses have since been held, summer and winter." The expenses of the school are met by students' fees.

The Library School of the Los Angeles Public Library, Los Angeles, Calif.
Marion Horton, Principal.

This school is an outgrowth of a course of training for library workers conducted by the Los Angeles Public Library from 1891 to 1914. In 1914 the training-class system was organized into a one-year professional library school. It is supported by public library funds.

The St. Louis Library School, St. Louis, Mo.
Arthur E. Bostwick, Director; Mrs. Harriet P. Sawyer, Principal.

The St. Louis Library School, a department of the St. Louis Public Library, was established in 1917, as an enlargement and extension of the training class of the St. Louis Public Library begun in 1910. It is supported from funds of the St. Louis Public Library. The director is librarian of the St. Louis Public Library.

University of California, Courses in Library Science, Berkeley, Calif.
Harold L. Leupp, Librarian.

Courses in library science in the State University were extended in 1919 to cover approximately the scope of the one-year professional library schools. Because it was considered that the university was the best place for the state supported library school, the California State Library School, established by the State Library in 1913, has now been given up. The library courses are given by members of the staff of the University Library and other libraries in the vicinity. It is hoped that the legislature will soon make a special appropriation for the support of a complete library school.

APPENDIX II

A. Specimen Entrance Examination Questions
LIBRARY SCHOOL OF THE NEW YORK PUBLIC LIBRARY

History

Answer question 2 and seven others.

1. To what nations are we indebted for the fundamental principles of our knowledge of any ten of the following:

Algebra	Government	Printing
Arithmetical notation	Law	Road making
Architecture	Music	Sculpture
Astronomy	Physics	Textile making
Building	Pottery	Theology
Gem-cutting		

2. *a.* Discuss in about 300 words the causes for the fall of Rome;
   or,
   b. Give in about 300 words an account of the feudal system;
   or,
   c. In about 300 words give the causes and consequences of the French revolution.

3. What was the Holy Roman Empire?

4. Give the names of five persons connected with the Renaissance, explaining briefly the part played by each.

5. Locate five of the following, giving briefly their historical associations:

Anjou	Helvetia	San Juan Hill
Byzantium	Ionia	Tours
Carthage	Jamestown	Tyre
Gaul	Runnymede	

6. Who were any five of the following:

Albigenses	Covenanters	Jacobites
Benedictines	Fenians	Know-nothings
Carbonari	Guelphs	Populists

7. Give briefly the historical significance of five of the following:

Alexander the Great	John C. Frémont	John Marshall
Simon Bolivar	Giuseppe Garibaldi	Carl Schurz
Edmund Burke	John Huss	John Wycliffe
John C. Calhoun	Niccolo Machiavelli	

8. *a.* Give a brief sketch of the history of the German Empire between 1870 and 1914;
   or,
   b. Discuss briefly the unification of Italy.

9. *a.* Give the causes and results of the Russo-Japanese war;
   or,
   b. What were the causes of the separation of Norway and Sweden?

10. Name three danger points in connection with its foreign relations that the United States has passed without resorting to war.

11. Write a brief account of one of the following:

Louisiana purchase	Missouri compromise	Northwest territory

APPENDIX 153

Current Events

Answer question 1 and five others, of which one must be either 4, 5, 6, or 7.

1. Name your home town, or that in which you have chiefly lived for the past twelve months. Give five matters of current interest which in that time and in that place engaged the thought or energies of any considerable number of its citizens.
2. *a.* Name ten organizations which work for the social welfare of the American people;
    or,
    b. Name five such organizations and speak of the program or the work of one of them in the past twelve months, or as advertised for the coming months.
3. Name ten men who have had public mention as possible presidential candidates, and give the party of each.
4. Name five persons immediately concerned with Irish, Italian, or Russian affairs, and state briefly their connection.
5. Describe two of the following:

    | American legion | Interchurch world movement | Non-partisan league |
    | Committee of 48 | National education association | |

6. What is the present status of the League of Nations? Name 15 states which are members of the League. Explain briefly the Council, the Assembly, the Secretariat.
7. Where are the principal oil-fields of the world? By whom are they owned? Explain the relation of oil to recent, present, and possible future events.
8. With what do you associate any five of the following:

    | Gabriele d' Annunzio | Alvarado Obregon | San Remo |
    | Lady Astor | Henry Morgenthau | William S. Sims |
    | Paul Deschanel | Glenn E. Plumb | Arthur Townley |
    | Morris Hillquit | | |

9. Through what periodicals or by what means do you personally keep in touch with current events?

General Information

Answer question 1 and four others.

1. Explain the allusions in any five of the following quotations:

    Talk to him of Jacob's ladder, and he would ask the number of the steps. *Jerrold.*

    Through the sad heart of Ruth, when, sick for home,
    She stood in tears amid the alien corn. *Keats.*

    The Meccas of the mind. *Halleck.*

    The Niobe of Nations. *Byron.*

    'T is Apollo comes leading
    His choir, the Nine. *Arnold.*

    Doubting Thomases at the convention. *Newspaper headline.*

    Was this the face that launched a thousand ships,
    And burnt the topless towers of Ilium? *Marlowe.*

    Earth proudly wears the Parthenon,
    As the best gem upon her zone. *Emerson.*

2. Characterize briefly two of the following, giving a somewhat longer account of a third:

    | Jenny Lind | Johannes Brahms | Edward A. MacDowell |
    | Stephen C. Foster | Fritz Kreisler | |

3. Characterize briefly five of the following:

    | Fra Angelico | Francis Seymour Haden | Ralph A. Blakelock |
    | John S. Copley | J. A. M. Whistler | Edwin A. Abbey |
    | El Greco | | |

4. Characterize in a single phrase (*e.g.*, English poet, American painter) ten of the following:

    Christopher Wren   Orville Wright   Herbert Putnam
    Augustus Saint-Gaudens   Augustin Daly   Sir William Osler
    George Grey Barnard   Charles A. Dana   Thomas H. Huxley
    Talcott Williams   John Stuart Mill   Joseph Chamberlain
    Junius Brutus Booth

5. Give an account of the development during the 20th century of a subject in science or economics in which you are interested.

6. Locate ten of the following:

    Belfast   Yukon   Santiago
    Durazzo   Hebrides   Johannesburg
    Fiume   Honolulu   Rio de Janeiro
    Congo   Vancouver   Versailles

Literature

Answer five questions.

1. *a.* Name five well-known translations of Greek or Roman classics;
    or,
  b. Tell the story of one of the Greek or Roman classics.

2. Supply the missing name in five of the following:
    —— and Beatrice; —— and Fanny Brawne; —— and Laura; —— and Highland Mary; —— and Stella; Abelard and ——; Mary Wollstonecraft and ——.

3. *a.* Give a brief account of the modern literary development of any country other than the United States and England, illustrating by some specific titles;
    or,
  b. Name five living dramatists, three of whom are continental writers, and give a list of the chief works of any one.

4. Discuss in about 300 words the literary work of any one of the following writers:

    Dante   Goethe   Hugo   Ibsen

5. Characterize briefly (*e.g.*, American novelist and poet) ten of the following:

    Joseph Conrad   Joseph Hergesheimer   John Masefield
    St. John Ervine   A. B. Housman   Graham Wallas
    Robert Frost   Vachel Lindsay   William Butler Yeats
    John Galsworthy   Amy Lowell   Archibald Marshall
    W. W. Gibson

6. *a.* What were the chief characteristics and who were the leading writers of the Victorian period of English literature;
    or,
  b. Discuss any similar group of writers in whom you are especially interested.

7. Give source of five of these quotations:
  a. The world is too much with us; late and soon.
      Getting and spending, we lay waste our powers.
  b. The light shineth in the darkness, and the darkness comprehendeth it not.
  c. A sorrow's crown of sorrow is remembering happier things.
  d. Oh to be in England
     Now that April's there.
  e. I saw the spires of Oxford as I was passing by,
     The gray spires of Oxford, against the pearl gray sky.
    f. Or like stout Cortez when with eagle eyes
      He stared at the Pacific, and all his men
      Looked at each other with a wild surmise,
      Silent, upon a peak in Darien.

APPENDIX

g. Or ever the silver cord be loosed, or the golden bowl be broken, or the pitcher be broken at the fountain, or the wheel broken at the cistern.

8. If you were to choose the first ten books to be printed in the new type for blind readers, what ones would you choose, and why?

B. Typical Entrance Examination Questions
VARIOUS SCHOOLS

History

What leagues of states or nations have existed at various times prior to the Great War? Give the object of each.

State briefly the event connected with each of the following dates: 480 B.C., A.D. 451, A.D. 476, A.D. 1066, A.D. 1688.

What Mediterranean races shaped the 20th century conception of the arts, law, religion, mathematics, and philosophy?

Show how the monastic orders benefited western Europe in other than religious matters.

Trace the development of the Mediterranean civilization from the earliest known history down to the Roman Empire.

Give an outline history of the 19th century in Europe, showing the principal changes that took place in the government and territorial possessions of England, France, Germany, and Italy.

Discuss the relations that existed between church and state in Europe during the Middle Ages. What great ideas underlay the conception of the Holy Roman Empire?

What were some of the immediate political results of the Protestant reformation?

What peoples of Europe are Celtic in origin? What are Teutonic? Which Slavic? Which Turanian? How does their origin affect their political sympathies and relations?

What progress toward constitutional government has been made among Asiatic countries in recent times? Write about half a page concerning one of those countries.

Give a brief history of the political parties in the United States showing the issues that led to the formation of each, naming their leaders and mentioning as many as you can of the presidents elected by each party.

Discuss the causes and results of the Wars of the Roses.

Give the origin of the "blood and iron" policy of Germany and the outstanding men who laid the foundation of the present German Empire.

Literature

Around what social questions were the following novels written?

| Alton Locke | Nicholas Nickleby | Hard Cash |
| Uncle Tom's Cabin | Daniel Deronda | |

In what books do the following characters appear? *Answer 10.*

Tiny Tim	Beatrix Fairfax	Gloriana
Maggie Tulliver	John Ridd	Nora Helmer
Bottom	Ben Gunn	Arthur Dimmesdale
Bathsheba Everdeen	Mrs. Proudie	Jeanie Deans

Who wrote the following and when were they written? *Answer 10.*

Don Quixote	Great Expectations	Idylls of the King
Tom Jones	Canterbury Tales	Pride and Prejudice
Paradise Lost	Quentin Durward	Pilgrim's Progress
The Divine Comedy	Pendennis	Stones of Venice
Barchester Towers	Old Wives' Tales	

156 APPENDIX

Give author and title and briefly characterize one important work in the literature of each of the following countries:

<table>
<tr><td>Norway</td><td>Russia</td><td>Italy</td><td>Spain</td><td>India</td></tr>
</table>

Name some of the men identified with each of the following literary groups:

<table>
<tr><td>English Lake poets
Pre-Raphaelites
Transcendentalists</td><td>Augustan age of English literature
French romanticists
Restoration dramatists</td><td>Scandinavian dramatists
Roman poets</td></tr>
</table>

What is an epic? What are the three great epics of classical literature? Give concerning one of these (a) Author and language in which written; (b) Historical foundation; (c) Theme; (d) Some of the qualities that determine its rank in literature.

Plan the chapter heads for a book to be called Literary Landmarks of America. What localities would have to be included and what names are associated with each?

What are some of your literary heresies; i.e., authors whom you enjoy reading but whose works do not rank with standard literature? Write a brief defense of one of them.

Who wrote (*answer ten*):

<table>
<tr><td>Montcalm and Wolfe
Emma
The Wandering Jew
Literature and Dogma</td><td>The Blessed Damozel
Jerusalem Delivered
The Life of the Bee
Lycidas</td><td>Antigone
Modern Painters
Woman and Labor
On the Heights</td></tr>
</table>

Discuss briefly the poetry movement of the present day.

What is meant by ten of the following terms: epic; stilted verse; miracle plays; conventional verse; genuine pathos; monolog; anthology; sagas; poetic license; psychological development; same thesis; plot; sustained interest; character delineation; realism; romanticism.

What is meant by ten of the following: Lake poets; Transcendentalists; Song of Roland; Nibelungenlied; Victorian age; Nature poets; Naturalists; Romance literatures; Celtic revival; Saxon influence; Renaissance; Mediaeval literature; Arthurian legends; Beowulf; Bede.

General Information

With what do you associate the following:

<table>
<tr><td>Bayreuth festival
Crédit Mobilier
Empirical
Mandatory</td><td>Non-partisan league
Program music
Psychoanalysis</td><td>Spartacans
Tanagra
Tara's Hall</td></tr>
</table>

Characterize briefly ten of the following persons, locating each by country and by century:

<table>
<tr><td>Wolsey
Cato
Xerxes
James Bryce
Garibaldi
Alexander Hamilton</td><td>Thomas à Becket
Noah Webster
Henry David Thoreau
Sobieski
Robespierre
Carmen Sylva</td><td>Auguste Rodin
Henry Davison
Henri Pétain
William James
Phillips Brooks
Rabindranath Tagore</td></tr>
</table>

Explain what is comprised in the following subjects (*answer eight*):

<table>
<tr><td>Chemical technology
Numismatics
Child psychology
Impressionism
Sanitary engineering</td><td>Counterpoint
Physiological chemistry
Meteorology
Psychotherapy
Bibliography</td><td>Archaeology
Economic geology
Pedagogy
Aesthetics</td></tr>
</table>

APPENDIX 157

Name the painter or sculptor of the following, and tell, when possible, the whereabouts (*answer eight*):

The Laocoön	The Horse Fair	Beatrice Cenci
The Man with the Hoe	Napoleon at St. Helena	Mona Lisa
The Descent from the Cross	The Greek Slave	Venus de Milo
	Die Heilige Nacht	

What are the favorable results hoped for from (*answer five*):

City planning	Conservation of water power	Self government in schools
Community pageants	Presidential primaries	Restricted immigration
Rural credits	Indeterminate sentence	

Write about a page on any one of the following subjects: Adamson law; Russian revolution of 1917; The situation as to Home Rule in Ireland; Recent movements in public education; French revolution; The Crusades.

INDEX

INDEX

ACADEMIC credit for library school courses, 69.

Accessioning: description of course, 20; hours of class-room instruction (table), 22.

Advanced study, *see* Specialized study.

American Library Association: *Catalog Rules*, 48, 49; *List of Subject Headings*, 48; *Manual of Library Economy*, 50; Publishing Board, 50, 51; as employment agency, 106; basis of membership, 125; committee on standardization and certification, 126; Committee on Enlarged Program, 127.

American Library Institute, 125.

Apprenticeship, 10, 36, 38.

Association of American Library Schools: standardization of terminology, 53; report on professional degrees, 70–71; organization and standards, 121–122; membership, 121; supervision over training agencies, 122, 129.

Atlanta, Carnegie Library of, Library School: field work in the curriculum, 56; support, 73; student fees in 1921, 74; maximum capacity, 75; enrolment in 1920–21, 75; number completing course in 1921, 75; average initial salary of graduates, 75; general statistics of graduates in 1921 (table), 78; general information, 150.

BIBLIOGRAPHY, Subject: description of course, 17; hours of class-room instruction (table), 22.

Bibliography, Trade: description of course, 18; hours of class-room instruction (table), 22.

Binding and Repair: description of course, 18; hours of class-room instruction (table), 22.

Book Selection: description of course, 13–14; hours of class-room instruction (table), 22.

Books for the Blind: description of course, 21.

Bostwick, A. E. (quoted), 26.

Budgets of library schools (table), 72.

Business library work: specialized study, 97–98, 100.

CALIFORNIA: compulsory certification of librarians, 126.

California State Library: correspondence course in cataloguing, 119.

California, University of, Courses in Library Science: joint course, 69; support, 73; maximum capacity, 75; enrolment in 1920–21, 75; number completing course in 1921, 75; average initial salary of graduates, 75; general statistics of graduates in 1921 (table), 78; general information, 151.

Carnegie Corporation: annual grants to library schools, 73.

Carnegie Institute of Technology, Pittsburgh: joint course, 69.

Carnegie Library of Atlanta, Library School, *see* Atlanta, Carnegie Library of, Library School.

Carnegie Library School, Pittsburgh, *see* Pittsburgh, Carnegie Library School.

Cataloguing: description of course, 12–13; hours of class-room instruction, 21, (table), 22; specialized study, 96; correspondence course given by California State Library, 119.

Certification of librarians: recognition of clerical grade of assistants, 11; relation to salaries, 85; recognition of specialized training, 99, 102; as stimulus to improvement in service, 110; as aid to county library system, 112; recommended by Minnesota Library Association, 123; compulsory in California, 126; laws relating to, 126; plan of A.L.A. committee, 126; present status of movement, 127–128. *See also* National Board of Certification for Librarians.

Chicago, University of: correspondence course in library science, 119; attitude toward correspondence study, 120.

Classification: description of course, 14; hours of class-room instruction, 21, (table), 22; specialized study, 96.

Class-room hours given to various subjects (table), 22.

College course: prerequisite to professional training, 4, 5, 24, 26–27, 79; most essential part of training, 6; as qualification for library school instructors, 34, 36.

Community Relations: description of course, 20; hours of class-room instruction (table), 22.

Correspondence study, *see* Instruction— Correspondence method.

Correspondence Study in Universities and Colleges, by Dr. A. J. Klein (quoted), 115–116, 120.

162 INDEX

County library service, 97, 100, 112, 131, 133–134.
Creech, J. L. (quoted), 83.
Current Events: description of course, 16; hours of class-room instruction (table), 22; place in the curriculum, 24.
Curriculum, 12–25; description of courses, 12–21; number of courses, 21; relative importance of different subjects, 21–23; hours of class-room instruction (table), 22; need for standardization, 23; evolution, 23; over-emphasis on pure literature, 24; reflects demands of professional workers, 24–25; annual library visit, 66–67. *See also* Field Work; *also names of courses*.

Decimal Classification, 48, 49.
Degrees, 70–71.
Drexel Institute Library School, 84–85.

Education for library work, 3–11.
Entrance examinations: discussion of present system, 27–29; uniformity desirable, 28–29; specimen questions, New York Public Library School, 152–155; typical questions, various schools, 155–157.
Entrance requirements, 26–33; age, 26; foreign languages, 26; bachelor's degree, 26–27; experience, 29–30; personal qualifications, 30–32; ability to use typewriter, 32–33.
Exchange of instructors, 46.
Experience as prerequisite to professional training, 29–30.

Fees, Student, in 1921 (table), 74.
Fellowships: for instructors, 51–52; for students, 109.
Fiction: hours of class-room instruction (table), 22; study as part of technical course, 23–24. *See also* Book Selection
— Description of course.
Field Work, 53–68; terminology, 53; aims and purposes, 54–55; amount and position in the curriculum, 55–57, (table), 56; as means of acquiring skill, 55, 59, 65; methods of making assignments, 57–58; as aid to placement, 59, 60; in one-year professional course, 59, 65; suitable conditions, 61–63; supervision important, 63, 64, 66; student reports, 63–64; for correspondence students, 116–117.
Filing: hours of class-room instruction (table), 22.

Godfrey, Hollis (quoted), 84–85.

High school education as preparation for library work, 4, 5, 28.
High school library work, *see* School Libraries.
History of Libraries: description of course, 17; hours of class-room instruction (table), 22.
Hughes, R. N., 90.

Illinois, University of, Library School: requirements for admission, 26–27; attention to undergraduate course, 28; attitude toward part-time instructors, 43; field work in the curriculum, 56; annual library visit, 66; academic credit, 69; degrees, 70, 71; support, 73; student fees in 1921, 74; maximum capacity, 75; enrolment in 1920–21, 75; number completing course in 1921, 75; average initial salary of graduates, 75; general statistics of graduates in 1921 (table), 78; specialized study, 92; salary statistics, 93–94; preparation for high school librarianship, 94–95; senior classes, 100; general information, 149.
Indexing: description of course, 20; hours of class-room instruction (table), 22.
Instruction: class-room hours (table), 22; higher standards desirable, 38, 51, 82, 89; use of syllabi, 39, 41, 49; methods, 40–47; part-time system, 42–44; special lectures, 44–45; coöperative, 45–47; use of reading lists, 49.
Correspondence method, 114–120; adaptation to library training, 42; need for text-books, 49, 116; as aid to improved library service, 111; as recruiting agency for schools, 117; for experienced workers, 117; attitude of library school principals, 118; restriction to one institution, 118; courses now offered, 118–120; application to specialized study, 120.
Lecture method: general discussion, 40–41; extensive use due to lack of text-books, 50.
Project method, 39.
See also Field Work.
Instructors, *see* Teaching Staff.
Inventory: hours of class-room instruction (table), 22.

Joint courses, 69–70.

Klein, A. J. (quoted), 115–116, 120.
Kroeger's *Guide to Reference Books*, 48.

LANGUAGES: description of course, 20; hours of class-room instruction (table), 22; requirement for admission to library schools, 26.
Lecture method of instruction, *see* Instruction — Lecture method.
Legislative Reference Work: special course at University of Wisconsin Library School, 92, 100.
Lending Systems: description of course, 17–18; hours of class-room instruction (table), 22.
Librarianship as a profession, 32–33, 81–82.
Library Administration: description of course, 15; hours of class-room instruction (table), 22; specialized study, 96–97.
Library appropriations: affected by lack of professional standards, 123.
Library Buildings: description of course, 19–20; hours of class-room instruction (table), 22.
Library commissions, 110–111, 134.
Library inspectors, 111.
Library institutes, 111–112, 134.
Library organizers, 111, 134.
Library schools: location in 1921 (map), *frontispiece;* limited resources, 25, 72; as employment agencies, 60, 103–106; fundamental responsibility, 60–61, 64; annual library visit, 67; graduate basis, 70, 86–90; 108–109; financial statistics, 72–74; utilization of existing plants, 74–76; need for increased number not justified by facts, 74–76, 82; as adjuncts to public libraries,86–89; statistics for 1920–21 (table), 75; as recruiting agencies, 107–108; standardization movement, 127–128; general information, 149–151.
Graduates: placement, 60, 63, 103–106; of joint courses, 69; total number, 76; men, 76, 77; women who have married, 77, 79; general statistics, 1921 (table), 78; salaries, 80–82.
See also Association of American Library Schools; Curriculum; Degrees; Entrance examinations; Entrance requirements; Instruction; Joint courses; Summer Schools; Teaching Staff; Training Classes; *also names of schools.*
Library technique: place in training for librarianship, 6–8.
Library work: two distinct types, professional and clerical, 3–11.
Library Work with Children: description of course, 15–16; hours of class-room instruction (table), 22; special courses, 92, 95–96.
Library Workers' Association, 105.
Loan funds for students, 109.
Loan Work, *see* Lending Systems.
Loans, Inter-library, 130.
Los Angeles Public Library, Library School: requirements for admission, 26–27; coöperative instruction, 46; field work in the curriculum,56; joint course, 69; support, 73; student fees in 1921, 74; maximum capacity, 75; enrolment in 1920–21, 75; number completing course in 1921, 75; average initial salary of graduates, 75; percentage of women graduates who have married, 77; general statistics of graduates in 1921 (table), 78; college graduates in 1921 class,79; general information,151.

MANN, C. R. (quoted), 91.
Matheson, K. G., 84.
Men with library training, 76–77.
Minnesota Library Association: report on college trained public librarians in the state, 122, 123.
Missouri, University of: correspondence course in reference books and their use, 119–120.

NATIONAL Board of Certification for Librarians: as aid to standardization of courses, 23; as agency for working out uniform admission tests, 29; as prize awarding body for encouraging preparation of text-books, 52; as placement aid, 106; recommended by A. L. A. committee, 127; financing, 127–128; analogy to American Medical Association Council on Medical Education, 129. *See also* Certification of librarians.
New York Public Library, Library School: purpose and scope of entrance examinations, 27; field work in the curriculum, 56; annual library visit, 66; support, 73; student fees in 1921, 74; maximum capacity, 75; enrolment in 1920–21, 75; number completing course in 1921, 75; average initial salary of graduates, 75; graduates engaged in library work, 77; general statistics of graduates in 1921 (table), 78; college graduates in 1921 class, 79; second year course, 100; favorable location for business library course, 100; general information, 150; specimen entrance examination questions, 152–155.

New York State Library School: requirements for admission, 26, 27; experience as prerequisite, 30; attitude toward part-time instructors, 43; field work in the curriculum, 56; annual library visit, 66; degrees, 70, 71; support, 73; student fees in 1921, 74; maximum capacity, 75; enrolment in 1920-21, 75; number completing course in 1921, 75; average initial salary of graduates, 75; men graduates, 77; general statistics of graduates in 1921 (table), 78; specialized study, 92; preparation for high school librarianship, 94-95; senior classes, 100; general information, 149.

Notes and Samples: description of course, 21.

OCCIDENTAL College, Los Angeles: joint course, 69.

Order Work: description of course, 18-19; hours of class-room instruction (table), 22; specialized study, 96.

PERSONAL qualifications for admission to library schools, 30-32.

Pittsburgh, Carnegie Library School: requirements for admission, 26; field work in the curriculum, 56; annual library visit, 66; joint courses, 69; student fees in 1921, 74; maximum capacity, 75; enrolment in 1920-21, 75; number completing course in 1921, 75; average initial salary of graduates, 75; general statistics of graduates in 1921 (table), 78; library work with children, 92, 95; general information, 149.

Pittsburgh, University of: joint course, 69.

Plummer, M. W. (quoted), 111-112.

Practice work: preliminary, for inexperienced students, 30; definition, 53.

Pratt Institute School of Library Science: field work in the curriculum, 56, 58; annual library visit, 66; support, 73; student fees in 1921, 74; maximum capacity, 75; enrolment in 1920-21, 75; number completing course in 1921, 75; average initial salary of graduates in 1921 (table), 78; "normal course," 97; general information, 149.

Printing and Publishing: description of course, 19; hours of class-room instruction (table), 22.

Professional literature: A. L. A. *Manual of Library Economy*, 50; as means of raising standard of instruction, 50; reasons for dearth, 50-52; suggested methods of encouraging preparation, 52. *See also* Text-books.

Professional organizations: hampered by limited funds, 112.

Professional standards, *see* Standardization and Certification.

Project method of instruction, 39.

Public Documents: description of course, 16; hours of class-room instruction (table), 22; specialized study, 98.

REAVIS, W. E., 46.

Recommendations of report, 136-148.

Recruiting for the library profession, 33, 51, 89, 107-109.

Reference Work: description of course, 14; hours of class-room instruction, 21, (table), 22; inadequacy of present training facilities, 95; correspondence course by University of Missouri, 119-120.

Research Work: inadequacy of present training facilities, 95.

Riverside Library Service School: coöperative instruction, 46; support, 73; maximum capacity, 75; enrolment in 1920-21, 75; number completing course in 1921, 75; average initial salary of graduates, 75; general information, 151.

Round tables, 111-112.

SABBATICAL years, 51.

St. Louis Library School: field work in the curriculum, 56; support, 73; student fees in 1921, 74; maximum capacity, 75; enrolment in 1920-21, 75; number completing course in 1921, 75; average initial salary of graduates, 75; general statistics of graduates in 1921 (table), 78; general information, 151.

Salaries, 83-85, 123; of teaching staffs (table), 73; of library school graduates, 79-82, (table), 80, 81.

Scholarships, 109.

School Libraries: description of course, 19; hours of class-room instruction (table), 22; specialized study, 94-95; correspondence course given by University of Wisconsin, 119.

Seminar: inappropriate use of term, 42.

Shelf Work: description of course, 20; hours of class-room instruction (table), 22.

Simmons College School of Library Science: field work in the curriculum, 56; joint course, 69, 70; degrees, 71; support, 73; student fees in 1921, 74; maximum capacity, 75; enrolment in 1920-21, 75; number completing course

INDEX

in 1921, 75; average initial salary of graduates, 75; percentage of women graduates who have married, 77; general statistics of graduates in 1921 (table), 78; general information, 149–150.
Small libraries, 130–135; need for trained librarian, 5–6, 133; recruiting staff, 10–11.
Special lectures, 44–46.
Special Libraries: description of course, 21. *See also* Business library work.
Specialized study, 91–102; failure of schools to provide, 91–92, 99; in one-year course, 93; subjects requiring, 94–98; coöperation with other institutions, 98; experience a prerequisite, 98–99; suggestions for organization, 100–102; cost of administration, 101–102; *in absentia*, 102.
Standardization and Certification, 121–129; A. L. A. committee, 126. *See also* Certification of librarians; National Board of Certification for Librarians.
Student self-help, 109.
Students in university: normal distribution, 89–90.
Subject Headings: description of course, 16; hours of class-room instruction (table), 22.
Summer Schools, 111, 113, 117, 134, 135.
Syllabi: extensive use in instruction, 39, 41, 49.
Syracuse University Library School: degrees, 70; support, 73; student fees in 1921, 74; maximum capacity, 75; enrolment in 1920–21, 75; number completing course in 1921, 75; average initial salary of graduates, 75; general information, 150.

Teacher training courses, 97.
Teaching Staff: 34–39; education, training, and experience, 34–37, (table), 35; difficulty in recruiting, 37; part-time instructors, 42–44; special lecturers, 44–45; exchange of instructors, 46; specialists for short intensive courses, 46; academic status, 71; salaries (table), 73.
Terminology, 23, 42.
Text-books, 48–52; for correspondence instruction, 116.

Training Classes: essentials of courses, 7–8; purpose and function, 10, 64–65, 76, 86; admission of students from other libraries, 11.
Training for Librarianship, by M. W. Plummer; rev. by F. K. Walter (quoted), 111–112.
Training in service, 110–113.
Tuition fees, 74.
Typewriter, ability to use, as prerequisite to library training, 32–33.

United States Bureau of Education, 36, 114.

Visiting lecturers, 44–46.

Washington, University of, Library School: field work in the curriculum, 56; joint course, 69; degrees, 70, 71; support, 73; maximum capacity, 75; enrolment in 1920–21, 75; number completing course in 1921, 75; average initial salary of graduates, 75; general statistics of graduates in 1921 (table), 78; general information, 151.
Western Reserve University Library School: field work in the curriculum, 56; joint course, 69; degrees, 71; support, 73; student fees in 1921, 74; maximum capacity, 75; enrolment in 1920–21, 75; number completing course in 1921, 75; average initial salary of graduates, 75; general statistics of graduates in 1921 (table), 78; library work with children, 92, 95, 100; general information, 150.
Wisconsin, University of, Extension Division: correspondence course for school librarians, 119.
Wisconsin, University of, Library School: experience as a prerequisite, 29–30; field work in the curriculum, 53, 55, 56, 67; joint course, 69; degrees, 71; support, 73; student fees in 1921, 74; maximum capacity, 75; enrolment in 1920–21, 75; number completing course in 1921, 75; average initial salary of graduates, 75; general statistics of graduates in 1921 (table), 78; legislative reference work, 92, 100; general information, 150.
Women in library work, 71, 107.

Z
668
W735

SEP 20 1971